NATIVE AMERICA

Native America

THE STORY OF THE FIRST PEOPLES

KENNETH L. FEDER

PRINCETON UNIVERSITY PRESS
PRINCETON & OXFORD

Copyright © 2025 by Princeton University Press

Princeton University Press is committed to the protection of copyright and the intellectual property our authors entrust to us. Copyright promotes the progress and integrity of knowledge created by humans. By engaging with an authorized copy of this work, you are supporting creators and the global exchange of ideas. As this work is protected by copyright, any reproduction or distribution of it in any form for any purpose requires permission; permission requests should be sent to permissions@press.princeton.edu. Ingestion of any PUP IP for any AI purposes is strictly prohibited.

Published by Princeton University Press
41 William Street, Princeton, New Jersey 08540
99 Banbury Road, Oxford OX2 6JX

press.princeton.edu

All Rights Reserved

GPSR Authorized Representative: Easy Access System Europe - Mustamäe tee 50, 10621 Tallinn, Estonia, gpsr.requests@easproject.com

Library of Congress Control Number: 2024953005

ISBN 9780691220451
ISBN (e-book) 9780691220475

British Library Cataloging-in-Publication Data is available

Editorial: Rob Tempio, Chloe Coy
Production Editorial: Elizabeth Byrd
Jacket: Katie Osborne
Production: Erin Suydam
Publicity: Alyssa Sanford
Copyeditor: Ashley Moore

Jacket Credit: Carver Mostardi / Alamy Stock Photo

Printed in the United States of America

10 9 8 7 6 5 4 3 2 1

For Jenn, Molly, Ellie, Josh, and Jacob
who took this journey with me.

CONTENTS

List of Illustrations   ix
Foreword   xv
A Practical Preface   xvii
Acknowledgments   xxi

Prologue: Crying Indians, Tipi Dwellers, and Other Stereotypes   1

1 Archaeology: A Way of Telling Stories   10

2 In Their Beginning   20

3 Are You Ready to Rock?   34

4 European Encounter with a "New World"   43

5 First Peoples: Origins   66

6 First Peoples: Clovis and Folsom   92

7 First Peoples: Older Still?   104

8 Learning to Live in a New World   114

9 More Than Maize: Native Farmers of North America   136

10 Into the Woods   156

11	Into the Cold	169
12	Monument Builders of the Midwest	191
13	City Dwellers	210
14	Great Houses and Cliff Castles	224
15	Northwest Coast: Ocean Farmers and Totem Poles	275
16	Art: History, Hunting, Sacred Imagery, and the Sky	291
17	War	322
18	Archaeology and Ethnic Cleansing	353
	Epilogue: A Story Still Being Written	372

Notes 375

References 383

Index 393

Color Plates follow page 200

ILLUSTRATIONS

Figures

2.1. Coyote depicted devouring the moon on the Tule River Indian Reservation in Southern California. 24

2.2. Coyote depicted in rock art (a petroglyph) in Nine Mile Canyon in eastern Utah. 30

3.1. A selection of stone tools from archaeological sites in the Farmington River valley of Connecticut. 38

4.1. Engraved section of John Vanderlyn's 1847 painting *Landing of Columbus*. 47

4.2. The Los Lunas Decalogue Stone in New Mexico. 59

4.3. The Newport Tower in Rhode Island. 60

4.4. A reconstruction of the large Viking house, excavated at L'Anse aux Meadows, Newfoundland, Canada. 63

5.1. Spearpoint recovered at Cooper's Ferry, Idaho. 81

5.2. Meadowcroft Rockshelter, western Pennsylvania. 82

5.3. Well-preserved human footprints discovered in White Sands National Park, New Mexico. 85

6.1. Skeleton of an extinct form of North American bison, *Bison antiquus*. 93

6.2. Fluted points: Clovis (*left and center*) and Folsom (*right*) with the flute extending nearly the entire length of the spearpoint. 94

x LIST OF ILLUSTRATIONS, PLATES, AND MAPS

8.1. A selection of copper tools made by the people who were the bearers of what we today call the Old Copper Culture in the area around the Great Lakes. 122

8.2. Basalt outcrop on Talcott Mountain, Avon, Connecticut. 125

8.3. A nearly five-thousand-year-old spearpoint finely crafted from hornfels, and a drill made of the same raw material. 127

8.4. A large chunk of steatite, or soapstone, at the Walter Landgraf Soapstone Quarry in Barkhamsted, Connecticut. 130

9.1. A domesticated variety of *Chenopodium* (goosefoot) seeds. 141

9.2. Sunflowers. 143

10.1. Replica of a Native American longhouse typical of the Iroquois people of the eastern woodlands. 159

11.1. Photograph taken of an Iñupiat family highlighting their winter clothing. 170

11.2. Modern Inuit man using a traditional kayak. 174

11.3. A little polar bear carved on a walrus tusk. 178

12.1. Ground view of some of the burial mounds enclosed by a wall made of earth at the Mound City necropolis. 200

12.3. A bird image cut from a flattened piece of copper by a Hopewell artist. 203

12.4. Drawing of the Octagon Earthworks, part of the Newark Earthworks in Ohio. 205

12.5. Aerial view of Serpent Mound located in southern Ohio. 208

13.1. An artist's conception of the Native American city today called Cahokia, at its peak at around 1200 CE. 212

13.3. This pendant cut from a shell and depicting what appears to be a soldier was recovered from the Etowah mound site in Georgia. 220

LIST OF ILLUSTRATIONS, PLATES, AND MAPS xi

14.1. The Betatakin cliff dwelling, Navajo National Monument, Arizona. 228

14.2. One of the Gila Cliff dwellings in New Mexico. 235

14.3. Mimbres ceramics. 236

14.6. Richard Kern's drawing of Pueblo Pintado, the first Chaco outlier Lieutenant Simpson's expedition encountered on their way into Chaco Canyon. 245

14.8. Casa Rinconada in Chaco Canyon, the largest of all kivas. 248

14.12. One of the Diné (Navajo) petroglyph panels in Crow Canyon, New Mexico. 268

16.1. The most famous of the so-called newspaper rocks in the American Southwest. 294

16.5. The Diné man Little Sheep painted this image in the early 1800s, showing the Spanish invaders, who killed his friends and family in Massacre Cave. 308

16.8. One of the giant one-thousand-year-old Blythe Intaglios in southeastern California. 316

16.9. A pictograph at Chaco Canyon showing what appears to be a depiction of the supernova that occurred in 1054 CE. 318

16.10. The "sun dagger" of light that bisects a spiral petroglyph on the summer solstice (June 22). 320

17.1. The so-called Resistance Kiva at Pecos Pueblo, used in a revival of Native religion following the Pueblo Revolt of 1680 CE. 335

17.2. The marker where General Custer of the U.S. Army Seventh Cavalry made his "last stand." 342

17.3. Markers memorializing two of the Native Americans who died during the Battle of the Little Bighorn. 343

17.4. Painting by the artist George Catlin showing Hidatsa Village along the Knife River in North Dakota in 1832. 351

Color Plates (after page 200)

1. The lower cliff dwelling at Tonto National Monument in eastern Arizona.
2. A 1960s Zuni pictograph in New Mexico.
3. The Grave Creek Mound, an Adena culture burial monument in West Virginia.
4. Monks Mound, the primary earthwork at Cahokia, is a truncated pyramid.
5. The multiroomed, multistory great house called Wupatki, considered to belong to the Sinagua culture.
6. Montezuma Castle in Arizona.
7. Largest of all the great houses in the American Southwest, Pueblo Bonito consisted of more than eight hundred rooms divided into apartments spread out across as many as five stories.
8. One set of steps, carved into the bedrock, leading travelers into and then back out of Chaco Canyon.
9. Square Tower House in Mesa Verde.
10. Cliff Palace in Mesa Verde.
11. Modern totem poles, Vancouver, Canada.
12. A well-preserved petroglyph located at McKee Springs in Dinosaur National Monument, Utah.
13. The Great Hunt Panel, a petroglyph that tells a story of hunting a herd of bighorn sheep.
14. A depiction of a bighorn sheep, its body pierced by three arrows at Three Rivers, located adjacent to a Mogollon village site.
15. The image of the great chief called Tsagaglalal, "She Who Watches," located near Horsethief Lake in Washington State.
16. Seven anthropomorphic pictographs located in a natural rock alcove in Horseshoe Canyon in Utah.

LIST OF ILLUSTRATIONS, PLATES, AND MAPS   xiii

Maps

0.1.	Native cultural regions of North America.	7
5.1.	Map of Beringia.	78
6.1.	Map showing the wide geographical distribution of Clovis sites.	99
8.1.	Map showing the many ecoregions of North America.	116
9.1.	Map showing the distribution of a sample of archaeological sites in North America where evidence of the use of domesticated plants has been recovered.	142
11.1.	Map showing the geographical distribution of the Paleo-Inuit and Inuit, from western Alaska all the way east to the coast of Greenland.	171
12.1.	Map showing the locations of earthworks sites discussed in this book, including Adena and Hopewell mounds; platform mound sites; and effigy mound sites.	192
12.2.	A map of the Poverty Point earthworks.	198
14.1.	Map of the American Southwest with sites and cultural affiliation indicated.	232
14.2.	Map of the great houses in Chaco Canyon.	243
16.1.	Map of a sample of rock art sites in North America.	298

FOREWORD

THIS BOOK BY Kenneth Feder is an engrossing, myth-busting, rollicking tale of the archaeology of native North America, beginning with the arrival of the first inhabitants more than twenty thousand years ago. It is also among the first books in our new series of archaeology books intended for readers fascinated by archaeology and what it reveals about the history of humankind—from amateur enthusiasts and general readers to seasoned scholars looking for a compelling and state-of-the-art synthesis.

This series, Unearthing the Past, was conceived back in 2019. During a conference keynote address, I challenged my archaeology colleagues to write more books and articles meant for the general public. I suggested that they begin telling their stories, each in their own way, about what they had found on their excavations, or what they found interesting about the ancient world, or what they would want most people to know about particular topics, whatever those might be. Based on my own experience, I reminded them that archaeology is one of the most captivating topics to many of the people we meet who always want to know more about what we do, how we do it, and what we find.

Feder has produced exactly the type of book that I had hoped for—this is not your dry and dusty archaeology textbook. Instead, it is a page-turner, eminently readable and jargon-free, full of interesting stories packed with genuine archaeological information and offering a behind-the-dig look at archaeological discoveries, reflecting Feder's long career of doing, studying, and teaching archaeology, as well as writing about it. Here, he paints a portrait of the deep history of Native North America, following the progress of its first peoples across the miles and millennia and showcasing the tremendous diversity of cultures that eventually spread across the land. Along the way, Feder surveys iconic sites and inventions, taking us from Chaco Canyon to Monks Mound and everything in between, from Clovis and Folsom stone weapons and tools to the invention and spread of maize and beyond, and explores a plethora of topics that bring to life what now remains of their material culture.

While extremely respectful of the people and places about whom he is writing, adding their voices to his, Feder also has his own inimitable style, for he is the consummate storyteller—you and he might just as well be having a conversation while sitting in front of a fireplace on a cold winter's day, with him cracking jokes and spinning yarns just this side of believable. But it's more than that as well, as Feder follows the story of Native America from its beginnings right up to the present day, illuminating a number of ongoing debates and taking a serious tone toward the end, including documenting more recent events in the grand scheme of things, such as the archaeology surrounding Custer's Last Stand, the Trail of Tears, Wounded Knee, and other actions taken by the government against Native peoples. As Feder shows, it is a history of adaptation, diversity, resilience, and continuity, for their descendants and resilient cultures are still very much present in the world today.

Without further ado, I now invite you to dig in and enjoy this journey into the past.

Eric H. Cline

A PRACTICAL PREFACE

I INTEND THIS "practical preface" as a very brief instruction manual for a couple of the practical approaches I apply in this book. Before I begin talking about stone tools and pots, cliff dwellings and great houses, pyramids and burial mounds, pictographs and petroglyphs—all enormously fascinating things that help tell the story of America's First Peoples—there are some terms and practical issues to dispense with right up front.

A Word About Measurements

The metric scale is infinitely superior to the English system most commonly used in the United States. There are literally only two other holdout countries in the twenty-first century that use the English system of feet, yards, and miles: Liberia and Myanmar, which most people couldn't identify on a map. I'm not sure I could either. I mean, come on: 10 millimeters in a centimeter; 100 centimeters in a meter; 1,000 meters in a kilometer. Easy peazy. Compare that with inches divided into fractions (1/64th of an inch? Seriously?); 12 inches in a foot; 3 feet in a yard; 5,280 feet in a mile. The system of measurement that we continue to use in the U.S.—along with good old Liberia and Myanmar—is certainly not intuitive or simple.

While I recognize that metric is the superior system of measurement, an exclusive use of metric by me here to, for example, convey the height of the pyramidal Monks Mound at Cahokia (chapter 13) or the length of Cliff Palace in Mesa Verde (chapter 14) would present a barrier (okay, maybe one just a few centimeters high—just a little metric humor to start your day) to most of the Usanians reading this book, who likely can picture what 100 feet looks like (the height of Monks Mound), but not necessarily 30 meters. My solution to this is pretty straightforward. I will present all measurements in metric first but add the English equivalent in parentheses. Yeah, we should all be using metric for sure, but I don't see any point in forcing the issue here.

A Word About the Calendar

As you certainly know, BC literally stands for "before Christ"—that is, before the birth of Jesus Christ. Despite the opinion of about one-third of the students I have ever surveyed on this point, AD does *not* stand for "after death" (after the death of Jesus Christ, which would leave a period of about thirty-five years of, I guess, DC, "during Christ"). AD actually stands for the Latin *anno domini*, literally "in the year of the Lord," meaning all of the years following the birth of Christ, including his lifetime.

The first issue when using that common and, let's face it, nearly universal reference system for year dates is that there is a minor technical glitch. By most historical analyses, the date applied to the year zero—that is, the year Christ ostensibly was born—was calculated by the monk Dionysius Exiguus in the sixth century and he was off by three years. Yup; as a result of his mistake, according to more accurate calculations, Jesus Christ was actually born in the year 3 BC, which makes absolutely no sense.[1]

Anyway, that's really just a bit of trivia. Of far greater significance is a recognition that there is built-in inequity in the system we use to designate a year date that has, as a zero point, the birth of Jesus Christ. Sure, that event is considered by Christians to be the most momentous one in history. However, Christianity, in its many forms, represents only about 32 percent of the world's population. That's the largest single percentage of religious followers (Muslims are a little more than 23 percent, Hindus 15 percent, Buddhists 7 percent, and about 16 percent follow other religions or say they aren't adherents of any religion at all), but it's not a majority of the population of our planet.

I will not argue with folks who respond, "Well sure, but we need a zero point, a temporal anchor in history, and everyone is familiar with BC and AD." It's a valid point. At the same time, it takes very little energy to use BCE (before the Common Era) and CE (the Common Era) instead, to at least recognize that for about two-thirds of the world's people, the birth of Jesus Christ is not that big of a deal and so, for them, makes no sense as a historical anchor point.

The good news here is you don't have to do any math as a result of my use of BCE and CE. The "Common Era" isn't some arbitrary point in time. Ironically, after my long-winded explanation, it conforms to the birth of Jesus Christ. So, gentle reader, at the risk of offending folks (something I likely will do here on occasion; oh well), I will be using BCE and CE throughout this book.

Additionally, you will see the occasional use of BP here and in other archaeology and history books. BP stands for "before present." That seems pretty straightforward and sensible but even here there is a complication. The present isn't a fixed point in time, it's an ever-moving target. To get around that, the "present" in BP is actually fixed at 1950! That's about the time radiocarbon dating was initially developed (see chapter 5 for a discussion of that dating method). Yeah, I know, it's messy. But as long as you understand what BCE, CE, and BP mean, you'll be fine.

ACKNOWLEDGMENTS

EVERY BOOK is a collaborative endeavor, and it would be remiss of me not to acknowledge the people who made this book possible. To begin, I had known archaeologist and prolific author Eric Cline, professor of Classics and Anthropology at George Washington University, through his works before I met him briefly at a conference. I am a huge fan and was thrilled when, years later, he invited me to contribute this volume to his archaeology series for Princeton University Press. I am forever grateful to him for that invitation.

The folks at Princeton University Press have been amazing companions in the journey of this book. I owe a debt of gratitude especially to my editor Rob Tempio. (I swear, Rob, I didn't intentionally exceed the figure limit. I'm lying.) Also, a big shout-out to my assistant editor Chloe Coy who really held things together and kept me on task (for which she deserves a medal). Thanks buckets to Elizabeth Byrd in production editorial and Erin Suydam in production. Copyediting can be a chore, but I find it an incredibly rewarding task when I am receiving wise counsel from talented and insightful editors. A big thanks to Melody Negron at Westchester Publishing Services. I've written a bunch of books, some in multiple editions, and have worked with a lot of copyeditors. The vast majority of them have been great to work with, but none better than Ashley Moore. She really was fantastic.

I also need to thank the reviewers of the raw manuscript I submitted to the press. Their suggestions, corrections, and kind words made my work so much better. Kristina Killgrove, Brad Lepper, Jay Levy—thank you to them all, even Reviewer #2. (That's just an inside reviewer joke.)

There are so many who have been inspirational in my approach to writing in general and writing about the archaeological story of Native

America in particular. I include in that list Isaac Asimov, Jeb Card, Brian Fagan, Alice Gorman, Guy Harrison, Kristina Kilgrove, Brad Lepper, Sarah Parcak, Jennifer Raff, Carl Sagan, and Holly Walters. As always, here's a special shout-out to my best friend and co-conspirator of more than forty years, Michael Park. Here's another one for our combined bookshelf, Mikey.

In a book written about the Native People of North America, their lives, their cultures, their histories, their survival, their agency, and their presence demands recognition and acknowledgment. I do so here. A special thank you to the wisdom shared by Kenny Bowekaty (A:shiwi), Coni Dubois (James Chaugham [Narragansett] descendant), Harris Hardy (Diné), Jay Levy, Trudie Lamb Richmond (Schaghticoke), and Kurly Tlapoyawa (Chicano/Nawa/Mazewalli).

Finally, always underlying my writing is the hope that when any of my kids—Josh, Jacob, Molly, or Ellie—open the pages of this book, however far into the future, they'll be able to point to a photo of a remarkable cliff dwelling or an intriguing petroglyph and say, "I remember dad taking us there."

And to my wife Jenn. This book, like our lives together, is a wonderful adventure. Let's go adventure some more!

NATIVE AMERICA

Prologue

CRYING INDIANS, TIPI DWELLERS, AND OTHER STEREOTYPES

IN A BOOK about the history of Indigenous People in North America, it makes sense first to address some of the common stereotypes many harbor about them. Perhaps the best-known preconception of Native Americans by non-Native people concerns the genuine and explicit reverence many of them have for the environment. This stereotype is so pervasive it was enshrined in a 1971 public service announcement, the "Crying Indian" television advert produced by an organization called America the Beautiful. The ad decried pollution, overcrowding, environmental degradation, and, adding insult to injury, littering.

The "Crying Indian" Ad

The ad in question begins with a scene of immense natural beauty in a thickly forested landscape. The thrum of tom-toms can be heard in the background. A Native American man, strikingly clad in buckskins and wearing a feather in his long black hair, paddles his birch-bark canoe along the pristine waters of a flowing river. As the one-minute spot proceeds, the man in the canoe enters a bay where, disturbingly in this seemingly Edenic paradise, he encounters modern garbage floating on the water's surface. Passing through the trash, he continues to paddle until he encounters the edge of a city beset with air pollution. Smoke wafts into the air while ugly smokestacks and steel girders pierce the sky. Beaching his canoe, he walks onto a garbage-strewn shore and then to the edge of an automobile-infested highway where, in the final insult, a callous occupant of one of those vehicles throws trash out of the window that lands at the feet of the Native person. This scene is accompanied by the narration, "Some people have a deep, abiding respect for the natural beauty that was once this country. And some people don't."

The scene then cuts to a close shot as the previously mentioned garbage lands at the Native man's feet. The narration ends on this final note: "People start pollution. And people can stop it." The final cut is a close-up of the man's face, where a single tear is rolling down his right cheek. Thus the name by which this ad is now sarcastically known: the "Crying Indian" commercial.[1]

I really hate being cynical about that PSA, but cynicism is hard to avoid. I don't want to tell you, but I will, that the man who portrayed the Native guy was an actor whose stage name was Iron Eyes Cody. Though he made a living portraying Native People in movies and TV, his given name was Espera de Corti. He was, in fact, an Italian American. Further, I don't want to tell you, but I will, the America the Beautiful organization wasn't a grassroots group of do-gooders and tree huggers hoping to save the environment. In fact, it was bankrolled by the beverage industry in an attempt to pass along the costs of environmental protection to the consumer for addressing the ultimate and systemic causes of pollution: the industry's reliance on single-use packaging. They wanted to avoid any burdensome regulations that might force them to play an active role in recycling, reusing, or renewing containers, all of which would have been not only disruptive to their business model but also very expensive.

As researcher Finis Dunaway states, the Native person in the ad isn't even a person; he's a symbol, an anachronism, a time traveler emerging from the wilderness like a ghost from antiquity. Further, in his confrontation with the modern world, he is a victim with no agency, no power, no control. Instead of, for example, showing the Native person organizing against environmental destruction, protesting, or suing the polluters, the ad shows him crying. This ad exploited Native American people based on a stereotype of their love and respect for the environment. But in that, they were not flesh-and-blood people; they were symbols used to elicit first pity and then guilt.²

Yes, many Native People espouse a philosophy that centers the environment, but in this book I hope to leave behind stereotypes—negative, benign, and positive. Each, in turn, treats Native People not as people but as symbols. There were and are literally hundreds of different Native American groups, each with its own indigenous economic system, social system, language, food base, technology, philosophy, and set of religious beliefs. The cultures of the Native People of the Americas were and are as diverse as those in Europe, Africa, or Asia. Even just saying, "Well, the Native People of North America believe . . . ," is to speak nonsense. The Pequot, Mohegan, Tunxis, Shinnecock, Creek, Aniyunwiya (Cherokee), Hopi, Diné (Navajo), Arikara, Seminole, Mandan, Sioux, Tule, Choctaw, Shoshone, Apache, Kwakwa̱ka'wakw (Kwakiutl), and Inuit, to name just a few of the peoples whose ancestors I will be discussing in this book, variously shared some things in common, but also exhibited fundamental differences. They are a people with a common heritage, but each had their own history and developed their own way of life. In my concentration on their histories, I will celebrate and center that variation through time and space.

Primitive, Lazy, Buffalo-Hunting, Tipi-Dwelling Nomads Who Are Drunk

Many other common stereotypes about the Native People of North America are harshly negative, defamatory, and, bottom line, based on racist generalizations. Indians are lazy. They're violent. They're drunks. Untrustworthy. Backward. Primitive. Sneaky. Some published descriptions of Native People, especially in the eighteenth and nineteenth centuries, are absolutely disgusting, and I see no point in repeating any more of them here. Certainly there are individuals in every ethnic group to which those descriptions I just listed might apply, but no entire group of people can or should be described in these ways. Those are libels and, even worse, they're lies. They're based on prejudice and, let's be frank, are racist by definition. Those beliefs led to the endless repetitions of some version of the phrase "The only good Indian is a dead Indian," spoken by generals and even a U.S. president (Teddy Roosevelt, in a speech he delivered in 1886; though he did say that it was true for only nine out of ten of them. Yay Teddy).

There also are stereotypes of Native Americans that appear to be benign, not positive or negative, but are really just caricatures that may be vaguely accurate when applied to certain individuals or groups, though they certainly are not universally true. For example, "Indians live in tipis." Well, some did, but housing styles varied regionally. Animal-skin-covered tipis certainly were used in the Great Plains, but in other regions entirely different house forms were the rule, including wigwams (dome-shaped houses made with a skeleton of saplings and coverings of bark or woven mats), longhouses (long versions of wigwams; chapter 10), snow houses (igloos; chapter 11), enormous pueblos made of adobe (chapter 14), and dome-shaped earth lodges (chapter 17).

And there's this: "Indians survived by hunting large game animals, especially the buffalo." Well, the American bison (technically, they're not buffalo, and the genus, species, and subspecies name of contemporary bison is, in fact, *Bison bison bison*, which makes it pretty easy to remember) was a vital source of food and hides for *some* Indigenous People, especially on the Great Plains. Even there, however, this subsistence focus was, at least in part, a product of the colonial period. The ancestors of the nomadic bison hunters had largely been sedentary agriculturalists who certainly hunted bison, but these animals were only one element in a far broader and far more varied quest for subsistence.

Okay, but isn't it true that "the horse was a vital part of Native culture in North America"? Well, it absolutely was but, again, only for some groups, and that reliance was a post–European contact phenomenon. Though species of wild horses were native to North America, they became extinct at the end of the Pleistocene or Ice Age, more than ten thousand years ago (see chapter 6). Native People may have hunted horses then but only developed an equestrian-focused way of life once domesticated horses were accidentally introduced into the New World by Spanish soldiers and settlers in the sixteenth century. Some of those domesticated animals escaped from Spanish control, formed feral herds, and were captured by Native People. Recognizing their usefulness through careful observation of the invaders, those Native People captured and tamed them, developing their own, distinctive horseback-riding technologies and skills. Recent research shows that this occurred in North America no later than the mid-1500s. The horse had already become a vital component of the way of life of the Native People of the Great Plains barely a hundred years later.[3]

These seemingly benign stereotypes of the first Americans aren't necessarily hurtful but, as noted, they are caricatures of the cultures of Native America. The stereotype of nomadic, tipi-dwelling buffalo hunters constantly engaged in war provided the basis for the portrayal of the Indigenous population of North America in Hollywood movies especially in the 1940s through, perhaps, the 1970s—think John Wayne—but it does a gross disservice to the enormous geographical and cultural diversity of Native Americans that I will discuss throughout this book.

There also are the salutary, even laudatory stereotypes of Native Americans that, while positive, are inaccurate and paint many different groups of people with an indefensibly broad brush. For example, "Indians are noble savages." The "savages" part sounds defamatory but, as originally conceived, it was applied by Europeans to people they viewed as pure, innocent, and inherently good because, in their primitiveness, they were uncorrupted by the negative influences of civilization. In this view, Native Americans weren't quite modern people but charming throwbacks to a time in humanity's infancy when all peoples were childlike and guileless. Sadly, but inevitably in this view, the "noble savages" who were Native Americans were viewed as being doomed to extinction when confronted by the ambitious, advanced, contentious, competitive, and far more advanced people who characterized the civilizations of the modern world—in other words, Europeans.

The People

The point of all this is to make clear that there is no homogeneous category of "Indians." Some were warlike. Some were peaceful. Some were egalitarian, living in societies where everyone in the same age and sex bracket had more or less the same or similar social and economic status, along with the same degree of control over their own lives. Some groups had highly stratified societies with rulers and followers, rich and poor, powerful and powerless. Some lived as "one-percenters," in modern parlance, kings and queens in socially and economically stratified societies where they were buried in splendor. Some people in those same societies died when their kings died, sacrificed to accompany their great rulers in death. In other words, the Native People of North America were just people, with all of their many and varied, glorious, ingenious, and complex ways of life. Putting them all in the same basket does a disservice to their history and their humanity.

So This Book Is About an Ancient, Lost World?

Nope. This is *not* a book about ancient people from the clichéd dim mists of time; at least it is not exclusively about ancient people. It certainly is not a book about extinct people. It is not a book about dead civilizations. It is not a book about quaint folk who exist only as faint memories in museum dioramas. It is not a book about a people whose time has come and passed and who have exited the stage of world history. And this is not a book about a people who can legitimately be characterized as weary and defeated, as James Earle Fraser depicted them in his famous 1894 sculpture where a pitiable Native American warrior is slumped over on a horse that can barely hold his weight. No. The Native People of America are not a group that has reached, as the name of that sculpture maintains, the "end of the trail." That canard will be discredited on virtually every page of this book.

This most decidedly *is* a book about the vibrant and myriad cultures of Native America from a broad and encompassing historical perspective (Map 0.1). It is, in a real sense, a history book about ancestors and

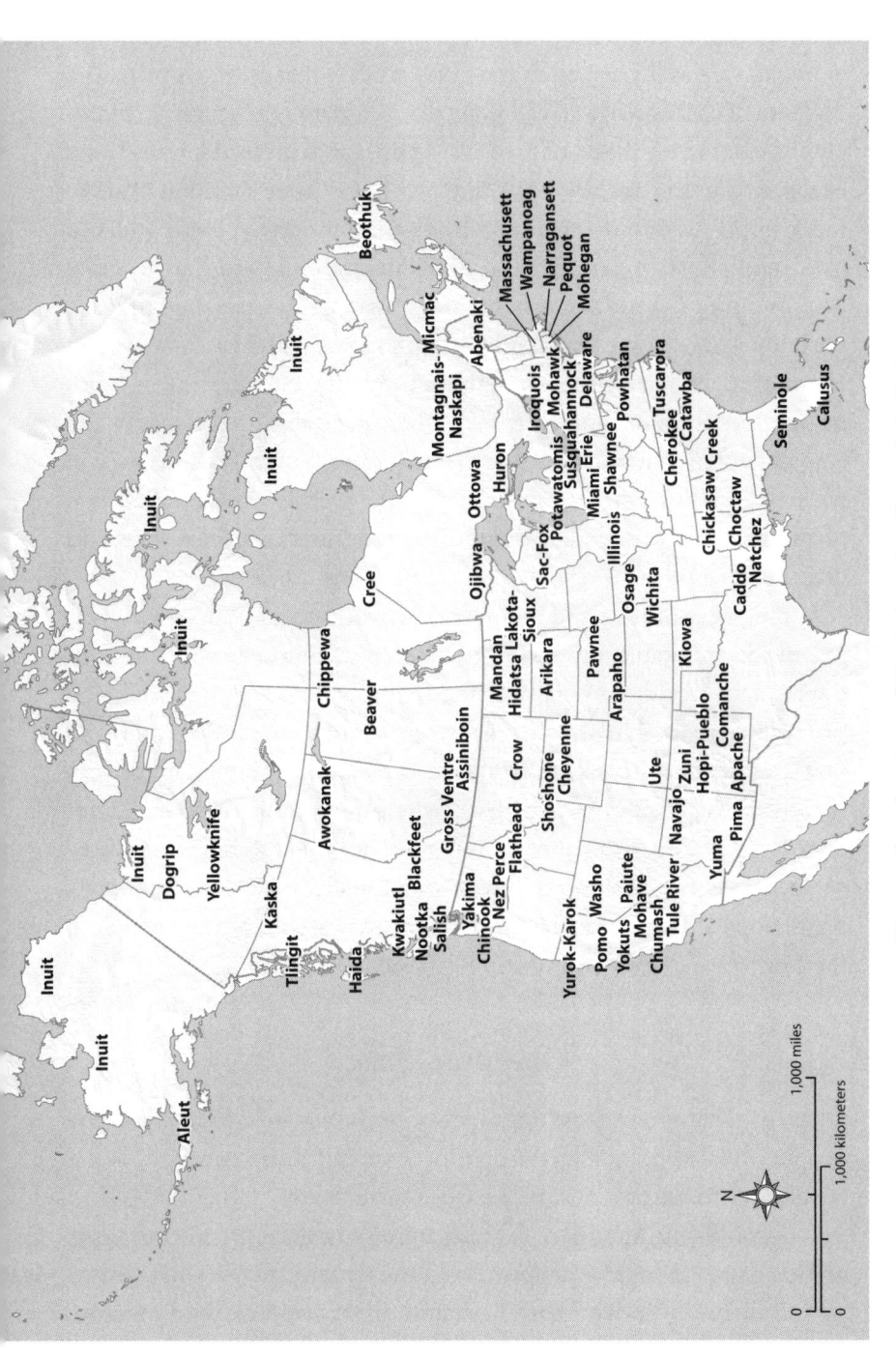

MAP 0.1. Native cultural regions of North America. Kenneth L. Feder

a continuing tale of living people, a people who—if I haven't been clear enough—are still very much here. It is a book that employs primarily the data of archaeology to tell their story, a story not written in hieroglyphs painted on sheets of papyrus, or markings pressed into wet clay, or words put on paper by a printing press. It is a story written in stone tools, in pieces of pottery, and in bones; in mounds of earth sculpted into sepulchers, pyramids, and enormous animal effigies; in great houses built of stone and mortar along with castles perched precariously in shallow caves carved by nature into sandstone cliffs; and in wonderful, artful, and even sometimes whimsical images scratched into or painted onto soaring canyon walls. These things constitute the language of archaeology in North America; they are the purview of the science that studies the past through the recovery and examination of the material things that people created, used, used up, lost, and discarded.

While these objects and buildings and works of art may seem at first to be indecipherable, mysterious, and even incomprehensible to us in the modern world, they are not, and they have the advantage of being beautiful, remarkable, and just really very bloody cool at the same time that they are enormously informative. This book is about a lot of very bloody cool and informative places where sites, tools, artwork, buildings, monuments, and entire cultures can be encountered and investigated. This is a book about the archaeological investigation of America's First Peoples. Thanks for electing to take the ride with me as we explore their historical legacy and continuing story.

One More Thing

Okay, so what is the most appropriate umbrella term to apply to the people who first populated the continent we call North America? What term or terms are the most respectful and accurate?

It is confusing, and there is no unanimity or even broad consensus on this issue among the people most directly affected. So what should we call them? Is "Indian" bad? Certainly, from a historical perspective, "Indian" is a misnomer attributable to Christopher Columbus's fundamental geographical error that led to his belief that in each of his four voyages he had reached the East Indies, a part of East Asia. So there is a reasonable argument that we should reject the use of "Indian" because we don't want to continue validating Columbus's mistake. Certainly, many **Native People** or **Indigenous People** think it's long past time to jettison that term. But not all. It is telling, I think, that the U.S. Smithsonian Institution's national museum dedicated to celebrating the story of America's **First People**—a museum that was designed and developed, at least in part, by and with **Native Americans** (itself an imperfect term since it incorporates the name of an Italian navigator, Amerigo Vespucci)—bears the official name the National Museum of the American Indian.[4] The current director (2024) is Cynthia Chavez Lamar, whose ancestors are Hopi, Tewa, and Navajo. In my home state of Connecticut, a wonderful organization that includes a museum, a place that exhibits a great reverence for the history and cultures of Native People and that involves them at all levels and in all of its programs, is called the Institute for American Indian Studies.[5]

There's no perfect approach, so I'll use a few collective names more or less interchangeably: Native Americans, Native People, Indigenous People, First Americans, First People, and maybe even, on occasion, Indian (especially in historical context). In so doing, I will likely not please everyone, but I use all these terms in the contexts of respect and admiration.

1

Archaeology

A WAY OF TELLING STORIES

SEVERAL SUMMERS ago I spent a bunch of time in my office in the Department of Anthropology at Central Connecticut State University following my archaeology field school. A work crew of carpenters and sheet rockers from campus was diligently reconfiguring our department offices and I got to interact with the guys, who were fascinated by my work as an archaeologist. As a user of modern power tools, one of the guys was deeply interested in how stone tools were made and used. But here's the thing. For the next few years, whenever I'd run into him on campus, his greeting was always the same: "Hey Dr. Feder! How's the dinosaur business?"

Damn! Dinosaurs! The notion that archaeology involves digging up dinosaurs is quite common and a difficult one to debunk, but here you go: WE DON'T DIG UP DINOSAURS. Full stop. Sorry for the shouting. Paleontologists dig up dinosaurs. Dinosaurs became extinct about sixty-five million years ago. I am an archaeologist. The focus of my discipline is on the human species. Our most ancient human ancestors evolved in Africa about seven million years ago, and the oldest sites I discuss in this book are much younger than that, maybe twenty-five thousand or thirty thousand years old at the most. So no. There are no dinosaurs in this book. Sorry. Now let me disabuse you of a few other and, to be honest, more harmful preconceptions you might have about a book with "archaeological" right there in the title.

Archaeology: A Way of Telling Stories

Believe it or not, though I am an archaeologist and "archaeological" is right there in the title of this book, I admit to feeling a little ambivalent about the use of that term to describe what this book is really about. At least in a sense, I am more comfortable describing this book as a work of "history," in the broadest sense of that term. That rich and temporally "deep" history reflects the story of the ancestors of peoples who are still here and, in many cases, continue to follow the cultural practices of their ancestors.

"History" with a Capital *H*

I think the subtitle of Madonna L. Moss's book about the Native People of the northwest coast of North America (chapter 15) applies to this book: *Archaeology as Deep History*.[1] My goal in this book is to provide a "deep history" of the Native People of North America with archaeology at the core of that history.

This book conveys the story of Native America primarily, but not exclusively, through the science of archaeology. So I will focus on more than just hardware here. Native People told and continue to tell their own histories, passed down across generations, providing their own version of past events. Furthermore, when Europeans arrived in North America in the sixteenth century, they recorded in writing their experiences here, including a description of the cultures of the Native People they encountered and a history of their interactions with them. The fact I am an archaeologist and that this book has "archaeological" in the title does not imply that I will or should ignore oral histories passed down by Native People or written histories told by non-Native explorers, soldiers, traders, missionaries, and settlers.

Archaeology: A History of People as Told by Landscapes, Places, and Things

Angeline Mitchell was a truly remarkable person. She was born in Bridgewater, Massachusetts, in 1854. Bridgewater is about 240 kilometers (150 miles) from my home in northwest Connecticut. So about

240 kilometers and 170 years separate Angie Mitchell and me, yet I feel like I know her because I have read the diary she kept describing her life, her exploits, and her experiences as a pioneer teacher in Arizona. Her diary is housed at the Sharlot Hall Museum in Prescott, Arizona; it has been published and, as I mentioned, I have read it. It is illuminating, fascinating, and simply quite wonderful.[2]

Here's what we know about her. When Angie was just a kid, her dad moved the family from Massachusetts to Kansas, where she later attended the University of Kansas at Lawrence. In 1873, at the age of nineteen, she obtained the equivalent of a teaching certificate there. With that certificate in hand, she taught at a number of schools in Kansas over the course of the next couple of years. When her mother and father moved west in 1875, she followed them to the pioneer city of Prescott, in the Arizona Territory (Arizona did not become a state until 1912), located about one hundred miles north of Phoenix.

She taught in Prescott for a few years and then, in 1880, when she was just twenty-six years old, she agreed to a position far to the east in an area sparsely populated by Anglos, deep in the wild area of what was then and is still called the Tonto Basin.

It took not a little courage for a young person to remove herself from the far more cosmopolitan confines of Prescott, with its population of 3,800, to what at the time was and still is pretty wild country, but Angie seems to have had both an adventurous soul and a commitment to teaching in an area sorely in need of a teacher. Though her mother and fiancé accompanied her initially to help get her settled in, they soon left her alone. In her own words, "Today for the first time in my life, I know what it is to feel utterly cast away and homesick."[3]

Once Angie adapted to her new surroundings, however, she embraced her life as a teacher in the wilderness, and she made multiple diary entries describing the educational adventures she took with her students, including one that is of the most interest to us here. On the field trip in question, Angie, with students in tow, encountered a fantastic, abandoned Native American cliff dwelling community consisting of two separate structures, one only partway up a cliff, the second higher up, and each ensconced in its own naturally eroded niche (Figure 1.1,

FIGURE 1.1, COLOR PLATE 1. The lower cliff dwelling at what is today Tonto National Monument in eastern Arizona. Teacher Angie Mitchell's 1880 visit to this site with her students inspired her to think about the connectedness of all people, whatever their culture. Kenneth L. Feder

Color Plate 1). Her description of the site is so detailed that, when rangers from the National Park Service were presented with a copy of her diary, they immediately were able to identify the place she and her students explored, cliff dwellings in what was designated Tonto National Monument in 1907.[4] If you're ever in eastern Arizona, I encourage you to visit it (it's about two and a half hours north of Tucson), walk in Angie's footsteps, and explore the houses lived in by Native Americans more than eight hundred years ago.

In the evening, with the moon rising in the clear, black, star-strewn sky, Angie wrote in her diary about the feelings that welled up in her as she thought about her day at the cliff dwellings that she and her students had just explored:

> It seemed so strange to be chatting and laughing so gaily in a house built unknown centuries ago by people unlike us in appearance but who had known joy and grief, pleasure and pain same as our race of today knows them, and who had laughed, cried, sung, danced,

married & died, mourned or rejoiced their lives away in this once populous town, or castle, or whatever one would call it! It made an uncanny feeling come over us as we rested till moon rise and talked of this long dead people and told the little we knew concerning them.[5]

Angie has done a marvelous job here reflecting on the "uncanny" feeling all archaeologists experience when they encounter the stuff left behind by human beings simply living their lives. She also remarkably expresses my own philosophy as an archaeologist, and what I hope to accomplish for the readers of this book and all of my other publications. I hope I can convey to you in these pages that same feeling of uncanny commonality and unity Angie so eloquently expresses in her diary about a people who, though removed from us in time and, for most of us, culture, are nevertheless fundamentally in step with our own humanity.

Angie died in 1909, two years after Tonto received its designation as a national monument and three years before Arizona became a state. Hers was a life well lived.

Who Owns America's Past?

I think it's fair to say that most people are proud of the unique heritage and history of their particular ethnic group, nationality, or culture. Most people feel great pride in their ancestors for overcoming the challenges they confronted, for their many achievements, and for the technological and social advances reflected in those deep histories. A small subset of people in these groups actually devote their lives to the study and celebration of their histories (in the broadest sense of that word).

For example, the famed but not uncontroversial secretary general of the Egyptian Supreme Council of Antiquities, Zahi Hawass, is an Egyptian archaeologist. Hawass spent his career excavating archaeological sites in Egypt, analyzing the written record of ancient Egyptians, writing books, participating in documentaries, and generally sharing his knowledge about ancestral Egyptians in myriad ways while, okay, also fronting for a sort of archaeology-chic clothing line. To reiterate, he is an *Egyptian* who works toward revealing the story of ancient *Egypt*.

Italian archaeologists often focus on the accomplishments of ancient Romans and Etruscans. K. C. Chang, a Chinese American archaeology professor who taught for years at Yale University, devoted his career to the analysis of Chinese prehistory. In these examples, the researchers focused on the roots of their own people, proudly telling their stories through archaeology and history.

The story of the history and archaeology of the Americas has been sadly different. The First People were, in large measure, displaced through disease but also undeniably through the political and military actions of an invading, colonial power (chapters 17 and 18). In large measure it is the descendants of those colonizers who have written the histories of Native People. In other words, that history, that archaeology, has been conducted by outsiders. Among those outsiders is, well, me.

Admittedly, the relationship between many Native People and outsider archaeologists has been problematic. Many Native People understandably view archaeology as simply another part of the colonialist program of usurpation and oppression. After all, Native People have their own histories, often handed down for generations. We'll talk about some of those histories in this book. Why do they need outsiders (like me) to impose a different story by digging holes in the ground and, too often, by disturbing their ancestors and treating them like things and not people? I get it.

As noted, I am one of those outsiders. I am not a Native person. My ancestors were Eastern European Jews who fled oppression and sought economic opportunity in the U.S. in the late nineteenth century. I am forever grateful for the safe haven America provided to my ancestors. I am alive and able to be an archaeologist and an author because of that gift. I am an archaeologist whose focus is Native America, not because archaeology affords me the opportunity to explore the history of my own people but because of my abiding interest in and respect for the cultures and histories of those Native People.

A New Archaeology

On the issue of "who owns the past," many non-Native archaeologists in North America have adopted a new approach and emphasis in recent years, no longer dictating Native American history without regard for the vast body of knowledge already possessed by Native People, and no longer ignoring how the work of archaeology affects those Native People. Labeled "archaeology's new purpose," the goal of this "new archaeology" is for Native People to be empowered to reclaim their past through the use of the discipline.[6] This new archaeology is far more likely to include the knowledge possessed by Indigenous folks, to collaborate with them, to involve them in all aspects of the work, and to recognize and incorporate their traditional knowledge with the nuts and bolts of archaeology. In some cases, in fact, non-Native archaeologists actually directly work for the Native folks who see the value of archaeology not in supplanting their knowledge but in supplementing it.

An Archaeology of Their Own

Another enormously positive development in the archaeology of the Native People of America is the fact that Native Americans themselves are becoming archaeologists and telling their own stories through their archaeological research.

Bertha Parker Pallan is often credited with being the first Indigenous archaeologist. She was of Abenaki and Seneca (East Coast) descent and first worked in the field in the 1920s. As such, some call Pallan the mother of all of the Native archaeologists who followed her. Though they continue to represent a very small percentage of the national organization of American archaeologists (the Society for American Archaeology), the number of Indigenous archaeologists is growing. For example, an ex-student of mine, and now friend and colleague, Jay Levy, was born to a Native family in South America. He was adopted as a baby by a white couple in Connecticut and later connected to his Native roots. Jay majored in anthropology at my institution, Central Connecticut State University; minored in archaeology; took every course I offered; and was a participant in my archaeology field school, helping excavate a one-thousand-year-old site in Simsbury, Connecticut. Jay is now the staff archaeologist in the Mohegan Tribe's Tribal Historic Preservation Office and is involved in research, preservation, and outreach on the Mohegan reservation, which is also in Connecticut.

I met archaeologist Kenny Bowekaty at the Pueblo of Zuni in central New Mexico in 2022. Though the people who live there today are commonly called Zuni, that name really refers to the place where their pueblo is located, on the Zuni River in New Mexico. In their language *zuni* simply means "beauty." Having been there, I believe the name is entirely appropriate. The people who live in Zuni Pueblo (also called Halona) actually call themselves A:shiwi, but they don't object to being called Zuni so I will use the two names interchangeably. It's like living in New York City and people calling you a New Yorker. We will visit Zuni Pueblo and highlight Bowekaty's work in chapter 14.

Kenny is A:shiwi, or Zuni, and a trained (at Stanford University), experienced archaeologist. He leads excavations on Zuni land, works in historic preservation, and conducts an amazing amount of outreach, sharing the story of his people with the world based on a combination of archaeology, history, and also the traditional knowledge passed down in his family. Kenny gives wonderfully informative and heartfelt tours of Zuni. His ability to combine the evidence he has collected through his archaeological research and the details of stories told to him by his grandfathers and grandmothers, and their grandfathers and grandmothers before them is extraordinarily important. When Kenny shared with us his knowledge of the ceremonies likely conducted at the sacred structures (kivas) at the archaeological site now called the Village of the Great Kivas, he did so from the perspective of a scholar with multiple channels of evidence. When he explained the meaning of the petroglyphs adorning the rock face that looms above the Village of the Great Kivas (dating to a far earlier period), he was able to do so from a Zuni perspective (chapter 16). And when he showed us a series of amazing painted images (pictographs) in a natural alcove at the top of the cliff, he knew they were a recent manifestation of a traditional practice of art because he lives at Zuni and the A:shiwi who live there know they

FIGURE 1.2, COLOR PLATE 2. A recent example (1960s) of a continuing artistic tradition (in this case, pictographs) among the Zuni people in their New Mexico homeland. Kenneth L. Feder

were painted in the 1960s by men working on the construction of a nearby reservoir (Figure 1.2, Color Plate 2).

Kenny Bowekaty is a great example of a new kind of archaeology in which traditional knowledge is seen as every bit as important and informative as that of the people with trowels and tape measures, maybe especially because he is fluent in both kinds of knowledge. If you have a chance to visit Zuni Pueblo (and you should!), make sure to contact their culture center and book a tour with him![7]

Jay Levy and Kenny Bowekaty are not the only Native People practicing archaeology. A list of others who are, in a sense, dragging the archaeological and biological anthropological professions along by moral force as well as by their application of science includes Dorothy Lippert (Choctaw; Smithsonian Institution); Kim Tallbear (Sisseton Wahpeton Oyate; University of Alberta); Joe Watkins (Choctaw; former president of the Society for American Archaeology); Paulette Steeves (Cree/Métis; Algoma University) (see chapter 7); Kisha Supernant (Métis/Papaschase/British; director of the Institute of Prairie and Indigenous

Archaeology and a professor in the Department of Anthropology at the University of Alberta) (see chapter 18); Norma Johnson (a citizen of the Kenaitze Indian Tribe; bioarchaeologist who works for the Chickaloon Village Traditional Council doing historic preservation work in Alaska); and Kurly Tlapoyawa (Chicano/Nawa/Mazewalli; a field archaeologist who, along with Ruben Arellano Tlakatekatl, hosts the fantastic podcast *Tales from Aztlantis*). The number of Native archaeologists is growing, and programs like the archaeology field school for Indigenous People in Canada are helping by presenting archaeology as a tool for "reclaiming" Native history.[8]

We can at least begin to address the grievances of the past, and we'll get a better, richer, and more inclusive archaeology as an increasing number of Native People embrace the discipline as a way of telling what is, after all, their story.

2

In Their Beginning

MY GOAL in this book is to share with you a vast story composed of many smaller ones. As a group, we human beings are good at storytelling. As children we tell our parents and caregivers about a dream or the source of a boo-boo. Maybe later we tell our friends stories about our pets and the funny things they do or about our siblings and the annoying things they do. As a parent, I tell my kids about my own childhood and about my grandparents, whom they never got to know. In my courses, I told my students stories about graduate school and working on my dissertation. I told them stories about my experiences at archaeological sites I have worked on and stories about the wonderful places I have visited for my books, encouraging people to visit archaeological sites that are open to the public.[1] You might say that as individuals, each of us is a large collection of experiences that we then make into stories that reflect who we are as individuals and as members of families. We are, in a sense, our stories, and many if not all of us enjoy sharing those stories in order for the people we encounter to know who we are.

Some of the stories we tell reach beyond the personal to include our collective selves. We tell tales about our nation; about how we overcame great challenges or how, against all odds, we defeated an implacable and powerful foe; or about how brave pioneers spread across an empty continent, conveniently leaving out the fact that the continent wasn't empty but home to millions of people bearing hundreds of cultures. I never promised that our stories were inclusive, complete, or even entirely true. The stories we tell as a nation, as a country, and as a people become our version of history that we teach in school and provide us with our holidays honoring the founders of our nation, the great victories won, and the sacrifices made. Some of these celebrations involve cranberry sauce.

Some of our stories reach beyond even that. Many groups, maybe most, strive to tell even more encompassing stories, not about just our individual selves, our families, or even our country or our people. Those stories concern where "it" all came from, "it" being the world itself, plants, animals, the moon, the stars, the sun, all of the elements of nature that provide the stage on which our personal and national dramas are performed. Many of these stories of the origins of everything of course include us, people. Where did people come from, not just us but all people?

Many scholars call these broad stories "origin myths," but I'm going to avoid using that phrase here since the term "myth" can be pejorative and elicits notions of something that simply isn't true or is just made up. In keeping with the theme here, let's simply call them origin stories, ways in which a group explains how the world came to be and where we all came from, how long ago, what our purpose is, maybe even what happens when we die.

And here's a key point: there are multiple ways of coming up with origin stories. Some we can fairly characterize as religious and involve some external or internal supernatural power or creative force, gods, a spirit or spirits, or a single omnipotent supernatural being. Religion is one way in which people attempt to write the story of who we all are in the broadest sense.

There is another way to come up with an origin story that involves direct observation of the world, a world that includes plants and animals, the stars, the sun, the moon, mountains and grasslands, rivers and oceans, and also human beings. We call that method science. Science is neither universally better than religion nor worse than it. It's just different, and the two methods can even be complementary, approaching the same questions and issues in entirely different—and entirely human—ways and providing entirely different insights about the nature of all that is. Science and religion can also aim their light on entirely different questions about the nature of the world and the fabric of reality.

They are not, or at least they are not destined to be, competitive or in opposition, though admittedly and unfortunately they often are.

It should come as no surprise that in writing this book, I will, as a trained scientist, attempt to provide the best scientifically sourced story of the First People of North America based on material evidence. I will base my discussion on the traditional approaches of science: observation, description, hypothesizing, testing, and explanation. But in no way will I attempt to denigrate or diminish the importance of the stories told by the people who are the focus of my scientific approach. For this reason, before I launch into the scientific consensus concerning the origins of the Native People of North America, I want to begin by providing a sample of their stories—"their beginning," as I phrased it in the title of this chapter—in an attempt to explain who they are and where they believe they come from. These stories aren't mine, they aren't based on science, but in a deeply important way, they're not wrong, nor can they be.

In Their Beginning: The Tule River People

The Tule River People are Native Americans living in Southern California, about 280 kilometers (175 miles) north and east of Los Angeles. Their reservation is located on nearly 245 square kilometers (60,000 acres) of mostly mountainous and entirely stunning forestland. It is absolutely a special place. I visited briefly in 2018 and the people I met were incredibly gracious and generous with their time and knowledge. I was given a tour of an amazing and sacred rock art site, and the tribal president provided me with a book of Tule stories concerning their history, published by the tribe in 2008, that compiled several of their most important traditional stories, including "When the World Began," in which they tell the story of the origin of human beings.[2] The recorded story was told by three Tule women, Beatrix Wilcox, Cecilia Silva, and Martha Tapleras. Though I did not have an opportunity to meet these women, I owe them and the tribe a debt of gratitude for sharing the story I am now about to share with you.

The tale begins in a time before the world we know was created. Eagle, working with Mountain Lion, instructed Dove to fly off and gather all the other spirit animals for a meeting. The purpose of the meeting, Eagle told the rest of the animals, was to create the first human beings. Intrigued by the task laid before them, the animals all shared their ideas about what they thought the most important characteristics of human beings should be.

The spirit beings came to a pretty clear consensus. Human beings should reflect a composite of the best features of each of the animals. Deer proposed, for example, that the humans should have eyes and ears like Deer, with their excellent vision and hearing in the forest. Fish suggested that, rather than feathers or fur, the humans should have smooth skin, enabling them to swim with ease, like a fish. Lizard chimed in with the idea that the humans should have long, dexterous fingers, enabling them to make baskets suitable for storing and even cooking food. (By the way, the Tule people are masters of basketmaking.) Those long fingers should also be useful for sewing deerskin clothing (the story makes no mention of how Deer felt about that).

Though the quality is not ascribed to any specific spirit animal, it's clear that, at least collectively, the spirit creatures conferred great intelligence on the humans, enabling them to learn how to live by observing the other animals. For example, the story states that humans learned to swim by watching Fish and they also learned to spearfish by watching Crane, who accomplishes it with its beak. Humans learned to weave baskets by watching birds make nests. They also learned to sing by listening to the birds. Finally, people learned to work together, collectively, to build their houses, collect food, and plant crops by watching, of all things, ants.

When it was Grizzly Bear's turn to contribute to the creation of human beings, he proposed that, rather than getting around on all fours like most animals, the humans should walk upright, on two feet, all of the time, just the way Grizzly Bear did when it suited him. In other words, Grizzly Bear hoped to confer on human beings a special ability that he, among all the animals, uniquely possessed.

In all of this industrious and creative work, most of the spirit animals felt useful, respected, and satisfied, and each was gratified that they were contributing an important and valuable part of themselves to the human

FIGURE 2.1. Coyote is an ambiguous spirit being for many Native People in North America. He's smart, mischievous, and untrustworthy. Here he is depicted devouring the moon, perhaps as he would during a lunar eclipse, on the Tule River Indian Reservation in Southern California. Kenneth L. Feder

being creation project. One animal, however, had been left out of the equation: Coyote, and he wasn't happy about it.

Coyote appears in lots of stories told by many Native People in North America and often is an ambiguous character. Like the actual animal, spirit Coyote is intelligent and clever, but also tricky and not especially trustworthy—a rogue, sure, but usually a lovable one. Sort of like some people. The same is true here in the Tule version of Coyote (Figure 2.1).

Coyote was especially displeased by Lizard's suggestion that the humans should have long fingers like him and even more upset, even jealous, about Grizzly Bear's proposal that they should walk on two feet, a way of moving around that Grizzly Bear possessed but Coyote did not. Coyote wanted the humans to be more like him, to have paws and claws, to walk about on all fours, and to use those paws to dig in the dirt for grubs. Attempting to defuse Coyote's anger, Eagle suggested a race between Lizard and Coyote, with the winner deciding paws or hands, upright or all fours. Coyote—not surprisingly, knowing him—tried to cheat to win the race. His attempt at subterfuge by taking a shortcut backfired and Lizard darted to the finish line ahead of Coyote, winning the race.

Grudgingly, Coyote then assisted Eagle in crafting the first six men and six women out of clay. These first people were able to walk on two legs and possessed all of the other characteristics and abilities cobbled together by the spirit animal committee. Each of these six couples were the ancestors of a different human group who then were sent out in different directions to populate the world. This is how human beings were created and how the Tule People, in particular, came to live in the land now called Southern California.

I really like that story. Consider how clever it is, how it's based on a very important observation about human beings that can be legitimately called scientific.

Physically, by and large, human bodies reflect the cliché, "A jack of all trades is a master of none." We are not the strongest animal; we're not the fastest on land or in the water; we're not the most dexterous; we can't see well in the dark like a cat or over enormous distances like a hawk or an eagle. We are, as the aphorism phrases it, "a master of none" of those abilities.

However, at the same time, and as the old saying continues, it can be argued that being a "jack of all trades" and a "master of none" is "oftentimes better than [being] a master of one." Our bodies are not really specialized for much of anything in particular, but they are pretty good at a wide variety of skills. We can run, walk for great distances, climb trees and mountains, swim, throw stuff, and manipulate material with our hands. Unlike most animals who might beat us in a specific task like running or swimming or climbing, we are passable in all of those abilities. Why, it's almost like nature took the most characteristic abilities of a bunch of different animals and put them together as an amalgam to produce us human beings. So the Tule provide a brilliant story that cleverly explains why human beings are the way we are.

In Their Beginning: The Inuit People

The Inuit (never Eskimo; see chapter 11) of the Canadian Arctic tell the story of "when things came to be" in this way. The world began when the Grand Sky People laid down the rocks and soil that became what we know as the earth. Life emerged directly from those rocks and soil in the form of plants and animals, and also human babies. In the Inuit story, all living things in this early stage of creation lived together harmoniously. "They lived with each other. Learned from one another. They were family."[3]

The first spirit people emerged at about this time as well. They looked like ordinary people, but they were incredibly powerful. Their mere thought was, by itself, a creative force. Anything these first people imagined or thought came into existence. It was at this time that the first people decided to divide themselves into two categories: male and female. These first males and females then began having families of their own. Oh, and as part of the creation by imagination, one of the first people kicked a pile of rocks, said "dog" in their language, and, behold, there were the first dogs. These dogs were destined to pull sleds and provide the first people with great mobility for traveling around their territories.

The Inuit had their own version of a biblical "fall from grace" when, soon, the people forgot that they represented just one group among many members of the family of all living things and began viewing themselves as superior to the animals. At the same time, individual people began thinking they were better or more worthy than other people.

This is also the time when hunting and eating animals started. As you might expect, the animals were more than a little put out by this but, being wise and understanding, recognized that for people to survive they needed to eat meat. So the animals decided that, as long as the humans treated them with respect, they would allow them to hunt them. The animals would die, their bodies would provide sustenance to the humans, and then the animals would be reborn in a cycle of birth, death, becoming food, and then being reborn.

It was around this time that death appeared for the humans. Intriguingly, according to the Inuit, the people themselves were the source of the idea. Before this, no one had imagined death, so no one had died yet. However, as people became old and weary, they tired of living and lay themselves down and imagined into existence an end of life. The bodies of those dead spirit people became mountains and hills.

There was a problem, however. The Inuit believed that these first dead people simply weren't very good at staying dead. Death was a new concept, and the first people's imagining of death simply wasn't strong enough. As a result, they would lie down to die, die for a little, but then, thoroughly annoyed by the process, wake up. In time, the incompletely dead people, like living people with insomnia who just say "ah, screw it" and get out of bed, simply gave up on the whole concept of mortality, whereupon they grudgingly got back up and began living again.

Through time, the first people's imagining of death became progressively stronger and clearer and death finally became a reality. The will of those who died had become so strong and so powerful that they were able to achieve permanent death and their spirits rose up into the air, where they can still be seen, colorfully dancing and shimmering across the sky as Aqsarniit, the Northern Lights. We've been incredibly lucky in southern New England this summer (2024) and have witnessed a few of these incredible natural light shows. It is of no surprise that the Inuit came up with an explanation for them.

The Inuit believe that it is just as well that today's people do not have the creative strength of the first people. Today's people simply cannot be trusted with the power to have their imagined worlds come into existence.

In the Inuit creation story, the first people created the world in which we all live simply by the power of their thoughts and imagination.

In other words, human beings weren't passive actors in the creation of the world, they were active participants. As dogs were and continue to be such an important part of their culture in terms of their mobility in the Arctic environment, it's not surprising that they are singled out in their creation story.

In Their Beginning: The Diné (Navajo) People

With a population of about four hundred thousand, the Navajo Nation of the American Southwest is the most populous Native American group (the Cherokee might argue that point, but they have a different set of rules concerning who is considered to be a member of their group). Most Diné, as they call themselves (it means "the People" in their language), live on a large reservation that takes up a substantial swath of northeast Arizona, a piece of northwest New Mexico, and a sliver of southeast Utah: 70,000 square kilometers (27,000 square miles); about the size of the state of West Virginia. You may be familiar with their magnificent works of art in the form of hand-woven rugs along with turquoise and silver jewelry produced by extraordinarily talented and creative Navajo artists.

The Navajo tell many stories about the origin of different elements of the world. This one may be my favorite and, once again, it involves that trickster and troublemaker Coyote.[4] When the world was new, only a few days old, and before there were ordinary people, there were First Man and First Woman. The world was a beautiful place back then. If you've ever spent any time on the Navajo reservation and surrounding lands, you won't be surprised by that appraisal. "Stunning" doesn't even cover it. But there was a problem. It was very dark at night after the sun went down. Having been on their reservation away from modern Navajo communities, I can certainly attest to that. Anyway, First Man and First Woman came up with a plan to both brighten the night and make the black silk dome of the nighttime sky even more beautiful and meaningful. The solution? Stars. First Man and First Woman decided to festoon the night sky with the twinkling lights of a large number of stars to help illuminate the darkness.

First Man and First Woman set about collecting bits of mica, a peculiar mineral that consists of thin sheets of translucent and highly reflective material that can easily be pried apart. First Man devised a plan to set the mica flecks in the sky in patterns that formed what amounted to a series of connect-the-dots designs—in other words, constellations—adding light, meaning, and beauty to the night sky. Together, First Man and First Woman piled these pieces of mica on a blanket and then, in an excruciatingly slow and exacting process, like artists producing a work of art across a vast canvas, they began meticulously positioning the sparkly pieces of mica on the vault of heaven. First they put one of the brightest flecks of mica in the north, fixing its position so that it could never move and always serve as a directional beacon for travelers. In other words, they began their work by placing what we today call Polaris or, more commonly, the North Star. Next, First Man grabbed seven of the shiniest pieces of mica and placed them very close to one another, a fantastic and highly visible bundle of lights. Today, Western astronomers call this cluster of stars the Pleiades or the Seven Sisters. The emblem on Subaru automobiles incorporates an image of the Pleiades star cluster (with only six readily visible stars; in fact, there are thousands in the cluster). First Man and First Woman then proceeded to position many other mica stars on their celestial canvas, all tracing recognizable shapes.

And then along came Coyote. Just as we saw for the Tule River People (and as we'll see among the people of the American northwest coast in chapter 15), the Navajo are ambivalent about Coyote. Coyote is smart but can be a pain in the ass. He was very curious about what First Man and First Woman were doing, and when they told him that they were lighting up the sky, he sort of invited himself to help. That was okay for a while, but the tedium of following First Man's meticulous plan began to grate on Coyote. So he decided to speed things up. When First Man and First Woman turned away, only briefly, to position more stars, it provided Coyote enough time to grab the edge of the blanket on which First Man and First Woman had stockpiled the mica flakes and, in one dramatic flourish, throw the lot of them into the air and blow them up into the sky with a mighty breath (Figure 2.2).

FIGURE 2.2. Here's Coyote again, depicted here in the middle of this piece of rock art (a petroglyph; chapter 16) in Nine Mile Canyon in eastern Utah, this time muddling up the patterns established by First Man and First Woman by throwing a profusion of stars into the sky. Courtesy of Prudence White

Well, Coyote had quickly and efficiently accomplished one of the tasks set out by First Man and First Woman; he lit up the sky with starlight. Unfortunately, Coyote's strategy for speeding up the process for positioning those stars created a chaotic mess, with bits of sparkling mica strewn randomly across the black canvas of the sky. First Man and First Woman indeed were angry, but Coyote was unsurprisingly unapologetic.

So the original patterns produced by First Man and First Woman remained, but with a superimposed profusion of tiny lights in no particular pattern at all. Look up at the night sky away from any city where light pollution washes out the heavens to see the handiwork of the impatient and impertinent Coyote.

Perhaps because I have a long-standing amateur interest in astronomy, I find that story compelling. Not surprisingly, the Navajo perceived patterns in the distribution of stars in the night sky and interpreted those patterns as intentionally created pictures and stories. The Navajo tale I've just related explains this as resulting from the original plan hatched by First Man and First Woman. Finally, the Navajo recognized that there was a large amount of chaotic background noise, devoid of any pattern, in what seemed to be a night sky otherwise filled with patterns and designs. Coyote was blamed for that.

The Navajo explanation of the night sky wasn't based on what we usually define as "science," but in this context, so what? It's a lovely story, and it certainly can still be characterized as the result of an abiding intellectual curiosity about nature, careful observation, a desire to explain what had been observed within the context of their culture, and a delightful and even poetic explanation. That's pretty damn good.

In Their Beginning: The Hebrews

Lest you think I am using the origin stories of the Tule River People, the Inuit, and the Navajo (and, by implication, the origin stories proffered by all Native People) in an effort to create a stark contrast between a modern, more "advanced" approach to the study of nature and the "simpler," anachronistic approach employed by Native People, consider the following origin story.

Another group of people believe that in the beginning there was nothing beyond a great and powerful presence who singlehandedly, over the course of six days and six nights, and simply by the force of his infinite will, created everything that constitutes our universe—the earth itself, light, dry land and vast bodies of water, the sun and the moon, trees and grasses, fish in the water and birds in the sky, and animals on the land. Last but not least, this supreme being fashioned out of clay a being in his own image, breathed life into him, and then placed him in a glorious garden where all of his needs would be met.

There were some strict rules concerning life in the garden, but it was a pretty sweet deal for this story's First Man—the Hebrew People called him Adam, from their word for the ground, *adameh*—and it got even sweeter when the great spirit gave First Man a companion, First Woman, who was originally called Chava, meaning "to live," but Adam changed that to Eve.

And there's more that follows. First Man and First Woman ended up breaking one of the important rules set forth by the creator when they ate the fruit from a forbidden tree growing in the garden that had been their world. They got evicted from that garden as a result and basically needed to fend for themselves for the rest of their lives, as did the generations that followed them. That includes us. Don't get me started about how their descendants got so vile that the "God" decided to drown the entire crew—people and animals alike—in a huge flood, only to relent at the last minute and save one righteous human family of eight people and a sampling of critters, which they loaded onto a boat to ride out the forty-day-long worldwide flood (see chapter 4).

By the way, that story was also used by believers to explain how different people populated different parts of the world after the flood, and that has direct relevance in this book. The patriarch of the saved family—of course, that was Noah—had three adult sons, each of whom had a wife, and after the flood those families migrated from what today is Turkey to Africa, Europe, and East Asia, each serving as the root population for one of those continents. Ironically here, since the writers of that story had no idea that there were two additional continents on the other side of the globe and that there were lots of animals and people living there, they never got around to explaining where they came from. Needless to say, the "discovery" of the people they ended up calling Indians was a real head-scratcher for them since there was no additional son of Noah to be their ultimate ancestor. The question of where those people came from, and when, is the focus of chapters 4, 5, 6, and 7.

Okay, obviously you saw what I did there. It wasn't exactly subtle. But here's my point. Millions upon millions of people—including millions of modern Americans—take that origin story at face value. They believe, and maybe you do too, that it reflects a real history of the world. Now, I'm not making light of any of these origin stories. Like the Native American origin stories I presented here, the story presented in Genesis in the Bible was a way people tried and continue to try to make sense of the world. Not better. Not worse. Different. And of intrinsic value.

Stories such as these, however, will not serve as grist for the mill of this book. I am a scientist, specifically an archaeologist, and as such, I hope it comes as no surprise that the story I present here is informed by the archaeological record.

3

Are You Ready to Rock?

I ONCE HAD a T-shirt emblazoned with the motto, "Love is fleeting but stone tools are forever." I'm not sure that archaeologists have a higher divorce rate than other people, but with T-shirts like that, you have to wonder. Anyhow, stone tools are such an important part of the archaeological record precisely because, while bone, wood, shell, and plant material decay to dust in many postdepositional environments (i.e., after they end up in the ground), stone tools are, indeed, forever. I will be talking about stone tools a lot, especially in the next few chapters. So let's tackle the general topic of stone tool technology here.

Stone Age People?

A disclaimer: you will often hear the Native folks of North America labeled as "Stone Age people." That misapprehension results in part from what I just discussed: stone tools are disproportionately part of the archaeological record because most of the other materials people used to make tools—wood and antler, for instance—have, under most conditions, disintegrated. But there is another aspect to the "Stone Age people" designation. While, yes, absolutely, stone was a very important raw material for the Native People of North America, I don't think I'm being overly sensitive when I say the term "Stone Age" is often used in a disparaging way, implying a level of simplicity, primitiveness, and even a primeval state that civilized people long ago abandoned.

If you harbor any conceit that stone tools are simple to make and therefore reflect the limited technological capabilities of a simple and primitive people, think again. Stone tools require a deep and sophisticated working knowledge of geology and practical physics.

First, stone tool makers need to know the characteristics of different varieties of rock to determine which can be used to produce sharp-edged, durable tools for cutting, scraping, piercing, engraving, and chopping. Sandstone, for example, is a nearly ubiquitous rock type in many regions; it underlies much of my own state of Connecticut and has even been designated our state rock. It has been used historically in construction; there are a bunch of churches in Manhattan made of Connecticut sandstone, and it's a primary building material for a lot of the city's fabled "brownstone" row houses. Walk around in old cemeteries in southern New England and you'll figure out in a hurry that sandstone was a preferred raw material for gravestones, especially in the seventeenth century before granite and marble became widely used. However, while it is a solid and attractive building material, most sandstone is pretty coarse, like a bunch of tiny fragments of rock all glued together. It's a sedimentary rock in which, even with the naked eye and especially under the microscope, you can see the individual grains cemented together because that's what it is. As a result of that graininess, you can't really make thin edges and, therefore, you can't really make very sharp edges, at least not sharp edges that hold up under any kind of use. Use the edge of a piece of sandstone to cut or scrape and the little grains just come apart.

The best stone for making sharp-edged tools exhibits what is called conchoidal fracture. Materials that exhibit conchoidal fracture break in the manner of glass, which, as you well know if you've ever broken a glass, produces dangerously sharp edges. If you cut your hand by picking up a shard of glass or pierce your foot by stepping on a shard, you should be able to understand that if you can learn to control the shape and thickness of bits of a glass-like material when you intentionally break it in a controlled process, you can make knives, scrapers, drills, and spear and arrow points and then haft them onto wooden shafts or handles to make highly effective tools.

The Good Stuff

Native People had to have a deep, applied knowledge of the geographic distribution of vital raw materials in their home territories, and one of those vital raw materials was stone. A recognition of the conditions conducive to the formation of various rock types contributed to their understanding of where the "good stuff" could be found if locally available. In many cases local folks also had to develop networks of contacts with people in other areas who were willing to trade the "good stuff" they had direct access to in their homelands.

Among the lithic raw materials exploited by Native People of North America were the following (this is not an exhaustive list):

- quartz: a hard, crystalline mineral
- quartzite: a metamorphic rock that began its life as sandstone and was later "metamorphosed," meaning transformed by heat and pressure
- flint: a cryptocrystalline (the individual crystals are so tiny they are hidden; *crypto* means "hidden" in Greek) form of quartz; a variety of chert
- chert: a cryptocrystalline form of quartz
- basalt: a volcanic rock
- rhyolite: a volcanic rock
- jasper: a microcrystalline variety of quartz, usually red or yellow in color
- chalcedony: a microcrystalline variety of quartz
- petrified wood: fossilized wood
- hornfels: a metamorphic rock that began its life as sandstone but was then metamorphosed by the application of enormous heat when it was covered by hot lava flows
- obsidian: not just a "glass-like" material but in fact glass, a variety made by nature in the bellies of volcanoes

Now, these raw materials can be heterogeneous and are of varying quality within a region. For example, some of the basalt flows in Connecticut are relatively fine grained and useful for making tools, but other flows are much coarser and not nearly as good. Having worked with them all in producing replicas of locally excavated stone tools as part of my course in experimental archaeology, I can attest to the fact that a lot of those locally available rocks are, well, just meh. Native People in the past knew that even better than I do and, likely through exploration and contact with neighboring groups, discovered that flint, a far superior, more glass-like rock type, was available in outcrops and mines to the west, in the Hudson River Valley. Especially in the Woodland Period (chapter 10), defined by archaeologists as the time that followed the Archaic (chapter 8), trade networks were established that brought enormous quantities of flint into Connecticut.

Rock Knocking

Stone tools all over the world were produced by a process called percussion flaking. In percussion flaking, a "core" of stone—the so-called object piece—is struck with a hammer that may be stone or antler, in an attempt to remove flakes that can serve as blanks to be further refined, often through a process called pressure flaking. In pressure flaking, instead of striking the object piece, there is a more controlled and precisely directed application of force in which a worker virtually peels off thin flakes by applying pressure to the edge, often with a "tine," the narrow tip of an antler. The goals in pressure flaking are to alter the shape of the edge of a tool and to make it progressively thinner and therefore sharper. Using a combination of percussion and pressure, stone tool makers produced cutting tools (knives), scraping tools (scrapers), engraving tools (gravers), and piercing tools (spear and arrow points and drills) (Figure 3.1).

Removing flakes from cores through percussion and then shaping those flakes by the application of pressure in order to produce a finished tool is not an arbitrary, casual, or random process of hitting a rock with another rock or pressing it with the tip of an antler and hoping for the best. It is a sophisticated and refined process informed by years of practice. Making a stone tool is an exercise in real-time problem-solving since you can't see the interior of the rock before you strike it hard

FIGURE 3.1. A selection of stone (quartz, quartzite, flint, hornfels, and slate) tools (spearpoints, knives, scraping tools, a shaft straightener, and a drill) from archaeological sites in the Farmington River valley of Connecticut. Kenneth L. Feder

enough to detach a flake or apply sufficient pressure to peel off a flake. Each strike or push reveals specific underlying features of the object piece that the toolmaker didn't know before and now needs to recognize and deal with, altering strategies on the fly.

I can make a pretty serviceable stone tool, but I'm mediocre at it overall. You know the cliché about it taking ten thousand hours of repetitive practice to perfect a skill like playing guitar or running a marathon? Becoming a highly skilled lithicist (sometimes called a flintknapper, even when raw materials other than flint are being used) works the same way and requires the same dedication to studying stone and learning how to control the size, thickness, and shape of flakes removed from cores and then sculpted into a final shape. People who become proficient at stone tool making possess a combination of both scientific and artistic skills. We see those skills exhibited in abundance by the stone tool makers of North America.

In the apocryphal tale, when asked what weapons might be used in World War III, Albert Einstein admitted that he didn't know the answer to that question, but he was pretty sure that in World War IV the weapons of choice would be sticks and stones. As I always told students in my experimental archaeology course, in the event of World War III, survivors (if there are any) who know how to make stone tools will rule us all.

A Point About Points

One common way in which archaeologists compartmentalize past peoples by time, place, and culture is by reference to the specific forms of the primary tools and weapons they produced. Projectile points are a major focus of analysis and interpretation.

First, the term "projectile point" is a generic term for any stone point that was used as the tip of a projectile. The generic term is used because we can't always differentiate, at least not initially, a dart point from a spearpoint or from an arrow point. "Projectile point" is simply a safer, inclusive term that makes sense to use unless we are certain of the kind of projectile we're dealing with.

Now, in my region of North America, here in the Northeast, archaeologists will drone on and on about arcanely named projectile point styles or types like Brewerton Side Notched, Levanna, Squibnocket Stemmed, Jack's Reef, and Orient Fishtails, which may be why we're rarely invited to parties. In fact, in the standard and venerable dictionary of projectile point forms in New York, William Ritchie's *New York Projectile Points: A Typology and Nomenclature*, which is used as a guide throughout the Northeast, Ritchie names and lists twenty-seven different projectile point types in the region, each representing a different culture, time period, and location.[1] So why is there so much variation in point form (see Figure 3.1)?

Here's the deal: there are not an infinite number of variables a toolmaker can take into consideration when making a stone point. Nevertheless, the number of combinations and permutations for making the point and have it still be effective is enormous. Straight edges, curved edges. Equilateral triangles or isosceles triangles. Side notched, corner notched, basally notched, or not notched at all. Straight base, concave base, convex base. Stemmed or unstemmed. Long, short. Wide, narrow. Flint, jasper, chalcedony, obsidian, and so on. Essentially, a point will be effective in dispatching an animal as long as it is pointy at the tip, its edges are thin and sharp, it can be hafted on a shaft of wood or reed, and it is aerodynamic. All of the other variables just listed often are just a matter of style, training, and preference and have little impact on the effectiveness of the weapon.

Nevertheless, there are general consistencies in the preferred point forms for a given place and time. In other words, while a stone tool maker has an enormous range of choices to make in crafting a spearpoint, dart tip, or arrowhead, people living in the same place and same time—for example, central Utah five thousand years ago, western New York State four thousand years ago, or coastal California eight thousand years ago—tended to make their tools according to local templates, and these templates may differ from those applied somewhere else at a different time.

Why is that? Let's speculate. Kids see their parents, grandparents, older siblings, and other adults in their orbit being competent members of their society who make stuff. Kids nearly always attempt to emulate the things they see adults do and so, in this scenario, if they see a parent making spearpoints, they may try their hand at it. At first, maybe, the parent takes sharp-edged pieces of stone away, hoping to protect their toddler, but at some point that same mentor may take the kid's hands and actively begin the process of training them in the craft of stone tool making, a skill that will be vital for them to learn for use in adulthood. It seems a reasonable assumption that many kids, but not necessarily all, want the end result of what begins as play to be consistent with what their dad or mom—or a grandparent, older sibling, aunt, or uncle—is doing and making. It makes sense, therefore, that a specific tradition of making stone tools, or any other tool, is passed down from parent to child, from mentor to mentee, from teacher to student. Now, many other parents living in other villages in the same region may actually all be able to trace their ancestry back to a founding family or closely related founding families, so the specific tradition of toolmaking isn't confined to a single village but may permeate an entire region. This would explain the geographic consistency of projectile point types within a region and within a time period.

There's a scene in the very well-known Broadway musical *Fiddler on the Roof* where the protagonist, Tevye, presents a list of things his people, Jews living in late nineteenth-century Russia, do in certain ways. He says, "You may ask, how did this tradition get started? I'll tell you. I don't know. But it's a tradition."

That answer is both funny and ironically insightful: "I don't know." Which inspires a song—a typical Broadway musical thing to do—the iconic "Tradition." Tevye admits that he has no explanation for the things he was taught, including the proper roles of boys and girls; the "tradition" of a man—"the papa"—being the "master of the house"; the responsibility of a woman to make a "proper home, a quiet home, a kosher home"; and the necessity to marry within the faith. Even though he can't explain these traditions, he feels no need to justify or even understand them while he continues to practice them and teaches his children to do the same, all because it constitutes "tradition," which is an important way by which people define themselves and distinguish themselves from people outside their group. Returning to Tevye: "And because of our traditions, every one of us knows who he is and what God expects him to do."

So if there's ever a Broadway musical focused on ancient people who make stone tools, when a little kid asks their mentor, "Why do we always put the notches on the sides and not the corners?" the teacher can admit to not knowing the answer but then focus on the importance of tradition!

Of course, there are always rebels in this scenario—like in *Fiddler on the Roof*, where Tevye's daughter falls in love with and marries a non-Jewish man—including creative people who ask, "Why do we always do that the same way? Maybe we should try something different." They may experiment and show their work to others, who may adopt their newfangled forms and methods or reject them. Over time, for reasons that may be practical but are also likely to be the result of serendipity, the common, accepted, or standard form for projectile points shifts, from side notched to corner notched, from straight edges to curved edges. And the point is (bad choice of words), consistency in point form and changes in point form are readily visible to the archaeologist, who then uses them to define a culture at a given period of time. We'll apply this perspective throughout this book.

One more thing. These social rules or norms applied to stone tool making apply to all of the other arts developed by Native People—and, to be honest, people everywhere. Ceramics, metallurgy, weaving, bone work, wood carving, building construction, and more are created, taught, passed down, and altered within a cultural framework that may be unique to each time, place, and group. Archaeologists study those objects, that material culture, and we glean from them the rules and norms reflected in their material forms as points and pots, rings and necklaces, clubs and knives, statues, houses, and on and on. We then use that knowledge to define at least the material culture of a group of people. I'll be doing that a lot in the rest of this book.

4

European Encounter with a "New World"

LIKE MANY AMERICANS, including many of you reading this book, I come from a family of immigrants. Three of my four grandparents were born in the U.S. in the late 1800s and early 1900s. The fourth, Mollie Feder (Fleischer), was born in Poland in about 1901. There are no birth records for her. Mollie, one of my favorite people in the world, was cagey about her actual age, going so far as to insist on an obviously false birth year on her gravestone so she would appear to cemetery visitors to be younger than she actually was—younger, in fact, than her younger sister. Go figure.

I get a kick out of tracing my family genealogy using federal census and state "vital" records (births and deaths). It was truly incredible to me to see my grandmother's name on the census rolls when she was a teenage girl and then a young woman who got married to Max (in 1922). In the 1930 census I found the name of their firstborn, a then five-year-old boy they named Murray (Grandma wanted to name him Maurice because of course she did). That little boy grew up to become a brilliant student, a soldier in World War II, and a husband; received a PhD from the University of California at Berkeley; and was a teacher, a scholar, a father to two children—my sister Karen and me—and ultimately a devoted grandfather. He was my dad.

Okay, so what was my intent in sharing a bit of my personal genealogy? I just wanted to show that for one category of Americans—people who came to America voluntarily—investigating the history of their presence here is greatly facilitated by official documents: ship manifests listing the names of immigrants; federal census records; the aforementioned vital records of births and deaths kept by states, counties, or towns; land records listing the names of property owners, including both sellers and buyers; tax records; church membership lists; school registers; and military rolls.

Personal records simply do not exist for other groups of Americans, so there's no paper trail to document their personal journeys to America and their stories upon arrival. For example, of the approximately 10.7 million African people who survived the Middle Passage, their involuntary voyage to the New World, most ended up as slaves in the Caribbean and South America. Close to 400,000 were shipped directly to North America, but they are represented by little more than gross numbers in the records of the slavers. Birth names, ages, marital status, and family relationships are missing though often passed down in family stories. Slave auctions record little more than raw numbers, identification of sex, and, in some cases, skills. Slaves generally were not treated as individual human beings with biographical lives worthy of documenting. They were commodities, valued not for their humanity but for their economic worth.

When it comes to the Native American people who are the focus of this book, written records are nonexistent for their initial settlement of America. It occurred long before writing had developed anywhere. Later documentation is sparse, generally little more than population numbers, and until recently it was kept by non-Native people with various agendas, often overseers of reservations. Very few Native People were enumerated in the federal decennial censuses from the initial one in 1790 through the 1840 count. Native People began to be regularly included in the federal census only in 1860, but not thoroughly or inclusively. Even after 1860, the federal census essentially ignored the largest segment of them, the Native People living on reservations. The attempt to include all Native People in the federal census, those living both on and off reservations, started only with the 1900 federal census. Even then, the counts are of questionable accuracy. That's not terribly surprising. Shamefully, Native Americans were not considered full citizens of the United States with the right to vote until passage of the Indian Citizenship Act of 1924, barely one hundred years ago as I write these words.

The best place to research the enumeration, or lack of enumeration, of Native People in the census is the National Archives website.[1] Again, for their initial expansion into the Americas, written documentation does not exist.

This, however, does not mean we have no sources of information to investigate the movement of the first people into North America. I will focus on a number of those streams of data in chapters 5 and 6, including geology, paleoclimatology, archaeology, and biological anthropology. These data will allow us to approach a number of questions, including the following: When did this first migration by people to the Americas occur? Where did they come from? How did they journey here? How did they survive once they got here?

I should add a point of clarification here. By opening this discussion with information about my family's arrival in America in the late nineteenth and early twentieth centuries, I am in no way implying that the original movement of people into the New World was just another example of immigrants showing up on America's shores, one in a bunch of equivalent population movements. There is no suggestion of equivalency here. The ancestors of today's Native People, as I will document in chapters 5 and 6, first arrived here likely more than twenty thousand and perhaps as much as thirty thousand years ago. Some argue for an even earlier entry date (chapter 7). Sure, I suppose that those first people in the New World can be labeled "immigrants," but I make no pretense that their migration was the equivalent of my ancestors' immigration of just a little more than 130 years ago or of yours if you are a non-Native, even if you can trace your ancestors back to Plimoth Plantation (original spelling) in Massachusetts (400 years ago), Point Comfort in Virginia (as slaves, 403 years ago, in 1619), Jamestown in Virginia (415 years ago), or St. Augustine in Florida (more than 450 years ago). We all are recent arrivals compared with Native Americans.

This is something Native People know absolutely. In my own research on the eighteenth- and nineteenth-century community in Connecticut, I encountered an 1855 newspaper interview of a woman who lived in the settlement called the Lighthouse, though the name of the village, located more than fifty miles from the coast, was metaphorical. When the woman, Polly Elwell, brought the reporter to the village cemetery, she told him that only one non-Native person was buried there. "He was a foreigner—like you." The reporter objected to this characterization of his lineage, claiming that his ancestors arrived on the *Mayflower*. Polly responded powerfully: "We were Americans when you foreigners came here."[2]

To rewrite the famous folk song penned by Woody Guthrie just a little, "This land was *their* land, from California to the New York Island, from the Redwood Forest to the Gulf Stream waters." The rest of us are, let's face it, foreigners and newcomers.

The Not Discovery of America

> Discover: to find information, a place, or an object especially for the first time.
>
> —CAMBRIDGE ENGLISH DICTIONARY

> Discover: to be the first person to become aware that a particular place or thing exists.
>
> —OXFORD DICTIONARY

I have on occasion written letters to the editor and freestanding essays for the *Hartford Courant*, by its own claim "America's oldest continuously published newspaper." I have shared in those letters and essays my anthropological and archaeological insights on some current topic or controversy recently reported on by the paper. I've commented on topics as disparate as nuclear war, designating English as our nation's official language, ancient and modern technology, evolution, and the use of animals in medical experiments, all from my position as a student of human antiquity.

None of these letters or essays elicited even remotely as strong a reaction, however, as did one I wrote in response to a previously published article in the paper about Columbus Day, of all things, concerning the

FIGURE 4.1. Engraved section of John Vanderlyn's 1847 painting titled *Landing of Columbus*. The original painting can be seen in the U.S. Capitol Rotunda. Bureau of Printing and Engraving, CC BY-SA 3.0

five hundredth anniversary in 1992 of Columbus's first voyage to the New World (Figure 4.1).

Everything I said in my letter was really quite innocuous, obvious, and certainly not original or groundbreaking. I ended my letter with this plea: "As we note this 500th anniversary of Columbus's voyage, we owe it to the Indigenous People of the Americas to also reflect on the destruction ultimately visited upon them by Columbus's accidental discovery of the New World."[3]

Truly, I didn't intend to provoke anyone but merely wanted to comment about our use of the word "discovery" when talking about American history. But it got someone righteously indignant, and the person who responded to me held nothing back.

My current attitude about Columbus is this: Go ahead, celebrate him all you want. Mark Columbus Day down as a holiday on your calendar. Have parades honoring his navigational achievements. If you are an Italian American, by all means take some ethnic pride in his nautical prowess and historical importance. Sure, maybe you should think about the fact that his treatment even of the Spanish colonists he oversaw in the Americas was egregiously bad. According to a report filed by Francisco de Bobadilla enumerating Columbus's offenses, this included cutting off people's noses and ears, selling folks into slavery, and forcing women to be paraded around naked as punishment for some offense.[4]

None of that was paramount in the mind of the person who wrote a response to my letter to the editor. The first giveaway that I must have hit a sore spot was the fact that her response was much longer than my actual letter to the editor. Even stranger, her letter was so off the rails, the newspaper declined to publish it, so she sent it directly to me accompanied by a handwritten notecard on which she accused me of telling "half-lies" about Columbus, "which is offensive to those who've studied history with an open mind." She continued, saying that I was prejudiced and I had "no right to propagate such prejudices." It didn't take much thought on my part to determine that she was a trifle upset with me.

What seemed particularly strange, however, was the depth of her extraordinary anger with the plea that was the main point of my letter: that, whatever you thought, felt, or said about Columbus, for pity's sake don't say he "discovered America." Because he didn't, for one mundane but significant reason and for one spectacularly foundational one.

The mundane reason it's clear that Columbus didn't "discover" America is this: Columbus, who made landfall in the Caribbean in 1492, was not even the first European to encounter the New World. That award, if they were giving an award for it, would belong to the Norse who beat Columbus here by five hundred years when they landed, explored, and briefly settled in eastern Canada, beginning a little before 1000 CE, as I will discuss later in this chapter. So even just consulting the European timeline shows that Columbus wasn't the first one here and thus did not discover America.

Of infinitely greater significance is the foundational reason I can present into evidence supporting my claim that Columbus did *not* discover America: there were already TENS OF MILLIONS OF PEOPLE (sorry for the shouting) living on America's continents. As Amerigo Vespucci—not Columbus, by the way—asserted in a letter written in 1503 to Lorenzo Pietro Francesco Di Medici, "It is lawful to call it a new world, because none of these countries were known to our ancestors, and to all who hear about them they will be entirely new."[5]

I simply cannot accept, nor should you, any interpretation of the term "discovery" that justifies its application to Columbus's achievement.

Imagine some random dude showing up at your house, planting a flag, proclaiming his "discovery" of your house and property, and then, to compound the injury, claiming this newly "discovered" territory for the king and queen of Spain or Fredonia or Pottsylvania or wherever. You'd rightfully have him hauled off and arrested!

Look, saying that someone other than the ancestors of the millions of people already living here discovered the lands (as will be discussed in chapters 5, 6, and 7) about twenty thousand and perhaps closer to thirty thousand years ago robs those Indigenous People of their historical achievement. It's a historical version of "stolen valor" and will not stand scrutiny.

This was the essence, phrased more politely I assure you, of my letter to the editor published just before Columbus Day in 1992—that whatever you think about him, hero, villain, or something in between, Columbus did not discover America. This obvious and to me self-evident fact is what so pissed off my correspondent. She began by saying, "Add a Professor Feder of CCSU to the list of detractors and malcontents who persist at tearing away at the achievements of Columbus like vultures at the kill."

What? I'm a "detractor" and a "malcontent"? Oh, and a "vulture"? Wow.

On my explicit objection to calling Columbus's achievement a "discovery," the letter writer chided me, responding, "To quibble about such things is to miss the point of man's daring and need to learn, all who came are to be credited for following the stars to their dreams."

Okay, beyond the terribly clichéd phrasing, this is where her letter gets totally scary and reveals what was truly at the heart of her perspective. Concerning very specifically the people already living in the Americas before Columbus arrived, the writer said, and this takes my breath away, "Whoever the men were, and whatever supposedly glorious civilizations existed, only traces remained and little came of them."

That's what is called "saying the quiet part out loud." In a single sentence, the letter writer dismisses all of Native American culture and refers to civilizations that even the Spanish conquistadores characterized as magnificent as only "supposedly glorious." So the Aztecs, the

Maya, and the Inca were some vague rumor and little came of them? Really? What about crops like corn, beans, and squash that continue to be mainstays in the modern world's diets; a calendar at least as accurate as the one developed by the conquerors; a number system with a zero; impressive and beautiful architecture; multiple writing systems; advanced irrigation systems; vast empires? Little came of the glorious New World civilizations?

It's nonsense and, just as bad, the writer's libel about New World civilizations is a non sequitur anyway. Her ignorance-based low opinion of New World peoples is entirely irrelevant. Even if it were accurate and reasonable (I repeat: it's neither), so what? They were here first. Full stop. That much is indisputable. *They* discovered, spread across, colonized, and thrived in a "new world" ("new" only to Europeans) consisting of two continents that provided a vast array of habitats, each challenging in its own ways, each of which required exquisitely crafted adaptations for survival, and they did this not hundreds and not thousands but tens of thousands of years before Columbus was even born.

Columbus did not discover America; he didn't even discover the capital of Ohio, though it is named for him. He did discover that if you anger the king and queen of Spain, they slap you in irons and throw you in jail. He also discovered that if you don't have the ear of the mapmaker, they don't even name the place you didn't actually discover after you; instead, they name it after that upstart Amerigo Vespucci, who figured out something you never did: that you made landfall not on Japan or China—that's what Columbus maintained until his death—but in a world new to Europeans. Well, it could have been worse. We all could be living now in Vespucciland. So there's that.

Okay, So Who Are These People Walking Around in This New World?

When Columbus first encountered people in the New World, there was no great mystery about the existence of people here because he didn't know it was a "new world." He just figured those folks were Chinese or

Japanese, or at least geographically and genealogically close to Chinese and Japanese people. When European thinkers began to delve more deeply into the issue, and certainly when Amerigo Vespucci recognized that Columbus was wrong and that he had not discovered a new route to Asia but had, instead, "discovered" (notice I'm using the *d* word in scare quotes) lands that were previously unknown to Europeans, significant questions were raised concerning the identity and source of the people he had encountered there.

Over the years since Vespucci's pronouncement, there have been a number of plausible (certainly not all equally so) or at least technically possible scenarios that might account for the presence of people in the New World in general and North America in particular. These proposed scenarios have reflected the dominant intellectual "paradigm" of the time. Think of a paradigm as a general consensus on a topic, but on steroids. Every science operates within its paradigm, its encompassing world view. Archaeology is no different. A paradigm provides the framework within which a particular science like archaeology functions. To be sure, a paradigm can be a restrictive box, and in the history of science, there are always people who think outside that box. Let's face it, some of those folks are delusional and end up either ridiculed in history or, perhaps even more sadly, entirely forgotten. However, some of those free thinkers have actually detected flaws in the reigning paradigm and moved science forward with new and better and more inclusive explanations. That is precisely how our understanding of the earliest human settlement of the Americas has improved and progressed. Since we're talking about how Europeans responded to their encounter with a world and a people whose existence they had not been previously aware of, let's start with the first paradigm applied to the source and timing of the Native population of the New World. It originates in the Bible.

The First Paradigm: Biblical

In the fifteenth century, the dominant paradigm of Europeans, the world view or framework within which the presence of a heretofore unknown people could be explained, was provided by the Bible. In other words, for Europeans, the true "History of the World, Part 1" (with apologies to Mel Brooks) had been written in the Old Testament of the Bible, especially in the book of Genesis.

I must digress briefly to acknowledge that at the time there was a school of thought—well, lack of thought—that denied the need to explain any newly discovered information related to nature or history, including the presence of people in a new world. This particular brand of anti-intellectualism viewed the Bible as inerrant, complete, and, therefore, sufficient for explaining everything. It was considered by some to be little more than conceit or hubris on the part of mere human beings to think that they needed to add to the knowledge already provided in the Bible, and it was considered practically blasphemous to believe that human beings even had the ability to explain on their own any element of God's creation. If there were people in the New World, it was sufficient to acknowledge that God put them there, and our job was to convert them to Christianity, not study the details of how God managed that trick. Theirs was a sort of "don't ask, don't tell" approach to the world. Just read the Bible. Everything you need to know is in there. Move on.

The brilliant seventeenth-century British Anglican theologian and scientist Rev. John Ray strongly opposed this view and summarizes that know-nothing attitude succinctly when, in the preface to his 1690 work *Synopsis Methodica Stirpium Britannicarum*, he notes, "There are those who condemn the study of Experimental Philosophy [what today we call natural history] as mere inquisitiveness and denounce the passion for knowledge as a pursuit unpleasing to God and so quench the zeal of the philosopher."

Ray defends our intellectual ability to grow our knowledge of the world and in fact interprets it precisely as a gift of God: "Those who scorn and decry knowledge should remember that it is knowledge that makes us men, superior to the animals and lower than the angels, that makes us capable of virtue and happiness such as animals and the irrational cannot attain." Ray, a devout Christian, even maintained that scientific inquiry was a method by which some people might worship God. The name of Ray's remarkable book published in 1691 explains his philosophy succinctly: *The Wisdom of God Manifested in the Works of the Creation.*[6] So in Ray's view, by studying God's work—in other words, by conducting science—you are actually worshiping God. This would include investigating God's creation of a world in which people were living in the Americas.

So while not all, a substantial number of scientists, philosophers, historians, and theologians embraced the effort to explain the presence of people in the New World, but always, always, always within a biblical framework that included the understanding that God had created the first people, Adam and Eve, and that all human beings were ultimately derived from that first couple. Beyond this, the biblical paradigm included a massive destructive event wrought by an angry God at some point after creation. This event, a global flood, killed off all terrestrial wildlife and all human beings except for those saved aboard an ark, the ultimate lifeboat, creating what amounts to a population bottleneck in human history. People were "fruitful and multiplied" after Adam and Eve were escorted out of the Garden of Eden, but the population of their descendants narrowed down considerably—like in the neck of a bottle—when the flood struck. The newly encountered, previously unimagined people—unimagined by Europeans—in a "new world," also previously unimagined by Europeans, must have, like everybody else in the world, descended from the folks saved onboard the ark. Figuring out precisely who and how were mere details, albeit details that fascinated many European thinkers.

Even before approaching the question of who the newfound people in the newfound world were and how they might be related to the people saved onboard the ark, European scholars first needed a determination of whether they actually were people or some kind of animal. Yes, that actually was a point of contention. Were the two-legged creatures seen walking about in the New World who possessed sophisticated languages, built imposing monumental structures, and had developed enormously productive agricultural systems actually humans or just some weird species of animals, perhaps apes? The question was so important, Pope Paul III felt compelled to weigh in on it in 1537 by declaring in a papal bull titled *Sublimis Deus*, "The Indians are truly men and they are not only capable of understanding the catholic faith but, according to our information, desire exceedingly to receive it."[7] How he knew that last bit about them, that they "desire exceedingly" to receive the "catholic faith," is an open question, but the good news is that in this same statement, the pope declared that, as real people, the Indians should never be enslaved or deprived of their property. Chalk one up for the pope on that determination, even if Europeans didn't always adhere to his opinion.

Once the pope had spoken on that point, it was understood that, like all other people alive in 1537, the Indigenous People of the New World had to be derived from Noah and Mrs. Noah, which led scholars to the determination that all people, including those newly encountered in the New World, had to be the descendants of one of Noah's three sons, Shem, Ham, or Japheth, along with, of course, their wives.

Before encountering the two continents they called North and South America, European scholars had counted three races of human beings and three sons of Noah. That could not have been a coincidence. Those same scholars went on to determine which of the three Noachian lines had led to each of those three known races: Japheth had given rise to the Europeans, Shem was the ancestor of the Asians, and Ham was the progenitor of the Africans. Since there was no fourth son who could have been the ultimate ancestor of the Indians as a separate, fourth race, the first speculations among Europeans concerning the derivation of the people of the New World concerned which one of those three specific, known bloodlines they could be traced back to. Was it Shem? Ham? Japheth? Each of those options was considered plausible, and each could be ensconced within the biblical paradigm.

European writers and thinkers in the fifteenth, sixteenth, seventeenth, eighteenth, and nineteenth centuries, and even into the twentieth, pumped out an enormous number of speculations concerning the downstream identity, long after the flood, of the Native People of the Americas. In other words, if Shem, Ham, or Japheth had been their great-great- (and however many more greats) grandfather, who were their more recent ancestors? Were they wandering Jews from the Middle East, perhaps members of the Lost Tribes of Israel who were descended from Shem? Were they transplanted Phoenicians from the northern coast of Africa and descended from Ham? Were they the descendants of wandering Vikings (Japheth), Scythians (Shem), Egyptians (Ham), Chinese (Shem), or Japanese (Shem)? In one extreme speculation it was even suggested that the founding population of Native America might be escapees from Atlantis upon its destruction. Many thinkers were indiscriminate and credulous in their speculations and supported all or any combination of these and more. But each and every one of these speculations was rooted firmly within the biblical paradigm, tracing America's Native People back through Noah's sons, Noah, and ultimately all the way back to Adam and Eve.

With all this speculating going on, one late sixteenth-century Jesuit missionary's hypothesis concerning the source of the human population of the New World, while still unabashedly biblical, was based on logic and precociously clearheaded thinking. He got pretty close to the modern consensus even though he did not possess the final piece of the puzzle, the geography of the farthest reaches of northeast Asia and northwest North America. I refer to a Spanish missionary who lived among the Native People of Peru in the sixteenth century, while making every effort to convert them to Catholicism. His name was Father José de Acosta.

In his book on the subject, *The Natural and Moral History of the Indies*, published in 1590, Acosta recognized that all of the terrestrial animals living in the aboriginal Americas must have drowned in Noah's flood, leaving those two continents completely devoid of animals when the biblical flood's waters receded after "forty days and forty nights." This posed a conundrum. Fifteenth- and sixteenth-century European explorers encountered large populations of animals in the New World. Where did those animals come from? Acosta made the deduction, consistent with his biblical framework, that since all living animals in the present (the sixteenth century for him) had to be descended from only the animals that survived the flood by being saved by Noah onboard the ark, the ancestors of the animals in the New World must also have descended from those same animals. Those animals, therefore, must have migrated to the New World after the flood, perhaps over many years, from the landing place of the ark in "the mountains of Ararat" to the New World. (By the way, the Bible does not say "Mount Ararat"; it refers to a region, "the mountains of Ararat," and the current Mount Ararat, in Turkey, wasn't called that until the Middle Ages.)

Based on world geography as known during Acosta's time, large oceans—the Atlantic on one side, the Pacific on the other—separated the Old World from the New World. Since animals cannot swim across vast oceans or build and navigate boats, Acosta reasoned that the descendants of the critters that survived the flood by hitching a ride on the ark must have been able to *walk* on dry land all the way from the mountains of Ararat to the New World, and this meant that, at least in some area of the globe, the Old and New Worlds were not separated by a large stretch of water but instead were joined. Acosta hypothesized, again based on existing knowledge of the configuration of the continents in the early sixteenth century (Magellan had already circumnavigated the world in the period 1518–22), that the only place the Old and New Worlds could have been close enough to facilitate animal movement simply by walking after the biblical deluge was the unexplored and unknown region (again, from a European perspective; local folks knew all about it) between northeast Asia and northwest North America. In other words, by what was essentially a process of deduction and elimination, Acosta reasoned that this region must be where the Old and New Worlds are joined.

Acosta therefore concluded that in scholars' attempts to determine how the human descendants of Noah made it to the New World, the animals saved onboard the ark might literally provide us with a pathway. If animals could migrate on dry land, over however long a period of time following the flood, and across however many miles from Ararat to America, so could have people, metaphorically following in those animals' footsteps. In Acosta's view, then, the Native People of the Americas must be transplanted northeast Asians.

Biological evidence already collected seemed to support this deduction. Years before Acosta reached his conclusion concerning the source population of the Indigenous People of the Americas, explorer Giovanni da Verrazzano sailed along the East Coast of North America from what we can determine was the modern border between North Carolina and South Carolina and then north and east to Cape Cod in Massachusetts in 1524. In his short memoir concerning this journey, Verrazzano described the physical appearance of those Native People he encountered along the way in terms of their skin tone, hair color and texture, and eye shape as being nearly identical to the characteristics of the Native People of Asia. Based on this, many scholars felt that this previous description of the Native People of the New World confirmed Acosta's precociously correct tracing of the Native population of the New World, a deduction that matches the modern consensus.

Of course, Acosta was technically incorrect, as the Old and New Worlds were not literally connected; however, they are very close in northeast Asia and northwest North America, separated by a strait of only about 80 kilometers (50 miles) at their closest. Remarkably, Acosta had largely figured this out almost sixty years before a Russian explorer, Semyon Ivanovich Dezhnyov, observed the proximity of the Old World to the New in northeast Asia and northwest North America when, in 1648, he saw that only a narrow sea strait separated them. Another Russian, Vitus Bering, did a more extensive study of the region in 1725, and it is his name that is applied to what we now call the Bering Strait and the surrounding waters of the Bering Sea. Of course, had anyone asked the Native People of the region, they could easily have reported on local geography and the proximity of two vast land masses. But the Russian Bering ended up getting the credit for that "discovery" (and yes, scare quotes again), so world maps bear his name for the strait and the sea.

What Acosta could not have known in 1590 is that the world has endured multiple cold periods when snow and ice have accumulated in vast amounts in northern latitudes and high elevations, removing large quantities of water from the oceans and exposing huge, broad swaths of land, including a vast plain now under the relatively shallow water of the Bering Sea that separates northeast Asia from northwest America. These cold periods occurred between about 1.8 million and 10,000 years ago during the geological epoch we now call the Pleistocene, colloquially called the Ice Age.

It would be nice to be able to say that Acosta's reasoning was so sound and sensible, especially once the geography of proximity had more or less been confirmed by Dezhnyov and then Bering, that the hypothesis of a northeast Asian source for the New World's human population became universally accepted. Alas, that was not the case, and speculations about pre-Columbian migrants from Egypt, Rome, China, Africa, Southeast Asia, and on and on continued unabated. Some actually continue to the present day. But they are just that: evidence-free speculations. No archaeological or genetic evidence supports any such claims. The Native People came from Asia at a time still being determined by scientists. More about that scientific consensus in chapter 5.

Messages in Stone

Is there any compelling evidence today that Europeans, Africans, or later Asians journeyed to and even settled in North America following the initial movement of people that I will focus on in chapter 5? Well, yes and no. Let's do a little exploring ourselves.

One variety of evidence that has been provided in support of the ancient visitation/colonization hypothesis is inscriptions. Especially in the nineteenth century, objects were claimed to have been found at archaeological sites in North America ostensibly bearing authentic inscriptions in Old World languages, often Hebrew (Figure 4.2).[8] In every case, linguists have raised serious questions concerning the authenticity of the writing and, of even greater importance for an archaeologist, no artifacts (other than the inscriptions themselves) have been found, none of the regular stuff beyond a written message that an archaeologist would expect to find if a group of foreigners had spent time in North America before Columbus, with one exception that I'll address later in this chapter. It is telling that these inscriptions were found predominantly during a period in American history when there was a lot of controversy about the "discovery" of America. Lots of archaeology has been done in the twentieth and twenty-first centuries and no one finds these inscriptions anymore. In all likelihood, they're all fake.

FIGURE 4.2. The Los Lunas Decalogue Stone is located in Los Lunas, New Mexico, about a thirty-minute drive from Albuquerque. The writing on the stone is a version of the Ten Commandments in Hebrew. Not reported until the 1930s, it is a modern fake. Kenneth L. Feder

Stone Structures

Along with inscribed artifacts, another category of evidence presented by those who believe there was a substantial presence of people from the Old World living in the New before the Columbus voyages are stone structures that to their eyes are strikingly similar to those dating to thousands of years ago in western Europe. Chambers, usually constructed with local fieldstone in courses of dry-laid stone masonry, are sometimes identified as ceremonial in nature, places of worship of ancient Celtic gods, and that may reflect astronomical alignments with the solstices and equinoxes. Sites like the Acton Stone Chamber and the Upton Stone Chamber, both in Massachusetts, are attributed to

FIGURE 4.3. The Newport Tower in Newport, Rhode Island. It was not built by Norse or any other pre-Columbian visitors to the New World. It was a windmill built by Benedict Arnold (the grandfather of the famous Revolutionary War traitor) in the mid-1600s. Kenneth L. Feder

these peripatetic, globe-trotting Celts. In another case, the base of a seventeenth-century windmill (the Newport Tower in Rhode Island; Figure 4.3) has been misidentified as an ancient Norse construction. There are, however, major problems with these attributions.

First, the chambers are often associated with typical nineteenth-century farm complexes—in other words, the remains of houses, the foundations of barns, stone walls, stone pens, and other outbuildings where the foundations mirror the stonework in the chambers.

Second, there actually are written, eyewitness accounts describing the construction of stone chambers by nineteenth- and even early twentieth-century farmers.[9]

Third, these same farmers are known to have built stone root cellars for the storage and preservation of root crops, ice houses for cold storage, and receiving vaults for the storage of dead bodies through the winter when the ground was too hard to dig graves. Those receiving vaults were used to preserve the bodies until they could be buried in the spring.

Fourth, and just as important, when archaeological excavations have been conducted inside and around these chambers, nineteenth-century artifacts associated with rural farm life have been recovered.[10] Excavation of the footings of the Newport Tower produced seventeenth-century artifacts.[11] No excavation has ever recovered any anomalous artifacts attributable to ancient Europeans—no bronze, for example, or out-of-place or out-of-time iron tools, no ancient ceramics, or anything else that reflects a time other than the eighteenth, nineteenth, or twentieth century (Figure 4.3).

The Real Deal

Am I telling you that there is no archaeological evidence for the presence of Europeans, Asians, or Africans in the Americas before the Columbus voyages? No! In fact there is documentary and archaeological evidence for the presence of one group of foreigners in North America about five hundred years before Columbus: the Norse.

While Leif Erikson gets all the love on this subject, it really is a compatriot of his, Bjarni Herjólfsson, who deserves the credit, or maybe the blame. Herjólfsson traveled to Iceland from his home in Norway to visit his father. When he arrived there, he was told that his dad had already migrated to a new land called Greenland.

Anyway, Herjólfsson was a farmer and not a mariner, and he got lost on the voyage to Greenland. He sailed south of the island, continued westward, and, much to his surprise, saw in the distance more land, land that the Norse had no previous knowledge of. Herjólfsson did a little exploring and identified three territories. He never made landfall, turned back to the east where he found Greenland, and finally tracked down his father.

We are aware of this story because the Norse wrote it down two centuries after the events I have just described transpired. The two books in which we find somewhat differing versions of Herjólfsson's exploits are titled *The Saga of the Greenlanders* and *The Saga of Erik the Red*.[12]

If you take at face value the words of the saga writers, the most likely lands Herjólfsson encountered if he traveled west of Greenland are the coasts of Labrador, Baffin Island, and Newfoundland in eastern Canada.

Remember, Herjólfsson was not an explorer or a mariner. He was a farmer looking to connect with his father. He never bothered to make landfall on any of these three lands; he never went ashore. He never had a bit of a walkabout to assess their potential for resources or colonization. But when he made his way to Greenland and told other Norse about his accidental expedition, it sparked great interest and one of them, Erikson, actually bought Herjólfsson's boat—because it would remember the way—and sailed off to the west to explore the lands Herjulfsson had described.

Erikson named the first of the lands he encountered Helluland, or Flat Slabs of Rock Land. That was almost certainly Labrador. Sailing past that, he next saw a heavily wooded coast and he called it Markland, or Forest Land. That was most likely Baffin Island. Finally, he arrived at the third land Herjulfsson had described. Erikson called it Vinland, or Vineland, which most likely was Newfoundland. Erikson made landfall on each of them, conducted brief explorations on the ground to determine what might make a good place to settle, and actually briefly settled. A couple of decades later, the Norse made a real effort to establish a colony on Vinland.

The key location in this discussion is a site called L'Anse aux Meadows, located at the tip of a peninsula on the northwest corner of Newfoundland in southeastern Canada, the island that is believed to be Erikson's Vinland.

While searching locations that might provide direct evidence of the Norse presence in Canada, archaeologist Anne Stine Ingstad arrived on Newfoundland in 1960, accompanied by her husband, Helge, who had been the governor of East Greenland. She was told by local people about a place at the tip of the aforementioned peninsula where there were the remains of abandoned buildings. Though the initial assumption was that the site might be aboriginal, soon after Ingstad began excavating, it quickly became apparent that it wasn't a recent historical

FIGURE 4.4. A reconstruction of the large Viking house, dated to just before 1000 CE (so about five hundred years before Columbus's first voyage to the New World), as excavated at the L'Anse aux Meadows site in northwestern Newfoundland, Canada. L'Anse aux Meadows is the only verified evidence of a Norse settlement of the New World before Columbus. Wikimedia Commons, Dylan Kereluk

site, nor was it a village of Native People. Excavations directed by Ingstad occurred from 1961 to 1964 and then again between 1966 and 1968.[13] Parks Canada returned to conduct additional excavations between 1973 and 1976. The place is now a national historical park (Figure 4.4).[14]

The material culture revealed in the excavations was foreign in the sense that it wasn't Native and it wasn't local. There were iron boat rivets. There was a ring-headed bronze pin. There was a soapstone spindle whorl for spinning wool, a raw material not used by local Natives. There was a bone needle and a stone oil lamp. There also was a small hearth where iron was forged. None of that reflected Native American culture on Newfoundland.

Ingstad located the footprints of eight structures at the site, including one large hall and an iron smithy. Those remains were very similar to the so-called Viking booths, the Norse houses seen on Greenland early in its occupation by the Norse.

Taken together, these archaeological data showed conclusively that the site was thoroughly Norse. There was no doubt about that. The question remained, however, how old was the occupation? Did its age conform to what the sagas said about Erikson's settlement on the island he called Vinland? In the most recent and likely the most accurate dating of the site, pieces of fir and juniper with scars left by iron blades (which the Norse had and the local Natives did not) have been radiocarbon dated (see the discussion in chapter 5) to 1021 CE, just a little more, as I write this, than 1,000 years ago and 471 years before Columbus's first voyage of exploration for the king and queen of Spain.[15]

So was the site at L'Anse aux Meadows the village established by Erikson? Was it a later, more ambitious attempt to colonize Newfoundland by another Norseman, Thorfinn Karlsefni, as discussed in the sagas? We likely will never know for certain. But the evidence is clear that the Norse were in America centuries before Columbus, and the kinds of evidence recovered at L'Anse aux Meadows can serve as a model for other hypotheses concerning the arrival of other foreigners on America's shores before Columbus, the kind of evidence, as discussed in this chapter, all other hypotheses lack at this point.

The L'anse aux Meadows settlement wasn't a one-off. There's also evidence of the regular movement of resources from North America to Greenland in the period from 1100 to 1400 CE in the form of timber. The only wood sources on Greenland itself are scrubby little trees that are entirely inappropriate for ship or house construction. A lot of the wood used for larger construction came from driftwood, which was also the case on Iceland. However, some of the sagas do discuss the importation of timber, and there is archaeological evidence that bears this out. In a recent study of wooden artifacts, branches, and sticks, among the more than eight thousand pieces of wood recovered from five Norse habitation sites on southwest Greenland, researchers were able to identify eight pieces of hemlock and jack pine.[16] Neither species is native to Europe or Greenland, but both grow in Canada. Some of the oak identified might be from North America as well, but oak also grows in Europe and one cannot be distinguished from the other.

Another resource the Norse coveted was walrus tusk, a kind of ivory, which was a very valuable raw material in Europe for decorative carving. Genetic analysis of some of those carvings indicates their source was walrus populations living in Arctic Canada. Either the Norse visited that region to obtain the tusks directly, or they traded for it with local Native People.[17]

By the way, according to the Norse sagas, one of the first things Erikson's men did on Vinland when they encountered local people, whom they called Skraelings, was kill them. That did not bode well for the Norse plan to colonize the new territory, as the Skraelings took offense at their behavior. In fact, conditions became so inhospitable for them, the Norse decided to abandon their Vinland colony entirely. The translators of Erik the Red's saga, Magnuss Magnusson and Hermann Pálsson, explicitly blamed that on the nasty Skraelings: "Karlsefni and his men had realized by now that although the land was excellent they could never live there in safety or freedom from fear, because of the native inhabitants. So they made ready to leave the place and return home."[18]

So while there is no evidence of a geographically widespread colonization of the New World by people from Europe, Africa, China, or Japan, the Norse were here, but they largely were a historical footnote. The big story of the exploration and settlement of the New World concerns the northeast Asians who arrived here more than twenty thousand years before the Norse. Their story is the focus of the rest of this book.

5

First Peoples

ORIGINS

WHILE MANY EUROPEAN thinkers continued to embrace the biblical paradigm discussed in chapter 4 in its assumption that a migration of people to the New World followed sometime after Noah's flood, a remaining question for those thinkers—and certainly one that also challenged people who had abandoned a biblically based view—concerned the precise timing of that movement. Whether you accepted the reality of a biblical deluge that cleaned the slate in the Americas, along with everywhere else, or you embraced a broadly evolutionary view in which human beings originated ultimately in Europe, Africa, or Asia and expanded across the globe from their evolutionary nursery, it remained an interesting question to consider the timing of the movement of people into the New World.

The Archaeology of the First People

Archaeology as a scientific discipline in the New World was initially fueled by general questions concerning the timing and identity of America's First Peoples and also the identity of the peoples who had constructed the profusion of earthen mounds encountered by European settlers as their population expanded through the Midwest. We'll focus on that latter issue in chapter 12, but suffice it to say that questions surrounding the source and timing of the earliest settlement of North

America inspired archaeological research in the United States throughout the eighteenth and nineteenth centuries. In fact, the first financial support earmarked by the federal government for archaeological research through the newly formed Smithsonian Institution (1846) was dedicated to a resolution of the identity of Native Americans and the authors of the mounds.

Based on this explosion of interest, a substantial amount of archaeology was funded and conducted and a wealth of data was produced. A broad consensus developed that the Native People of the New World were, just as Father Acosta had deduced in the sixteenth century (chapter 4), from northeast Asia and that this migration had occurred relatively recently, certainly after the flood and probably no more than a few thousand years ago.

Among scientists in the late nineteenth and early twentieth centuries, the primary champion of the hypothesis that America's Indigenous population had originated in northeast Asia relatively recently was the Harvard-based physical anthropologist Aleš Hrdlička. Hrdlička based his conclusions, essentially, on the study of anthropometry, the metrical analysis of skeletal anatomy, that was conducted between 1898 and 1903. This is not surprising, as he was, after all, not an archaeologist but a biological anthropologist whose focus was the human skeleton. When he compared the skeletal remains of Native People that were then being excavated by archaeologists in great numbers with the bones of contemporary Native People (early and mid-twentieth century), he found them to be essentially identical. At the time, there were very few controls in place that regulated the excavation of Native American remains, and cruelly, museum vaults were filled with the "specimens" that sometimes were the parents, grandparents, and great-grandparents of living people.[1] Issues concerning the excavation of human burials would ultimately be addressed on a federal level with the passing of the Native American Graves Protection and Repatriation Act in 1990.[2]

Based on his reading of the osteological data as a physical anthropologist, Hrdlička was skeptical that this degree of similarity could have been maintained for a lengthy span of time. The geographical separation and, therefore, genetic isolation of two populations of a species has long been viewed as a factor in those populations going their separate ways in their separate and different environments. Geographically and genetically separate from their source population in northeast Asia, the Native People of the Americas would have, Hrdlička maintained, been subjected to the vicissitudes of natural selection along with random mutations and would therefore exhibit distinct and recognizable differences from their Asian ancestors. Charles Darwin had figured out this process of differentiation when he investigated the eighteen different-looking species of finches that inhabited the Galapagos Islands, all of whom had originated from a single species in South America. But at least the osteological remains recovered in North America that Hrdlička examined, however ancient, looked very much like the bones of modern Native People and the modern Native People of northeast Asia. They didn't appear to have changed much at all. He took this to mean that only a rather short period of time separated contemporary Indians from their earliest ancestors in the Americas and from their source population in northeast Asia.

Though Hrdlička's legacy at this point is viewed with more than just a little ambivalence by modern anthropologists, during his tenure at Harvard and his time as the curator of physical anthropology at the U.S. National Museum (the Smithsonian National Museum of Natural History), and as the founder of the primary disciplinary journal of the American Association of Physical Anthropologists (now the American Association of Biological Anthropologists), he had an outsize impact on the discipline, including on the careers, especially, of young scholars. He had an enormous influence, directly and indirectly, on their getting hired, obtaining funding for research, and then having that research published, especially in the journal he founded. As a result, to an extent, publications became an echo chamber of Hrdlička's views about the earliest settlement to the New World and many scholars were reluctant to contradict or confront him. At the same time, it is important to acknowledge that there was no accepted method for accurately dating sites, artifacts, or skeletal remains, including those of the bones on which Hrdlička was basing his conclusions, so it was difficult for archaeologists to rock his boat and contradict the recent arrival paradigm. It would take a giant leap in the ability to determine the age of sites to relegate this consensus to the dustbin of prehistory. Archaeology is all about physical evidence, and even Hrdlička's skepticism couldn't withstand an onslaught of exactly that. We'll discuss that evidence in this chapter and the next.

First People

Scientific consensus is forever changing as the result of new data, new methods of analysis, and new interpretations of existing data. That's precisely the way science is supposed to work. We propose hypotheses, ways of explaining the existing data, and then confirm, modify, or throw the whole thing out and start anew when new data are collected. As we'll discuss in chapter 6, Hrdlička's view wasn't definitively overturned until archaeological sites were discovered where tools were found together with the bones of extinct animals. This led to a new consensus in American archaeology that the first Native American settlement of North America occurred a bit before ten thousand years ago, right before the end of the Ice Age or Pleistocene Epoch. These people produced a tool technology called Clovis based on a spearpoint type named for the town in New Mexico where it was first identified (chapter 6). Clovis First, the notion that the people making Clovis points represented the first settlers of the New World, served as the dominant explanation—a paradigm—for the earliest human settlement of the New World for good reasons. As seen in chapter 6, Clovis sites were multiple, geographically widespread. Stone tools had been found in profusion and in undisturbed contexts. Dating, especially as derived from the radiocarbon method (see the next section of this chapter), was firm, and different dating methodologies were mutually confirmatory. It all seemed to hang together and it made sense.

All along, there were older outliers, to be sure, glimmerings that there were sites older than the oldest exhibiting Clovis technology, but the evidence for them seemed considerably weaker than for Clovis or somewhat later Folsom sites (I'll talk about those sites in chapter 6). They tended to be one-offs, unique sites in terms of stratigraphy or artifacts. None of them appeared to be examples of a larger context of sites with similar dates and similar-appearing technologies. So some of those sites were rejected by skeptics who proposed either that the dating was simply wrong or even that the material presented as artifacts, things made by ancient human beings, weren't artifacts at all, just fortuitously shaped items made by nature and sometimes disparagingly called geofacts (see chapter 7). Certainly, there were scientists, including archaeologists and geologists, who strongly questioned the validity of Clovis First, and they kept looking, kept excavating, and kept pushing. James Adovasio at the Meadowcroft Rockshelter site in Pennsylvania and Tom Dillehay at Monte Verde in Chile were two of the strongest voices crying out in the Clovis First wilderness. More about Meadowcroft later. Science is an entirely human enterprise, and there were pretty vicious arguments, there was a ton of resentment, and the Clovis Firsters were unflatteringly called the Clovis Mafia by some.

But this is exactly how science works and how it must work. Well, other than the "mafia" accusation. Scientists are supposed to be skeptics but not cynics; science should be about doubt, not denial. If a new, revolutionary hypothesis is presented, most scientists will apply the adage popularized by astronomer and science communicator Carl Sagan: "Extraordinary claims require extraordinary evidence," with that essential philosophy having been articulated by the French scholar Pierre Simon Laplace (1749–1827): "The weight of evidence for an extraordinary claim must be proportioned to its strangeness." Of course, he said it in French. The point is there will be—and there should be—skepticism, vigorous debate, back-and-forth, and arguments, but ultimately a resolution will be reached. As the second president of the United States, John Adams, phrased it, "Facts are stubborn things; and whatever may be our wishes, our inclinations, or the dictates of our passion, they cannot alter the state of facts and evidence." In another aphorism, "Everyone is entitled to his own opinion, but not his own facts."[3] Eventually, the facts of an occupation of the Americas that predated Clovis and Folsom, an occupation that predated the end of the Pleistocene, were sufficient to negate that skepticism. This chapter is about a handful of those sites. Jump ahead to Map 6.1 in the next chapter for the locations of these pre-Clovis sites.

About Radiocarbon Dating

Carbon dating is a mainstay in archaeological dating, and it's worth a brief diversion here to discuss the technique used to date many of the sites mentioned in this chapter and, for that matter, throughout this book.

Radiocarbon dating is also called carbon dating, ^{14}C dating, and carbon-14 dating. The "14" represents the atomic number, the combined number of protons (6) and neutrons (8) in the nucleus of the radioactive (unstable) isotope (variety) of carbon. Regular, stable carbon has an atomic number of 12, for 6 protons and 6 neutrons. The unstable ^{14}C decays to nitrogen at a known rate, thereby providing a sort of atomic clock or calendar for dating something that once was alive; carbon is one of the building blocks of life.

The amount of ^{14}C that was in a piece of wood, seeds, nutshells, bone, teeth, antler, and shell, among other remains, when those were part of living organisms (trees, plants, animals, fish, shellfish) can be estimated. The amount that's left when determined in a radiocarbon lab can be measured, and that measurement is used to calculate the amount of time that must have passed since the living thing died and stopped incorporating fresh carbon.

The best analogy I can provide is this. Think of radiocarbon atoms as being the sand grains in the top of an hourglass. In this hourglass, the sand is cascading into the bottom (that's the ^{14}C on top decaying to nitrogen on the bottom) but is constantly being replenished from the top (in the analogy, that happens by the plant breathing in carbon in the form of carbon dioxide from the atmosphere or the animals eating plants or other animals). So the sand (^{14}C) is in a sort of equilibrium when the organism is alive. Once the organism dies, however, the top of the hourglass is sealed off and the sand on top is no longer being replenished. The sand continues flowing to the bottom and, without replenishment, there's less and less of it on the top. An hourglass is called that because the amount of sand put into it is calibrated to last for about an hour when you flip it over. If you know the rate at which the sand is pouring out of the top and then encounter the hourglass with some sand on the bottom and some still flowing from the top, you can calculate about how long ago it was flipped. With the hourglass metaphor as used here, that amount of ^{14}C that remains reflects about how long ago the organism died.

In radiocarbon dating, the rate of decay is known as the half-life, how long it takes for half of the ^{14}C to decay to nitrogen. Physicists have calculated that: 5,730 years. So if we measure the amount of radioactive carbon left in the remains of a plant or animal, we can accurately calculate how long ago the organism died. Obviously, if the date is derived from a human remain, that date shows us how long ago that person lived. If it's wood from an ancient fireplace, or the bone of an animal hunted by a human being, or an antler carved into a sculpture, the age of the organic remain tells us the age of the site in which it was found.

With its wide usage after its discovery in about 1950, radiocarbon dating has been a real game changer for archaeology. Remember in the practical preface where I said that in the phrase "before present" (BP), the "present" is fixed at 1950? That year was chosen because that's when radiocarbon dating became a standard way of dating archaeological objects. It has proved to be very accurate, can be applied widely, and is now a relatively inexpensive procedure. It generally costs only a few hundred dollars for a date. There are, however, limitations. If not enough time—less than a few hundred years—has passed since the organism died, not enough of the ^{14}C has decayed for an accurate determination of age. If too much time has elapsed since the organism died—more than fifty thousand or sixty thousand years—effectively all of the ^{14}C has decayed away, so that represents about the maximum age for which the technique can be accurately applied. In other words, as long as something is more than three hundred or four hundred years old and less than sixty thousand (some would say fifty thousand) years old, radiocarbon dating is a very useful technique and accurate when applied to just about anything that was alive. There are other challenges with radiocarbon dating, including technical issues involving variations in ^{14}C in the atmosphere over time and contamination of samples with older carbon (we'll deal with a specific instance of this in this chapter). Despite these limitations and challenges, radiocarbon dating has been a boon to archaeological research all over the world. Most of the dates I provide in this book were derived through radiocarbon dating.

How Old Could the Oldest Archaeological Sites Be in North America?

On one point we can be nearly certain (scientists can be "nearly certain" but reject the notion of absolute certainty): any new paradigm must be based on the understanding that the Native People of the New World could not have gotten here more than three hundred thousand years ago, for the simple reason that there were no anatomically modern human beings—just a technical way of describing human beings whose anatomy, in all important respects, is identical to our own—anywhere in the world before that. The earliest fossil evidence for anatomically modern human beings is found in Africa, in particular at a number of sites in the north. For example, fossil crania found at the Jebel Irhoud site in Morocco, including those of three adults, an adolescent, and a child (their ages determined variously by tooth eruption, the fusion of the end caps of their long bones, and cranial sutures, all of which present us with time posts of an individual's development), have been dated to about three hundred thousand years ago.[4] Beyond this, Morocco is thousands of kilometers overland to Alaska, creating an additional delay. So unless new evidence surfaces for an even earlier appearance of anatomically modern human beings, three hundred thousand years ago is technically our absolutely maximum point in time for the earliest settlement of the Americas, and it is actually considerably less than that if we factor in the time it would have taken for these first humans to spread across that vast distance.

Siberia

This brings us back to exactly the same question asked by the Spanish cleric José de Acosta in the late sixteenth century (chapter 4): What avenue could people have taken to get to the New World?

First, could the first settlers of America have simply sailed across the Atlantic to arrive, like a very precocious Columbus, on the shores of the New World? Well, technically, yes, they could have, except there is no archaeological evidence for oceangoing vessels until about seven thousand years ago. So while hypothetically people may have traveled to the New World from Africa, Europe, China, or Japan after that, they would not have been the first people to reach the Americas (and see chapter 4 for the general lack of evidence for such movements of people closer to Columbus's arrival).

That leaves us with the question, What would have been the most plausible overland route from, ultimately, the Old World to the New World, fully recognizing that these first people had no idea that a "new world" separate from Africa existed, how far away it was, and no reasonable motivation for migrating there?

True to form when it comes to the "discovery" and naming of a place, the Native People of Siberia and what was to become Alaska were well aware of the geographic configuration of the region that Acosta only imagined in 1590, and they regularly traveled back and forth. Mentioned in chapter 4, the land under and surrounding the strait that was exposed during periods of glacial ice buildup on land has been called the Bering Land Bridge or Beringia. It was a vast and long-lasting region in more or less continuous existence during a period when glaciation was at a peak, a period called the Late Glacial Maximum, between about forty thousand and eleven thousand years ago.

That narrow strait is located in the Arctic, and this fact gave scholars who followed Acosta (chapter 4) another data point in their attempt to explain, to source, and to date the human presence in the New World. It also meant that for human beings to have entered into the New World through what is now Siberia, they must have previously been able to survive in Siberia's Arctic climate, which takes a certain set of adaptations certainly not possessed by our first ancestors in Africa. In other words, to figure out when people entered the New World from the Old, we need to know when eastern Siberia was settled.

Northern Siberia is not the easiest place on the planet to conduct archaeology. Fieldwork in Siberia can be a challenging enterprise—the territory is vast and unforgiving, the field season when the ground isn't frozen and can be excavated is short, and expenses are very high.

Given those challenges, nevertheless, a substantial amount of archaeology has been conducted in Siberia, including northern Siberia near the closest approach of the land in easternmost Asia to the land in westernmost North America. That archaeology suggests that the earliest human occupation of what would have essentially been the embarkation point for people heading to the east and into the New World dates to about forty-five thousand years ago and not much before that, with the older sites located not in far eastern Siberia but in the central part of the region. For instance, the SK Mammoth site (including the bones of a butchered woolly mammoth) dates to forty-five thousand years ago and is located in north-central Siberia. On the Yana River, the Yana River RHS occupation is closer to what would have been the land bridge to the New World. The site dates to about thirty-two thousand years ago. Ikhine is farther south but still reflects a human occupation and adaptation to the climate of Siberia at close to thirty-four thousand years ago.

There's no real point to my reciting a litany of the oldest archaeological sites in central or eastern Siberia. Suffice it to say that we know that modern human beings (people who look like us) had developed adaptations that allowed them to survive and thrive in Siberia only after about forty-five thousand years ago and not appreciably before that. That implies that the source population for Native America in all likelihood cannot be dated to before that date. So forty-five thousand years ago is another data point in our discussion.

Pathway to a New Land

I admit to being tempted at this point in the book to write a lyrical, romantic, even poetic introduction to my discussion of the original peopling of North America. My tale would be replete with those clichéd "hardy hunters," braving the elements in a windswept land, bravely exploring newly discovered territories to the east. Their path led through a hellish Arctic and into a brave new world teeming with a menagerie of dangerous—but delicious—Ice Age beasts. Marching, marching ever onward, fulfilling an ancient version of manifest destiny. Something like that.

It has long been a common conceit of mostly first-world people living in continental climates in the Northern Hemisphere that the physical environments that characterize where they live are, by some metric, "better"—richer, more pleasant, more salubrious, but also presenting just the right amount of challenge, making us more capable of progress—than the environments of non-Westerners, which are seen as either too easy and therefore incompatible with progress or too harsh or too difficult, so much so that all the people who live there can manage is to provide enough food for their survival. In this scenario, very common in the nineteenth century and labeled "environmental determinism," people are "primitive" as a result of the harshness of their environment.

Again, that's a conceit. Human beings are experts at adaptation, crafting ways of life that enable their survival when confronted with all manner of environmental conditions. Folks who have for generations lived in the Arctic tundra—a mostly treeless expanse populated today by large animals like bison, caribou, and musk ox—perfected their hunting techniques and their material technology involving tools, clothing, and housing. They love their homelands and don't sit around thinking, "Man, this place really sucks. I wish I lived in Miami." The people living in northeastern Siberia after forty-five thousand years ago were supremely well adapted or well adjusted to living in the Arctic tundra. They were really good—in fact brilliant—at living there, under conditions that I freely admit would kill me because I didn't grow up experiencing those conditions and learning how to cope with living there to the point of even loving to live there.

My key point is this: it is unlikely that the people living in Siberia after forty-five thousand years ago were looking for something different or "better" (which is a meaningless term here). They were just exquisitely adapted to their environment and acutely aware of changes in their territory, an awareness that was a crucial survival skill. That awareness led groups of people to investigate those changes because they were very smart, very curious, and very much concerned with how changes in the landscape might affect their ability to survive. Around forty thousand years ago they surely noticed something new, interesting, and potentially very important. In stories told by elders to younger adults and adults to children, they passed along their observation that across the great water, off in the direction of the rising sun, and every year more visible, every year closer as the tide went out a little farther and came back in, there was a new territory, a territory that might be rich in food and other resources. A territory that must have demanded investigation by a nomadic group of hunters and foragers who certainly were always looking for resources and food sources.

A Beringian Pathway

What the residents of Siberia were experiencing were the effects of what geologists call the Pleistocene Epoch. During the Pleistocene, colloquially called the Ice Age, large swaths of the northern latitudes and higher elevations became covered with ice that did not melt off in the spring. That ice originated from the world's oceans as water evaporated and fell as ice and snow but then didn't melt off as the planet cooled. This concentration of water that came from the oceans caused a decline in sea level. That decline is what exposed a land connection between northeast Asia and northwest North America.

The timing of the exposure of this land we have named the Bering Land Bridge or Beringia is crucial in this discussion, and we have strong, well-dated evidence that shows it was available for travel, both through the interior of a wide platform of land and along its coast, beginning at about 33,000 years ago, perhaps at a maximum in its extent between about 26,500 and 19,000 years ago, during the period called the Late Glacial Maximum (Map 5.1).[5]

A slow melt-off of the ice and concomitant incremental inundation of Beringia began after about nineteen thousand years ago and accelerated after twelve thousand years ago, and its modern configuration as a sea strait emerged after eleven thousand years ago. In other words, the initial appearance of a land connection between northeast Asia and northwest North America follows the initial appearance of people in northeast Asia based on archaeological evidence by a few thousand

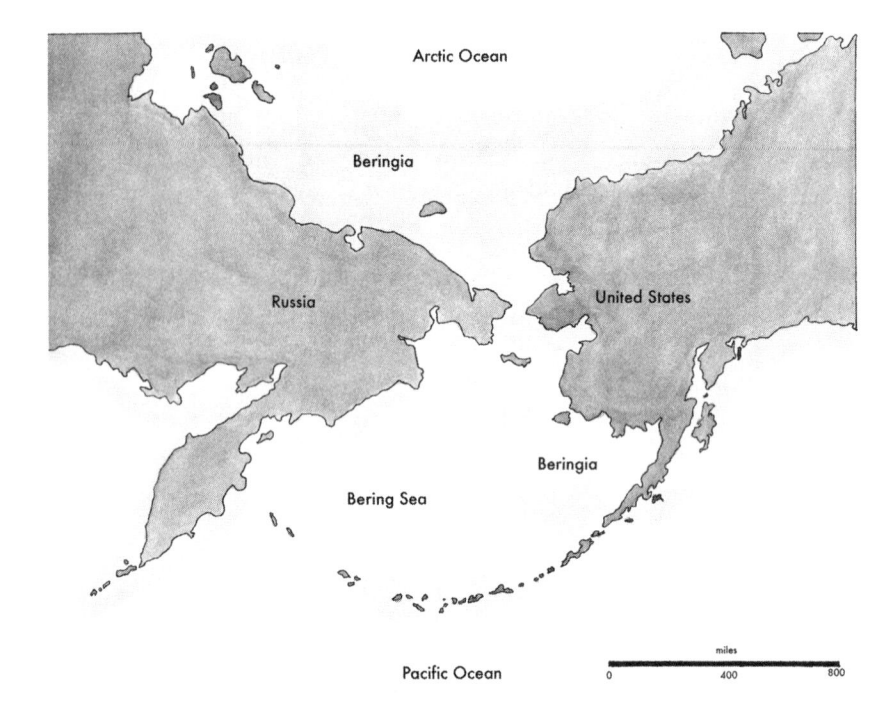

MAP 5.1. Map of Beringia. The current configuration of the coast is in dark gray. The land exposed during glacial maxima of the Pleistocene Epoch is light gray. During glacial maxima, northeast Asia and northwest North America were a single, continuous area of land across which animals and people could move. Jennifer Davis

years. The Institute of Arctic and Alpine Research has created a very cool animation of the waning of the land bridge beginning twenty-one thousand years ago.[6]

While the presence of the land bridge certainly facilitated migration into the New World from northeast Asia for both terrestrial animal species and people, there is a complicating factor. When glaciation and Beringia were at their peak, there was maximum expansion of two enormous bodies of ice in North America: the Laurentide ice sheet centered in north-central Canada and the Cordilleran, which originated in the higher elevations of the Rocky Mountains. We know that during glacial maxima, the Laurentide, expanding toward the west, and the Cordilleran, expanding to the east, coalesced, meeting in the middle.

It's ironic: the very conditions rendering it easiest for people to enter the New World from northeast Asia made it impossible for them to travel south into the American heartland. As the coldest temperatures of the Pleistocene declined, and as the North American ice sheets diminished in size, an "ice-free corridor" between the Laurentide and Cordilleran ice sheets appeared, but this happened only after 14,800 years ago. Even then, environmental conditions through what was fundamentally a chasm between two huge bodies of ice were likely not conducive to the movement of human beings or the animals they might have been chasing after. Not unexpectedly, there are no verified archaeological sites of people living in that corridor until a millennium after its initial appearance. Therefore, archaeological sites in North America that date to much more than 14,800 years ago and, based on the initially difficult conditions in the ice-free corridor, even much before 13,000 years ago probably were not those of people whose ancestors traversed the corridor. Those people more likely entered along the southern Beringian coast, expanding by traveling along that coast or, conceivably, more quickly by boat, and then only later expanded eastward, into the American West, Midwest, and ultimately East.

South of the Ice Sheets

Alaska presents its own challenges when it comes to archaeology as well, but there is at least one ancient site that reflects a relatively early settlement of the shoreline south of what would have been the Beringian coast I just mentioned. The site is called On Your Knees Cave as a result of the fact that you need to be literally on your knees to enter it.[7] In 1996, researchers encountered a human skeleton in the cave in a layer that was radiocarbon dated to approximately ten thousand years ago. An analysis of the human bones found in the cave produced an isotopic signature that proves, not surprisingly, that the individual relied on a maritime food base for their subsistence. So, while not being the oldest site in the region, it certainly shows that human beings were there no later than the end of the Pleistocene.

Cooper's Ferry

Further south still, dating to about 16,500 years ago, the Cooper's Ferry site in Idaho appears to represent the remains of a settlement of a people whose ancestors had migrated along the southern Beringian coast, whereupon, at some point after traveling south of the southernmost extent of the glaciers, they made a left turn, heading eastward for about 600 kilometers (370 miles) into what turned out to be a vast, mostly uninhabited continent.

Excavation of Cooper's Ferry has produced twenty-seven beautifully flaked stone tools, including projectile points with stems on their bases for hafting onto wooden spears and hundreds of stone flakes that resulted from the manufacture of those tools (Figure 5.1).[8]

The eighty-six animal bone fragments recovered at the site were too broken up and small for definitive species identification, but they pretty clearly represented medium-sized to large mammals, possibly extinct horses. So the people at Cooper's Ferry were, minimally, making stone tools, killing and butchering animals, and then cooking their meat. The most exciting aspect of the Cooper's Ferry site relates to its pretty firm dating: as mentioned, it was occupied beginning about 16,500 years ago. In other words, it represents a firmly dated and identified occupation of North America that is older than Clovis by about 3,000 years. Its location is south of where the Cordilleran ice sheet is calculated to have been at the time. The age of the site is especially significant because it represents a human settlement south of the coalesced ice sheets 2,000 years before there was an ice-free corridor through which people might have traveled.

Other Sites

Other archaeological sites have been found and excavated south of the margins of the late Pleistocene ice sheets in North America. At the Manis site on the Olympic Peninsula in Washington State, a vertebra of a woolly mammoth displays an imbedded fragment of a bone point used in the hunt. Radiocarbon dating shows that the mammoth was hunted more than 13,800 years ago. Also occupied about 13,000 years

FIGURE 5.1. Spearpoints recovered at the Cooper's Ferry site in Idaho. The site has been dated to about 16,500 years ago. Davis et al. 2022, CC BY-SA 4.0

ago is the Meadowcroft Rockshelter, located in far western Pennsylvania, 3,700 kilometers (2,300 miles) east of the Pacific Coast of North America (Figure 5.2). Meadowcroft Rockshelter revealed a long sequence of occupations of, not precisely a cave, but an overhanging rock that would have afforded inhabitants protection from the weather.

People came back to this valuable place again and again, with multiple occupation layers separated by soil and rock deposits that had blown into the cave. The earliest of those deposits that produced human-made objects, including stone spearpoints, has been dated to at

FIGURE 5.2. Meadowcroft Rockshelter, western Pennsylvania. Archaeologist James Adovasio identified a series of occupations of the rock shelter, the oldest of which dates to more than thirteen thousand years ago. Kenneth L. Feder

least thirteen thousand and perhaps closer to sixteen thousand years ago, close in time to the dates derived for Cooper's Ferry. An interpretation of even older material at Meadowcroft, dating to as much as nineteen thousand years ago, is not widely accepted but not out of the realm of possibility.

Far to the south, in Texas, the Gault site shows clear stratigraphic evidence of stone tools below and therefore older than a level with Clovis points (see chapter 6). Radiocarbon dating of that layer indicates a date in excess of fifteen thousand years ago.

The Trail to White Sands

Footprints are remarkably evocative and, at the same time, can be remarkably informative. For example, in many of Arthur Conan Doyle's Sherlock Holmes stories, Holmes, with magnifying glass in hand, hurtles himself onto the ground in order to pore over the tracks left behind either by the victim of a crime or by the presumed perpetrator. From his careful study, Holmes can determine whether the person was walking or running, was tall or short, was light or heavy, had a disability that resulted in a limp, used a crutch, or even had a prosthetic leg. Based on the shoe worn or even the shape of the foot, he also is ordinarily able to distinguish between footprints of a man and those of a woman.

Taking a page from the great "consulting detective," archaeological detectives similarly attempt to coax information from footprints that have preserved for hundreds, thousands, and even millions of years. Perhaps the most famous example comes from the Laetoli site in Tanzania in eastern Africa, where a couple of ancient human ancestors walked across a bed of ash that had been only recently deposited by a nearby volcano. After their stroll, the ash was rained on, solidified like concrete, got covered up, lay undisturbed and preserved for many, many years, and was only encountered in the 1970s by paleoanthropologists Mary Leakey (we'll talk about her again in chapter 7) and Tim White. The age of the solidified ash itself has been determined through the application of a technique called potassium/argon. It dates to 3.6 million years ago. The two sets of footprints, so close together as to suggest the individuals were striding arm in arm, are virtually identical to those left by modern human beings in soft sand. This clearly shows that even at this very early date, our ancestors' primary mode of locomotion, how they moved around, was unlike that of a chimpanzee or gorilla who gets around on all fours, but very similar to that of a modern human being with our bipedal (two-legged) gait. Holmes would have come to the identical conclusion, I am certain.

Conditions have to be nearly miraculously perfect for ancient footprints to preserve into the present, and there are relatively few examples. One of the most recent and most intriguing sets has been found at White Sands National Park in southeastern New Mexico. They speak to the questions surrounding the timing of the first human presence in the Americas.

White Sands is a glorious place. For years it was a national monument but "graduated" in 2021 to the status of national park. Imagine a vast, imposing, and starkly beautiful desert marked by enormous, ever-shifting sand dunes, but the dunes aren't the standard-issue tan or light brown of most deserts. The White Sands dunes, as their name indicates, blindingly glisten white in the scorching New Mexico sun. Like snow. But it's sand. I was there in the spring of 2023 and, well, wow! Beautiful and alien.

In 2021, researchers announced the discovery of sixty preserved, fully human footprints in one of the corners of the park (Figure 5.3).[9]

Applying the methods of Sherlock Holmes—and biological anthropologists—based largely on their length, the estimated eleven to fifteen people who left behind the footprints mainly were kids with estimated ages of between about nine and fourteen. Researchers also found in the same deposit the footprints of a woolly mammoth and a possible wolf.

The researchers carefully exposed the surfaces on which the footprints were located, recovering abundant evidence of plant life, particularly in the form of seeds of the plant *Ruppia cirrhosa*. Sure, that may seem like a minor detail, but it is an important one. That species is an aquatic plant so, unlike today, when the area is a starkly beautiful desert, at least right where the people were hanging out, it had been a wetland with lots of plant life. This also helps explain the preservation of the footprints: the moisture in the ground facilitated that preservation as the sand cured like concrete in the hot sun and was then covered by subsequent deposition, which protected it from deterioration through erosion.

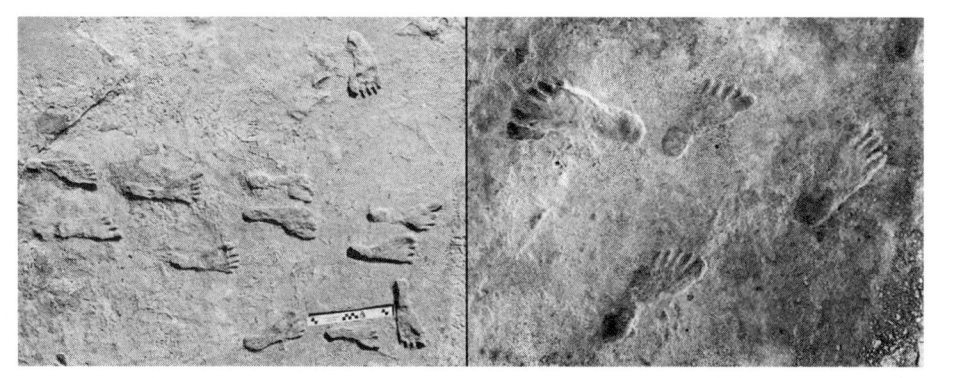

FIGURE 5.3. A sample of the remarkably well-preserved human footprints discovered in White Sands National Park in southeastern New Mexico. Organic material and quartz crystals found in association with the footprints indicate an age of more than twenty-one thousand years. Bennett et al. 2021. Reprinted with permission from AAAS

It is truly amazing to consider that these footprints provide the clichéd "snapshot" of a brief interval of time—effectively, a moment—when a bunch of kids, maybe just fooling around as kids do, walking and running over a glorious, sandy landscape near a wetland a very long time ago, made an eternal mark on that landscape with their footsteps. The key question to ask here is, How long ago?

The researchers believe they know, and their result is staggering. They collected the preserved seeds from the *Ruppia* found between the layers of the footprints. The stratigraphic positioning of the seeds and the prints shows that the prints were below each of the eleven clusters of seeds that provided radiocarbon dates. The footprints, of necessity, therefore were *older* than those seeds. Those carbon dates showed that the seeds and thus the footprints dated to between 21,130 and 22,860 years ago, rendering the site among the oldest in North America.[10]

Stunning. And remember, this is southern New Mexico, so if the people who left the footprints arrived in the New World via Beringia, they must have walked into Alaska considerably before that, likely thousands of years before. So yeah, stunning.

So case closed? People were in New Mexico more than twenty-one thousand years ago? Some were skeptical of the original report. The stratigraphy is clear; there are footprints stratigraphically positioned under, and therefore older than, some of the seeds. That juxtaposition has not been questioned. What has been questioned is the validity and extreme age of the dates on the seeds. The question relates to a technical problem that the authors of the study acknowledge, which concerns the plants from which the carbon dates were obtained and which I hinted at earlier in my general discussion of the complexities of carbon dating.

For context, let me tell you a fascinating story I was told by a geologist on this general topic. An assembled group of geologists at a banquet were served a meal of fresh fish where the bones of the fish had been removed, radiocarbon dated, and shown to be thousands of years old. Shocking, right? How could fish that were recently alive generate carbon dates that implied they lived and died thousands of years ago? While I have no idea if that story is actually true, the science is legitimate and reflects a well-known challenge when deriving carbon dates from aquatic species, particularly those living in water bodies that flow through a landscape characterized by the presence of deposits of limestone.

The discussion is a little "inside baseball" but it's important, so please bear with me. Terrestrial plants obtain their carbon from the atmosphere, and the proportion of radiocarbon (^{14}C) to plain old carbon (^{12}C) in the plant when it is alive matches the proportion in the air.

The same is true for animals who eat those plants, incorporating their carbon into their bodies (including their bones).

Here's where the possible contamination of carbon dating samples rears its ugly head. Limestone often consists of a lot of ancient corals and shells. Those corals and shells were parts of living things and contain a lot of carbon, but it's "dead" carbon, so ancient that the ^{14}C has long ago decayed to nitrogen. When a stream passes through a landscape with ancient limestone deposits, water passes over that limestone and dissolves it. When an aquatic plant, or an animal like a fish, incorporates that dead carbon into its leaves, roots, fruits, and seeds and when an animal eats that plant, it increases its percentage of ^{12}C and thus lowers its percentage of ^{14}C, which, if you apply carbon dating, results in a spuriously old radiocarbon date. Like the fish at the apocryphal banquet and, just maybe, the dated seeds at White Sands being used to date the footprints.

In other words, there is a potential problem with the carbon dates derived from the *Ruppia cirrhosa* seeds and relating those dates to the White Sands footprints. The dates may be inaccurately old if those plants incorporated a substantial amount of "dead" carbon from the dissolved limestone rocks through which a stream flowed.

Researchers skeptical of the claim of the great antiquity of the New Mexico site as derived from those seeds interspersed with the New Mexico footprints ran a little experiment.[11] They took a sample of *Ruppia* that was collected in 1947 from a spring near where the footprints were found and that had been curated in a lab ever since. Then they radiocarbon dated it. The result? The remains of the plant that we know was alive only about seventy-five years ago produced a carbon date of about seventy-four hundred years old!

This process is precisely the way science is supposed to work. A new, potentially revolutionary discovery is made, researchers publish their work, and their colleagues read those publications and then think about them and ask probing questions. Have the researchers ignored an important problem with their conclusions? Are there alternative explanations that might better explain their conclusions?

The original researchers were inspired by the skepticism of their colleagues to return to the proverbial drawing board to assess the possibility presented by those skeptics that the original dates they derived for the seeds, and therefore the footprints, had been inaccurate.[12] They applied a separate dating method to the footprints and they radiocarbon dated organic material associated with the footprints that would not have been affected by the carbon offset presented by aquatic plants. First, they determined the age of quartz grains in the layer of the footprints using optically stimulated luminescence. That method produced a date of 21,500 BP. Next, the researchers collected pollen, again from the same level as the footprints. The pollen grains they used (in bulk) in the procedure were terrestrial—not aquatic—species, primarily from conifers, so there was no concern about dating dead carbon. The result was a date between 23,400 and 22,600 years ago. This new round of dates nearly perfectly matched the original dates, lending strong support for an age in excess of 21,000 years for the human occupation of White Sands in New Mexico.

So a bunch of kids just walking around what in 2021 would become White Sands National Park have been immortalized through their footprints, providing scientists who live more than 21,000 years later a way of dating what is one of the oldest archaeological features in North America.

Genetics

You've probably watched any one of a number of police procedurals on TV where an individual, either a victim or a possible perp, is identified on the basis of the genetic material they have inadvertently left behind in their blood, semen, or hair. You've also probably seen ads for genetic tests that might enable you to trace your ancestry by comparing your genes with those in a large genetic database. For example, I submitted a sample of my saliva to a commercial lab and, unsurprisingly, the results strongly showed that my ancestors were from eastern Europe, specifically traceable to a largely endogamous (they tended to marry within their group) subset of Europeans calls the Ashkenazi Jews. Also unsurprisingly, when my younger son independently submitted his saliva to another commercial lab, his results reflected that part of his genetic heritage passed down by me and my ancestors.

In an analogous way, the genetic analysis of both modern people on each side of the Bering Strait and genetic material derived from the bones of people long since passed away has been used to address some of the questions approached by archaeologists: What is the source population for Native Americans? Where did they come from? And how long ago?

Biological anthropologist and geneticist Jennifer Raff's wonderful book *Origin* has summarized the results of that analysis.[13] Essentially, that work shows very clearly that the source population of the first Americans lived in Asia, including especially the ancient people of Siberia, with genetic signals coming, directly or indirectly, from Japan.

Remember that when Aleš Hrdlička looked at the degree of difference between the skeletal morphology of the first Native Americans and modern people, there was little difference, so he hypothesized that a relatively short period of time had passed since their initial migration into the New World? Well, when geneticists examine the genetic echoes of the first Americans in their ancient skeletons, they see enough evolutionary change to hypothesize that more than twenty thousand years, perhaps twenty-four thousand years, have passed since the Native population of northeast Asia and the Native population of the Americas separated, perhaps in Siberia, becoming genetically isolated with no or very little genetic admixture. Those numbers, at least twenty thousand and perhaps as much as twenty-four thousand, were derived entirely independently from the archaeological record and represent a remarkable confirmation for a rough age for the initial human entry into the New World that I mentioned earlier in this chapter. So, in both timing and geography, the genetic record of both past and modern people and the archaeological record support the current archaeological consensus of the peopling of the Americas.

From the Bones of Children

You really can't consider the importance of the bones of a little boy found on the Anzick family farm in Montana in 1968 without thinking about the family that raised him and doubtless loved him during his very short life. He was only about a year old when he died and was buried, likely by those who grieved for him. And this happened about 12,500 years ago.[14]

The skeleton was investigated by researchers from the National Institutes of Health with the support of local Native People. Remarkably, one of the scientists involved in the study was a woman whose name is Susan Anzick. She is the daughter of the farm owners and was just two years old when the little boy's remains were recovered in a layer beneath one that included Clovis-era artifacts. In other words, the stratigraphy or layering at the site indicated that the boy perhaps lived before the time of Clovis. A genetic analysis of his bones showed great similarities to modern Native People and similarity to the genetic signature recovered from the bones of yet another little boy of similar age, this one found in Siberia at the place called Mal'ta.

The bones of two more small children were recovered at the Upward Sun River site in Alaska. Again, the research was supported by local Native People who named the children Xach'itee'aanenh t'eede gaay (Sunrise child-girl) and Yełkaanenh t'eede gaay (Dawn twilight child-girl). Radiocarbon dating indicates that these two precious infants died about 11,500 years ago and were buried with both love and respect. Their bodies had been covered in the mineral red ocher and offerings of stone and antler tools had been placed alongside their tiny bodies. DNA recovered from one of the girls shows, as it did at Anzick, a close relationship both to modern Native People in North America and to the Native People of Siberia. In a detailed analysis of the genetic affinities of people on either side of Beringia, and by calculating the most likely rate of genetic change, it has been determined that the ancestors of the Upward Sun River children diverged from the Native People of northeast Asia approximately twenty-two thousand years ago.[15]

This all reminds me of a pictograph (see chapter 16) I saw a few years ago in Fremont, Utah. It is a beautiful painted image of a blanket, placed artfully on the white rock outcrop. The story told about the painting is that many years ago a Paiute woman gave birth there but, sadly, the baby died. She buried the remains of her child at that spot and then followed her people on their yearly round. That's when the dreams started. Her baby was cold. Her baby was lonely. Haunted by those sorrowful dreams, the mother returned to that spot and painted the image of a blanket to keep her baby warm in the spirit world.

As a parent four times over, that story breaks me. And it is genuinely heartbreaking to remind ourselves that the Fremont baby, the Anzick boy, Xach'itee'aanenh t'eede gaay (Sunrise child-girl) and Yełkaanenh t'eede gaay (Dawn twilight child-girl), and the little boy buried at Mal'ta aren't just specimens. They are the remains of actual children, babies who tragically died—very long ago, of course, but that doesn't make their deaths any less tragic. They came into the world, as all babies do, wrapped in blankets of family, love, and hope. Despite that family, love, and hope, they lived short lives and each of them certainly left holes in the hearts of those who had already grown to adore them. As sad and as short as their lives were—and I'm sure it would have given no comfort to their families—they have nevertheless attained a level of immortality in teaching us in the present, non-Native archaeologists but also the children's descendant family, about the history of their people. As Native American biological anthropologist Dorothy Lippert brilliantly puts it regarding the study of the skeletal remains of Native People, the study of their remains provides those ancestors with a "voice made of bone."[16] We are all of us in archaeology greatly indebted to the Anzick boy, the Mal'ta boy, and Xach'itee'aanenh t'eede gaay and Yełkaanenh t'eede gaay. They have spoken to us in that "voice made of bone" and we have listened. In a version of the old expression of support for the grieving, "May their memory be a blessing."

6

First Peoples

CLOVIS AND FOLSOM

LET'S TURN the clock back to 1908. Remember the view of biological anthropologist Aleš Hrdlička that the Native People of North America had been here for, at most, a few thousand years? In that year, a cowboy who was a self-taught archaeologist and a direct descendant of slaves, George McJunkin, happened upon a remarkable site while investigating damage after a severe flood in Wild Horse Arroyo near the town of Folsom, New Mexico.[1] With an abiding interest in and experience conducting archaeological research, McJunkin immediately recognized the significance of his discovery. The flooding had revealed the skeletons of no fewer than thirty-two bison. That was amazing enough but there was more. The bones were not those of modern bison, the species *Bison bison bison* I mentioned earlier in the book. The bones discovered by McJunkin were much too large to be representatives of that species.

Make no mistake, modern bison in North America are enormous animals. An adult male may be 2 meters (6 feet) tall at the hump on his back directly behind its neck and weigh about 900 kilograms (2,000 pounds). Huge indeed, but the extinct variety represented by the skeletons discovered by McJunkin dwarfs even that. The bones of the extinct species called *Bison antiquus* are of an animal 25 percent taller, as much as 2.3 meters (7.5 feet) tall at that same hump, and weighing about 1,600 kilograms (3,500 pounds) (Figure 6.1). It certainly was an imposing

FIGURE 6.1. Skeleton of an extinct form of North American bison, *Bison antiquus*. The remains of multiple animals of this species were found in 1908, along with stone spearpoints bearing channels on both faces, at what became known as the Folsom site in New Mexico. This site became the linchpin in the argument that human beings settled the New World at least as early as the end of the Pleistocene. Nikhil Iyengar, CC BY-SA 4.0

animal. I cannot even imagine staring one of those down while all I'm holding is a stone spearpoint hafted onto a wooden shaft. I think at that point I would have seriously considered the benefits of a vegetarian diet.

It was a remarkable paleontological discovery on its own and it raised the question, Had people been responsible for the deaths of those bison who had died in Wild Horse Arroyo? Although there was no way at the time to date the bones precisely, existing evidence suggested that *Bison antiquus* had become extinct at the end of the Pleistocene (Ice Age), and that was believed to have occurred more than ten thousand years ago. So if there was any evidence of a human presence in the bone bed, it would provide proof that humans had been in North America long before the existing paradigm had allowed for.

FIGURE 6.2. Fluted points: Clovis (*left and center*) and Folsom (*right*) with the flute extending nearly the entire length of the spearpoint. Replicas; Kenneth L. Feder

In part to assess the possibility of an ancient human involvement with the bison remains found in Wild Horse Arroyo, archaeologists from the Colorado Museum of Natural History (now the Denver Museum of Nature and Science) launched a full-scale excavation of the site in 1927. To the surprise and delight of the archaeologists, sharp-edged stone tools and flakes were found in the thousands, including about two dozen sharp-edged spearpoints, each with distinctive channels or "flutes" on both of their faces (Figure 6.2).[2]

Those channels allowed for a firm hafting onto a likely wooden shaft and, perhaps, aided in the aerodynamic characteristics of the spears. One of those points was found nestled within one of the skeletons, specifically in the ribcage, at least appearing to have been the murder weapon. Later, in an even more dramatic and telling discovery, excavators found the tip of one of those fluted points actually embedded in one of the vertebrae (a backbone) of one of the bison. There can be no clearer smoking gun (which, I admit, is a strange figurative phrase in this case) than this. A human hunter had pierced the hide of a now-extinct bison who must have lived more than ten thousand years ago, a guess date from 1927 definitively confirmed when radiocarbon dating was developed and applied to the bones of extinct bison in the early 1950s.

A Late Ice Age Occupation of North America

Based on radiocarbon and other dating techniques derived from samples all over the world, it is now recognized that the Pleistocene Epoch, or Ice Age, ended about ten thousand years ago and that time period reflects a vast die-off of large mammals—megafauna—in North America. So the extinct bison species represented at the Folsom site must have been dispatched during the Pleistocene. This doubled, tripled, or even quadrupled the previously accepted maximum date for a human presence in the New World. Subsequent radiocarbon dating of sites with similar spearpoints, now called Folsom points, shows their first appearance as being somewhere between 12,900 and 12,740 BP.[3] A plethora of radiocarbon dates derived from organic material found in association with these points indicated that they were the standard hunting weapon for a period of about four hundred years. Folsom is not the name of a tribe; it is the name of a particular stone tool technology employed by people living in the western region of North America between the previously mentioned dates and about 12,000 BP. Hunting was a major, but certainly not the only, component of their diets, and bison were an important focus of their hunting.

Following McJunkin's discovery, the archaeological floodgates opened up as more skeletons of extinct animals were found associated with stone spearpoints and knives and scraping tools—including more bison and also woolly mammoths and mastodons, horses, and ground sloths, among others. As must ultimately happen when new data become available that contradict the existing view, the paradigm shifted, pushing back the entry of people into the New World to at least the end of the Pleistocene. Beginning in the 1950s with the widespread application of radiocarbon dating, direct dates were obtained from the bones of those animals people hunted, along with the charcoal found in hearths people used to cook the meat obtained from those animals, and resistance to the developing new consensus evaporated. Literally thousands of stone spearpoints that looked similar to the one found among the *Bison antiquus* bones at the Folsom site were found, as were hundreds of places where the people who made these weapons also made other stone tools, hunted and gathered wild foods, and lived and died.

A number of Folsom sites show that my reluctance to confront a giant bison with nothing but a stone-tipped spear is somewhat misguided. Recognizing the foolhardiness of going *mano a* bison, Folsom hunters devised a clever, sort of diabolical approach in their hunting strategies. In this approach, which is exemplified at the Casper site in Wyoming, hunters bearing Folsom spearpoints recognized that bison would panic and stampede when spooked. With this understanding of animal behavior in hand, they initiated a stampede at the Casper site and, likely using loud noises and perhaps controlled fires, directed the animals toward what amounted to a natural sand trap. With their enormous weight concentrated on relatively small hooves, bison possess an effective adaptation for running quickly on the hard surface of a prairie. However, it was a terrible design for soft sand, and at Casper they sank into that sand, becoming ensnared. The more they struggled, the deeper they sank. This doomed them and created a virtual shooting gallery, a killing field where, while maintaining a safe distance, hunters could dispatch the trapped bison with their spears, producing a huge quantity of meat.[4]

The scene is unimaginable, as these terrified megabeasts struggled and likely bellowed in abject terror when they recognized their dire situation. As spears began piercing their thick hide, the smell of blood and their enormous pain likely increased their feeling of panic, causing them to accelerate their struggle, which only continued to further envelop them in the sand.

Other sites in North America dating to the Paleoindian period show another strategy. Instead of chasing bison into a sandy trap, hunters stampeded them over a cliff—for example, at the Olsen-Chubbuck site in Colorado. There, archaeologists recovered the nine-thousand-year-old remains of a grouping of about 200 bison, including 16 calves, 65 immature bulls and cows, and 109 adults, both male and female.[5] The bison remains recovered here are of an extinct species labeled *Bison occidentalis* whose remains have been found dating to between 11,700 and 5,000 years ago. The animals had been driven, likely with noise and perhaps fire, toward and then over the edge of an arroyo. The animals were killed or severely wounded by the fall and crush of other members of the herd. The stone tools found at the site postdate those at Folsom. There are no fluted points, but there are beautifully flaked spear tips defined as the Cody type.

Historical references to more recent bison kills like the ones at Casper, Olsen-Chubbuck, and others suggest that, after the killing ceased, the people engaged in a huge feast, gorging on fresh meat.[6] After they had their fill—those same historical records claim that some adults ate, in a single sitting, a few pounds of meat and then slept for hours—they then dried and stored huge quantities of meat to feed their compatriots for an extended period of time.

The Folsom people appear to have been nomadic, but not randomly so. There is some evidence that suggests that small bands of people traveled regular routes across vast distances over the course of a year. We know this because of our ability to trace the sources of raw materials used for their hunting equipment. For example, at the Lindenmeier site in north-central Colorado, the natural glass forged in the crucible of ancient volcanoes—a material called obsidian (chapter 3)—that was used to make their Folsom points could be traced to at least two separate geographical sources in the western plains.[7] Materials like obsidian possess a distinctive and diagnostic chemical fingerprint. In other words, to the naked eye, all of the obsidian tools and flakes recovered at Lindenmeier looked pretty much the same—they all looked like highly reflective black glass. However, when those obsidian tools and flakes were assessed for their chemical constituents, the precise concentrations of "trace elements" or minor contaminants like tiny amounts of copper or arsenic differed sufficiently to show that they fell into two distinct groupings traceable to two separate obsidian sources. When those two distinct trace chemical signatures were compared with those derived for raw obsidian sources in the west, it was determined that the artifacts matched the signatures at two different sources, one about

560 kilometers (350 miles) away from Lindenmeier in northwest Wyoming and the other about 680 kilometers (425 miles) away in central New Mexico. While trade is a possible explanation for this, it is at least plausible that two different groups of Folsom people gathered at Lindenmeier during mammoth-hunting season about 12,300 years ago. Each had passed by one or the other of those two sources during what amounted to their seasonal travels, collected obsidian from those sources, made tools from the material, and brought them along for the joint Colorado hunt, where they lost, discarded, or put their spearpoints away for safekeeping. Luckily for archaeologists, the residents of Lindenmeier never retrieved those tools and they remained at the site, where, twelve millennia later, archaeologists were able to recover them, analyze them for the trace chemicals of their raw material, and deduce the most likely locations for their geographic sources.

An older variety of fluted point was discovered subsequent to the discovery at the Folsom site. These spear tips tended to be longer than Folsom points and, while sharing the distinctive technology of fluting or channeling on both faces, the channels of these older points extend up only about one-third of the way from base to tip (see Figure 6.2, left and center). This variety is named Clovis for the New Mexico site where it was first found and identified, and that became the general name used to label that projectile point form. Again, like Folsom, Clovis isn't the name of a tribe or even a particular group of people. It is the name of a technology that was geographically expansive, including much of North America and reaching as far as the southern tip of South America. Radiocarbon dates indicate a date range of between 13,050 and 12,750 years ago (Map 6.1).[8]

Whereas Folsom points tend to be associated with the remains of extinct bison, as at Folsom, Casper, and Lindenmeier, Clovis points are found in association with the remains of woolly mammoths and mastodons. Mammoths and mastodons were even bigger than the extinct species of bison hunted by people bearing Folsom points. Based on skeletal remains, a large adult mammoth might have measured about 3.5 meters (11.5 feet) tall and likely weighed more than 7,000 kilograms (15,000 pounds, or more than 7.5 tons). That's pretty much the size of an adult African bull elephant. Again, it's vegetarian time for me.

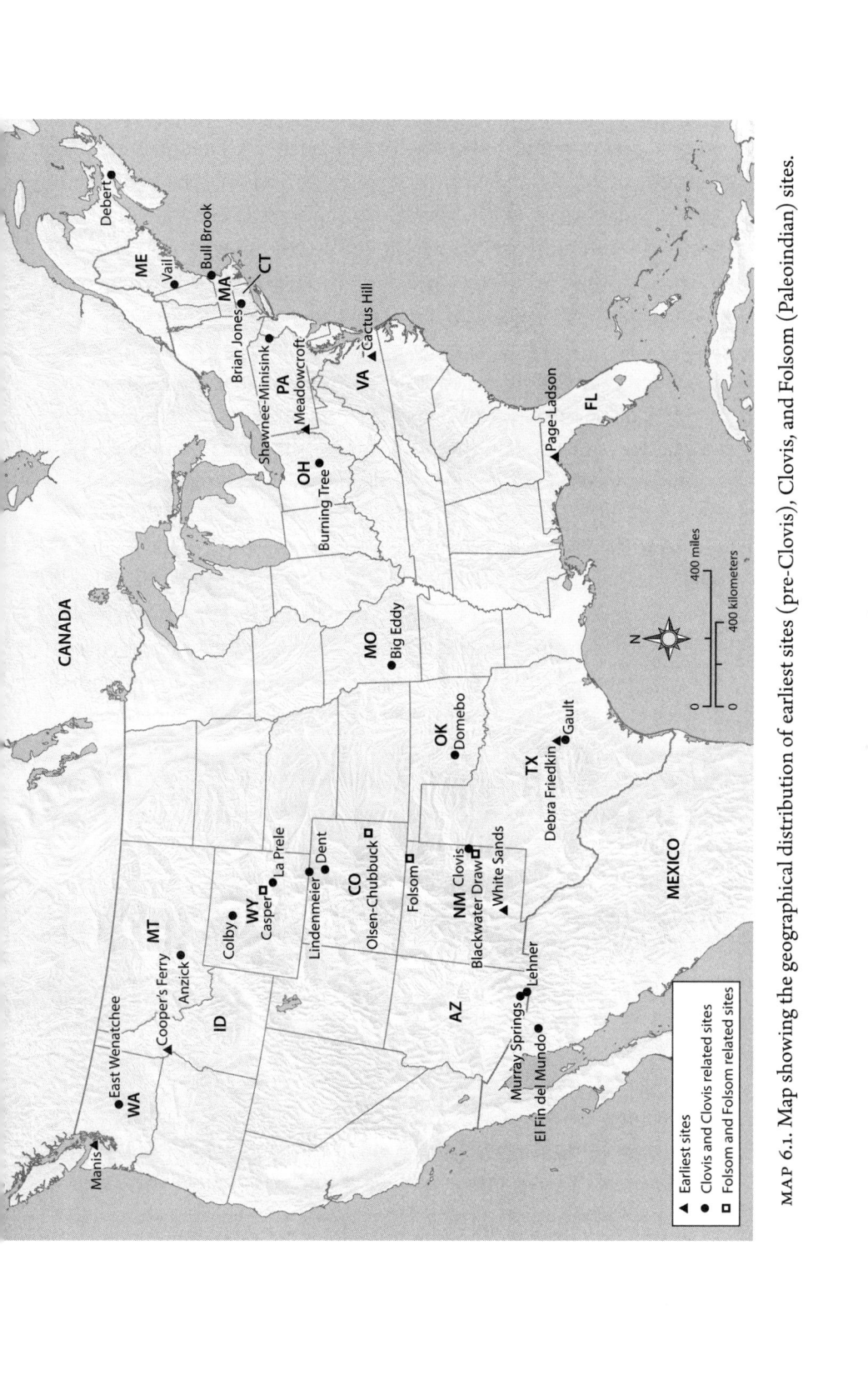

MAP 6.1. Map showing the geographical distribution of earliest sites (pre-Clovis), Clovis, and Folsom (Paleoindian) sites.

The prospect of even a group of hunters confronting an angry and panicked prehistoric elephant seems, well, nuts, but here too the hunters employed a clever and effective strategy. For example, about thirteen thousand years ago at the Lehner site found along the shore of the San Pedro River in southern Arizona, over a relatively short period of time, hunters chased down nine immature woolly mammoths (singling out young animals may seem cruel, but it's actually a pretty smart strategy), a bison, a horse, and a tapir, tricking them to walk into a trap, the waterlogged and muddy soil of a swampy section adjacent to or part of an arroyo.[9] Unable to extricate themselves from the gloppy, wet soil of the swamp, the animals were easy pickings for the human hunters, who were safely positioned at the margins of the quagmire, where they could wait out the struggling and exhausted animals and then kill them with their large fluted points, producing a bonanza of fresh meat, some of which could be feasted on immediately and the remainder dried and preserved for future use. Thirteen quite beautiful, graceful, artfully made Clovis instruments of death, along with a handful of sharp-edged butchering tools, were recovered during excavations in the mid-1950s conducted by archaeologists from the Arizona State Museum. A number of those points were found right in the middle of the bone deposit. The excavators also encountered two hearths filled with charcoal and bone. The hearths show that some cooking of the meat occurred right at the kill site and also provided organic material in the form of charcoal from pine, ash, and oak for radiocarbon dating. The site represents a virtual moment in deep time when Clovis hunters, producing food for their families, successfully killed enormous, Ice Age beasts.

The La Prele Mammoth
Clovis Site

The La Prele site in Wyoming represents a place where a group of hunters butchered a woolly mammoth about thirteen thousand years ago, leaving behind the bones of the six-ton beast and a wealth of stone tools. The great majority of the tools, including a couple of Clovis points with their typical channels or flutes, stone knives and scrapers, and more than thirty thousand small flakes (the results of stone tool making; see chapter 3), were of a rock type called chert.[10]

Away from the butchered mammoth skeleton itself, excavators found patterned clusters of these stone tools and waste flakes in rings that, they suggest, might reflect the outline of the interior walls of three circular structures about 3 meters (10 feet) in diameter. Historically, people have a tendency to move their stuff to the interior walls of such circular, one-room structures, leaving a debris-free center for a hearth and sitting area.

Though the tools and flakes were all chert, when researchers investigated the precise chemical makeup of the artifacts they recovered, they determined that the stone found within the margins of two of the possible houses was obtained from a source about 120 kilometers (75 miles) away in eastern Wyoming. The source of the chert found in the third possible house was even more remote, located in southwest Wyoming, about 400 kilometers (250 miles) from the site. As was likely the case at Lindenmeier, as I discussed previously, this may indicate that at least two families, traveling separately and widely through what today is Wyoming and adjacent states in their yearly walkabout, joined forces at La Prele to communally hunt mammoths.

Another fascinating discovery at the site was the presence of thousands of pieces of the mineral ocher. When ground down, ocher produces a powder (usually red but sometimes orange, sometimes yellow) that historically people often combined with a binder like grease or albumen to create a paint (see chapter 16). The researchers at La Prele didn't find any painted objects and can't be sure what the purpose of the ocher may have been (body paint?). They do know this, however: at least some of that ocher was obtained from a source about 95 kilometers (60 miles) away. So whatever its purpose or significance, it was important enough to collect a lot of it and schlepp it the 95 kilometers to the site. It is clear from both the chert and ocher sourcing at La Prele that Paleoindians were a peripatetic people, which is just a fancy way of saying they moved around a lot and across great distances to obtain the necessities of life.[11]

Excavators at La Prele have also identified fragments of at least four bone needles. They were able to identify the bones used to make the needles as canid (likely fox), felid (wild cat), and hare. Eyed needles are known from other Late Pleistocene sites in North America, attesting to the presence of sewn, tailored clothing instead of just robes or capes. It's ironic, I think, that the small, fur-bearing animals used to make warm clothing were sewn together using the bones of small, fur-bearing animals.[12]

Since the initial discovery and definition of Clovis and Folsom points, literally thousands of fluted points have been found across the United States and Canada. Clearly the toolmaking tradition that involved fluting on projectile points used to hunt large game animals (megafauna), including species that became extinct at the end of the Pleistocene, was widespread and remarkably successful. It isn't a great surprise that archaeologists once thought that Clovis and then Folsom represented the sites of the first human settlers of the New World, as their archaeological signal was virtually everywhere dating to the end of the Pleistocene, perhaps masking evidence of the presence of people who were here earlier still.

Too Much of a Good Thing?

You likely have noticed that you don't see woolly mammoths, mastodons, or *Bison antiquus* traipsing around at Yellowstone National Park in Wyoming, Glacier National Park in Montana, or Aulavik National Park on Banks Island in the Northwest Territories of Canada, though you might see moose, caribou, herds of modern bison, or musk ox. Why is that? What happened to those Ice Age beasts?

One hypothesis explains the extinction of megafauna in North America as the result of Late Pleistocene hunting. The appearance of the Clovis culture in North America was quickly followed by the extinction of thirty-five genera of large mammals, including woolly mammoths, mastodons, horses, and *Bison antiquus*. For all of these there is unambiguous evidence of hunting by human beings.[13] While it is true that correlation isn't necessarily evidence of causation—the fact that these extinctions occurred on the heels of the development of weapons exquisitely crafted for hunting those animals does not necessarily indicate that the extinctions were caused by that development—it is nevertheless suspicious. The so-called overhunting hypothesis is based on the belief that, perhaps, large animals in the New World had no experience with puny two-legged, spear-wielding hunters. Such large animals have long gestation periods, so it was difficult for them to respond to a population dip that may have resulted from increased predation. Add this to the fact that, as a result of climate change at the end of the Pleistocene, these larger animals were already suffering a significant amount of stress, and it becomes clear that maybe a combination of factors caused their populations to drop precipitously, leading, in relatively short order, to their extinction. However, the timing is imperfect, direct evidence is sparse, and many remain unconvinced by the data marshaled by supporters of the overhunting hypothesis.

What is indisputable is that the people who left behind all of those fluted points successfully spread across North America and adapted quickly to the many specific habitats they encountered and to the changes wrought by the warming that occurred when the Ice Age ended.

7

First Peoples

OLDER STILL?

IS THERE a new paradigm on the horizon? Will future archaeologists look back with a combination of nostalgia and pity at the current growing consensus I presented in chapter 6 about the timing of the first human settlement of North America, much in the way today we look back at both Aleš Hrdlička's formulation and then the Clovis First view? Could our current paradigm be overturned with even older sites from an even older migration? Well, yes, it is possible. But how likely is it?

Archaeologist Paulette Steeves thinks the evidence is clear and archaeologists have not yet caught up to the already existing data of a much older appearance of people in the New World.[1] She compiled a list of sites she argues are already sufficient to do precisely this, although, in fairness, most of the sites on her list, while thoroughly debunking the Clovis First consensus, don't appreciably contradict the current opinion. But some do, by a lot. Let's consider a site that she discusses and has long been pointed to by those who espouse a new paradigm, one that includes a human presence in the New World far more than forty thousand years ago: the Calico Early Man site.

Calico Early Man Site

The Calico Early Man site is located in the Mohave Desert of Southern California, a little less than two and a half hours from Los Angeles and near the small town of Yermo.[2] The site was first brought to the attention of the world when in 1959 local archaeologist Ruth DeEtte Simpson showed famed paleoanthropologist Louis Leakey—he of Olduvai Gorge in Africa fame—what she believed were stone scraping tools recovered from a stratigraphic layer that was deemed initially to date to more than 100,000 years before the present. Later excavations revealed the presence of chipped stone from as much as twenty-six feet below the current surface with a likely date of deposition of more than 200,000 and as much as 350,000 years ago. As noted in chapter 5, that early date *predates* the appearance of anatomically modern-looking human beings—the direct ancestors of modern people—anywhere in the world by tens of thousands of years!

Obviously, if the pieces of chipped stone recovered at Calico were actually tools made by human beings and if the dating of the deposit from which they were extracted is correct—those are big claims and would need extraordinarily strong evidence to be accepted—the Calico site would be of enormous significance, older by a factor of ten, than the next-oldest accepted archaeological site in North America. It could even provide evidence for the presence of premodern human beings—Neanderthals were one variety of premodern humans—in the New World. Talk about needing to rewrite the textbooks.

It is true that when human beings chip raw stone to produce tools—knives with sharp edges for cutting; steep-edged tools for scraping; symmetrical, sharp-pointed weapons for hunting—they do so methodically, and they follow a sequence and a set of rules (see chapter 3). Those methods and rules can be discerned by archaeologists, especially those trained in lithic analysis, the study of stone tools. Specialists in stone tools usually spend an inordinate amount of time attempting to replicate stone tool technologies, and they become fluent in the processes ancient people developed and then applied to make durable tools before the development of metallurgy.

Those lithic specialists also know full well that nature also has the ability to break stone, but you can ordinarily distinguish stone chipped by human toolmakers from the often more random chipping produced by nature when stones smash into other stones as a result of falling from heights (off a cliff, for example) or when a torrent of water (for example, a river) carries along stones that then crash into other stones located in the channel. Those same lithic specialists also know that it simply isn't possible to always distinguish stones broken by people from those broken by nature, especially when, as is often the case, at least some of the tools made by people are simple and merely "expedient," made for a simple task that requires nothing more than a sharp edge without a need for symmetry, precision, or beauty. It must be admitted that such tools, requiring only a few flakes and not needing to adhere to any particular template or form, may be indistinguishable from stones broken by nature.

Therein rests the problem with the Calico assemblage. There's again far too much "inside baseball" (well, "inside archaeology") about the arguments concerning the chipped stone at the site for this book, but the general consensus is that the Calico assemblage of stone cobbles and flakes—much of it chert and chalcedony, which are wonderful raw materials for making stone tools—is largely natural, not artifactual, and in those cases where the tools might be genuine, the dates are far more recent, well within the current archaeological consensus for the peopling of America.

Much of the chipped chert and chalcedony has been found in a "fanglomerate," a geological feature with tens of thousands of stone cobbles that were part of an alluvial fan deposited by flowing water at the mouth of an ancient river. Swiftly flowing water in an alluvial fan possesses sufficient energy to move rocks around pretty violently, causing them to smash into other rocks with more than enough force to break them. The angles (usually obtuse, or greater than ninety degrees) at which stones smash into other stones through natural processes ordinarily don't match a human approach, where, grasping a hammerstone in one hand, the worker applies percussive force (hits it) at an acute angle to produce sharp-edged flakes from a core (see chapter 3). But that's not always true, and where you have millions of stone cobbles bashing into one another for hundreds of thousands of years, you're bound to get pieces that look like tools. Sure, a bunch of chimpanzees banging away at a computer keyboard likely won't replicate a Shakespeare play, but a river smashing lots and lots of rocks together certainly can produce things that look like simple stone tools. But poring over thousands upon thousands of stone flakes and then focusing only on those that share some characteristics with stone tools likely is an example of confirmation bias. It's cherry-picking (well, stone-flake-picking), concentrating only on the sample of flakes that appear to confirm your hypothesis while ignoring the vast majority that doesn't.

World-renowned paleoanthropologist Mary Leakey, married to the aforementioned also world-renowned paleoanthropologist Louis Leakey, diagnosed this exact problem when she first viewed the chipped stones in the early 1960s. She noted that the pieces identified as human-made tools by the Calico researchers were, in fact, cherry-picked—in her terms, an "infinitesimal" proportion of all the busted-up rock in the ancient alluvial fan that, by sheer coincidence and as a result of the huge numbers of broken stones present in the deposit, looked like tools.[3] Understand, none of the objects identified as tools were beautiful, symmetrical artifacts. They all simply were stone nodules or flakes with a handful of flake scars on their edges. If you walked over the deposit, it likely wouldn't even occur to you that there were human-made tools.

There's one more element behind the skepticism of the majority of archaeologists concerning Calico: it is most decidedly a "one-off." There aren't other sites in Southern California or elsewhere with similar assemblages dating to more than one hundred thousand, two hundred thousand, or even three hundred thousand years ago.

Where are the rest of the sites dating to this period in California? Where's the trail of the ancestors of the Calico "people" leading back to wherever they must have come from? Unless the Calico "people" arrived by helicopter, they must have come overland from somewhere. And Southern California isn't exactly a local stop on the express train from Beringia. Nope; it makes sense to be highly skeptical about the Calico Early Man site.

I suspect that, had Louis Leakey not bestowed his name, fame, and abilities to attract grant money to the site (National Geographic kicked in money for excavation), the controversy wouldn't have received nearly as much attention among archaeologists as it did. Louis Leakey was of the opinion that the languages of Native America were too diverse to have developed from a small group of migrants from northeast Asia just ten thousand, twenty thousand, or even thirty thousand years ago. Perhaps, as a result, he was less skeptical than he should have been about the chipped stone and the associated dating at Calico. As noted previously, Mary Leakey—who was, of the two of them, far more knowledgeable about stone tools than was her husband—was dismissive of the identification of the battered stone cobbles and flakes at Calico as human-made, going so far as to say her husband's embrace of Calico was "catastrophic to his professional career and was largely responsible for the parting of our ways."[4] Wow; she thought it was so wrong, it contributed to their separation and ultimate divorce.

For a time, according to the now defunct website of the Friends of Calico, there was at least some uncertainty about who or what was responsible for the chipping of stone (though there was a pretty clear leaning toward them being artifacts, as many as sixty thousand of them).[5] Though the Friends group cited lots of dates—ranging from a few thousand years ago to hundreds of thousands of years ago—they recognized that while those dates related directly to geological deposits, it can't be assumed they also apply to what they believe are artifacts. I can pick up a piece of basalt today on Talcott Mountain in Avon, Connecticut, and make a stone tool. The basalt itself can be dated to about 180 million years ago, but my tool will be only a day old. At least in recognizing the dating challenge, there has been a backing away from the certainty that the site is hundreds of thousands of years old, but some of the artifacts—especially the Wren Biface found in the general area, which is clearly human-made—might be more like fourteen thousand years old, which would still be very important.

When I was there, sometime in the 1980s, I saw pieces of chipped stone in the small on-site museum that, I must admit, I would not have thought twice about had I recovered them at an archaeological site whose excavation I was directing. Some appeared to be simple, expedient tools—nothing fancy, to be sure, but showing two or three flakes removed from an edge. But in archaeology, context is all-important; it's one thing to find a chipped flake at a verified site (in association with symmetrically flaked tools, fire hearths, etc.), and it's quite another to find what appears to be a chipped flake in the middle of an alluvial fan where millions upon millions of stones had been deposited and broken by flowing water. In fact, as I walked around the site, I saw other pieces of chert and chalcedony sitting on the surface that, again, had I found them in context, in an archaeological stratum at a site, I would have assumed were waste flakes that could have been used expediently as simple cutting tools. But again, context is all-important, and finding these things in a natural deposit where there had been a lot of water moving around energetically makes it incredibly challenging to distinguish artifacts from naturally chipped rock. Today, the site is administered by the Bureau of Land Management and, after a closure of several years, is again open to the public.

The ghost of Carl Sagan would like to chime in with his previously mentioned aphorism: "Extreme claims require extreme levels of evidence." Sagan isn't suggesting that we automatically reject claims that are outside a given paradigm; he is simply demanding, as it says on Missouri's license plates, that supporters "show me!" And that demand to "show me" has not been met in the minds of the vast majority of archaeologists. Sure, it's possible, but we just don't have sufficient evidence to overturn the existing paradigm or forge a new one. Calico and the other claimed sites proposed to replace our current consensus at this point simply don't hold up.

Other One-Offs

There are other outliers, to be sure, sites with much older dates than those derived for the sites I discussed in chapter 5. One of the more recently proposed ones is the Cerutti site in Southern California, dated by its investigators to be 130,000 years old.[6] Cerutti has been proposed as a game changer and paradigm breaker, but as at Calico, the evidence presented, in this case not of stone tools but of broken-up mastodon bones, simply is not convincing to the majority of archaeologists. Remarkably, for a site that received so much positive press, there are no chipped stone tools at Cerutti. None. At all. No cutting tools. No scraping tools. No piercing tools. That alone makes an archaeologist's spidey senses tingle with skepticism. The identification of the broken-up woolly mammoth bones found there is based entirely on their configuration, which the researchers at the site maintain can best be interpreted as the result of having been processed by human beings as part of a pattern of food preparation.

But are there other sites that match what is seen at Cerutti reflecting this heretofore unrecognized pattern of food preparation? Nope. However, there are other possibilities, not involving intentional exploitation of mammoth meat by human beings, that might explain the configuration of the bones. The area where the bones were found was seriously disturbed during road construction with the use of heavy equipment that likely was capable of and might have been responsible for breakage of the ancient bones. Again, extreme claims—and a human presence in California 130,000 years ago is extreme—require extreme evidence, and Cerutti, at least for now, does not exceed that bar of initial skepticism.

It is no surprise, therefore, that because older outliers like Calico and Cerutti are relatively few in number compared with sites dating to the late glacial and early postglacial periods, because they present unique remains without a broader context of similar sites, and because they are outliers in terms of both time and artifacts, they are viewed by most archaeologists as anomalies that can safely be set aside at least *for the time being* unless and until additional supporting and convincing evidence is forthcoming. Remember, Calico was first reported in the late 1950s, more than seventy years ago, and no confirming evidence in the form of additional, similar sites has been found. Draw your own conclusions there, but for me that's pretty damning evidence that Calico is not an authentic pre-Clovis or pre-pre-Clovis archaeological site.

One more point. Knee-jerk skepticism sounds like a bad thing, but it's how science needs to work, at least as an initial reaction. In any science, when someone announces a discovery, proposes a novel interpretation of existing data, or suggests that we need to flip the table of a current consensus and start from scratch, the vast majority of scientists are going to react negatively. And yes, people being people, with all of their biases, preconceptions, and even conservatism (not the political kind, just the thinking kind), can be real jerks to anyone brave enough—or foolish enough—to try to overturn a paradigm. It takes time. There will be arguments. There might be yelling. There likely will be hurt feelings. But none of that matters all that much in the end. If the proof is there, it will prevail and the skeptics will either be convinced or become irrelevant. Again, this is as it should be. The consensus will wait here, patiently or not, until such time that this convincing evidence is presented.

A Separate Creation?

I've saved the "best" for last. What if the presence of people in the New World has an entirely different explanation? Maybe asking the question, When did people first arrive here? deflects us from considering what actually happened. I hesitate to even ask the question, but could the human beings we today call Native Americans have evolved right here as an entirely separate and independent variety or even species of people? This would mean Native Americans didn't come from anywhere else. They have, in a sense, always been here.

This is by far the most unlikely scenario addressed thus far. I have seen it mentioned or suggested, at least tangentially, on some social media platforms, so I might as well discuss it briefly here. Is it possible? The answer is easy: not so much. The hypothesis of a separate evolution is easy to dismiss on two fundamental grounds. To begin, the Native People of North America, like people on each of the other continents, are genetically extraordinarily similar to the people on all of the other continents. Human beings may look superficially different on the outside—skin color, hair texture, facial features, bodily proportions—and those differences may be more or less geographically distributed and patterned, but we are genetically very closely related. Our differences are, literally, skin deep. Based on the genetic unity of humanity, one group of modern human beings, including the Native People of the Americas, could not plausibly have evolved separately from any or all of the other groups. Our genetic differences are minor and often just a matter of statistics, like frequency of blood types, details of tooth shapes, or percentages of eye colors. Take human beings from two different parts of the world—for example, northern Africa and the southern tip of South America—and sit them down next to each other and, sure, there will be details of appearance that vary between them, but they will be far more alike than different, and recognizably the same species. Fossil specimens—including those given the names *Australopithecus afarensis*, *Homo habilis*, and *Homo erectus*—are ancestral to the first modern-looking human beings who evolved in Africa and only Africa. Europeans, the Native People of North and South America, Asians, Australia's Aboriginal People, and the people of the Pacific Islands are all descended from those Africans. We are, all of us, transplanted Africans.

At the same time, the osteological evidence, both in living species and in the fossil record that we see for evolution in Africa, simply doesn't exist for North or South America. Ancient ape species and the ancestors of ancient humans diverged approximately seven million years ago. Our line's divergence is marked by the ability to habitually walk on two feet. But there are no apes in the New World, and no fossil evidence has been found indicating there ever have been. So an ape species—distinguished from the monkeys by having proportionally larger brains and greater intelligence, dexterous hands, and no tail—that could have served as a source population for a bipedal, large-brained, and highly intelligent primate that relied on culture for its survival does not and has never existed in the Americas.

In fact, all primates—the family of animals that includes monkeys, apes, and people—in the New World (other than people) are *Platyrrhini* monkeys (technically that's the name of their pavorder), which have broad, flat noses with nostrils pointing out to the side; these monkeys, in fact, are more distantly related to human beings than are Old World *Catarrhini* monkeys, which have humanlike, projecting noses. Genetic evidence supports the hypothesis of a split between the platyrrhine and catarrhine monkeys about forty-four million years ago, and this meshes pretty well with the oldest fossil evidence for monkeys in the New World, which clocks in at about thirty-six million years ago in Peru.

Old and New World monkeys also differ in the details of their tails. New World monkeys, unlike those in the Old World, have prehensile tails with which they can grab things. If you see a monkey using its tail to hang on to branches as it moves through the trees, it's a New World monkey and never an Old World monkey. Further, tooth configuration is different. New World monkeys have three premolar teeth in each quadrant of their mouths (upper left, upper right, lower left, lower right). Apes and Old World monkeys, like human beings, have only two premolars in each quadrant. Though the canine teeth of Old World monkeys and apes tend to be substantially larger than in humans, the kinds of teeth and the number and configuration of those teeth are the same—two incisors, one canine, two premolars, and three molars in each quadrant. Finally, monkeylike critters including tarsiers did live in North America, but they became extinct here more than twenty-five million years ago, long, long before the first distinguishable species in the human genealogy, the hominins.

Based on fossil evidence, all in Africa, as noted, it is estimated that the evolutionary line that led to modern chimpanzees, the animal most closely related to modern humans, and human beings diverged into separate lineages beginning about seven million years ago. There is no evidence at all for the existence of such an evolutionary "cousin" to human beings in the New World. So, no, the Native People of the Americas did not evolve in North America. They and the Native People of Europe, Asia, Australia, and the Pacific Islands are all evolutionarily related to one another and descended from the earliest human beings, who, evidence clearly shows, evolved in Africa.

8

Learning to Live in a New World

IF YOU'VE ever driven across the U.S., you have been eyewitness to a fundamental fact about the landscape of America: it is enormously diverse. I did it in 1982 and it was a trip both literally and figuratively, as well as very revealing about America's natural diversity. Leaving the forested, hilly landscape of my home state of Connecticut, we drove south, passing through more hills and deciduous and mixed forests of the mid-Atlantic states. Next, heading due west from there, we passed through the Appalachians of North Carolina and crossed the broad, flat, enormously rich floodplain of the Mississippi River, eventually hitting the grasslands and plains of Kansas, a place so flat I jokingly maintain that when you enter the state at its eastern border, driving along on I-70, if you squint you can see the western border some 680 kilometers (424 miles) away. Not really, but the plains of Kansas seem unremittingly flat to the eyes of this New Englander. Continuing west, we encountered the foothills of the Rockies in Colorado. We passed over the Rockies on the border between Nevada and California, following the general route of a group of migrants today called the Donner Party, who were made famous by the fact that in 1846 they got trapped east of the mountains there, where half of them died of starvation and at least some of them managed to survive by eating the bodies of their dead compatriots and even a couple of Indian guides. Our car, my old Datsun five-speed, was none too happy overcoming the elevation of the Rockies, but admittedly we had an easier time than the Donner Party. We survived on fast food, chips, and Cokes rather than the dead bodies of our companions. In California we encountered rich and fertile agricultural lands redolent with their harvest of oranges, melons, and avocados. After walking the hilly streets of San Francisco and dipping our toes into the Pacific Ocean near Los Angeles, we turned east again, heading into the American Southwest. There we encountered the iconic saguaro cactus landscape of Arizona's dry, scrubby deserts, and then on to the shimmering white desert in New Mexico mentioned in chapter 5 and enshrined in what was then White Sands National Monument and now is White Sands National Park.

My point here—and admittedly our drive included only a relatively small portion of the American landscape and didn't include Alaska—is that America is both vast and marked by extraordinary ecological, geographic, climatological, and geological diversity: old mountains covered in forest; sandy beaches along clichéd "wave-tossed" coasts; broad grasslands once teeming with herds of large animals, especially bison; young, tall mountains with jagged peaks that have permanent ice fields at their summits; humid, subtropical forests; glacially scarred landscapes; flat plains; arid deserts—we have it all, or nearly so (Map 8.1).

This was the variety that confronted America's First People as they entered and spread across the landscape of their new world as their population grew, especially as the Pleistocene waned and the modern world, with its current climates and plant and animal communities, became established. The archaeological record shows this very clearly, and it reflects a particular element of the genius of Native People: their ability to, from a common cultural source, exquisitely adapt to each of these many and varied habitats by adjusting their existing ways of life to conform with the new and changing conditions presented in the Holocene, the modern geological epoch. But what do I mean by the verb "adapt" and its noun form "adaptation"?

"Adapt" is, indeed, a verb that generally means to develop a set of behaviors within the context of an encompassing "culture" or way of life that enables a group's survival under a given set of environmental circumstances. People may need to adapt in response to the conditions and challenges they face in a new territory into which they have

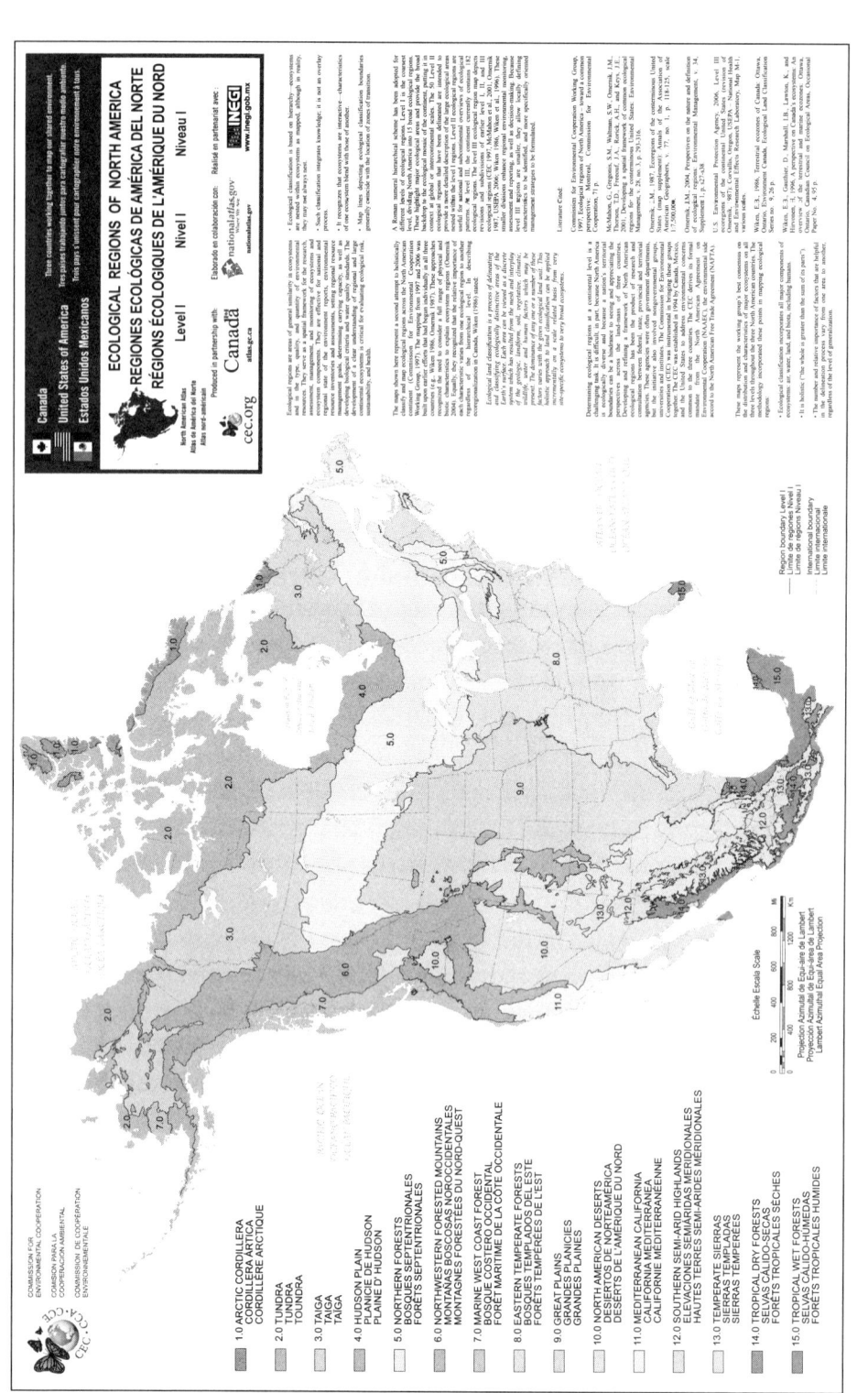

MAP 8.1. Map showing the many ecoregions of North America. The continent is ecologically diverse. The strategies Native

entered—they have to invent a new way of life. In some instances, once they have created a strategy for living in a place, they may need to adapt or adjust their way of life further in response to the new conditions and challenges posed when the area in which they live experiences a change in the environment; that environment includes other people. An "adaptation" is the sum total of those behaviors.

Compare human beings' adaptations with the extremely focused and restrictive adaptations of koalas in Australia or pandas in China. The adaptations of those animals are incredibly narrow, with little wiggle room or tolerance for change. Koalas eat eucalyptus leaves and little else. If the environment changes and eucalyptus trees don't survive, goodbye koalas. They can't replace eucalyptus leaves and survive on a diet of popcorn and string cheese. It's eucalyptus or nothing. Pandas survive on bamboo. Without bamboo, no pandas. They can't accept substitutes. Their biology won't allow it. When environmental conditions change and a region is no longer conducive for the growth of eucalyptus or bamboo—or if humans, with our voracious appetites for land for agriculture and the extraction of other resources, clear-cut eucalyptus forests or denude areas where bamboo grows—those animals can't simply shift their diets or change their subsistence patterns. They can't figure out another way to survive. They die. When this happens enough, they become extinct, at least in the wild. They're not being uncooperative, stubborn, or stiff-necked like a kid who refuses to eat broccoli or spinach. It's a question of their biological requirements.

Human beings aren't like that. We are omnivorous and the broadest of generalists, able to survive in almost every habitat on Earth, and not by evolving specialized biological adaptations, because the most significant of our biological adaptations, our large and complex brain, affords us the ability to invent ways of surviving on the fly, nearly instantly.

A theme underpinning the migration of human beings into North America is the ability to adapt on multiple levels. The first people entered into terra incognita, a land with conditions, resources, dangers, challenges, and opportunities entirely unknown to them. And there wasn't just one unknown land with a specific climate and set of resources and challenges, there were dozens or even hundreds to be encountered as they spread across two continents characterized variously by Arctic tundra, deserts, mountains, plains, prairies, woodlands, and rainforests. Beyond this, the habitats they encountered were not static. They were, particularly at the end of the Pleistocene, marked by great change as the continent warmed up and ice melted off in the North, which resulted in great changes in weather patterns in the South. Those Native People had to, essentially, continually redefine themselves, continually reconfigure their adaptations, and continually update their cultures in order to survive. The evidence of that redefinition, reconfiguration, and revision is seen in the archaeological record for the time period that is the focus of this chapter. We call this time the Archaic Period.

It is a testament to the creative genius of America's First People that they developed successful and vibrant adaptations to the myriad habitats they encountered as they spread across two continents. They didn't fall into these adaptations or emulate other people or animals. They invented from scratch ways of life that were congruent with the natural conditions they encountered. The Archaic Period that marks the post-Pleistocene of North America, beginning about nine thousand years ago and usually seen as ending about three thousand years ago, is all about the First People settling into their many different ways of life in their new world.

Diversity

The term Archaic is applied to a time in North America following the end of the Pleistocene when Native People developed adaptations to the many different environments that were established after the ice. All of the Archaic peoples were hunters of wild animals (including fish and shellfish) and gatherers of wild plants, basing their subsistence on the resources they encountered in their home territories. It's fair to say that most of the Archaic peoples were practical and generally used any and all of those resources that were available to them. They were "generalists." They were expedient foragers; if it was food, it was eaten.

At the same time, it is clear that in the many different environments in which they found themselves, there were uniquely useful, abundant, and valuable resources that were not necessarily available in other regions. In those instances where people lived along the coast, for example, or had a major river in their territory, or a large lake, or an abundance of a particular kind of stone or metal, they used and even emphasized these unique resources in their adaptations. In other words, while they tended to be generalists, they recognized what was especially useful or valuable in their territory and exploited the hell out of it.

In recognition of the extraordinary diversity of adaptations devised by the Archaic peoples of North America that resulted from the extraordinary natural diversity of North America, instead of just a couple of cultural designations based on stone tool technology (like Clovis and Folsom), archaeologists apply a host of terms to their various adaptations and, therefore, cultures geographically distributed across the landscape. Here in the Northeast we have the Mast Forest Archaic, Maritime Archaic, and Lake Forest Archaic. Farther south there is the Shell Mound Archaic. In the American Southwest they have the Desert Archaic. North, into Canada, is the Shield Archaic (named for the geological feature called the Canadian Shield, a flat expanse east of the Rockies that is characterized by volcanic bedrock). Farther north, the Paleo-Arctic Tradition represents the Archaic in the Arctic (chapter 11). In the flat grasslands of the North American plains there is, not surprisingly, the Plains Archaic. In recognition of the dominance of the Mississippi River across the American Midwest, archaeologists define the Riverine Archaic. I will not discuss every one of the Archaic adaptations in depth. Instead, I will focus on examples that serve as models for how each of those distinct adaptations reflects the ability of the Indigenous People to craft a way of life based on the post-Pleistocene resources available in their home territories.

The Cultures of the Archaic Period

As just mentioned, in the broad classification scheme developed by archaeologists to define and name the different adaptations of post-Pleistocene northeast North America are the following: Mast Forest Archaic, Maritime Archaic, and Lake Forest Archaic. The Mast Forest

Archaic is centered in New York State and much of New England (excluding the coast of Maine), and south through Virginia and to North Carolina; the Maritime Archaic homeland is the Atlantic coast of Maine and eastern Canada; the Lake Forest Archaic is identified in sites around the Great Lakes.

Note that these distinctions are applied by archaeologists. These three groups were not walled off from one another, and the geographical interfaces among them were permeable and likely shifted as a result of small-scale, perhaps even year-to-year, fluctuations in local climates. Applying these names is simplistic and, to an extent, overly so, but it does reflect genuine, coherent differences in subsistence focus and artifact styles related to differences in the resources available in their territories and various historical traditions of toolmaking.

Lake Forest Archaic

Living in the vicinity of the Great Lakes and along the St. Lawrence River in the northern U.S. and southern Canada afforded local people access to abundant lacustrine (lake) and riverine resources, with an emphasis on fish. Moreover, the region is rich in mammalian resources, including deer and moose, and wild plants. These resources are important, but something else characterized the Lake Forest Archaic, and that unique feature concerns one of the raw materials people used to make their tools.

The application of the term Stone Age to describe and define the Native People of North America, even if unencumbered by any implied bias (see chapter 3), isn't factually accurate. The Native People living around the Great Lakes, especially Lake Superior, discovered extensive deposits of "native copper," not as an ore that required smelting but in the form of raw and pure natural copper.

As a people experienced and skilled at making stone tools explored their territory in the quest for valuable resources, they hoped for good rock for making sharp-edged implements (again, see chapter 3) but they found something decidedly different: a rather strange-looking shiny orange or green "rock" that didn't flake when struck with a stone hammer but, instead, absorbed the blows and actually changed shape. This "rock" couldn't be flaked, but it could be reshaped into a desired form.

For some, the "it smooshes but doesn't break into sharp flakes" characteristic of the new material ended the story. It was a big nonstarter for them. But others were intrigued by it. Through experimentation, they figured out that this process of shaping was greatly facilitated by softening the "rock" through the application of heat. In so doing, they discovered that they could create durable, sharp-edged tools that were the equal of any they could craft from stone by the application of percussing and pressure (chapter 3). In other words, they became metallurgists.

Beginning about ninety-five hundred years ago, and initially using a technique called cold hammering where nuggets of raw and pure natural copper were beaten into shape with thin, very sharp edges, Native toolmakers produced spear and arrow points, knives, ax heads, and other tools out of copper in the culture called the Lake Forest Archaic (Figure 8.1).

Copper was found in glacial boulders but also in underground seams that local people extracted, sometimes in actual mines where they left pillars in place to serve as support beams for the roofs. Copper became such a crucial raw material and was used so extensively in the Great Lakes region, archaeologists have named and identified the Old Copper Culture there.

Mast Forest Archaic

The "mast" in the name Mast Forest Archaic is a reference to one of the major food sources in the Northeast: the nuts produced by local trees, including acorns, chestnuts, walnuts, and hickory nuts, that are jettisoned from the trees in the fall. Those nuts—the mast—accumulate on the forest floor, where they serve as a major food source for people as well as for animals like deer. Those animals, in turn, serve as a food source for people as well. So, obviously enough, trees growing in the mast forest of the Northeast include oak, chestnut, walnut, and hickory, along with maple, birch, and elm among the deciduous trees and pine, spruce, and hemlock among the conifers.

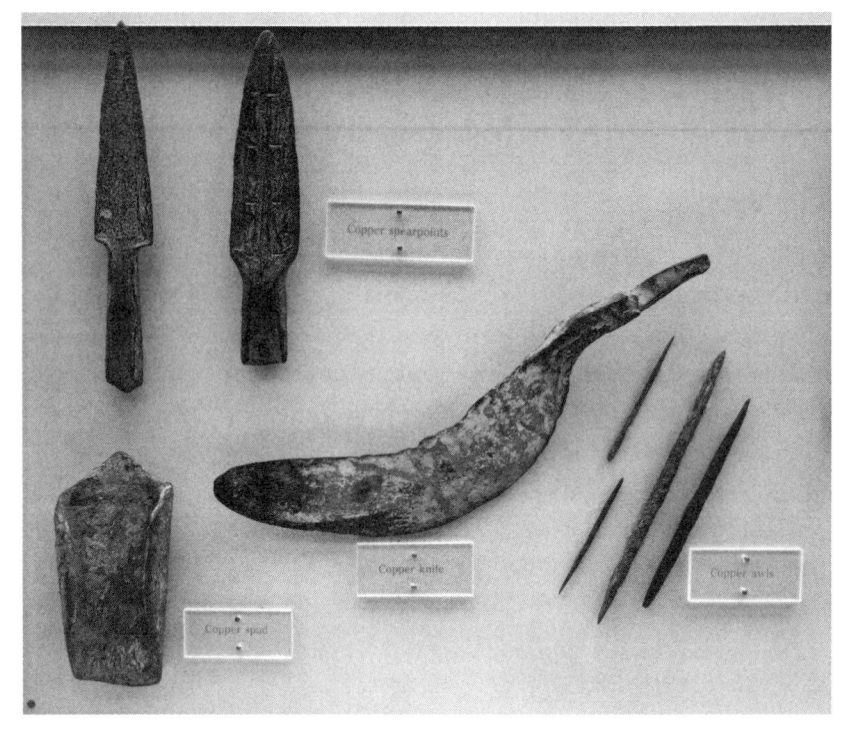

FIGURE 8.1. A selection of copper tools made by the people who were the bearers of what we today call the Old Copper Culture in the area around the Great Lakes. Daderot. Wikimedia Commons.

Unfortunately, soils in the Northeast tend to be acidic and biologically active. This means that organic materials including seeds, nutshells, and bone tend to decompose pretty quickly as a result of acidity and the fact that animals, including microorganisms in the soil, eat those remains, often leaving very little for archaeologists to recover and identify. Fortunately, when organic material is burned, for example in the process of cooking, preservation improves dramatically. Burned or "calcined" bone can better withstand acidic soils, and burned wood and carbonized seeds and nutshells are similarly removed from the natural recycling of their constituent parts. This is why the excavation and careful recovery of material in cooking hearths is such an important part of dietary reconstruction in the Northeast. As well as providing evidence of diet, the recovery of preserved, carbonized wood provides material for radiocarbon dating.

Based on organic remains found in cooking hearths and in storage pits where material has fortuitously been preserved, often as a result of burning but also when it has been waterlogged (which eliminates aerobic microorganisms that might otherwise eat the remains), we have a pretty good idea of the subsistence practices of the people of the Mast Forest Archaic. It should go without saying that the people who represent an adaptation to the post-Pleistocene mast forest of the Northeast relied on those chestnut, walnut, and hickory trees for their carbohydrate-rich nut meats. Acorns can be eaten as well, but they need to be processed to remove the tannic acids in their nutmeat. Along with the trees, other food sources in the northeastern forests include the seeds, leaves, and roots of wild plants, especially those growing in the disturbed habitats along river banks where the sun isn't blocked out by tree canopies. Freshwater fish and shellfish provided important sources of protein. Perhaps most important, the deer attracted to the mast on the forest floor were a nearly perfect source of food and provided the triple bonus of meat, hides for clothing and shoes, and antlers, the tines (tips) of which were especially useful as pressure flakers in stone tool making, as described in chapter 3. Fur-bearing animals including foxes, beavers, wolves, and bears were an important part of the economy as well.

The Northeast also has extensive coasts from the mid-Atlantic states north to and then east along the shorelines of Connecticut, Rhode Island, and Cape Cod in Massachusetts. Once past the cape, the coast runs northward across eastern Massachusetts and into southern Maine, where it merges with the region characterized by the Maritime Archaic. Sites along that coast often show a reliance on shellfish, with a focus on oysters, quahog, and scallops. In fact, before modern development, the coast of southern New England was characterized by numerous "shell middens," large mounds of shells that had been discarded in the local people's version of the shellfish industry.

Alsop Meadow

The Alsop Meadow site is located in an open field adjacent to the Farmington River in Avon, Connecticut. The location was prime real estate for Archaic people, right along a river and bracketed by a couple of glacial features called eskers. Eskers are fascinating features consisting of sediment deposited by water in tunnels carved by the water's flow inside glaciers. As such, when seen from the air, eskers look like rivers, but instead of meandering channels, they're meandering hills. The eskers demarcating the meadow where the Alsop Meadow site is located likely provided a measure of protection to residents.

I directed the excavation of Alsop as part of the Farmington River Archaeological Project, run out of Central Connecticut State College (now University). Unfortunately, we found little organic material at the site other than burned wood. We found no calcined bone, but we did recover some burned shells of hickory and chestnut. Radiocarbon dates for the site indicated an age of 4,950 years, placing it firmly within the beginning of the Late Archaic.

In an area of just a little more than one thousand square meters (about a quarter of an acre), we recovered over sixteen thousand stone tools and stone flakes. As we expected at a Late Archaic site in southern New England, the people living at Alsop Meadow relied on locally available stone to make their tools. Some of their tools were made from volcanics, one of the three basalts available as layers of nearby Talcott Mountain, interdigitated by layers of sandstone, and located only about three miles away. The toolmakers at Alsop clearly recognized the presence of two separate volcanic flows on the west side of the mountain, today called Holyoke and Talcott. They also clearly understood that the Holyoke basalt had a finer grain than the Talcott and was therefore preferable for making tools. We actually found a couple of large blocks of that material at the site. Those blocks look exactly like those that are today visible, eroding out of an exposure toward the top of the mountain (Figure 8.2).

Even more interesting, the Alsop toolmakers discovered that in some places where the black rock appeared to be superimposed over the gritty

FIGURE 8.2. Basalt outcrop on Talcott Mountain, Avon, Connecticut. The prismatic shape of the basalt chunks that eroded out of the exposure made them convenient cores from which sharp flakes could be removed and then made into tools. Kenneth L. Feder

red rock that represents the sandstone strata, there was another, even better rock for making tools. As we understand it now, in a process similar to the production of glass by heating grains of silica to a great temperature, when molten lava (that's what became the black basalt) overrode the sandstone (the red rock), it heated it to a great temperature. This baking of sandstone metamorphosed or transformed it into a different kind of rock exhibiting different characteristics. In other words, nature transformed red, grainy, crumbly sandstone—a rock not especially useful in the production of sharp-edged and durable tools—into a black, very fine-grained, and flint-like rock called hornfels. Hornfels exhibits conchoidal fracture and is very useful for making sharp edges and durable tools (chapter 3).

The vast majority of tools and waste flakes we recovered at Alsop were hornfels. Now think about that. Five thousand years ago, people living in this part of the Farmington Valley in northwest Connecticut followed an animal trail to the top of what we today call Talcott Mountain.

Perceptive and aware of their environment because their lives depended on it, in their geological explorations they noticed the presence of alternating layers of rock as they climbed, beginning first on a red layer of soft, crumbly rock. After a while, they found themselves walking on a geological bench of hard, black-and-gray, coarse-grained material. They almost immediately recognized that this rock would be pretty tough to make into sharp-edged tools. Once they passed over that rock, they encountered more of the coarse and crumbly red rock. They recognized that the red rock might be useful for hearth circles, but useless for most tools.

Climbing closer to the pinnacle of the mountain, which is all of 300 meters (about 1,000 feet) high, they noted the existence of another black-and-gray layer, but this was a significantly finer-grained material and a pretty good rock for making stone tools, so they collected some of the blocks that eroded out of exposures toward the top of the mountain, perhaps the same really impressive one the modern trail brings you to today, with its accumulation of prismatic chunks still eroding out of the mountain (see Figure 8.2).

They also learned something more in their investigation of the mountain. In a few isolated spots there were pockets of a dark gray or black rock with a very fine texture and smooth surfaces, much finer and more glasslike than the second layer of basalt encountered on their climb. Perhaps they noticed that this different rock could be found directly under the layers of the dark grey hard rock and actually seemed to belong to the same layer as the red rock. This was pay dirt (well, pay rock).

Using their own rock hammers, they extracted what they could and brought it down the mountain to show other people in their village, the place we today call Alsop Meadow. Nodding in approval, the other toolmakers congratulated their friends and began using the rock for making stone tools. Countless return visits to the good rock were made to collect more of this superior raw material.

Among the complete tools we recovered at Alsop were spearpoints, knives, scraping tools, and drills. Some of these tools are pretty clunky, and the clunkiest are always made of basalt. However, some of the hornfels tools are among the most artfully made artifacts I have ever

FIGURE 8.3A AND FIGURE 8.3B. A nearly five-thousand-year-old spearpoint finely crafted from hornfels, a metamorphosed form of sandstone (a). On the right is a drill made of the same raw material (b). Recovered at the Alsop Meadow site in Avon, Connecticut. Kenneth L. Feder

excavated at a site in Connecticut, showing what a skilled knapper can produce when given some really good rock to work with (Figure 8.3).

A special note for all you New York State archaeologists: All of the symmetrical, "bifacial" tools recovered at Alsop—these are tools that were flaked on both faces of the large flakes removed from cores and that then were made into spearpoints and drills—had a base for hafting that was about one-quarter the length of the tool and was concave on both sides. This gives the base of these tools the appearance of a fish tail. While similar points are found in New York State dating to two thousand years after Alsop was occupied—those points were first defined by their discovery at a site near Orient Point on Long Island and are called Orient Fishtails—I think the Alsop fish tails were entirely independently developed and are not genealogically related to the Orient Fishtails. The Alsop points exemplify what Tevye from *Fiddler on the Roof* taught us in chapter 3: within the community of people who lived in Alsop Meadow nearly five thousand years ago, the traditional way of making the base of tools that were to be hafted involved not notches but instead inwardly curved sides. That curving created room for what likely was the sinew wound around the wooden shaft to make that connection of spearpoint to shaft as strong as possible.

Soapstone

People of the Archaic faced a significant challenge: they had not yet developed ceramic technology (chapter 10). No ceramics, no pottery. Without pottery, there are a limited number of ways of cooking food, especially soups or stews, over an open fire, and they are all cumbersome, time consuming, and not particularly efficient. Very tightly woven baskets and carved wooden bowls can be used, but neither can be placed directly over a fire, which greatly complicates the cooking process. The contents of the vessel can be warmed by placing rocks directly in a fire, heating them up, and then picking them up (with some sort of tongs) and gingerly dropping them in the vessel. Unfortunately, while it works, it's a pretty inefficient and problematic process, as hot rocks may shatter when they are placed in the cold contents of a basket or wooden vessel, leading to bits of rock in your food. Additionally, as one of my students figured out in an experiment he conducted, it's a very, very slow process.

There was another option open to people who had access to a mineral called steatite or, colloquially, soapstone. Steatite is a very soft rock. On a simple 10-point scale of relative mineral hardness (called the Mohs scale after the German geologist who invented it), diamond is assigned a 10 and steatite is only a 2 (your fingernails are 2.5). Steatite, therefore, is relatively easily extracted from its parent rock and also easily carved to shape. Here in Connecticut, we commonly find quartz and quartzite tools, purposely shaped to the form of picks, at soapstone quarries. On the aforementioned Mohs scale, quartz and quartzite are about a 7.5.

At the same time, steatite is highly resistant to thermal shock, meaning it is good at sustaining a quick change in temperature without shattering. Steatite tends to heat up slowly and to then radiate that heat slowly and evenly. Modern woodstove makers have figured this out and some build stoves with a cast-iron framework onto which they affix flat panels of polished steatite. Having owned two soapstone woodstoves, along with polished soapstone being quite beautiful, looking for all the world like marble, I can also vouch for the fact that while the stone certainly gets hot to the touch—you wouldn't want to leave your hand on it for terribly long—it doesn't approach the extreme temperatures of cast-iron stoves. Of even greater importance, because it maintains the heat it stores from the fire and radiates it relatively slowly, the stove is still radiating heat into your room long after the fire has gone out.

As well as its being exceptionally heavy, the most significant problem with steatite is that it simply isn't widely available. That was a good thing if you lived near, had direct access to, and could, in a sense, monopolize this valuable resource as a result of your and its geography. Connecticut has, for example, a relatively small number of known steatite sources.[1] Just as was the case with the discovery of hornfels on Talcott Mountain, Native People explored their territories and gathered geological knowledge. During that exploration, they found deposits of soapstone and set up quarries where they proceeded to mine the material for the manufacture of cooking vessels, platters, spoons, cups, and even smoking pipes. There's direct, archaeological evidence for the quarrying of soapstone at those sites beginning more than three thousand years ago, just before the appearance of clay pots (Figure 8.4).

As a result, until ceramic technology was adopted, steatite was a highly sought-after, highly valuable raw material. Demand for the mineral was high, but supply was low or, at least, geographically restricted. Yet soapstone vessels are found throughout the state, including in lots of sites at the end of the Archaic and the beginning of the Woodland (usually dated to before three thousand years ago) that are located a great distance from the known quarries. In fact, evidence is being collected

FIGURE 8.4. A large chunk of steatite, or soapstone, at the Walter Landgraf Soapstone Quarry in Barkhamsted, Connecticut. Native People quarried the material here about 2,850 years ago. You can make out several "unharvested" bowl forms in the soapstone. The scale is one meter long. Courtesy of Astana R. Heath

now by Dan Wilcox, a graduate student in archaeology (and a past student of mine), showing that at least some of the soapstone artifacts recovered in excavations on the north shore of Long Island, across Long Island Sound from the Connecticut shore, a place where there are no sources of soapstone, may have originated in northern Connecticut.

As we will see in chapter 10, ultimately, steatite represented a stopgap raw material. It was useful and worked well for its intended purpose in cooking over an open fire, but its patchy availability was a significant problem for the people of the Archaic. A new raw material and a new technology would change everything: ceramics. I'll talk more about that in chapter 10.

Maritime Archaic

You can see the pattern clearly during the Archaic: people settling in and adapting to what were, effectively, regionally differentiated modern habitats in North America, exploiting the resources, especially lithic (but including copper), that were useful in making tools and, importantly, the plant and animal resources that were also regionally distributed. This certainly applies to the Maritime Archaic, whose heartland is located along coastal Maine and eastern Canada, as seen especially in Newfoundland by about seven thousand years ago, southern Labrador by about five thousand years ago, and northern Labrador by about four thousand years ago. By that time, the archaeological sites located along the Atlantic coast from central Maine and then north along virtually the entire coast of Canada all reflect a subsistence base related directly to the unique richness of the coast—thus the name Maritime Archaic. Archaeologist Bruce Bourque rightly describes them as an "ancient American sea people." His book *The Swordfish Hunters* is a wonderful presentation on the fascinating Maritime Archaic people.[2] His full-color photographs of the obviously effective but also wonderfully and artfully crafted tools are fantastic.

Where preservation has been high, the hearths excavated at Maritime Archaic sites reflect a diet rich in fish. Some of the fish remains reflect species that did not dwell right along the coast. These species are labeled "pelagic," and it would have required the use of boats capable of sailing some distance away from the coast to encounter them and then carry them home for dinner. Maritime Archaic subsistence also included sea mammals; among the very sophisticated tools found at Maritime Archaic sites are toggle harpoons, which were designed to twist after penetrating the thick hide of a seal. As the seal twists or turns in an attempt to escape, the harpoon head simply gets more deeply and inextricably embedded. Bad for the seal, good for the hunter. We'll see the development of a similar technology among people of the far north in chapter 11.

Make no mistake: though focused on marine resources, the Maritime Archaic people did not rely exclusively on the sea. Evidence shows that they also hunted caribou. In some cases, people cleverly used piles of stones to create "drive lanes" through which panicked animals would tend to run while being chased by hunters. Those piles were positioned increasingly close until they created a choke point at which the animals would become trapped in what amounted to a killing field, where hunters hiding in wait could dispatch them. I'll discuss them in more detail in chapter 11.

Along with stone spears, lances, and harpoons, ax heads and gouges show that Maritime Archaic people were also expert woodworkers. As their homes—semi-subterranean pit houses early in the period and bark-covered longhouses toward the end—were made with a skeleton of saplings and logs, the ability to work wood efficiently was an important skill.

Most of the stone tools produced by Mast Forest and Lake Forest Archaic people were made by shaping stone through the application of a combination of percussion and pressure. People of the Maritime Archaic were using that same technology, often using Ramah chert found in Ramah Bay in northern Labrador, to make spearpoints, knives, and scraping and engraving tools. However, Maritime Archaic people also produced sometimes elegant, long spears called lances as well as a tool called an *ulu*, a knife with a semilunar (half-moon) shape (the word *ulu* is taken from the Inuktitut language spoken by the Inuit Native People of northeastern Canada), through a process of grinding and polishing, usually of a softer stone than chert, particularly slate.

Okay, I've saved what you likely will find the most interesting element of Maritime Archaic culture for last: their ceremonial and religious life as indicated by their treatment of the dead. At the seven-thousand-year-old L'Anse Amour site in southern Labrador, archaeologists found the burial of a child who was about twelve years old when they died. The grave required a significant amount of labor in what can reasonably be interpreted as an act of love. The child was buried under a low mound of stone more than thirty-five feet in diameter. Grave goods were found in the burial, including food remains in the form of fish bones—nourishment for the afterlife?—an antler handle for a tool, a harpoon head, and the tusk of a walrus.

A later cemetery, Port aux Choix, dating to between forty-four hundred and thirty-four hundred years ago, was discovered in Newfoundland. Archaeologist James Tuck encountered fifty-six separate burials at the site, likely an accumulation of graves over a period of time in a communal cemetery. As was the case at L'Anse Amour, grave goods were associated with the burials. Most of these were related to woodworking.

Elaborate burials also characterize the manifestation of the Maritime Archaic farther south in Maine. Their treatment of the dead between five thousand and three thousand years ago was so distinctive, it lends its name to the culture: the Red Paint People. The "red paint" in this instance refers to the large quantities of red ocher with which they decorated the bodies of the deceased upon their burial.

Like other people of the Maritime Archaic, they based a significant portion of their subsistence on maritime resources including fish and shellfish. Like their contemporaries farther north, they must have had boats to catch pelagic fish, as evidenced by their inclusion of swordfish snouts—their eponymous "swords"—in red paint burials.

Desert Adaptations

Archaeological evidence, as shown in chapter 5, proves that human settlement of the Southwest began more than twenty-one thousand years ago as the descendants of northeast Asians who crossed over or sailed along the coast of the Bering Land Bridge spread across North America in the Late and post-Pleistocene world. As discussed here, as the Pleistocene waned and more or less modern climate regimes took hold, the descendants of those first peoples crafted adaptations, ways of surviving, in the context of those newly established environmental conditions. In the Southwest this meant, in large measure, adapting and adjusting to the hot and dry conditions that currently characterize the region. You know, when people tell you the Southwest is hot but it's a dry heat, they neglect to tell you that a dry 110 degrees will still melt your eyeballs right out of their sockets. But that's another story.

The period beginning about eight thousand years ago marks the establishment of a modern climate in the Southwest. Certainly throughout much of the Archaic, the so-called Desert Archaic people were nomadic hunter-gatherers guided by the geographical distribution of food resources by season. They lived in small, impermanent settlements, building semi-subterranean structures called pit houses; archaeologists have found lots of these in the region. They hunted large animals like pronghorn antelope, mule deer, bison, and bighorn sheep and smaller critters like jack rabbits and cottontails. Part of the subsistence quest focused on wild plants that produced nutritionally rich seeds. As much as seventy-five hundred years ago, people across the Southwest used handheld pounding or grinding stones against platform stones—in other words, manos and metates—to produce flour.

The dryness of the region makes the reconstruction of diet a bit more direct than in other regions as a result of the preservation of what, I get it, isn't the most romantic of archaeological remains: paleofeces. Yes, as the title of one of my kids' books declares, everybody poops. Further, the human digestive system cannot process everything that we ingest, so bits of seeds, tiny bones, nutshells, and, yes, even entire kernels of corn simply pass through and are shown the door. You probably already knew that. In other words, the stuff that remains unprocessed is excreted. Where conditions are dry enough, those excretions remain intact for the discerning archaeologist to recover and then analyze. Called paleofeces and, when fossilized, coprolites, they really do supply a wealth of dietary information. Researchers have found bits of piñon nuts, juniper berries, mesquite beans, and cactus fruits in paleofeces recovered in sites ascribed to the Desert Archaic.

Riverine Archaic

I'll end this chapter with a brief mention of a site that is iconic for the Archaic Period in the American Midwest: the Koster site, located near the Illinois River in west Illinois, about 80 kilometers (50 miles) northwest of St. Louis, Missouri. As in all of the various manifestations of Archaic ways of life discussed, beginning directly in the post-Pleistocene period about nine thousand years ago, the people of Koster exploited a wide variety of wild foods. Included in their diet were waterfowl; deer and other small mammals; nut foods including hickory, acorn, and hazelnut (without which my coffee would be intolerable); river resources including freshwater fish and freshwater shellfish; and natural fruits like pawpaws and persimmons.

In providing this list of subsistence sources on which the inhabitants of Koster relied, I have "buried the lede"—meaning, in my application of this old newspaper phrase, that I intentionally left out what might be the most significant of the food remains found at Koster, not in terms of number of calories provided but in terms of historical implications. Beyond the foods just mentioned, the people at Koster also collected the seeds of numerous wild plants, including sunflower, goosefoot, smartweed, pigweed, and marsh elder. Now while, with the exception of sunflower, those foods may be wholly unfamiliar to you, you might have never even heard of them, and you certainly cannot pick some up at the grocery store, not even Whole Foods, those are important plant species because they ultimately formed part of what became an independent, local "agricultural revolution" on the part of North America's Indigenous People. I'm going to discuss that subsistence revolution in the next chapter.

9

More Than Maize

NATIVE FARMERS OF NORTH AMERICA

MOST OF YOU likely are familiar with the term "natural selection" as used to describe the engine of biological evolution. Some of you might know it was a term that Charles Darwin introduced in his magnum opus *On the Origin of Species* in 1859.

Natural Selection

Though commonly used, it actually is a misleading term, implying an active process by which species evolve through a process of active "selection." No, the Goddess of Nature does not look down upon her creation and consciously or actively "select" which individuals in a plant or animal species live or die. Natural selection is a passive process. Here's how it works.

There is inherent diversity in every wild plant and animal species. In every generation there are differences among individuals. These differences appear randomly and are baked into the genome, the overall gene pool, of the species. They don't appear as the result of a particular need. They just are. The mixing of these traits through sexual reproduction in the wild is like Forrest Gump's "box of chocolates": you never know what you're going to get.

Some of those differences in the characteristics of individuals in the same wild plant or animal species, by sheer accident, by the luck of the draw, happen to confer an advantage on those individuals in the struggle for survival in nature and under a particular set of environmental conditions. Individuals possessing those advantageous characteristics are more likely to survive and then pass down those characteristics to subsequent generations.

For example, some plants may produce seeds that germinate later in the spring than others in the same species, even in the same plot. Plants that grow from these late-sprouting seeds may not flourish as the earlier growers come to dominate the seedbed. Now suppose that the climate changes and the area where the plants are growing begins to experience frequent late frosts in the spring. In this new scenario, the early germinators tend to die off as a result of those hard freezes early in the spring but late growers, safely ensconced in the soil and therefore protected from those late frosts, germinate after the final frost of the spring and then thrive. They pass down the characteristic of later germination to subsequent generations and that characteristic comes to dominate the population. That's natural selection.

Artificial Selection

The term "artificial selection" is a play on the term "natural selection." The "artificial" in the term isn't a reference to anything fake or pretend. It simply means that, instead of nature passively "selecting" individuals with advantageous characteristics in a given environment, it's people who do the selecting, both intentionally and unintentionally, and this selection is based not on what is inherently best for the plant or animal but on what is most beneficial for the people who rely on them for their livelihoods.

For example, in most wild seed plants, the connection between the seed and the stalk becomes brittle as the seed ripens—so brittle, in fact, that even the force of a benign breeze, a gentle rain shower, or an animal wandering through the area is sufficient to cause the seed to detach from the plant and deposit itself on the ground, where it can sprout in the next growing season. So seeds develop a tenuous connection to the plant after they mature, which is advantageous, and nature "selects" for that characteristic. Remember, nature doesn't think, "Ooh, I know. I'll give seeds a brittle connection to their stalks because they need them." Nope. A brittle connection is the result of random genetic forces and it is only coincidentally advantageous and passively selected for in the natural struggle for existence.

A brittle connection, however, is problematic for people harvesting a wild seed crop. The very act of grabbing a stalk or cutting it with a sickle imparts enough force to shatter the connection and scatter the seeds all over the place, producing a mess and creating additional work in collecting the profusion of seeds on the ground.

Think of it this way. Imagine picking up some M&Ms that are stored in a very weak, brittle bag that disintegrates as soon as you attempt to pick it up, scattering the candy all over the floor. It creates a mess, and an inconvenient mess at that if you have your heart set on eating a big bowl of M&Ms. Now, if the bag holding the candy-coated chocolate deliciousness is strong and durable, it may be harder to gain access to the candy because it's difficult to open, but at least the candy doesn't end up all over the floor. This discussion is making me hungry. I'm going to go get me some M&Ms now. The dark chocolate kind. I'll be right back.

Okay. Craving satisfied. Getting back to the issue at hand, plants with a nonbrittle, flexible connection (that connection is technically called a rachis)—which is disadvantageous in nature because the seeds are less likely to disconnect from the plant, fall to the ground, and then grow in the next season—are preferred by humans. It's like the strong bag holding the M&Ms. Those seeds are more likely to adhere to the stalk while being harvested and therefore more likely to make it back to the village, where, when removed, they are more likely to then fall to the ground or even be stockpiled as seed stock for next year's crop. In this example, human beings are, both intentionally and accidentally, encouraging the growth of wild plants that would be disadvantaged in nature but are preferred by human beings. That's artificial selection.

Archaeobotanists, scientists who study plant remains at archaeological sites, apply this in an attempt to distinguish domesticated crops from their wild antecedents. When we find examples in archaeological contexts of a dominance of plants with a nonbrittle connection to their stalks, or where seeds larger than those of wild varieties are found, or when the bones of smaller and therefore less dangerous adult animals are found, or when bones are recovered of animals with smaller jaws and teeth, we conclude that some level of artificial selection has been applied. In other words, where we find lots of evidence at an archaeological site of the remains of individual plants or animals possessing characteristics that would have been problematic in the struggle for survival in nature but that would have made them advantageous to humans and, therefore, preferred, we consider the possibility that they possess those characteristics because human beings selected them for their own selfish reasons. Beyond this, genetic evidence can also be used to show that a species is different enough from its wild relatives to suggest domestication. Finally, when archaeologists find examples of plants at sites located far from the home territories of the wild species, it may be inferred that people brought them into new territories without the natural features of their home regions and where people would need to tend them for their survival.

North American Domestication

Especially after the end of the Pleistocene and as modern climates became established in our postglacial world (chapter 8), people all over the world recognized the value of playing an active role in encouraging the growth of certain members of economically important plant species or the survival of certain members of economically important animal species (less aggressive, richer pelt, better milk producer). So they began to select those plants and animals that exhibited advantageous characteristics for special treatment, to encourage their survival and propagation. After generations of focused assistance to those individuals in plant and animal species with advantageous characteristics, those species can be considered "domesticated." The characteristics of plants and animals are controlled by their genes, and by artificially selecting plants and animals for survival based on their characteristics, people were indirectly modifying the genomes of the populations with which the people interacted. Some domestications are so extreme, with the characteristics selected for so deleterious in nature but great for humans, these species would have a very difficult time in the natural world and can survive only with the intervention of human beings.

Domestication was a geographically widespread process, but archaeologists and historians generally count six major hearths of selection and domestication:

- the Middle East (the Fertile Crescent) in the development of wheat, rye, oats, and barley as well as sheep and goats
- Africa, south of the Sahara, in the development of sorghum and millet as well as cattle
- East Asia in the development of rice and pigs
- Central America in the development of corn (maize), beans, and squash
- South America in the development of potatoes as well as llamas and alpacas
- eastern North America in the development of squash, sunflower, and a number of other, less well-known seed crops

It's that final one on the list that often surprises people. Sure, everyone knows about the Native American use of corn (maize) but, as I'll discuss later in the chapter, maize was domesticated in Central America and only later brought north into what today is the U.S. and Canada. Nevertheless, before the expansion of maize agriculture to the north, Native Americans in eastern North America were already in the midst of their own, largely independent agricultural revolution. The development of what is called the Eastern Agricultural Complex isn't as widely known for two reasons: corn agriculture here is very well known and the trope of maize-growing Indians is pervasive, and the crops domesticated by Native Americans in the Mississippi Valley and east, with a single exception, simply are not very well known in our modern diet even, as I mentioned in the last chapter, if you shop at Whole Foods (Figure 9.1).

FIGURE 9.1. A domesticated variety of *Chenopodium* (goosefoot) seeds has been found in archaeological sites in North America dating to as much as thirty-four hundred years ago. Kenneth L. Feder

The Eastern Agricultural Complex

Remember my mention of wild seeds found at the Koster site in Illinois? Some of those same species, along with a few additional ones, have been found at more recent sites in the Midwest. For example, the carbonized seeds of plants including marsh elder, knotweed, and goosefoot (I get it, those aren't likely part of your diet) have been found in cooking hearths at several archaeological sites in the American Midwest, such as Napoleon Hollow in Illinois; Newt Kash Hollow, Cloudsplitter, and Salts Cave in Kentucky; and Higgs in Tennessee (Map 9.1).

Here's the most interesting thing about that. The seeds recovered at these sites have somewhat different characteristics from those produced by their wild ancestors recovered at Koster: they are larger and the seed attachments have been tweaked so those seeds are less likely to simply detach when jostled. Those differences likely were the result of a

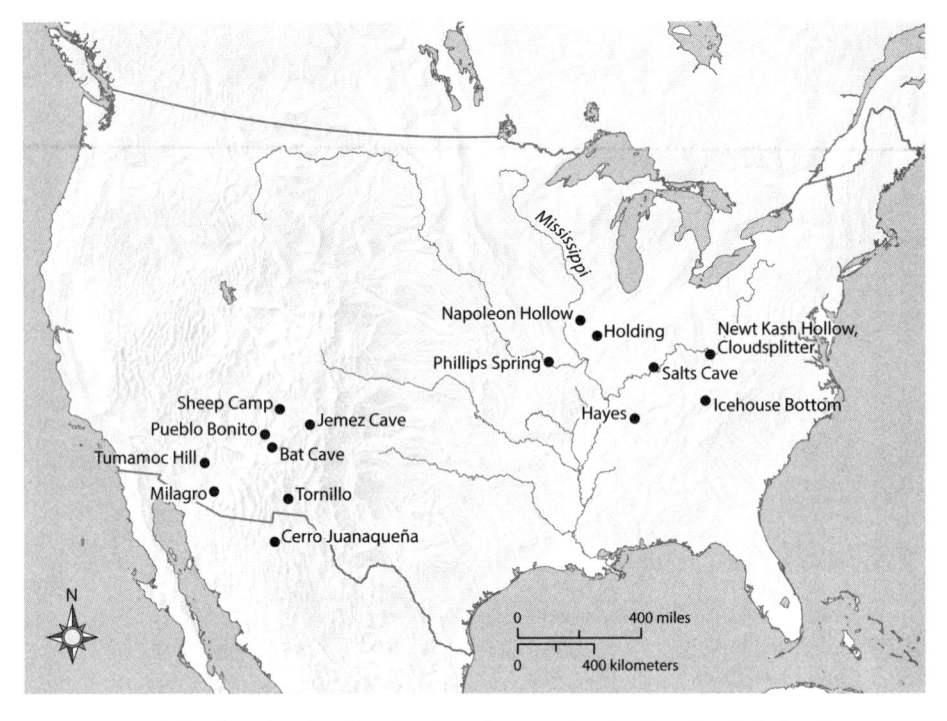

MAP 9.1. Map showing the distribution of a sample of archaeological sites in North America where evidence of the use of domesticated plants (including squash, sunflower, marsh elder, goosefoot, little barley, knotweed, and maize) has been recovered. Kenneth L. Feder

concerted application of artificial selection to increase the productivity and utility of these plant foods. These sites all date to as much as four thousand years ago.

And then there's sunflower. Ethnohistorical information in eastern North America clearly shows the cultivation and use of sunflowers for their seeds. The French explorer Samuel de Champlain described cultivation of sunflowers and the processing of their highly nutritious seeds into flour by Native People of the Great Lakes region during his visit there in 1615 CE.[1] However, there has been some controversy concerning the original hearth of sunflower domestication, largely because the San Andres site in Mexico has actually produced preserved seeds of domesticated sunflowers that appear to predate those found at a number

FIGURE 9.2. Sunflowers were a significant crop independently domesticated by Native Americans as much as five thousand years ago and at least as early as thirty-eight hundred years ago. Kenneth L. Feder

of sites in eastern North America. Plant geneticists who have studied this have concluded that, despite the currently extant radiocarbon dates, eastern North America was the home of wild sunflower growth and its most likely hearth of domestication (Figure 9.2).[2]

Wild sunflower seeds have been recovered in archaeological contexts dating back to at least fifty-eight hundred years ago and perhaps as much as eighty-five hundred years ago at the Koster site in Illinois.[3] The earliest evidence of seeds that are significantly larger than those produced by wild plants has been found at Hayes in Tennessee, Riverton in Illinois, Newt Kash Hollow in Kentucky, and Marble Bluff Shelter and Eden's Bluff in Arkansas. Hayes dates to as much as five thousand years ago. The other sites listed date to between about thirty-eight hundred and three thousand years ago, and there was continued use of Eden's

Bluff until fifteen hundred years ago.[4] All of this transpired long before the appearance of corn in the eastern United States.

Whatever controversies may still exist concerning the precise location of the domestication hearths of plants in North America and the chronology of that domestication, this much is clear: the Native People of North America were full participants in the worldwide process that led to the agricultural revolution and engaged in their own, independent version of that revolution beginning as much as five thousand and certainly by three thousand years ago. Their preexisting knowledge and appreciation of the domestication process through artificial selection and their attendant appreciation for those selected plants and animals predisposed them to recognize the potential of a new crop when it moved in from the south.

Maize

I assume that most of you know—you should—that corn is a gift from the agricultural people of the Americas, but you may not know that the name "corn" actually is a misnomer. When English-speaking people first entered into New England in the seventeenth century, they didn't have a name for the yellow crop with rows of deliciously edible kernels on large cobs, so they called it "corn," which is a word from Old English that is simply a generic name for *any* cereal crop or grain. Wheat is a corn. So is rye. So is barley. An old English folk song, "John Barleycorn," anthropomorphizes "barleycorn," depicting the harvesting of barley for the production of whiskey as the murder and torture of this fellow John. Old English folk songs use some wild metaphors. Anyhow, the word "corn" was applied to the many-rowed, large-cob crop because it was a grain, but the English colonists didn't know what specific name to call it. Native People in the Caribbean, the Taino, called it *mahiz*, which the Spanish transformed into *maize*. So the crop most of us call corn is more properly called maize. Maize, along with beans and squash—sometimes called "the three sisters"—was a major agricultural component of the diets of many Native People of the Americas, including those who lived in North America.

Maize Stereotypes

The image of "Indian corn," especially the varieties with colorful kernels that people use to decorate their doors in the fall, is iconic. Are you familiar with the Mazola brand of cooking oil? It's made from corn, and the name Mazola is just a play on the word "maize." In fact Mazola aired a television commercial in 1977 that used a Native American woman as their spokesperson. In the commercial she holds a freshly picked ear of corn and says, "You call it corn. We call it maize. We knew about the goodness of maize—corn—before America was America."[5] In a truly awful follow-up to that commercial, continuing its Native American theme, a group of young Native men are running across a grassy plain as the sound of a beating tom-tom fills the ear and a flute can be heard playing quietly in the distance. While this is happening—and oh my, this is tragically silly—a chorus of Indian men is chanting, "Mazola, corn goodness." Because, you know, that would really happen.[6] I'm not making this up, and it really is as embarrassingly bad as it sounds. However, the ad did reflect a recognition that an important, even vital part of the modern human diet, and the crop underlying Mazola's product, had been developed by the Native People of the New World.

Making Maize

The existence of maize as a fundamental food crop for the world in the twenty-first century is a testament to the remarkable skill of Native agronomists and also to a couple of extraordinary strokes of genetic good luck. The wild plant that provided the raw material for the process of artificial selection that led to our modern corn is a tropical species called teosinte. Teosinte continues to grow as a wild crop in Central America, but it looks nothing like modern corn. The edible part of teosinte is a spike of triangular seeds. The seeds are nutritious but small and, inconveniently, they fall off relatively easily when jostled by the wind, an animal passing by, or a person attempting to harvest it.

However, in a stroke of good luck, the morphology of the area of seed attachment in teosinte is controlled by very few genes. One mutation makes those seeds more likely to stay attached, and only a few genes control the number and size of those seeds. It appears that beginning more than seven thousand years ago, people collecting teosinte in Central America, perhaps intentionally, perhaps accidentally, began selecting those individual plants that by chance possessed seeds that stuck on, were more numerous, were larger, and had seed spikes that looked like small cobs. This rendered teosinte a far more productive and convenient crop and source of food.

Both archaeological and genetic evidence has been used to pinpoint the region where maize domestication most likely occurred, in the Rio Balsas region of southern Mexico beginning as much as nine thousand years ago.[7] The earliest fossil cobs of a very primitive, teosinte-like maize have been recovered there, dating to sometime later, about 6250 BP.[8] Unfortunately, there is a lack of direct evidence for maize in the region between the period of six thousand and nine thousand years ago, so the archaeological evidence can't confirm the older date derived through genetic analysis. For our purposes here, at least we know maize was a food staple in Mexico more than six thousand years ago, but the process of maize domestication began far earlier than that.

By continued selection of plants that were better from a human perspective, teosinte crossed the line from being a tended wild crop to being one that relied absolutely on human intervention because those sticky seeds posed an enormous disadvantage in an entirely natural setting. Those plants relied on people to extract the seeds and then plant them. As noted previously in this chapter, it's pretty typical in the process of domestication for people to select characteristics that are beneficial from a human perspective but disadvantageous in nature. Years later, the Aztecs of central Mexico recognized the connection between teosinte and maize when they named the plant. In the Aztec language Nahuatl, *teosinte* means "God's corn."

Moving Maize

Okay, that explains how a tropical cultigen was domesticated in a tropical environment and how it became an important food source for people living in the tropics. But how did maize manage to become a major source of food across the broad expanse of North America and in areas like my state of Connecticut, where the climate is decidedly nontropical? It turns out that maize possesses a tremendous amount of genetic diversity and flexibility. In other words, there is a lot of variation in the species, a lot of raw material for agriculturalists to exploit through artificial selection, enabling them to choose individual plants that happen to be well suited to grow in wet environments but also in dry environments, in areas with a long growing season but also in places with a short growing season.

Finding Fido

Use the domestication of the dog as a model. Their wild ancestor is the wolf, but look at the remarkable diversity of dog breeds. Big dogs, little dogs. Furry dogs, short-haired dogs. Mellow dogs, ferocious dogs. Energetic dogs, couch dogs. Those variations are all intrinsic; they exist as genetic instructions in the wild population of wolves. Little, mellow, and lazy wolves might not go far in wolf world, but people appreciated those characteristics in a captured wolf pup that has been abandoned by its mother. People might take it in, leading to its survival. It may then mate with another pup with those same characteristics and produce a generation of wolf-dogs more to the specifications of breeders than to those of nature. The oldest evidence for domesticated wolves—in other words, dogs—in the New World has been found in Alaska and dates to more than ten thousand years ago.[9] Based on a genetic study conducted on the remains of dogs found here, these animals are descended from a source in Siberia, so it appears that when people expanded into North America from northeast Asia, they brought their pups with them. The dogs found in aboriginal North America are not the result of a separate domestication of North American wolves.[10]

Apply the same selection process applied to wolves to a malleable and diverse wild plant like teosinte and you have the genetic raw material necessary to create an enormously important crop with a wide range of varieties, each well suited to survival in a different environment.

First Encounters

It is amazing to note that when English-speaking people first settled the northeast coast of North America in 1620 at a place they named Plimoth, in the modern state of Massachusetts, the settlers found the agricultural fields of Native Americans rich with an enormous maize harvest, in an area with long, hot, dry summers and long, cold, snowy winters, a far cry from the conditions of the crop's ultimate source in the tropical regions of Central America 3,200 kilometers (about 2,000 miles) away.

As you can well imagine, since Central America is the geographic source of maize, New England was not the first place it appeared north of Mexico. The oldest evidence for maize north of Mexico, in fact and not surprisingly, has been found in the American Southwest at a number of sites just north of the border with Mexico dating to more than three thousand years ago. Sites like Milagro in Arizona and Jemez Cave and Tumamoc Hill in Arizona all produced maize kernels in archaeological features like hearths and storage pits dated to between three thousand and forty-one hundred years ago. These early corn adopters had been predominantly hunter-gatherers, relying for their subsistence on the wild plants and animals that lived in their dry environment. Maize provided them with a supplementary food source that had enormous potential and over which they could assert more control. If you need more food, plant more. If it's too dry for the crop to flourish, provide it with water. Maize became a real game changer pretty quickly in the Southwest (see chapter 14).

Making Maize What You Want It to Be

The presence of maize in the American Southwest more than three thousand years ago brings us back around to the question, How could a tropically adapted crop be cultivated at all in the dry environment that predominates there, much less become a major food source for the people who lived there?

As previously noted, one thing that distinguishes maize from most other plant species is its extraordinary genetic diversity. Long cobs, short cobs; long growing season, short growing season; tropical adaptation, drought tolerance; yellow kernels, white, red, purple, black, and mixtures of colors. This treasure trove of diversity is present in the genome, seemingly sitting there waiting for human beings to find those varying characteristics and to breed those through artificial selection in a way that suits the needs of those human beings. As people attempted to introduce the tropical cultigen maize into a new territory like the Southwest, people had a vast genetic reservoir to experiment with through breeding, amplifying features hidden in the genome that they could use to create a new variety or "race" that might thrive in that new territory.

Here's some context. If you've ever gone to the nursery and selected seeds to plant in your garden, you may have noticed a map on the back of the packet showing the distribution of "growing zones" (or "planting zones" or "hardiness zones"), indicating where the species will grow. Using that map, you'll know if the flowers or vegetables you're hoping to grow (outside a greenhouse) will thrive in the area in which you live. If you were to create a combined map based on all of the current races of maize, the map would show that maize was a match, essentially, for the entirety of the United States and reaching as far north as 58° north latitude, which includes about half of Canada along with all of China and a large swath of Russia. I can't emphasize this enough: that is astonishing for a cultigen whose wild parent species, teosinte, is a tropical plant.

Granted, maize isn't infinitely flexible. There are places where it cannot grow and there are no existing variants that can survive in those places. But maize is so malleable it can be grown over much of the world. For 2021, the most recent year of records compiled by the Food and Agriculture Organization of the United Nations, maize provided people (and animals eaten by people) with more food than rice (number three) or wheat (number four) (sugar cane is number one in terms of tonnage produced).

Across Native North America there were many different varieties or "landraces" of maize. In a sense, each of those landraces was a GMO, a genetically modified version of teosinte. The genetic modifications here were accomplished through a combination of maize's inherent variability and the diligent application of artificial selection by the brilliant agronomists of Native America.

Trade, Diffusion, Migration

How did maize make it from southern Mexico to north of the Rio Grande? There have long been two competing hypotheses to explain the process. In the first explanation, it is suggested that the maize moved with migrating people. In other words, a people moving north, perhaps as a result of population growth and the need for new territory, brought maize along with them as they did so in an effort to maintain their traditional agricultural economy. Crossing over into what is now Arizona and New Mexico, they continued their ordinary practice of preparing fields, planting corn kernels, perhaps watering their crops, and then harvesting. In this scenario, local folks encountered the new immigrants, saw them practice an unknown technology of not only collecting food but actively producing it, appreciated the potential of the new technology, and adopted it for themselves.

It's an interesting suggestion but it suffers for the reason that, other than the maize itself, there is no direct, material evidence to support it. One might expect that a group of immigrants would have brought along their material culture in the form of artifacts made in their distinctive way, different and distinguishable from those of the resident population. Archaeologists haven't found their trail north of the modern border between Mexico and the U.S., no foreign tools or other objects that might suggest the presence of a group of foreigners. In that way, the hypothesis fails the archaeological test.

In the other explanation, it is proposed that it wasn't people who moved north, it was just the maize and the agricultural technology that accompanied it. No, maize didn't grow legs and migrate north. Instead, people at the northern margins of maize agriculture more than four thousand years ago encountered their neighbors to the south and witnessed their very different way of providing food. They recognized that the new agricultural technology involved quite a lot of preparatory labor and quite a bit of maintenance, but there was a big payoff in terms of the amount of food provided and the increase in food security that accompanied producing rather than collecting your food. So these folks would have obtained some corn kernels from their neighbors and then they would have invested some time and energy in providing at least some of their subsistence with the new food. Their facility with the new technology would have improved with practice, and they ultimately would have relied on it for most of their subsistence. In turn, neighbors even farther to the north would have seen their neighbors to the south, been fascinated with the newfangled food-producing technology, and initiated their adoption of it, and this process would have been repeated again and again as the technology, not the people, moved north. It took many generations and centuries, if not millennia, but with the adoption of the new way of providing food, everything changed. Populations could grow, populations could become more concentrated, and other assistive technologies, especially irrigation, made the new mode of subsistence ever more reliable, so long as there wasn't a major drought. And all along, because of the enormous genetic variations seen in the crop, it became increasingly able to survive and even flourish in the different environments into which it was introduced.

That same process of expansion by the process usually called diffusion, the movement of ideas without necessarily a concomitant movement of people, occurred to the north and especially to the northeast of the American Southwest. That process of expansion again took many generations. Technological advances, new ways of doing things that are more productive and safer, still have to overcome a conservative reaction that finds safety in doing things the way they always have been done. In fact, the appearance of an agricultural subsistence system highly reliant on maize, while the population is still farming local crops like sunflowers and collecting food through hunting, fishing, and gathering wild plants east of the Mississippi, is rather late in this story, likely not much earlier than about 1,700 years ago.[11] Maize kernels have been found at Icehouse Bottom in Tennessee (1,775 years ago), Edwin Harness in Ohio (1,720 years ago), Grand Banks in Ontario (1,570 years ago), Site 211-1-1 in New York (1,130 years ago), and Holden in Illinois (925 years ago) (see Map 9.1). Farther north, in the Great Lakes region of Ontario, there may be evidence of a minor penetration of maize as much as 2,300 years ago, but it's clear that maize did not become a major part of the local diet until 600 years ago.[12]

The agricultural system with many acres of cornfields surrounding the Native communities, as reported by the Spanish in the Southeast and the English in New England, had been adopted by the Native People probably no more than about twelve hundred years before first contact. When Europeans arrived in the East, they were witness to a subsistence system still in flux. Unfortunately, the European presence interrupted that process, especially through the coincidental spread of European diseases for which Native People had no resistance.

An Agricultural Evolution

Clearly, the introduction of maize in the American Northeast woodlands did not lead to an immediate "agricultural revolution." As is the case in virtually every instance across the globe, when domesticated crops first entered into the area, adoption was slow, proceeded in fits and starts, and reflected an evolutionary, not a revolutionary, process. A plausible scenario for the American Northeast beginning twenty-three hundred years ago—that's the age of the oldest archaeological evidence mentioned previously for maize in the region—runs like this.

The dominant variety of maize moved in from the south and could survive in the Northeast, but it likely didn't thrive there. It simply was not well adapted to the local climate. In all likelihood, the Native People of the Northeast first became aware of maize as a food basis to the south through trade and travel. As they were accomplished agriculturalists of local seed crops (like amaranth, lamb's quarters, and especially sunflower, as mentioned earlier in this chapter), their curiosity about the crop was likely piqued and, in an effort to determine its viability as a food crop, they may have obtained maize, eaten some, and ended up deciding it was worth their while to grow some in test plots to assess its viability.

As practiced agronomists of local plants, they well understood how to manage a crop and how to determine whether it could survive in their region. After several years of growing test plots of maize, they would have recognized that, though many individual maize plants died off in a first planting because the growing season wasn't long enough, because temperatures were too cold at night, or because the humidity wasn't high enough, a small number of individual plants managed to survive in those first few years of experimentation. These individual plants were hardier for the environmental conditions into which they had been introduced and could withstand what the rest of the plants could not.

Those survivors weren't enough to produce a viable subsistence crop, but they were enough to convince some Native agricultural researchers that by replanting the kernels produced by the survivors in subsequent years, more of the planted individuals made it through the next growing season.

They also recognized that some of the maize plants, including ones that couldn't make it through the shorter growing season of the Northeast, had advantageous characteristics from a human perspective. For example, maybe they produced bigger cobs with larger kernels, and if you planted them side by side with the plants that could ripen in a shorter growing season, you could produce some plants with both advantageous characteristics. Today we call this process "hybridization," and it can happen through insect pollination (most commonly by bees) or—and there's little reason to assume that Native agronomists didn't understand the process—by people moving pollen by hand from one plant to another. Think about the creation of dog breeds as an analogy.

In other words, beginning likely more than two millennia ago, the Native People of the Northeast were conducting agricultural breeding experiments in an effort to see if maize could be made to be a good fit for their growing region and if, through artificial selection and hybridization, they could engineer a crop that could thrive in their homeland. In this manner, in a sort of old-school genetic modification through artificial selection and hybridization, Native People in the Northeast bred a maize variety today called Eastern 8-Row maize and, later, Northern Flint with lots of regional subvarieties.[13] In so doing, they greatly improved the utility of maize, creating an enormous, positive change in their economy. That change had a significant impact on their cultures, and their lives.

Native Agronomists

The process of observation, investigation, and experimentation took time, and the perceived value and utility of maize increased slowly. Initially and for an extended period of time, maize was viewed as a valuable addition or supplement to the diet, one of a large number of food sources, but certainly not the dominant one. This is clearly seen in archaeological data recovered from cooking hearths and food storage features. Even long after the initial introduction of maize, archaeology in the Northeast continues to show, for example, the enormous significance of deer hunting in the diet. Other mammals were of continuing importance, as shown by the recovered beaver, muskrat, and bear bones in archaeological hearths. Locally domesticated seed-producing plants including sunflower, smartweed, lamb's quarters, and amaranth are also abundant at these sites, along with evidence of the use of wild berries like elderberries and blueberries as well as nuts. Evidence of the domestication of a local variety of squash shows its use as far back as a little more than three thousand years ago in Pennsylvania and New York State. The third "sister," beans, appears to have been a later arrival in the area, with the earliest archaeological evidence seen no earlier than by about seven hundred years ago, or around 1300 CE.

Although we can't interpret the numbers cited by archaeologist Timothy Abel literally, as a direct indicator of the percentage of the diet inferred from seed percentages at Iroquoian archaeological sites (chapter 10), his numbers are an important illustration of the broad spectrum of plant foods in the diet of the people and of the growing significance of maize to local diets: there was pretty close to a 50-50 split between maize and local domesticated, as well as wild, plant foods.[14]

Another nonfood element of the plants utilized by the precontact people of New York State was tobacco. Lots of tobacco seeds were recovered from archaeological sites, and an abundance of ceramic smoking pipes have been excavated. At least historically, smoking was not a recreational behavior—people didn't just kick back and smoke a bowl after a long day in the cornfields—but rather a formal and ceremonial practice, and it is reasonable to assume that tobacco smoking had a similar role in Iroquoian society in the mid-1400s CE, in other words a couple hundred years before the Jesuits described it in their reports to their superiors in Montréal and Québec (chapter 10).

My most important point in this extended discussion is this: the Native People of North America weren't passive actors in this process. They were not simply the recipients of an agricultural system based on maize, beans, and squash gifted them by generous or advanced neighbors to the south in Mexico. They weren't simply exposed to the new crop and immediately inspired to jettison their previously effective mixed subsistence system of locally domesticated seed crops, wild fruits, and wild game all for this new maize-based system. It would have been foolish—and they were certainly not foolish—to have done so. How could they be certain that a crop that grew under very different environmental conditions would survive, much less thrive, in their region? They couldn't take that risk, there was no need for them to take that risk, and they didn't take that risk. They approached the potential of the new crop scientifically and patiently. And, in the end, they scored a huge success.

10

Into the Woods

IN CHAPTER 8, I focused on the period labeled the Archaic in the story of the Native People of North America, a time that began with the waning of the Pleistocene glacial ice, the beginning of the establishment of modern climatic conditions, and the readaptation of Native People to the climatic conditions presented in the eastern woodlands (Mast Forest Archaic), the Atlantic coast (Maritime Archaic), the Great Lakes region (Lake Forest Archaic), the desert west (Desert Archaic), and the other Archaic cultures. The beginning of the Archaic, therefore, is a point in time with an objective, observable, and fundamental change in the lives of people, in this case a change in the environmental conditions to which they needed to adapt. It makes sense to mark the end of one period of cultural adaptations and the beginning of another period by reference to the end of the Pleistocene about ten thousand years ago. Sure, it wasn't instantaneous, and no, Native People didn't get a memo alerting them to the need to overhaul their lives on, maybe, Tuesday, April 1, 10,000 BP, because the Ice Age was ending and everybody needed to adapt. Nevertheless, the end of the Pleistocene was an objectively environmental game changer, so using it as a time post makes sense.

The end of the Archaic and the beginning of the subsequent Woodland Period, however, ordinarily set at three thousand years ago, has no convenient or obvious temporal guidepost. The climate didn't change dramatically three thousand years ago, Europeans didn't arrive en masse (or at all) three thousand years ago, and no, extraterrestrial aliens didn't arrive at that point to change the fundamental conditions of life in North America. Instead, two significant features used by archaeologists to demarcate the end of the Archaic and the beginning of the Woodland were the following: the invention and spread of fired clay objects (in other words, ceramics, generally in the form of pottery) and, even more significantly, domesticated crops. Certainly domestication changes everything, altering one of the most fundamental of human behaviors: how we feed ourselves (chapter 9).

But there's a complication here. Those two defining features of the Woodland Period didn't appear everywhere or at the same time. First, among the Native People of North America, there were groups who, especially either due to the limitations of their habitats or, ironically, as a result of the incredible wealth of wild food sources in their territories (chapter 15), never embraced agriculture. At the same time, there were people who, for various reasons, didn't develop ceramic technology. Also, even in those places where agriculture and ceramics did develop, these technologies didn't necessarily appear together at the same time. For example, as we've seen in chapter 9, the Native People of North America initiated their own version of an agricultural revolution at or a little bit before three thousand years ago. However, the adoption of at least an early phase of an agricultural subsistence system based on local plants doesn't appear in, for example, my home state of Connecticut until well after 1000 CE, perhaps as late as the 1300s. Despite the lack of evidence for agriculture of any kind here much before that, Connecticut sites that date to after three thousand years ago are still considered to represent the Woodland Period.

Ceramics

While they required an entirely different skill set, fired clay pots had one enormous advantage over steatite as a raw material, as discussed in chapter 8: clay is pretty close to being ubiquitous. It's available nearly everywhere. In other words, while you might have to travel a great distance to a soapstone quarry and trade valuable stuff to the folks who live there in order to obtain the material, clay was nearly everywhere for the taking.

Economists use a term, "disruptive innovation," to describe an invention or a development—in other words, an "innovation"—that turns things upside down, that is "disruptive" to the status quo, and that leads to significant changes in people's lives. The automobile was a disruptive innovation. Microchips were a disruptive innovation. Perhaps for the Native inhabitants of North America, the development of fired clay vessels was a disruptive innovation that defined the birth of the Woodland Period.

Haudenosaunee

Okay, I've started here by defining the Woodland Period and talking a bit about how we define and demarcate it and why we use three thousand years ago as a point of demarcation for the cultures of the Native People who lived in the woodlands of eastern North America. Now let's continue on to what may be the most recognizable and even iconic culture of the Woodland Period in eastern North America, the Haudenosaunee. You more likely know them as the Iroquois.

Long before the American Revolution in 1776, leaders in the British colonies of North America were discussing the best format for a government within which the geographically, economically, and politically disparate colonies might best come together and organize themselves. In fact, as early as 1744, representatives from the Maryland, Pennsylvania, and Virginia colonies met in Lancaster, Pennsylvania, for a conclave to discuss issues of cooperation among the colonies and how to create a governmental structure that might unite all of them under a single umbrella, creating a united front for dealing with the British. The organizers of the conference hoped to obtain the wisdom of a person with experience on this issue, so they invited someone whom they considered to be an expert in creating and maintaining a governing format that would work expeditiously in placing a number of independent political entities under a single, unifying political structure.

That expert was not a British political functionary or philosopher. He wasn't even some well-respected intellectual chosen from among the colonists. Instead, the invited expert was a man called Canassatego.

FIGURE 10.1. Replica of a Native American longhouse typical of the Iroquois people of the eastern woodlands. Institute for American Indian Studies, Washington, Connecticut. Photo by Kenneth L. Feder

He was a Native person of the tribe called the Iroquois by the French colonists to the north, in Canada. The Iroquois people called themselves the Haudenosaunee. The New York State Museum has created a video that provides an explanation of the origins of those names.[1] As Tsadeyohdi (Denise Waterman; Turtle Clan) points out in the video, Iroquois was a term applied by European settlers; it was a "word that they brought with them that they identified with us; Haudenosaunee is what we identify ourselves." Haudenosaunee means "People of the Longhouse," which reflects their standard residential construction: long, relatively narrow houses, parabolic in cross section, with saplings used for framing, and surfaced with bark (Figure 10.1).

The colonists had invited Canassatego to share his wisdom on the issue of governance because he was a political leader in a system that appeared to offer a useful model for the situation the British colonists faced. The Haudenosaunee consisted of a consortium of first five, and later six, tribes that had long ago been wracked by internecine conflict but had reached a consensus to end that conflict by creating a system of governance in which each of the individual tribes in the consortium maintained a degree of autonomy and independence, and each had an equal say on issues that affected all of the separate groups while also accepting an overarching governmental structure, including a body consisting of representatives of each tribe. That "congress" met regularly to determine policy for the "league of nations" and to adjudicate disputes among its members peacefully by talking it out, voting, and accepting the results of those votes. In other words, Canassatego was there to discuss the representative democracy created by the Haudenosaunee in which a consortium of distinct but closely related people joined together under the banner of a single nation—like states in a confederacy. His wise counsel was translated into English, recorded for posterity, and published by none other than Benjamin Franklin: "Our wise forefathers established a union and amity between the Five Nations. This has made us formidable. This has given us great weight and authority with our neighboring Nations. We are a powerful Confederacy and by your observing the same methods our wise forefathers have taken you will acquire much strength and power; therefore, whatever befalls you, do not fall out with one another."[2]

Clearly Franklin was very impressed by Canassatego's words, thought long and hard about them, and used them for inspiration in his thinking about a similar system of government for the colonies. Seven years after the conference in Philadelphia, referring back to the words of the Haudenosaunee representative, Franklin wrote a letter to his publishing partner James Parker in New York City: "It would be a very strange Thing, if six Nations of Ignorant Savages should be capable of forming a Scheme for such an Union, and be able to execute it in such a Manner, as that it has subsisted Ages, and appears indissoluble; and yet that a like Union should be impracticable for ten or a Dozen English Colonies, to whom it is more necessary, and must be more advantageous; and who cannot be supposed to want an equal Understanding of their Interests."[3]

Okay, bad form about the whole "ignorant savages" libel, but maybe Franklin was speaking ironically? Maybe? In any event, he crafted a statement for another conference, this time in 1754 and held in Albany, New York, on the same topic of the best format for a government that would bind the colonies together. Called "Short Hints Towards a Scheme for a General Union of the British Colonies on the Continent," it lays out the particulars of a federal government for the colonies and owes quite a lot to the nature of the government practiced by the Haudenosaunee.[4] It was no accident or coincidence that, once again, representatives of the Haudenosaunee were invited to attend the conference for the assistance they could provide. The fact that the colonists repeatedly sought advice from the Haudenosaunee would seem to belie the whole "ignorant savage" canard. Okay, so who were the Haudenosaunee, what does ethnohistory tell us about their culture, and what does archaeology tell us about their origins in the Woodland Period?

Jesuit Relations

We know quite a lot about the Haudenosaunee and, by inference, the end of the Woodland Period because Europeans wrote extensively about them. It largely traces back to the Jesuits. The Jesuits are a Catholic order of priests whose members served as missionaries in the region of southeast Canada and the northeast United States, especially New York State and Pennsylvania. Living among the people they called the Iroquois and the Wendat (more widely known as Huron, but that was a derisive name applied to them by the French) as well as related groups, the Jesuits hoped to convert the people to Catholicism. But the Jesuits were intellectuals, in many ways a sect of the Church that embraced science as a way of furthering what they perceived to be the will of God. Their conscious and explicit strategy in the conversion process included the careful observation of the people to be converted while keeping a detailed record of those observations. The Jesuits believed that by better understanding a people and their native culture, it became easier to convert them.

Those recorded observations of the Native People were presented as yearly reports by the missionaries on the scene between 1632 and 1673 back to the Church leaders in Montréal and Québec. Those reports were called *The Jesuit Relations* (in the original French, *Relations des Jésuites de la Nouvelle-France*). We know a lot about the culture of the Haudenosaunee—and you can't miss the irony—because the scientifically inclined Jesuits, to facilitate the elimination of Native religious beliefs and practices, studied and wrote extensively about them.

Certainly, many of their reports concerning the religion of the Native People whose existence it was their goal to expunge must be interpreted with great skepticism. However, aspects of Native culture observed and described, sometimes in obsessive detail, by those Jesuit missionaries, including Native architecture, subsistence, and technology, are likely reasonably accurate since there seems little in the Jesuit agenda that would have caused them to misrepresent those elements of Native life.

As noted, the now translated and published *Jesuit Relations* provide archaeologists with a rich and richly descriptive database, often focused on the elements of Native material culture that constitute so much of the archaeological record.[5]

By the way, the Jesuits were not alone in providing detailed discussions of the Native cultures of the American eastern woodlands. There also are the journals written by or for French explorers like Jacques Cartier, who first encountered the Native People of Canada in 1535, and Samuel de Champlain, who visited what became New York State in the early 1600s. These sources add up to a substantial database of ethnohistory that informs archaeologists concerning the cultures of the Native People of the northeastern woodlands of North America, especially for the time not coincidentally labeled the Woodland Period.

One of my favorite instances of this occurs in Champlain's journal, where he reports on a battle he joined on one side of an Indian war, during which he was wounded: "I was wounded as I was shooting the first time into the side of their barricade, by an arrow shot which slit the end of my ear and entered my neck. I took hold of it and pulled it out; it was barbed on the end with a very sharp stone."[6] So in the midst of a battle in which he's SHOT IN THE NECK, Champlain calmly removes the arrow and then dutifully notes the form and raw material of the weapon. I'm not sure if, having just been SHOT IN THE NECK, I would have retained my composure like that. But at least we can be grateful to the French explorer for his eyewitness testimony concerning the efficacy of Native archery.

Now, rather obviously and rather sadly, the archaeological record can't be used to test the veracity of Haudenosaunee history. But it can be used to examine the material culture observed and reported on in *The Jesuit Relations*. That record, along with the accounts of explorers like Cartier and Champlain, describes a material culture that is very similar to what the archaeological record reveals for the period of more than five hundred years preceding contact. The domiciles of the Native People described by the Jesuits, for example, are elongated dwellings made of bent-over saplings covered in bark, much in the form of Quonset huts, with a center hallway and multiple apartments lived in by nuclear families, each of which was related to every other one. These "longhouses" described by the Jesuits are reflected in the archaeological record by the preserved remains of the buried posts of the bent-over saplings.

People of the Longhouse

The name Haudenosaunee is aptly descriptive; it means "People of the Longhouse," and the domestic structures of the people, the homes in which their extended families lived, were indeed "long houses" (see Figure 10.1). The Jesuits described them in that way, and the archaeological record shows that the Haudenosaunee had been building them for hundreds of years before the arrival of Europeans. The wooden structures themselves have long ago disappeared through fire and decay, but the layout of preserved "post molds," sometimes little more than stains in the soil representing the eroded posts of the superstructure of the longhouses, show the existence of enormous structures averaging 61 meters (200 feet) in length. The largest one on record is twice that long, more than 122 meters (400 feet) in length; in other words, true to its name, it is a really "long house," a hundred feet longer than a football field. Some Haudenosaunee villages were nucleated, meaning that the residences were clustered, consisting of multiple longhouses that were placed in proximity to one another and together encompassed by a palisade, a fence of small logs. So say the Jesuits, and so says the archaeological record. The oldest radiocarbon dates for longhouses in New York State indicate that their construction began in the early 1100s, but they don't appear to have become the dominant form of houses until about one hundred years after that.

Based on the testimony of the Jesuits, Haudenosaunee families appear to have been matrilocal. This means that related women remained with the families into which they were born and their husbands moved in with them from other families and other communities to live with their wives' extended families. In other words, within a single longhouse, all of the women were related to one another; there were mothers, daughters, sisters, grandmothers, aunts, and female cousins all of whom were born in the same village, grew up together, stayed with their family upon marriage, and raised their sons and daughters where they had themselves been raised. Upon reaching adulthood, a man would look for a wife in another village and then move into that community. It is believed that the pattern of matrilocality the Jesuits described in the 1600s and 1700s was long standing, initiated long before the arrival of Europeans in the region.

The historical Haudenosaunee were an agricultural people with a reliance on the stereotypical "three sisters" of maize, beans, and squash (chapter 9). However, archaeology in the Northeast shows that this reliance was not exclusive and maize was not embraced immediately by the ancestors of the Haudenosaunee.

As shown in chapter 9, the roots (unintentional pun) of the cultivation of maize in the Northeast can be traced back to about twenty-three hundred years ago. Phytoliths, opal silica bodies formed by plants with forms that are diagnostic of each species, have been recovered at archaeological sites in the Finger Lakes region of central New York State (I have flown over them and they sure look like monumental fingers!). Some of those phytoliths have been identified as maize and associated with radiocarbon dates of that age. Archaeologist John Hart has shown that evidence from the region indicates that maize was a consistent part of subsistence.[7] It's not until nearly a thousand years later, about 650 CE, that skeletal evidence shows that at least some people were eating substantial amounts of maize.[8]

The Six Nations

As previously mentioned, historically the Haudenosaunee consisted of a confederacy of first five, and later six closely related groups or nations. These were the following:

- the Onondaga, the People of the Hills
- the Oneida, the People of the Upright Stone
- the Cayuga, the People of the Great Swamp
- the Seneca, the People of the Great Hill
- the Mohawk, the People of the Flint
- the Tuscarora, the Shirt Wearing People

Other nations, including the Delaware, the Wyendot, and the Tutela, joined the confederacy later on. Related nations in the Northeast that were not part of the confederacy but spoke the same language as the Six Nations or a similar one include the Erie, the Conestoga, the Meherrin, the Nottoway, and the Tionontati. Another closely related group, with whom the confederacy had a competitive and downright hostile relationship, were the Huron (Wendat) in Canada.

Though they did not employ a writing system, the Haudenosaunee have maintained an oral history for centuries, telling and retelling a consistent story across the generations. I will briefly summarize it here. The separate nations that today make up the confederacy had been in a debilitating state of nearly constant warfare beginning as much as a thousand years ago. Then, at some point in their history, perhaps as early as 1142 CE but probably more recently than that, there arose an individual whose name has been passed down as Skennenrahawi or Deganawida but is most widely known as the Great Peacemaker, who realized that for the benefit of all the people of all the then five nations, warfare needed to cease. The leader of the Onondaga, the fabled Hiawatha, joined with the Great Peacemaker, along with Jigonsaseh, now known as the Peace Queen of the Seneca. Together they visited the leaders of each of the nations in the role of peace envoys.

One imagines an airing of grievances, expressions of anger and resentments, but also the recognition that all of that must be set aside, transcended for the good of the thousands of people whose lives had been so adversely affected by the constant preparation for war, the endless need for heightened vigilance about the possibility for war, and the actual grinding conduct of those wars.

Ultimately, wisdom prevailed. Draw your own ironic conclusions about modern politics and conflict. At the conclusion of the peace mission, the representatives of each of the groups agreed to the Great Law of Peace, in which it was decided that each nation would retain a measure of independence and sovereignty, each maintaining its own individual leadership structure. At the same time, the detailed agreement created a broader political structure called the Grand Council of Chiefs that included each of the leaders of the independent nations as a sort of overarching federal government in which joint decisions were made that affected all of the people by a vote of the council. This democratic reform resulted in a long and lasting peace that, while it may not have been perfect, was far superior to the state of perpetual conflict that had prevailed previously. Most decisions now were made by a vote of the leaders rather than by the arrows of warriors.

The format and organization of the Great Council of Chiefs served as a model for Benjamin Franklin and his compatriots, as discussed earlier, first for the creation of a federal government for Great Britain's colonies in North America and then, after the American Revolution, for the government of the United States.[9] Table 10.1 presents a comparison between the Haudenosaunee confederacy and the government created by the American colonists. Obviously, both consciously and explicitly, the Haudenosaunee government was inspirational to the British colonists in America.

The Great Law of Peace agreement, by the way, did not prevent the different nations from choosing different sides in the conflict between French and English settlers in their region, nor did it prevent them from fighting alongside the group with which they allied themselves.

TABLE 10.1. Comparison of the U.S. Constitution and the Iroquois Great Law of Peace

Iroquois Confederacy and the Great Law of Peace	United States Constitution
Restricts members from holding more than one office in the Confederacy	**Article I, Section 6, Clause 2**, also known as the **Ineligibility Clause** or the **Emoluments Clause** bars members or serving members of Congress from holding offices established by the federal government, while also barring members of the executive branch or judicial branch from serving in the U.S. House or Senate.
Outlines processes to remove leaders within the Confederacy	**Article II, Section 4** reads "The President, Vice President and all civil Officers of the United States shall be removed from Office on Impeachment for, and the conviction of, Treason, Bribery, or other High Crimes and Misdemeanors."
Designates two branches of legislature with procedures for passing laws	**Article I, Section 1**, or the **Vesting Clauses**, read "All legislative Powers herein granted shall be vested in a Congress of the United States, which shall consist of a Senate and House of Representatives." It goes on to outline their legislative powers.
Delineates who has the power to declare war	**Article 1, Section 8, Clause 11**, also known as the **War Powers Clause**, gives Congress the power "To declare War, grant Letters of Marque and Reprisal, and make Rules concerning Captures on Land and Water;"
Creates a balance of power between the Iroquols Confederacy and individual tribes	The differing duties assigned to the three branches of the U.S. Government: Legislative (Congress), Executive (President), and Judicial (Supreme Court) act to balance and separate power in government.

The Archaeology of Democracy?

The Haudenosaunee are not the only Native Americans who organized their nations according to democratic principles. The Muskogee people of the American Southeast have a long-standing tradition of what we can fairly describe as a representative democracy. Family groups called clans take care of their own business, but the Muskogee also have an overarching political structure to organize and coordinate the relationships among those clans and to oversee the actions of their nation as a whole.

In essence, and as recorded by the Europeans who entered Muskogee territory in the sixteenth, seventeenth, eighteenth, and nineteenth centuries, clans sent representatives to meet together in a central place to deal with disputes and to decide on joint and combined actions of the clans. The meeting place traditionally was a large, round structure or a square building with rounded corners. Some of these "council houses" were truly gigantic, with examples ranging between 12 and 37 meters (40 and 120 feet) in diameter. These structures weren't houses. No one lived in them. They were spaces dedicated to assemblies of clan representatives. In a way, our Congress meeting in the Capitol building to address national issues is an example of something quite similar.[10]

Here's the thing: archaeologists working at the Cold Springs site in the Oconee Valley in northern Georgia have now been able to trace back the practice of the ancestors of the modern Muskogee people of building large, round or square structures to more than fifteen hundred years ago.

In the telling of their own history, the Muskogee people speak of their development of what certainly sounds like a representative democracy in their deep past, as well as their construction and use of dedicated structures for the political meetings of clan representatives where they would reach consensus on issues democratically without decisions imposed by an elite or ruling class. Although it cannot be proved definitively that these round or square structures are archaeological examples of historically documented council houses, between archaeology and local history, it seems a reasonable suggestion that the Muskogee practiced representative democracy beginning more than fifteen hundred years ago.

11

Into the Cold

FIRST, A WORD about words. You are probably very familiar with the term "Eskimo" as a label for the Native People of the Arctic, the people who live in the snow with their igloos, parkas, and kayaks—words, by the way, derived from their native language for things they invented. Their words for those inventions have worked their way into common usage in English, and the inventions, at least parkas and kayaks, enrich the lives of both Native and non-Native people in the modern world. Then there's Eskimo Pies, Eskimo kisses, and probably more things Eskimo.

However, as is so often the case, the Native People who are labeled Eskimo by outsiders generally don't accept that term, as it is not even in their own language (Figure 11.1). It's not absolutely certain, but it may be based on a word in the language spoken by the native Innu people of eastern Québec, identifying them as "netter of snowshoes." Eskimo has long been applied to them mostly by white colonists.

As is also often the case, the label imposed by outsiders, Eskimos, is at best overly broad and ignores the inherent diversity in groups that live across more than 4,800 kilometers (3,000 miles) of northern Alaska, Canada, and Greenland. At worst, it's at least implicitly insulting to name a people with a term applied to them by outsiders, similar to the application of the Diné label Anasazi to the ancestors of the Pueblo people, as discussed in chapter 14. In my opinion, for what it's worth as an outsider, it is simply a reflection of respect for a people to call them by the name they prefer, and yes, those people get to change their minds

FIGURE 11.1. Stunning photograph taken of an Iñupiat family highlighting their winter clothing. Photo taken in 1929 by Edward R. Curtis

about what that name should be. Though I freely acknowledge that there isn't unanimity among the Native People of Alaska, northern Canada, and Greenland, the nearest thing I can find that might qualify as a consensus is Inuit for the people of Alaska and Canada (Inuit is the plural form for the word *inuk*, which simply means "person") and Kalaallit for the Native People of Greenland. You will often see the Native People of Greenland referred to as Thule (or Thule Eskimo), but the people themselves who live there have never referred to themselves by that term and many reject its use.

To complicate matters further, many of the various groups of Native People who live in the American Arctic don't accept a broad, umbrella term since it ignores their diversity. Many prefer being referred to by their own designator for themselves—for example, the Inupiaq of northwestern Alaska, the Yu'pik of southwestern Alaska and eastern Siberia, and the Sugpiaq of the Kenai Peninsula in southern Alaska.

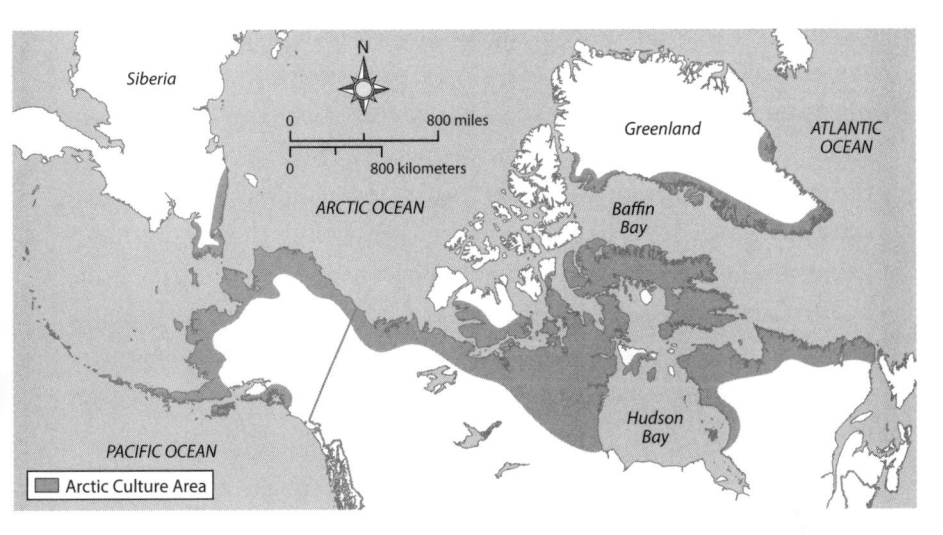

MAP 11.1. Map showing the geographical distribution of the Paleo-Inuit and Inuit in the Arctic Culture Area, from western Alaska all the way east to the coast of Greenland. Redrawn based on S. J. Crouthamel

Oh—and I'm sure you didn't want yet another complication to this—the Native People of the Aleutian Islands who live in an archipelago at the southwestern terminus of the Alaskan Peninsula are culturally and historically distinct from their mainland Inuit neighbors. Though usually referred to as Aleuts, they far prefer the term Unangax̂. The archaeological site called Anangula, located on the island with the same name in the Aleutian Islands, is the oldest excavated village in the Aleutians and was occupied more than nine thousand years ago. Its location has been described as an occupation of what had been the coast of Beringia as the land bridge was being inundated.

Genetic evidence indicates a common heritage for the Unangax̂ of the Aleutian Islands, the Iñupiat of northern Alaska, and the Inuit of Arctic Canada and Greenland.[1] These people are genetically distinct from the Native Americans living to the south—the "Indians"—and appear to have arrived in the New World as part of a separate migration subsequent to the initial settlement of North America by Native People (Map 11.1).

Naming people and cultures becomes even more problematic when we are dealing with archaeological sites. Archaeologists have a tendency to subdivide people based on "the material remains of human behavior," the catchall definition for archaeology I presented in chapter 1. We are practiced at drawing figurative circles around groups separated in space and time and assigning each a unique name or label, all on the basis of the differences seen in the artifacts we recover at their archaeological sites. It is one of the vexing challenges of archaeology that we don't have a time machine allowing us to directly observe people in the past. Without that science fiction device, we are stuck describing human behavior and defining different human groups who lived in the past based on the things people made, used, lost, and discarded while conducting those behaviors.

The People of the Arctic

I realize the stereotype of "Eskimos" includes a focus on the hunting of marine mammals, but the archaeology of the Inuit people who populated the Arctic beginning about five thousand years ago shows their reliance on a far broader spectrum of animal resources including large land mammals like musk ox and caribou and small mammals like foxes, birds, and also fish. Using animal-hide boats to ply the Arctic's coastal waters, the people of the North also hunted large marine mammals like seals, sea lions, and walruses. Weapons used included harpoons and spears, some of which were propelled by a tool called an *atlatl*.

Known by various names the world over ("throwing stick," "throwing board"), *atlatl* is the Nahuatl (Aztec language) word for a device used to enhance the distance and accuracy of a thrown spear. The atlatl was, effectively, used as a way of artificially increasing the length of the hunter's throwing arm. If you're a baseball fan, you know that pitcher Randy Johnson, a six-foot-ten lefty in the period 1998–2009, could throw fastballs that were amazingly accurate and very, very fast. His speed and accuracy were facilitated, at least in part, by his very long arms. An atlatl or spear thrower artificially lengthens the arm of the thrower and makes them more like Randy Johnson.

The working end of ancient Inuit spears and arrows consisted of often very small, sharpened pieces of stone. The small size of the spear or arrow points provides archaeologists with the unimaginative name of the toolmaking tradition: the Arctic Small Tool tradition, also known as the Denbigh Flint Complex. The shapes and diminutive size of these artifacts are reminiscent of those made in eastern Siberia, suggesting that the technology originated there and was then brought across the Bering Strait by migrants.

Though snow houses called igloos also fit in the stereotype applied to the people of the Arctic, and at least some groups certainly relied on them in the winter months, there simply is no direct archaeological evidence for snow houses in the ancient Arctic, for the obvious reason that they don't leave any material evidence of their existence. They melt. It is likely, however, that the people of the Arctic did build them for their winter homes. There simply aren't a lot of other options for home building in the treeless expanse of the Arctic. As seen at the Ak&lungiqtautitalik (that is the actual spelling) site in Ukkusiksalik National Park, located above the Arctic Circle on the northwest shore of Hudson Bay in Canada, summer houses do leave material traces in the form of stone rings positioned to hold down animal skins used in circular dwellings. Dating to about four hundred years ago, these summer homes were of a size that suggests they were domiciles for nuclear families or, perhaps, small extended families with parents, their children, and a grandparent or two.

Belying the stereotype of "primitiveness" as applied to nomadic Arctic hunters, the Native People clearly were masters of technology. Archaeological evidence shows that they were master boatbuilders, producing hide-covered craft we all know today as kayaks (Figure 11.2).

They also were brilliant inventors of hunting equipment, including barbed, toggle harpoons that would virtually glide into the body of a seal coming up for air in the ice.

Of necessity, the people of the North were very successful clothing designers for the relentlessly cold winter conditions of their territory. They produced coats with built-in head coverings—in other words, hooded parkas (see Figure 11.1). While the old tale that you lose half (or three-quarters) of your body heat through your uncovered head isn't true, we can all still appreciate hooded coats in the dead of an Arctic

FIGURE 11.2. Modern Inuit man using a traditional kayak. Ville Miettinen, CC BY 2.0

winter. The Native People of the Arctic also created waterproof undergarments by sewing together the stomachs and intestines of animals they hunted. Long before there were Uggs, they also made warm and waterproof, fur-lined footwear (*mukluks*), perfect for walking in snow. Though they had no glass, tinted or otherwise, they were able to make sunshades for their eyes from pieces of bone or ivory, carved into a shape that could wrap around a person's face and rest on the bridge of the nose, and into which they cut thin slits at eye level. Those slits provided a technologically aided squint that made it far easier to see in the bright conditions of a sunlit snowfield. A snow-blind hunter is at an extreme disadvantage, and this bit of tech likely made the difference between success and failure in a hunt on a brightly illuminated snowscape.

The Settlement of the Arctic

As noted in chapters 5 and 6, the first settlers south of the Arctic were migrants from northeast Asia who crossed the Bering Land Bridge interior or along the southern coast of Beringia before twenty thousand years ago, likely more than twenty-five thousand and perhaps as much as thirty thousand. Though adapted to life during the Late Glacial Maximum, these first people generally avoided the Arctic. It really says something that people who had adapted to Ice Age conditions gave a big "nope" to living above the Arctic Circle. As noted by Canadian archaeologist Robert McGhee, the American Arctic was "the last major environment on Earth that was unoccupied by humans."[2]

The first ancient people of the western Alaskan Arctic are labeled the Paleo-Inuit. Archaeological evidence indicates that they entered into the New World from the Kamchatka Peninsula in Russia around fifty-five hundred years ago. This is long after the submersion of the Bering Land Bridge, so the only way to get from there to here was by boat. To survive in much of the Arctic, exploiting sea life is an absolute necessity and having seaworthy watercraft provides people with a big advantage. The use of watercraft as an important aid in subsistence therefore facilitated the movement of people between northeast Asia and northwest North America in a post-Beringia world.

These first migrants into the American Arctic were, in a very real sense, the inhabitants of two continents, Asia and North America, and they likely regularly moved back and forth across the Bering Strait and spent time on either side. Their territory reached from Chukotka (the easternmost region of Russia) across all of northern Canada, traversing multiple time zones and modern national borders (Russia, the U.S., Canada, and Denmark; Greenland is Danish territory) (see Map 11.1). The Paleo-Inuit clearly had a sophisticated culture extraordinarily well adapted to environmental conditions that, let's face it, would seem to be quite daunting and dangerous to those of us used to far more equable climes.

Recognizing the valuable resources available in what was now their new world, the Paleo-Inuit spread through the interior of Arctic Canada and ultimately all the way to Greenland (where they are generally called Pre-Dorset and then Dorset), arriving there between five thousand and forty-five hundred years ago, only about five hundred or one thousand years after their initial foray into Alaska, as evidenced by archaeology, which is remarkably quick. As geneticist Jennifer Raff describes it in her absolutely wonderful book *Origin*, the "archaeological footprint" of that initial migration and spread is faint, reflecting, as she suggests, both a small population moving across the landscape and the rapidity with which that migration and expansion took place. Beginning about five thousand years ago, the Paleo-Inuit expanded like a swiftly moving, faint ripple across the landscape of the Arctic.[3]

Hunting

Different animals respond differently to the possible presence of a predator, and the nature of that reaction has a significant impact on hunting strategies. White-tailed deer (*Odocoileus virginianus*), for example, the large mammals who are very common in the deciduous forests of eastern North America, tend to travel singly except when mothers are with a little one or two. These deer exhibit what is called a "freeze and flee" response. That means at their first inkling of a threat, they cease all movement lest they confirm their presence to a predator that might not yet fully realize that they are there. Only if the deer sees the predator continuing to approach their fixed position, appearing to be stalking even after the deer has frozen in place, does it attempt to run quickly away. I wonder if this explains the trope of a deer that is hypnotized in the headlights of oncoming cars moving swiftly on a highway, whereupon the poor driver's insurance is going to become more expensive and the deer is going to be roadkill. The deer isn't hypnotized by the light; it's just behaving as it should when confronted by a presumed predator in the forest. That strategy, unfortunately for the deer, isn't very useful when the enemy isn't a wolf or a mountain lion but two tons of steel bearing down on it at sixty-five miles an hour. There's not enough time in that scenario for the "flee" part of the strategy to kick in.

Caribou (*Rangifer tarandus*), a major food source in the Paleo-Inuit diet, on the other hand, aren't loners like deer; they live in sometimes quite large herds that reach into the thousands, tens of thousands, and even hundreds of thousands spread out over a vast territory. Caribou react communally to a threat not by freezing but by immediately initiating warp-drive panic mode, with the herd's members collectively playing follow-the-leader and running like hell away from the source of a threat. The behavior of a prey animal living in large groups and ready to run en masse when a threat appears presents certain challenges but also great opportunities for the hunter.

The Paleo-Inuit recognized and brilliantly exploited this aspect of caribou behavior. Realizing they certainly couldn't outrun a caribou, and not wanting to get in front of thousands of panicked animals running toward them, they developed a clever technological and behavioral approach to isolate a manageable number of animals and then control the direction in which those animals would run. They accomplished this by setting up piles of stone called cairns in a large V shape to create a "drive lane," thus producing a directed, managed, or even forced escape route that started at the wide top of the V to snare a substantial but limited number of animals who would run into the narrow part, bunch up as they attempted to flee, and thus slow down and even stop altogether in what amounts to a caribou traffic jam at the base of the V.

Continuing the traffic jam analogy, I'm sure you have experienced something frustratingly similar on a highway that begins with six or more lanes but narrows down to five, then four, then three, two, and then maybe even one. Traffic jams up as the road narrows and cars have to merge into fewer and fewer lanes. The Paleo-Inuit accomplished this effect with their rock cairns. Hunters positioned at the end of the drive lane, with its very narrow passageway, could easily shoot their arrows at and kill the traffic-stalled caribou. It's brilliant and just a little evil (again, from the caribou's perspective), but it reflects the skill and intelligence of the Paleo-Inuit people.

Resource Extraction

There is a common conceit that people who rely on hunting for their subsistence have little time or desire to do much more than hunt because there isn't the time to do much of anything else. This is nonsense. In fact, the Paleo-Inuit weren't just accomplished hunters, they also were

FIGURE 11.3. A beautiful little polar bear carved on a walrus tusk. dalbera, CC BY 2.0

extremely skilled artists, producing remarkably beautiful carvings in stone, bone, and ivory (not from elephants but from the long upper incisors of walruses) (Figure 11.3). Their subjects often were the animals that characterized their Arctic home, such as polar bears and seals, but also included human faces.

When you live in the Arctic, your access to many resources common in areas to your south may be very limited. For example, there are no trees in the so-called barren ground that characterizes the Arctic. Something people to the south take for granted, wood, used for the framing of structures, in the shafts of spears or arrows, and, crucially, as material to fuel the fire so necessary in their very cold world, is very hard to come by. The Paleo-Inuit recognized that there were considerable quantities of driftwood along the coast, and it was a very important source of wood in construction and for fuel. They also were adept at using the large bones of animals like the caribou as a substitute for wood in construction. They built houses using driftwood or bone for the framing, which they then covered in animal hides.

Ukkusiksalik

David F. Pelly is a wonderful Canadian author and researcher who has lived and traveled in the Arctic for more than forty years. His book *Ukkusiksalik: The People's Story* is a fascinating tale of his experiences in a place that lends its name to his book.[4] Pelly focuses on the archaeology and ethnography of this community located at the northwest margin of Hudson Bay, above the Arctic Circle. The Inuit residents of the community, whom he has befriended and who have befriended him, are marvelous storytellers. They generously shared their life stories and history with Pelly, who, in turn, shared them with the broad audience of his readers.

According to Pelly, archaeology in the region shows a substantial population of Pre-Dorset and later Dorset (regional variants of the Paleo-Inuit) people dating to after 500 BCE. Researchers have identified some 440 sites in a broad region in the Ukkusiksalik area. Twenty of these are residential sites consisting of round or oval hut rings of sometimes substantial boulders, each one as much as about a meter (three feet) high. These often were quite heavy and used to hold down the bottoms of animal hides that had been positioned on a framework of bone. One of these rings was larger than the others and showed evidence of being compartmentalized in a way that is reminiscent of other excavated Dorset archaeological sites. In the same region archaeologists identified six smaller stone structures that likely were used essentially as meat lockers, caches where meat was stored for the winter. Semi-subterranean structures were identified with walls of boulders on top of which were fixed a framework of large bones. On that framework the builders positioned animal hides for the walls.

According to Pelly, the modern Inuit residents of the region, known historically as the Aivilingmiut, report that their ancestors—and they count those who left behind the archaeological sites in their region among them, calling those ancestors Tuniit—hunted caribou and musk ox in the summers and caribou again in the fall during their seasonal migration. Seal and walrus were also hunted along the interface of ice and sea in the summers and also in the spring when these sea mammals warmed themselves on sunlit beaches. Seal and walrus provided an important source of not only meat but also blubber, which was used to fuel soapstone lamps called *qulliq* that provided both light and sufficient heat to warm the people's small, cozy houses. As noted, the large canines of walruses were used to sculpt images of the animals and people in their territory and were a valuable trade material in their dealings with the Norse (see chapter 4). The people also relied on fishing for Arctic char, often where rivers drained into the local bay. So, not surprisingly, the people living in the Aivilingmiut who shared their lives with Pelly were supremely well adapted to life in the Arctic. They relied on a broad spectrum of foods as they became available on a seasonal basis. Beyond this, they developed storage facilities for those foods to preserve them and therefore extend their window of availability.

Testimony from the modern Inuit in the region indicates that in the old days, before the coming of the Qablunatt (white people), the subsistence was provided entirely by hunting and fishing and this necessitated a nomadic existence. Elders spoken to by Pelly for his book tell stories passed down from their grandparents of frequent moves to relocate to where animals or fish were most abundant, as well as of acceptance of a feast-or-famine existence—both during the year and over the course of many years—that necessitated the stockpiling of food in times of plenty in what was effectively cold storage, those rock-lined caches just mentioned, to get the people through the lean times. Of necessity, the people who lived in the Arctic were careful observers of their environment, studied and understood the behavior of the animals on which their subsistence depended, and developed technologies and strategies to facilitate their survival. They were, in fact, brilliant at surviving. Pelly's book is a wonderful example of how modern, ethnographic work among a living people provides direct help in interpreting the archaeological record.

Inuit

Long after the initial Paleo-Inuit expansion across the Arctic, sometime between eight hundred and one thousand years ago, a new culture likely resulting in part from an in-migration of a new people emerged, and it has been identified by archaeologists based on evidence of new and novel technologies that seem only indirectly related to what had been seen previously among the Paleo-Inuit. These new people, the Inuit, were accomplished sea hunters, going after seals and walruses but also even whales. I simply can't imagine the challenge of a handful of people in boats, brandishing nothing more than spears and harpoons, taking on even a small whale. Ahab in the novel *Moby Dick* has nothing on these Inuit hunters.

While there is some evidence for the prior presence of dogs, likely used in hunting among the Paleo-Inuit, the Inuit were responsible for the use of the novel technology of the dog sled, which made them uniquely mobile in the snow-covered landscape of the Arctic. All those Iditarod mushers owe the existence of their dog sleds—and sled dogs—to the Inuit. Remember the Inuit origin story I shared with you in chapter 2: dogs were singled out in the story as a special part of creation.

The Inuit also used *umiaqs*, skin-covered boats much larger than kayaks. These were not used by individual hunters searching for food but were for moving groups of people and their stuff across large expanses of coastline. Combining their use of *umiaqs* with oars and paddles, the Inuit could move whole communities seasonally or even as part of a longer and more permanent expansion into new territories. The Inuit were also known to have manufactured sails from animal intestines, which they sewed together and attached to their *umiaqs* to facilitate sea travel. Traditional Inuit still manufacture and use *umiaqs*; these days they attach outboard motors to them. The Inuit have long been perfectly comfortable embracing new technologies that make their work easier or more efficient and effective.

Another invention of the Inuit was the semilunar slate knife with the working edge, the curved half circle of the half moon, ground down into a razor-thin edge, and a bone or wooden handle fixed to the straight edge of the tool. Called by the Inuit an *ulu*, these knives were extremely useful, especially for gutting a fish or animal carcass. A simple twist of the wrist slices open a fish. The ulu became a widespread tool used in butchering; the Native People along the coast of Maine and the Canadian coast of Labrador, New Brunswick, and Newfoundland used it as well (see chapter 8).

The Inuit were also inventors of highly effective hunting equipment, including the barbed, toggle harpoon I mentioned previously, a weapon that could penetrate even the thick hide of a seal, sea lion, or walrus, slicing its way deep into the body of an animal as the creature came up for air in the ice, embedding itself in its body, and disengaging from the shaft, all while still connected to the hunter by a strong rope made of animal gut. The more the animal struggled, the more deeply embedded the harpoon head became, and the more the animal struggled, the more exhausted it became, all while the hunter held on to the rope attached to the harpoon embedded in the animal's body. Eventually, the exhausted animal surrendered to death and the hunter's family could feast.

The Inuit spread from Alaska across the Arctic by essentially following the same route used by the Paleo-Inuit. The Inuit likely are the direct ancestors of the modern people of the American Arctic, the folks who used to be called Eskimos.

It's very interesting that when the Inuit relate their own histories, they include reference to a people they encountered who were already living in the American Arctic as they expanded their territory. The Inuit call the people they encountered the Tuniit. Their descriptions of the Tuniit are obviously difficult to assess with certainty. The Inuit sometimes characterize the Tuniit as strong but smaller than the Inuit, and in other versions they are described as being extremely tall. Nevertheless, researchers view the Inuit stories about the Tuniit as reasonable eyewitness accounts of the Paleo-Inuit people filtered through a complex mix of myth and memory. One thing that can be confirmed is that the Inuit also report the existence of the stone cairns discussed previously and used by the Tuniit to funnel caribou fleeing from hunters. That makes sense of course. As the Inuit, who were careful and curious investigators of their territory, expanded into new territory, they certainly noticed the substantial and patterned stone piles and, not surprisingly, wondered what they were, what their purpose was, who built them, and how long ago. In a very real sense, the Inuit were asking archaeological questions and, if their stories of encountering the Tuniit are even remotely accurate, ethnographic questions as well.

It has long been thought that the Inuit replaced the Paleo-Inuit so quickly and so completely that there simply wasn't sufficient time for a blending of cultures and people. This seems largely to be true, and the cultural replacement signified by the disappearance of typical Paleo-Inuit artifacts and their replacement by tools made in an Inuit style occurred over just a few generations.

Despite the replacement of Paleo-Inuit culture, it does appear certain that the Paleo-Inuit and Inuit were not entirely separate peoples but at least distant relatives, cousins separated by time and space and sharing a common ancestor traceable back to Siberia. Anthropological geneticist Jennifer Raff participated in a study that, with the complete cooperation of Native People, extracted samples of mitochondrial DNA (mtDNA), a form of DNA that occurs in the mitochondria of our cells and is passed down only in maternal lines, from mothers to both their sons and daughters, from 137 living Iñupiat Inuit from the North Slope of Alaska.[5] The researchers determined that one of the mtDNA varieties—technically, one of the haplogroups—called D2a, found in the living Inuit, while atypical for them, has been extracted from the bones of Paleo-Inuit people. The presence of an atypical haplotype may be explained by tracing it back to Siberia, where the Paleo-Inuit and Inuit both originated, having been derived from a common source population, albeit a few thousand years apart.

The diversity seen in the archaeological record of the Paleo-Inuit is repeated in the case of the Inuit. This should not be surprising considering that over the course of between five hundred and one thousand years, the Inuit spread across an arc of territory encompassing northern Alaska and Arctic Canada and extending all the way to and including the west coast of Greenland, a distance of about 3,400 kilometers (more than 2,100 miles) in total. The last stretch of that distance is the Nares Strait, a body of water more than 320 kilometers (200 miles) across, stretching from Ellesmere Island in Canada to the coast of northwestern Greenland.

As a result of differences in food preferences, housing, trading patterns, art, and religion, archaeologists distinguish separate subgroups within the Inuit that are sufficiently different to warrant separate names.

For example, there are the Iñupiat (the North Slope of Alaska), Nuvugmiut, Ipiutak, Saqqaq, Thule Inuit, and Yu'pik. I will avoid assaulting your senses with a detailed enumeration of how these named subgroups of the Inuit have been differentiated. Suffice it to say that under the Inuit umbrella term was a diverse series of cultures, each of which had developed finely honed ways of life in response to the environments presented by the North American Arctic.

What Is Behind the Replacement of the Paleo-Inuit

It is a bit perplexing why the Paleo-Inuit, a people who seem to have been so well adapted to life in the American Arctic, were so quickly and apparently thoroughly replaced by another group of people, the Inuit, bearing a distinctively different culture. You will often see references to the more advanced technology of the Inuit, but I've never been entirely comfortable with that explanation.

Another possibility relates to climate change. While today anthropogenic climate change is affecting the earth far more quickly than previous, natural episodes, smaller, naturally inspired climate changes have affected human life in multiple instances in the past. Perhaps coincidentally, perhaps not, sometime around the time that the Paleo-Inuit faded away, between 950 and 1250 CE, the world experienced a kind of global warming called the Medieval Warm Period. We recognize this warm period through various proxy measures of worldwide temperature increase. There is evidence of a melt-off of ice in the Arctic. Areas that were not previously navigable because of icebergs became iceberg-free. Areas that had been too cold for agriculture became viable for agriculture. Writers in Europe recorded experiencing rising temperatures during this time period.

Though something like a dramatic change in climate is an easily understandable and conveniently simple explanation for the Inuit replacement of the Paleo-Inuit, it's difficult to see how the Inuit, who were supremely well adapted to the existing climate of the Arctic before the warming period, would have benefited from that warming while the Paleo-Inuit, also supremely well adapted to the existing climate of the Arctic before the warming period, would have been adversely affected. Add to this the fact that, though the world was generally warmer during the time between 950 and 1250 CE, a more nuanced view indicates that the warming wasn't universal and didn't necessarily occur simultaneously or to the same degree all over the world. So did the warming people experienced during the Medieval Warm Period contribute to the Inuit replacement of the Paleo-Inuit? Were the Inuit simply more flexible and better able to rapidly adjust their subsistence focus more readily than the Paleo-Inuit? It is an interesting hypothesis, but one that simply cannot be confirmed at this time.

A Native Age of Exploration

In his book *Ancient People of the Arctic*, archaeologist Robert McGhee calls the movement of people across the American Arctic "the great exploration."[6] In so doing he makes an important point. When the question is posed, Why did ancient people expand across an unknown landscape? it is often proposed that it was primarily an economic decision fueled by necessity in the search for resources or the need for space to accommodate an expanding population. That makes intuitive sense, I guess, and necessity certainly played a role in many historical instances of the expansion of a group into a new (to them) territory. However, it's always important to at least consider how human curiosity likely fueled exploration and expansion. We are an intelligent species, and part of that intelligence is reflected in our inquisitiveness. "Hmm. I wonder what adventures lie on the other side of that mountain? Or downstream on this river? Or across that vast body of water?" are questions that people ask pretty regularly. Curiosity is, I firmly believe, an important element of intelligence.

The fact that, once they settled in North America, the Paleo-Inuit people and later the Inuit managed to spread themselves across the vast expanse of the Arctic is a testament to their adaptive skills. But why did they spread so far and so fast?

Again, I am in no way denying that there were practical considerations for the human exploration of and sometimes movement into territories unknown to them. Certainly the so-called Age of Exploration among Europeans in the fifteenth, sixteenth, and seventeenth centuries was predicated on economic considerations. The "race to the moon" in the 1960s between the United States and the Soviet Union was fraught with political and economic motives, as each side was attempting to prove that its system—capitalism versus communism—was the superior one. However, let's not forget that the individual human beings involved in the literal ground game, or space game, were excited by the possibility of new experiences and challenges that transcended considerations of the practical value of those explorations. What was true for Columbus was true for Neil Armstrong and was true for the Paleo-Inuit and later the Inuit families who looked out toward a vast horizon, wondered what they would find there, and decided to take the risk and head out in the context of their own age of exploration.

The Iron Age . . . from Space!

I'm not saying it was aliens because—spoiler alert—it wasn't aliens. I just used the "Iron Age . . . from Space!" heading as a printed version of clickbait, intentionally making it sound like I've lost my mind and am about to embrace *Ancient Aliens*. Nope. I provided an intentionally misleading heading to pique your interest.

Oh, the iron age I am referring to literally was from space, but not in the form of intelligent beings from another planet visiting Earth and schooling the natives. These extraterrestrial interlopers were in the form of meteorites. You likely have seen bits of space matter evanescently streaking across the sky. Those are meteors. Some meteors are large enough that they don't fizzle to bits but actually crash into the surface of the Earth. A gigantic and impressive example of one of these can be seen west of Winslow, Arizona, at what today is called Barringer Meteor Crater.

Technically a meteor that survives entry and actually crash-lands is called a meteorite, and when conditions are right, some very large fragments survive. Some meteorites consist of a natural alloy of iron and nickel and provided a raw material valuable to the Paleo-Inuit and subsequent Inuit people, along with the Pre-Dorset and Dorset.

As was true throughout North America, Native People of the North were exquisitely careful observers of their homeland. They had to be to survive. And when they saw a bright light streaking across the sky, they investigated those occurrences. Along the way, they discovered places where those bright lights, those large meteorites, had fallen to Earth and had survived the collision with our planet. Almost certainly in a scenario similar to the one I proposed for the Old Copper Culture of the Great Lakes (chapter 8), Native People investigated the material characteristics of those meteorites, ultimately extracting pieces from them, and then in a process of experimentation figured out that by heating and pounding pieces of this strange new raw material, they were able to produce sharp-edged cutting and piercing tools including knives and spear tips. In other words, with a little help from nature, the Paleo-Inuit had access to iron without needing to smelt the metal from ores and, as a result, engaged in their own iron age. Those with direct access to the meteoric iron traded it and iron artifacts are found throughout the Arctic, including at sites at great distances from known sources. By the way, other people in the world discovered sources of meteoric iron and figured out the same thing the Inuit had, that you can make sharp-edged tools from the material. A dagger recovered in the nearly intact tomb of the pharaoh Tutankhamun, the boy king of ancient Egypt, was made of meteoric iron from a local source.

If you visit the American Museum of Natural History (AMNH) in New York City, which I did countless times as a child, you can see one of the most impressive of these North American Arctic meteorites. In what is today the museum's Arthur Ross Hall of Meteorites, there is an enormous, thirty-four-ton, quite beautiful, highly eroded and pockmarked iron meteorite on display that was found on the Cape York Peninsula of Greenland. It was of such importance, both economically and spiritually, to the Native People of Greenland—the Inughuit, a local Greenlandic subgroup of the Inuit—that they named it, calling the four large pieces of it located in their territory Woman, Dog, Savik I, and Tent. The meteorites are estimated to have fallen to Earth in a single-impact event, perhaps sometime between five thousand and ten thousand years ago, but dating the impact is problematic. When I was a kid

I witnessed an enormous meteor streaking across the summer night sky over Long Island in New York on April 25, 1966. It was astonishing. I can scarcely imagine what it must have been like seeing the fall and impact of the Cape York meteor if people had been there to witness it.

Unfortunately, and reflecting the age-old trope that something isn't discovered until Euro-Americans encounter it, the website of the AMNH says, "Discovered in 1894 in Greenland, this iron meteorite slammed into Earth 10,000 years ago."[7] Um, no. The Paleo-Inuit and Dorset people discovered the meteorite on display at the museum, along with its companions, while establishing a village in the area about a thousand years ago and almost immediately began using it as a major source of iron in tool production. That's hundreds of years before the American Robert Peary encountered it in 1894. Beyond this, even ignoring the fact that local people were using the meteorites for raw material in tool production for hundreds of years, he didn't personally "discover" it in any sense of the word. He was told about it and taken to it by a Native person.

Okay, but what is this beloved bit of cultural patrimony from Greenland—I mean, come on, the Native People even named it!—doing in a museum in New York City? Woman, Dog, and Tent (called Ahnighito by Peary, but that is not what the Inughuit called it) were appropriated (a nice way of saying stolen) from the Native People and moved to the AMNH in 1895. Once the large meteorites were removed, the economy of the Inughuit was upended and they became dependent on Europeans for their iron. Certainly that was an unintended consequence of Peary taking the meteorite, but it sucks regardless.

If you're interested in the details of this story, please check out the social media thread (on X) by my brilliant colleague Erin Thompson, a professor of art crime (I love the title) at the City University of New York.[8] By the way, along with the meteorites, Peary brought several Inughuit people back to New York with him. Upon his arrival he decided to monetize those people and, after docking at the Brooklyn Naval Yard, he opened his ship to the public, putting them on display. He charged people twenty-five cents to see the Native People, as if, like the meteorites, they were mere scientific specimens valued for their ability to entertain the general public. The Peary-MacMillan Arctic Museum has created a virtual exhibition that tells the tragic story of one of the two Inughuit survivors of their cruel exhibition, a seven-year-old boy named Minik who was adopted by a superintendent of the American Museum of Natural History.[9]

A Story

One more thing. Though Inuit culture, like all cultures, has changed through time, including the period immediately after they encountered European explorers and then settlers, the Native People retained many of their traditional beliefs and behaviors while embracing introduced technologies that they found useful. As an example, when I was in graduate school in the 1970s at the University of Connecticut, where there was a robust program focused on the Arctic in the Anthropology, Biocultural Anthropology, and Biological Anthropology Departments, I met an Inuit guy, a visiting student at the university, who regaled our cohort of graduate students in anthropology with stories of his life experiences as a modern Inuit who still practiced more or less traditional hunting. For example, he was an avid subsistence hunter back home, as was the practice of his people, but he didn't use traditional weapons like a spear or a bow and arrow. Instead, he used a rifle. When he traveled across the ice and snow in search of animals to hunt, he didn't move about on a dog sled. He used a snow machine (snowmobile).

My favorite story of his reflected both his embrace of non-Native technology he found of value and his knowledge of living in the Arctic. He told of an instance in which he was hunting on the ice, miles from home. The day had seen temperatures rise above freezing but then dip down, all while the air was saturated with a cold mist. So wet and bitter.

During his excursion, he encountered a polar bear that took umbrage at the intrusion into its territory. My Inuit friend attempted to outrun the bear with his snow machine. He thought that he had done so successfully and breathed a sigh of relief, not looking for a fight with a 680 kilogram (1,500 pound) bundle of violence. Unfortunately, later in the day, he saw the bear again, which was tracking him by, I assume, following the smell of the vehicle's exhaust. I guess the bear held a grudge. So the hunter decided that he had no choice but to dispatch the bear with his rifle. He described raising his gun, aiming it, and then attempting to pull the trigger. We all sat on the edge of our seats when he told us, shockingly, that as a result of the freezing moisture in the air, the trigger wouldn't budge. It had locked up, frozen in place.

Now, mind you, this happened as a polar bear with evil intent continued his relentless pursuit. The dude realized that one way of unfreezing the mechanism would have been to call a time-out, light his Coleman stove, melt some snow, continue heating it until it got nice and warm, and then pour it over the trigger, thus defrosting and unlocking it. At that point, he might call an end to the time-out, aim, and fire. I once actually had to use the same strategy to unfreeze a locking gas cap for my car. Well, except for the fact that the car wasn't trying to kill me.

Apparently, polar bears aren't good sports when it comes to defending their territory from offending Inuit hunters, and it wouldn't agree to a time-out. So, as our storyteller hilariously told us, he clearly understood that he had only one immediate and readily available source of warm liquid. Urine. So, yes, he unzipped and proceeded to pee on the trigger. That worked like a charm and freed it up, allowing him to bring the rifle to his shoulder, aim it by leaning its pee-soaked stock against his cheek (gross), and then fire. It worked, and the polar bear would bother him no more.

Now, I need to be honest. First, my Inuit acquaintance told a ripping good tale, and how tall his tale was, I cannot say. I make no pretense that any of what he told us was possible, plausible, or even made any sense. I am not a hunter, and the last time I used a gun it shot nerf balls and not bullets. So the lesson in his story may simply be that the Inuit are marvelous storytellers. I like to believe, however, that the other lesson here merely exemplifies what I already knew, that the modern Inuit, along with their direct ancestors, their Paleo-Inuit distant cousins, the Pre-Dorset, the Dorset, the Kalaallit, and all of the other iterations of Native People of the American Arctic, were and are capable people amply prepared to live in the Arctic. That, and they have a wonderful sense of humor.

12

Monument Builders of the Midwest

WHEN YOU THINK of impressive monuments built by ancient people, you probably imagine great structures made of stone: the triad of pyramids of Giza in Egypt, Stonehenge in England, the monuments of central Mexico or of the Maya in Mexico, Guatemala, Costa Rica, El Salvador, and Nicaragua. These monumental structures are absolutely stunning, clear evidence of the remarkable architectural, engineering, and mathematical abilities of ancient people.

When you think of remarkable ancient monuments, you likely don't include the United States, but you should. The Native People of North America built spectacular monuments, not in stone but of earth. Conical burial mounds; gigantic, four-sided, flat-topped platform mounds (often called "Temple Mounds"); extensive walls enclosing and distinguishing large, open areas; and effigies in the shapes of animals and birds (Map 12.1). Beginning in the eighteenth century, white settlers in the American Midwest and Southeast encountered thousands of these monuments and were mystified by them.

Remember back in the prologue when I decried the practice of stereotyping, the broad-brush (and inaccurate) painting of all Native Americans as nomadic, tipi-dwelling buffalo hunters? Well here's an instance in which a pernicious stereotyping of the Native People of the Americas as being primitive, lazy, and backward actually led people to irrationally deny the technological accomplishments of the Native

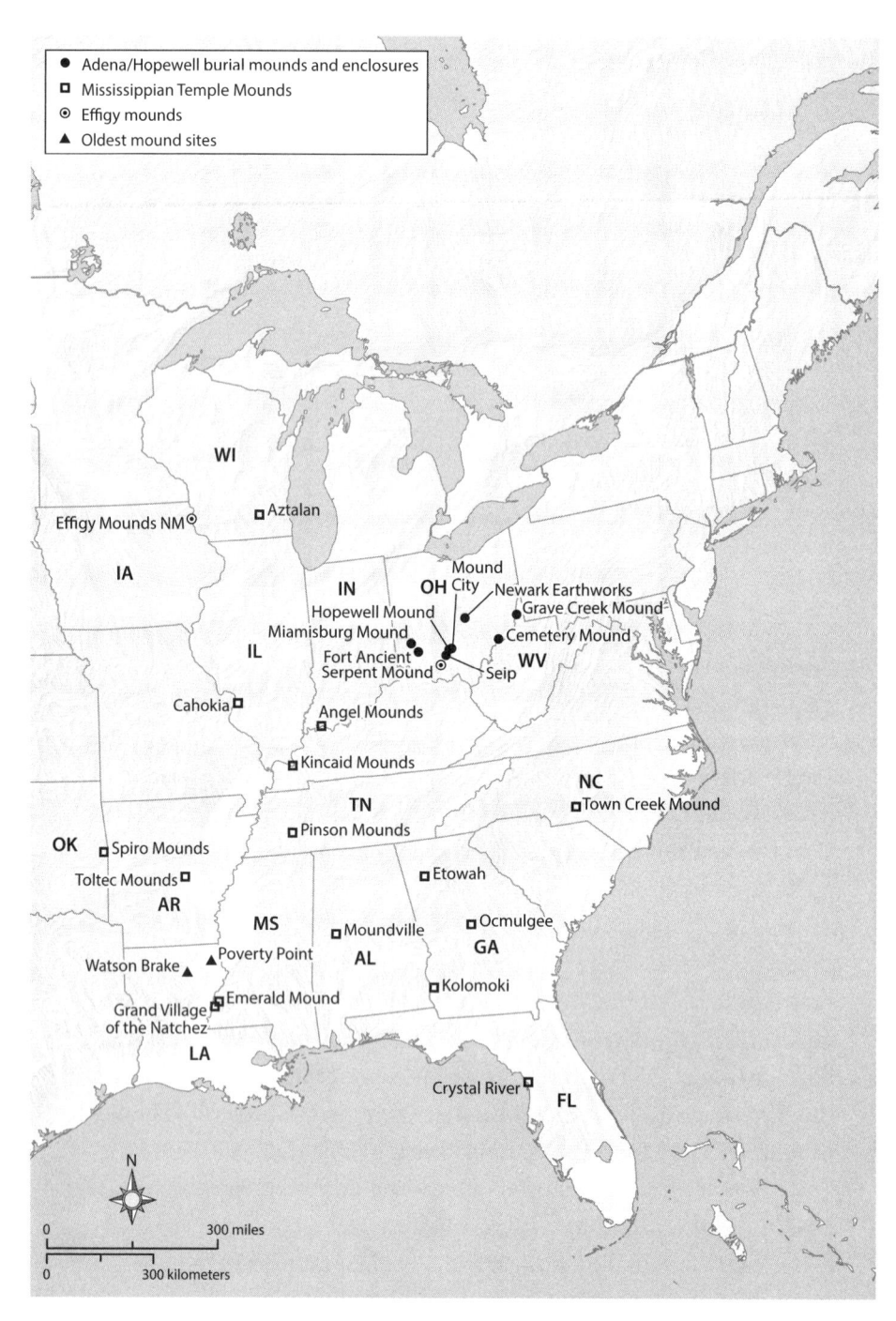

MAP 12.1. Map showing the locations of earthworks sites discussed in this book, including Adena and Hopewell mounds; Mississippian temple mound sites; and effigy mound sites. Kenneth L. Feder

People of North America that they could readily observe, actively and intentionally disassociating them from archaeological sites found in North America, all in an attempt to rob Native People of their accomplishments. Yup, Europeans entering into the American Midwest encountered remarkable examples of monumental construction that could have been accomplished only through the application of diligent, hard work, work that had to be highly organized and well planned, work that had to be accomplished through the concerted efforts of a highly skilled and persistent workforce, and—get this—work that Europeans actually witnessed among Native People to the south!

So how did these European settlers interpret the clear evidence of the communal labor of Native People to produce magnificent monuments of enormous scale? They made up a story about a phony-baloney lost race of probably white people who had arrived in America before the Indians and who had made all the impressive burial mounds, effigy mounds, and platform mounds but who then were wiped out by the nasty and brutish Indians. Those Indians, so the myth stated, arrived on the scene maybe fifteen minutes before—well, more realistically, just a few decades or maybe centuries before—the current wave of Europeans arrived here just in time to reclaim the New World from those nasty Indians who had taken it from the previous wave of European immigrants who had gotten here first. If your head is spinning from that bit of logic, good.

If that all sounds a little loopy and a lot convoluted, you are right, but I am not making any of it up. In his 1872 book, *Ancient America*, J. D. Baldwin expressed the sentiments of many when he said, "It is absurd to suppose a relationship or connection between the original barbarism of these Indians and the civilization of the mound builders."[1]

Leaving aside the fact that Baldwin was arguing in the negative—you know, that the Native People could not have built the mounds because, um, the Natives could not have built the mounds—and leaving aside his general disdain for Native Americans, did the people supporting the myth present any affirmative evidence for the existence of a culture other than that of Native Americans who built the mounds? Well, yes, but the "evidence" (yeah, I used scare quotes) was garbage.

- Iron or maybe bronze swords have been found in the mounds! Or maybe brass? And these metals were unknown to the Native People of America. Well, no. Iron or bronze or brass artifacts, swords or otherwise, were never found in any North American mounds. That claim was based on misinterpretation and misrepresentation. The metal artifacts recovered in and around the mounds invariably were copper and rarely silver, both from natural, raw sources of those metals available in North America and known to have been used by Native People (see chapter 8).
- Artifacts bearing written inscriptions in ancient Old World languages had been found in the mounds. And again, no. There were a handful of claims of the discovery of inscriptions in Hebrew or Phoenician or Egyptian, or some truly weird amalgam of Old World scripts. All of them, I mean ALL OF THEM, were easily proved to have been fakes planted in or near the mounds. The Newark Holy Stones, the Grave Creek Mound Tablet, the Davenport Stones, and the Bat Creek Stone, alluded to in chapter 4, are examples of these fake inscribed artifacts planted in actual mounds.

"But Feder," you might say, "you mentioned eyewitness accounts written by Europeans who saw earth mounds being built by Native People. Wasn't that conclusive evidence that the Native People of North America were capable of constructing the earthworks and proof that they had?"

Yes on all counts. Seventeenth- and eighteenth-century accounts published by Spanish and French explorers of the American Midwest and Southeast saw mounds being built and wrote down descriptions of the process and purpose. You might reasonably ask, "But how could anyone, especially some very learned people, ignore those eyewitness accounts and claim that the mounds were a big mystery and that a non-Native people had been responsible for their construction?" All I can say is that eighteenth- and nineteenth-century writers appear to have subscribed to the philosophy that you should never give up a good story about a lost race just because there is evidence that shows it's nonsense. I mean, come on! Who needs to consider overwhelming evidence when you have a precious combination of bias and hope? I will demur from making any comparisons between this and issues plaguing the modern world.

With many—not all, but many—writers, historians, and other thinkers in the American Midwest in the eighteenth century finding it inconceivable that the ancestors of the people they encountered in the flesh had been capable of the communal and coordinated labor necessary to build the monumental mounds, their solution was genius (I intend that as irony). They made up a story about a mound-building race whose presence in America predated the Indigenous People. A white race. Totally white.

As Robert Silverberg points out in his classic 1968 book on the subject, *The Mound Builders*, the myth of a race of white mound builders was quite convenient and even "comforting to the conquerors."[2] Denying Native People the obvious sophistication of the culture of those who had built the mounds gave European settlers an excuse to deny the sophistication of the people they were displacing. The argument seems to have been, hey, we may be displacing the "Indians," but we don't need to feel guilty about that because what have they ever accomplished in this rich land and, oh well, march of civilization and all that. If you recognize that argument, remember that this bias still exists; go back to chapter 4 and read the words of the woman who wrote me a hilarious letter deriding me for suggesting that maybe, just maybe, Columbus had not discovered America.

At the same time, the myth of a lost race of white mound builders allowed European settlers to play the role of the aggrieved party in their actions vis-à-vis the Native People because, after all, the advanced culture that was responsible for the mounds had likely been European or, at least, white people (maybe the Lost Tribes of Israel), and those ancient settlers had themselves been forcibly displaced by the savages, so we are only wreaking a deserved vengeance on those who destroyed our brothers and sisters of yore. Hey, if you're going to make stuff up, why not go full-bore bullshit about it?

Okay, this book is not about this topic, so I'll move on here. If you'd like to know more, Jason Colavito has written the definitive guide: *The*

Mound Builder Myth: Fake History and the Hunt for a "Lost White Race."[3] I provide a shorter summary of the mound builder myth as a chapter in my book *Frauds, Myths, and Mysteries: Science and Pseudoscience in Archaeology*.[4] Suffice it to say that Native Americans, the descendants of the people who first settled North America more than twenty thousand years ago, were the mound builders and the creators of the spectacular artifacts found in association with the earthworks. The historical legacy is theirs and theirs alone.

Monuments Made of Earth

The tradition of bringing together large groups of people to create what amounts to monumentally scaled sculptures of soil began in America thousands of years ago. The oldest evidence of monumental mound building has been found at the Watson Brake site in Louisiana. Watson Brake has been dated to about fifty-five hundred years ago on the basis of twenty-seven radiocarbon dates obtained on organic materials recovered at the site. The site itself consists of eleven accumulations of earth, mounds, arranged in an oval, surrounding what amounts to a broad, open plaza that, at least we can imagine, was used as a place where a large number of people could have gathered for ceremonies or as a marketplace. The Watson Brake mounds come in a variety of sizes from less than 1 meter (2 feet) to 7.5 meters (25 feet) in height. Several of the mounds, the equivalent of elevated nodes, are connected by a low ridge of earth that represents the arc of the oval. Again, based on radiocarbon dates, the site wasn't thrown up overnight; mound building was carried out over a period of as much as five hundred years.[5]

The builders were not agricultural but clearly had enough time on their hands to complete the construction project, along with a social and political system capable of coordinating and organizing a sizable group of people who willingly worked together on a project that offered no personal, direct, material benefit to them as individuals but who believed that by working together, by subordinating themselves to an overarching authority, they were benefiting as a group in some ineffable way that is not clear to those of us in the present who are not members of their culture. This is not unlike people in the European Middle Ages—or today, for that matter—providing support and labor for the construction of a magnificent cathedral. Those people gave up some of their wealth, time, agency, and personal sovereignty to participate in and support a project they believed was important at least in part because it was bigger than any of them and bigger than anything they could have accomplished on their own.

An even more monumental earth construction is seen at the Poverty Point site, also in Louisiana. Poverty Point is an amazing place and unique in its configuration. It dates to more than thirty-five hundred years ago and was built over the course of several centuries, during which its residents constructed a series of six massive, parallel, concentric, nested, and segmented ridges of earth configured in a sort of half circle, looking like a giant letter C and butting up against a wetland today called Macon Bayou (Map 12.2).

The ridges themselves range from just a few centimeters (a bit more than an inch) to 1 meter (about 3 feet) in height. Each ring segment is between 15 and 25 meters (50 and 80 feet) wide. The low areas between each ring and its adjacent one are between 18 and 30 meters (60 and 100 feet) wide. The outermost of the parallel circular ridges has a diameter of about 125 meters (400 feet). The innermost of the six ring circles has a diameter of about half that, about 60 meters (200 feet). Four causeways cut across the mound rings and converge at what is close to being the center of those circular rings, at the edge of the water. The specific numbers here aren't so important; there won't be a test. What's important is that the entire thing is enormous, a lot of planning went into it, and the result is both impressive and beautiful.

In addition, there are five separate large individual mounds, the most massive of which is over 18 meters (60 feet) high and, from above, sort of looks like it was intended to represent a giant bird, perhaps an eagle or other raptor. If you pull up its image by typing in "Poverty Point" on Google Earth, have a look at what is labeled Mound A. All I will say is, at least at this point, the claim that it is the image of a bird of any kind is a real stretch.

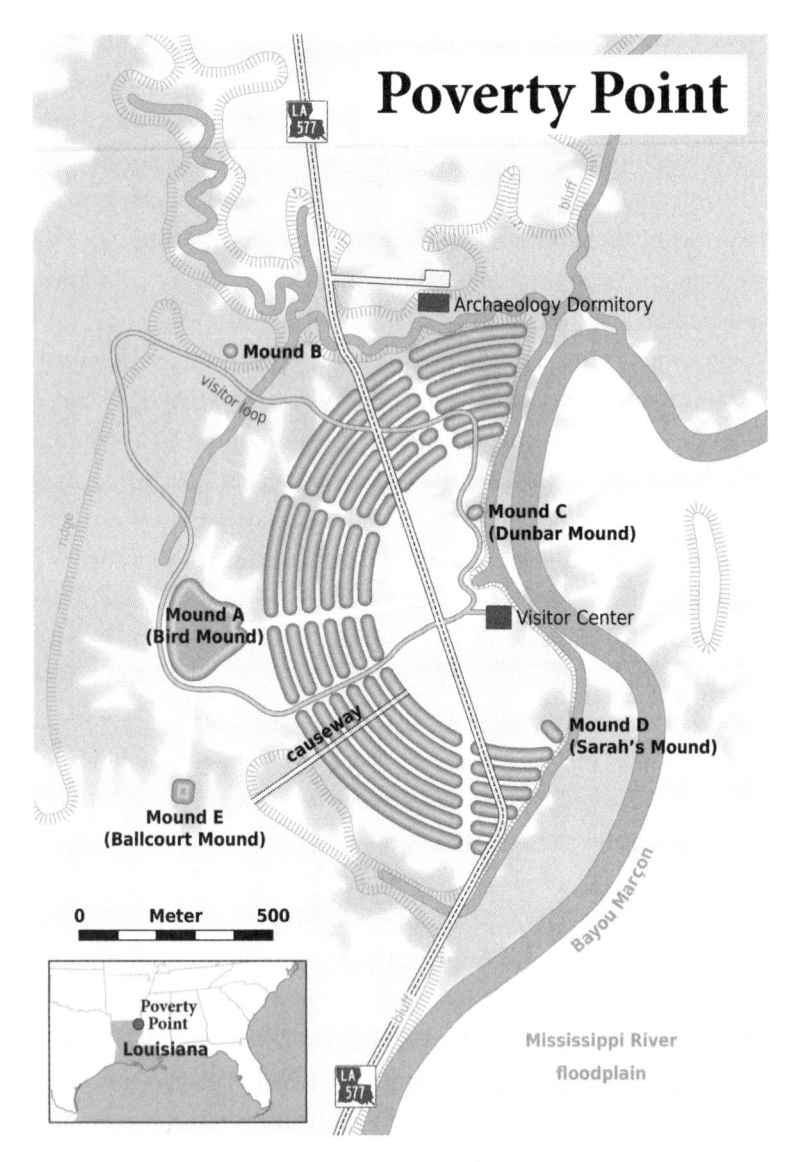

MAP 12.2. A map of the Poverty Point earthworks. Maximilian Dörrbecker, CC BY-SA 2.5

It is difficult to deduce what Poverty Point's precise function was. Could it simply have been a residential site, with the concentric mound ridges intended merely to raise up the living surface above the flood stage of the river? Maybe, but that doesn't really explain the geometrical nature of the mounding, which looks far more artistically designed than a simple and practical flood control project. Was Poverty Point intended instead as an impressive, communal, artful sculpture in soil accomplished by the joining together of a large number of people who wished to memorialize a central place that reposed in the heart of their nation? It could have been, but that cannot be proved.

Poverty Point's massive and literally monumental scale, its substantial age, and, to be honest, the remaining mysteries concerning its purpose together contributed to the successful nomination of the site to an honor roll of places with worldwide significance maintained by the World Heritage Center of the United Nations. That list includes more than one thousand places worldwide, honored for their historical, cultural, or natural significance. Stonehenge and the Pyramids of Giza are also on the list. In this book, I discuss a few more sites in North America that are on this list, including the Hopewell Ceremonial Earthworks (Ohio), Cahokia (Illinois), Mesa Verde (Colorado), Chaco Canyon (New Mexico), Taos Pueblo (New Mexico), and L'Anse aux Meadows (Newfoundland, Canada).[6]

Mounds of Death

The word "necropolis" is ordinarily associated with sites in ancient Egypt and maybe especially Greece. The word, in fact, originates in Greek and literally means "city of the dead." A necropolis is, for the most part, a formal cemetery, often with structures called sepulchers or mausoleums, buildings constructed to house the bodies and, perhaps, the spirits of the dead.

Traditionally called by the absurdly descriptive name Mound City, this centerpiece site of the Hopewell Culture National Historical Park, administered by the federal agency the National Park Service, is located in Chillicothe, Ohio, and is a Native American necropolis. Mound City is one of the specific sites included in the aforementioned Hopewell Ceremonial Earthworks enshrined in the World Heritage Center list (along with Great Circle, Octagon, Hopewell Mound Group, Hopeton Earthworks, High Bank Works, Seip Earthworks, and Fort Ancient, all in Ohio).

Mound City consists of twenty-five burial mounds. Most are conical in cross section and have circular footprints (one exception is a large

FIGURE 12.1. Ground view of some of the burial mounds enclosed by a wall made of earth at the necropolis rather mundanely called Mound City, part of the Hopewell Culture National Historical Park and now contained within the World Heritage Center's Hopewell Ceremonial Earthworks. Kenneth L. Feder

mound with an oval base topped by a ridge). The mounds are positioned in a more or less square plaza of about seventy thousand square meters (seventeen acres) demarcated by an earth mound a little more than a meter (a few feet) high. It's really quite impressive on the ground, but from the air it's a genuine work of art (Figure 12.1).

The mounds in the enclosure house the burials of individuals who almost certainly were socially important and politically powerful members in a culture archaeologists call Hopewell. Understand that we have no idea what these people called themselves; the name Hopewell derives from the name of a nineteenth-century settler in Ohio, Mordecai Hopewell, who had a mound on his property that became the defining example of the culture. Similar mounds in the region with a similar suite of stone tools and pottery have been included in the Hopewell culture. The consistent appearance of the mounds they built, similarities in artifact styles, and a common subsistence base indicate that the sites we

PLATE 1. The lower cliff dwelling at what is today Tonto National Monument in eastern Arizona. Teacher Angie Mitchell's 1880 visit to this site with her students inspired her to think about the connectedness of all people, whatever their culture. Kenneth L. Feder

PLATE 2. A recent example (1960s) of a continuing artistic tradition (in this case, pictographs) among the Zuni people in their New Mexico homeland. Kenneth L. Feder

PLATE 3. The quite impressive Grave Creek Mound, an Adena culture burial monument in West Virginia. The mound is over 19 meters (62 feet) high and 73 meters (240 feet) in diameter, and its footprint covers an area of 16,700 square meters (nearly 180,000 square feet or a bit more than 4 acres). Multiple human burials were found in the mound. Kenneth L. Feder

PLATE 4. The truly monumental Monks Mound, the primary earthwork at Cahokia, technically is a truncated pyramid. The house of a ruler stood at the apex of the mound, about 30 meters (100 feet) above the city. Kenneth L. Feder

PLATE 5. The multiroomed, multistory great house called Wupatki. Considered to have been built by the Sinagua people. Kenneth L. Feder

PLATE 6. Montezuma Castle in Arizona. It may not be the largest cliff dwelling, but it certainly is one of the most impressive and accessible. This is another Sinagua site. Kenneth L. Feder

PLATE 7. Largest of all the great houses in the American Southwest, Pueblo Bonito consisted of more than eight hundred rooms divided into apartments spread out across as many as five stories. This view is from the ridge overlooking the canyon. Kenneth L. Feder

PLATE 8. Pictured here is one set of steps, carved into the bedrock, leading travelers into and then back out of Chaco Canyon. Kenneth L. Feder

PLATE 9. Square Tower House in Mesa Verde. It really does look like a castle tucked into a natural niche in the vertical wall of the mesa. The view from the top the mesa (shown here) is spectacular. The National Park Service also conducts guided tours down into Square Tower House. Kenneth L. Feder

PLATE 10. Cliff Palace is the largest and perhaps the most beautiful of the six hundred or so cliff dwellings in Mesa Verde. It was the first of the cliff dwellings encountered by Richard Wethcrill and Charlie Mason, having been told about them by local Native People. Kenneth L. Feder

PLATE 11. Iconic of the Native art of the American northwest coast, these modern totem poles can be found in Stanley Park in Vancouver, Canada. Kenneth L. Feder

PLATE 12. This absolutely stunning and well-preserved petroglyph was made in the Fremont style, depicting an anthropomorph with broad shoulders and a narrow waist who is holding what looks like a shield. It's located at McKee Springs in Dinosaur National Monument in Utah. Kenneth L. Feder

PLATE 13. One of the most photographed petroglyph panels, and unlike many other large panels (such as Newspaper Rock in figure 16.1), the Great Hunt Panel tells a single, coherent story with hunters bearing bows and arrows hunting a herd of bighorn sheep. Kenneth L. Feder

PLATE 14. Three Rivers is located adjacent to a Mogollon village site. Among the more than twenty thousand individual pieces of rock art, this depiction of a bighorn sheep, its body pierced by three arrows, may be one of my personal favorites. Kenneth L. Feder

PLATE 15. The quite moving image of the great chief who traded her life for the ability to watch over her people for eternity. She is now called Tsagaglalal, "She Who Watches." Located near Horsethief Lake in Washington State. Kenneth L. Feder

PLATE 16. Seven anthropomorphic pictographs among a couple dozen, many life-size, located in a natural rock alcove in Horseshoe Canyon in Utah. Part of the Great Gallery, these armless and legless images, often with eyes wide open, are in the Barrier Canyon style. It doesn't matter what religion, if any, you subscribe to—this place is sacred. Kenneth L. Feder

MONUMENT BUILDERS OF THE MIDWEST 201

FIGURE 12.2, COLOR PLATE 3. The quite impressive Grave Creek Mound, an Adena culture burial monument in West Virginia. The mound is over 19 meters (62 feet) high and 73 meters (240 feet) in diameter, and its footprint covers an area of 16,700 square meters (nearly 180,000 square feet or a bit more than 4 acres). Multiple human burials were found in the mound. Kenneth L. Feder

today designate as Hopewell were created by communities of folks who would have recognized each other as one people.

Who were the Hopewell? They appear to represent the culmination of an even older mound-building culture, the Adena, which flourished between about 800 BCE and 100 CE. The Adena were the role models for the Hopewell in at least some of their mound-building practices, constructing sometimes enormous burial mounds. Miamisburg Mound in western Ohio is Adena, and at about 20 meters (65 feet) high and 245 meters (800 feet) around at its base and with a footprint of more than 4,000 square meters (1 acre), it is one of the largest burial mounds in the U.S. Grave Creek Mound in West Virginia is a similarly massive Adena mound and also contains multiple burials (Figure 12.2, Color Plate 3).

Archaeologists define cultures and assign sites to a culture or group based on their ages and the artifact assemblages found at their sites. We hope that we've captured something real, different characteristics and practices that maybe the past people themselves would have recognized as legitimate ways of distinguishing their group from others. It isn't easy to definitively distinguish Adena from Hopewell. Impressionistically, Hopewell material culture seems more complex than Adena, and massive earthworks that were not intended to house the remains of the dead, the enclosures to be discussed later, are a hallmark of the Hopewell.

Most Hopewell sites are located in Ohio, but sites designated as Hopewell are also found in Kentucky and Illinois. The Hopewell culture dates to between 200 BCE and 500 CE, but its true flowering occurred between 125 and 400 CE. Along with the communal labor needed to build burial mounds, those buried in them were interred with grave goods, artifacts often made of exotic material, stuff not native to Ohio but that needed to be traded for, like copper or mica (Figure 12.3). Many of these objects are exquisite, finely made works of art produced by highly skilled artisans who almost certainly were afforded the opportunity to learn and perfect the requisite skills for producing those objects.

Most Hopewell residential sites, their villages, are nothing extraordinary, quite small and each with a resident population of just a few families. Though they did plant crops, the Hopewell did not rely exclusively on agriculture for their subsistence and didn't cultivate maize at all. They practiced a broad-spectrum variety of subsistence, hunting deer and other small mammals, fishing, collecting an abundance of wild plants in their home territory, and planting some of the local agricultural crops mentioned in chapter 9, including sunflowers, a local species of squash, and goosefoot.

Archaeologists don't find much social stratification or economic inequality in Hopewell residential sites. For example, archaeologists have not identified families that had a larger or fancier house than others, and no one alive at the time had a concentration of fancy stuff that required the work of a specialist artist or that was made of particularly valuable raw materials. In other words, there do not appear to have been Hopewellian kings or queens, no class of wealthy noblemen and noblewomen reflected in the archaeological reconstruction of village

FIGURE 12.3. A beautifully crafted bird image, cut from a flattened piece of copper by a Hopewell artist. Kenneth L. Feder

life. Overall, their society seems on its face to largely have been egalitarian. In life, everyone, at least those in the same age and sex categories, seems pretty much to have been equal to everyone else in terms of material wealth. Obviously, some people were singled out for special treatment, but then only in death. Everybody else was simply cremated. A chosen few, perhaps people who were religious functionaries, were laid out in wooden structures, accompanied by remarkable works of art, and then at some later time had their burial locations covered with a mound of earth. These are the folks buried at Mound City and other

Hopewell and also Adena burial sites. For a very informative book-length treatment of the Adena and Hopewell of Ohio—and for scads of beautiful photographs—check out Bradley Lepper's book *Ohio Archaeology: An Illustrated Chronicle of Ohio's Ancient American Indian Cultures*.[7] Five stars!

Sacred Spaces

Along with burial mounds, the Hopewell used relatively narrow and tall earth mounds to demarcate spaces in a way that appears to have been an effort to isolate and differentiate those enclosed spaces from the surrounding area. Some of these encompassing mounds followed the irregular path delineating the flat top of a bluff, thereby enclosing the irregular space at the top of the bluff. Some of these mounds reflect, on a sometimes huge scale, a geometric delineation, enclosing a round, rectangular, square, or even octagonal space.

For example, in Newark, Ohio, one element of the Newark Earthworks State Memorial is the Great Circle Earthworks. Those earthworks represent, just as the name implies, a mound enclosing a circular space of more than 100,000 square meters (26 acres). The mound encircling the space is generally about 2.5 meters (8 feet) high. Piling up that dirt created what amounts to a moat about 1.5 meters (5 feet) deep around the entirety of the space. The mound-enclosed circle is about 365 meters (1,200 feet) in diameter, and the circumference is 1,150 meters (3,800 feet; in other words, the circular mound is that length around). I have seen a jogger running along the top of that ridge, which is a little more than one kilometer. So a decent workout. In the center of the space is a low-lying mound that seems to resemble an effigy of a bird, perhaps an eagle—though, as at Poverty Point, erosion makes that difficult to confirm.

The Octagon Earthworks is another part of the Newark Earthworks State Memorial. It consists of a series of segmented linear mounds that together enclose a vast octagon of about 200,000 square meters (50 acres). At the southwest side of the octagonal enclosure is an opening, a break in that part of the enclosure. The break (about 20 meters, or 70 feet, wide) is flanked by two linear mounds that run at about ninety

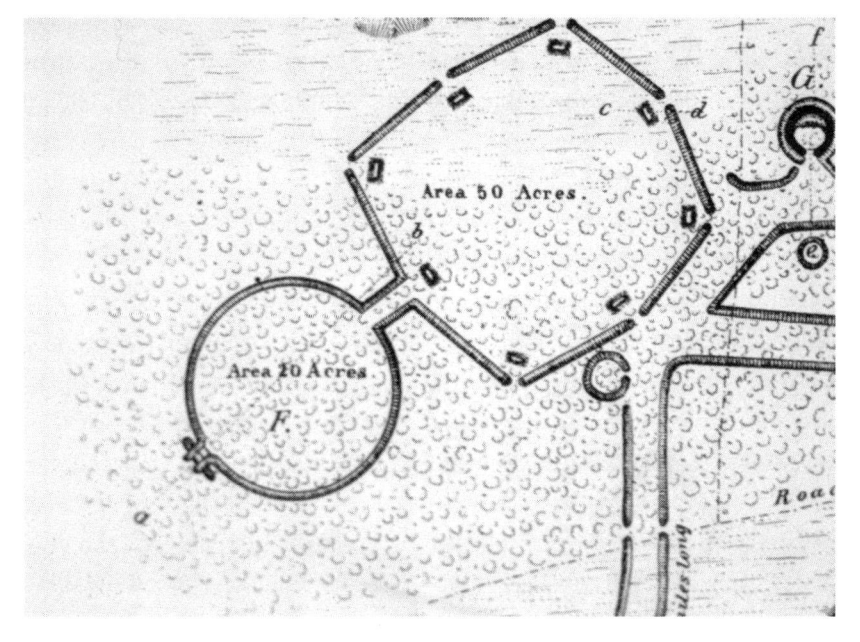

FIGURE 12.4. Drawing of the Octagon Earthworks, part of the Newark Earthworks in Newark, Ohio. As you can see in the drawing, the octagon encloses an area of 50 acres (over 200,000 square meters). The attached circular earthwork encloses an area of 20 acres (80,000 square meters). From Squire and Davis 1848

degrees from the adjacent octagon walls and connect the octagon with another enclosure, this one circular and measuring about 80,000 square meters (20 acres). Part of the southwest wall of the circle is a mound far more massive and taller than the rest of the enclosure walls. The entire site is truly stunning and looks like, and is, a beautiful landscape sculpture (Figure 12.4).

Unfortunately, more than one hundred years ago the State of Ohio signed a lease with a country club for their use of the double enclosure as, believe it or not, a golf course. So yes, in the middle of a site certainly deemed sacred by its builders and still deemed sacred by the Native People of Ohio who trace their ancestry back to those builders, there was an active golf course that most days of the year had been closed to nongolfers, who could only view the monument from a platform located at the margins of the enclosures or on the few days each year that the course was closed to golfers. Fortunately, as the result of an extended legal battle, the golf course has closed down and will move to another location, and the associated earthworks will be open to the public in 2025 with the former golf course reconfigured—no more sand traps, no more greens—into a parklike setting. The reconsecration of this sacred site represents the concerted work of a large number of people, Native and non-Native alike.

Why did the Hopewell create these and the other enclosures? Enclosing, demarcating, and differentiating a space deemed sacred and separating it from the ordinary and profane activities of everyday life is a common practice in both the ancient and the modern world. There is no evidence of habitation of the enclosures built by the Hopewell, no evidence of everyday life. They don't encircle the lived-in space of a community. Though it cannot be confirmed definitively with the evidence available to archaeologists, it is believed that sites like the Great Circle and Octagon Earthworks were places where people gathered for religious ceremonies.

The long axis of the double enclosure just described runs from the bottom of the circle at the top of the large mound, travels through the middle of the walled avenue that connects the circle to the octagon, and then passes through the center of the far side of the octagon. That axis is aligned with a compass direction of 51.5° (east of north) and is about 800 meters (0.5 miles) long. The direction 51.5° might sound like a random number for the builders to have aligned that long axis with, but it's not. That compass direction points to the rising of the moon on a key day in the lunar cycle, the northernmost point of moonrise over a cycle that lasts 18.6 years. In other words, if you were standing on the pinnacle of the large mound at the far end of the circular enclosure and saw the moon rising directly over the center of the part of the octagon at the farthest point from your viewing location, you would know with some certainty that you had reached a fixed point in that 18.6-year lunar cycle. Calculating the timing of that point in the lunar cycle would have required years of careful astronomical observation. Just for context, there is some evidence that the 18.6-year lunar cycle was also baked into the design of Stonehenge in England. This means that, along with being architects and engineers, the Hopewell people were astronomers engaged in long-term observations of the moon.

The area around Newark and Chillicothe, Ohio, was clearly a hub of Hopewell culture, and their archaeological sites are found throughout that territory. Interestingly, from aerial photographs and by ground truthing, we know that the Hopewell appear to have constructed what amount to wide avenues bounded by long, linear earth walls spanning nearly 10 kilometers (6 miles). Ohio archaeologist Bradley Lepper suggests that this road, called the Great Hopewell Road, represents a ceremonial avenue, a sanctification of the physical and spiritual connection among the various sacred sites, including burials and enclosures, that resided at the core of Hopewell religion.[8] In this enormous investment of labor in symbolizing those connections, the Hopewell show us their ability to marshal the forces of a large cohort of members of their community who, for at least a part of their year, and over the course of years, devoted their labors to the construction and maintenance of monuments that were more focused on spiritual life than the material necessities of this life.

What happened to the people who built the mounds? While they may have stopped building earthworks, they didn't disappear. They didn't move away. They are not an extinct people. In fact, their descendants continue to live in the American Midwest as members of a number of different Native American groups, including the Chippewa, Delaware, Kickapoo, Miami, Ottawa, Peoria, Potawatomi, Seneca, Shawnee, and Wyandot. Notice that a number of those names have become the names of geographical places in the United States and Canada.

Thunderbirds, Bears, and Snakes, Oh My

Perhaps the most interesting and whimsical of the earth monuments constructed by the Native People of the American Midwest are effigy mounds, gigantic sculptures in earth of animals, generally bears, birds, and at least one snake. In fact, there is a national monument devoted to a cluster of these effigy mounds in Iowa in the appropriately named Effigy Mounds National Monument.

FIGURE 12.5. Aerial view of Serpent Mound in southern Ohio. This effigy mound is more than 435 meters (about 1,430 feet) long from mouth to coiled tail. Google Earth

The most impressive effigy mound is located back in southern Ohio. Called Serpent Mound, it is, obviously enough, a monumentally scaled representation of a snake with its tail neatly coiled and its body sinuously running along the top of a bluff above Ohio Brush Creek. From the tip of its tail to its apparently open mouth about to swallow what some interpret to be a representation of the sun, Serpent Mound is 435 meters (about 1,430 feet) in length and its body is generally about 1 meter (about 3 feet) tall (Figure 12.5).

Several other mounds dot the immediate landscape and may be part of a broader story. Archaeologist Brad Lepper and his colleagues argue that the image of the snake was an element in the Siouan origin story concerning a serpent who impregnates First Woman, thereby creating human beings.[9] Together, the layout at Serpent Mound and its associated mounds may in some ways be replicated in a pictograph in Picture Cave in Missouri that tells that same story.[10]

There are a number of long-standing arguments concerning Serpent Mound's age, with one group of researchers arguing that it is more than two thousand years old and attributable to the Adena culture discussed earlier in this chapter. Lepper contends that, in fact, the site dates to about one thousand years ago and reflects what archaeologists in the Midwest label the Fort Ancient culture, named for an enormous mound enclosure site also in Ohio.[11]

Whatever its exact age and meaning, Serpent Mound is an astonishing work of art. The site is administered by the state agency the Ohio History Connection. It is open to the public, and there is an on-site museum and an open tower visitors can climb to obtain a bird's-eye view of the serpent.

Is Serpent Mound, along with the bears and thunderbirds seen at Effigy Mounds National Monument and all the other earth effigies seen in the American Midwest, a work of art or a work of worship? The answer is clear: it is both.

13

City Dwellers

I MAKE very infrequent sojourns to "the City." Just about everyone who lives near New York City refers to it as "the City," because, well, what other city is there? When I do go, I drive from my house in the wilds of northwestern Connecticut to New Haven, where I park my car in a commuter lot. From there, I take the train—Amtrak—into Manhattan, where it disgorges riders into Grand Central Terminal, a beautiful, very well-maintained, and highly functional train station, the largest in the world (by area and number of platforms), opened in 1913 and still exhibiting a marvelous art deco vibe that has never gotten tired. It's a very impressive place.

My feeling of anticipation is always the same as I walk through the corridors of the terminal and finally reach the glass doors that lead out onto East Forty-Second Street. That moment when I open the door and walk out into the explosion that is New York is transformative. It feels like I'm entering a world entirely different from my everyday existence. It's like in the movie *The Wizard of Oz* when everything turns from black and white to color when Dorothy enters Oz. Upon exiting Grand Central Station, it's abundantly clear in every imaginable way that you're "not in Kansas anymore." You are instantly enveloped by a blanket of the sounds and smells that are New York—of buses and construction; diesel fumes and roasting chestnuts; knishes, hot dogs, and falafel; people wearing way too much perfume or cologne and others not wearing nearly enough; street musicians pounding on their Home Depot buckets while others regale passersby with classical violin sonatas; itinerant preachers warning us all to avoid the temptations of Sodom (and, man, are they in the right place!); folks who either took too many drugs that morning or maybe not enough. People. Everywhere people. Naturalist Charles Darwin characterized life on our planet as a "blooming and buzzing confusion," and that characterization applies perfectly to New York City and likely just about any city on Earth. It's the essence of sensory overload. It's exhilarating and exciting and more than just a little terrifying to this denizen of the woods of Connecticut, where my senses are used to the smell of my neighbor's rescue horses and the sound of snowblowers or leaf blowers, depending on the season, and my nearest neighbors are raccoons.

New York City is arguably the social and economic capital of the United States, though, admittedly, the people who argue that are probably New Yorkers. It certainly is a central node, a hub of American society. There is no more convincing evidence of that than this: when, on September 11, 2001, murderous terrorists hijacked four commercial jetliners and used them as weapons to attack the core of America, their targets were Washington, D.C. (our actual political capital), and New York City. Love or hate the city, but those terrorists knew that they were striking at our core, at the heart of America.

"The City" Eight Hundred Years Ago and in Illinois

Now come with me in my time machine and let's travel back some eight hundred years and visit a Native American community in the Mississippi Valley, in what is today Collinsville, Illinois, just east of that state's border with Missouri and a little less than seven miles east of the great river.[1]

Certainly the scale is far different. The population is not in the millions but in the tens of thousands. The structures are wood, not brick; the monuments are made of earth and not granite; and we travel by foot and not rail. Nevertheless, we encounter a "blooming and buzzing confusion" of a city overloaded with its own unique sights and smells and sounds. Just as central as New York City is to modern America, the place we today know as Cahokia (we do not know what its people called it)

FIGURE 13.1. An artist's conception of the Native American city today called Cahokia, at its peak at around 1200 CE, during what is called the Mississippian Period. Cahokia Mounds State Historic Site, artist William Iseminger

was the heart of social, political, and economic life in the American Midwest between about 1050 and 1400 CE (Figure 13.1).

We walk through this Native American metropolis of at least ten thousand and as many as thirty thousand people and are buffeted by the sounds of manufacturing by copper workers, stoneworkers, and weavers. The air is heavy with the smoke billowing out from pottery kilns and cooking hearths. The smells of venison roasting on open fires, fish drying on wooden racks, and unhusked corn roasting on stone platforms are everywhere. In the distance we see workers piling up basket load after basket load of earth, constructing a flat-topped pyramid more than 10 meters (32 feet) high, on the top of which the house of a noble family will be built. Their elevated social, economic, and political status is symbolized by the elevation of their home, the equivalent of the penthouses of wealthy New Yorkers on high looking down on the common rabble.

The dull thud of stone axes chopping off the branches of straight-trunked trees, each over 6 meters (20 feet) tall and transported to the city from the surrounding countryside, reverberates through the morning. Those trees are being used by workers performing maintenance on the central palisade, a walled enclosure of more than 800,000 square meters (200 acres) demarcated by more than twenty thousand logs. The palisade is marked by a series of bastions from where soldiers can keep watch on the surrounding territory. Within the enclosure are a series of eighteen impressive earthworks on which the elevated houses of the highest of Cahokia's noble class are situated. In other words, at the heart of the city is, effectively, a gated, protected, and fortified community of Cahokia's political, economic, and social elite. I am not intending to be snarky here, but it is unclear whether this neighborhood of Cahokia has been fortified to protect its elite residents from foreign invaders with evil intent or to protect the rulers and noble classes from its own citizens in the event of a revolution.

Looming over the entire cityscape are more than 120 geometrically precise platforms of mounded earth, some conical, most trapezoidal in the manner of pyramids with flat tops (technically "truncated pyramids," pyramids but with their tops cut off). The largest of these platforms is in the palisaded enclosure and today is called Monks Mound, named for the monastery of Trappist monks built on one of its flanks in the mid-eighteenth century. Monks Mound is enormous and literally monumental, a multiplatformed, truncated pyramid of earth reaching over 30 meters (almost 100 hundred feet) in height at its apex. Its footprint alone covers 65,000 square meters (16 acres), and it is estimated that its volume contains 625,000 cubic meters (22 million cubic feet) of earth (Figure 13.2, Color Plate 4). That footprint, by the way, is similar in its extent to that of the largest Egyptian pyramid, the burial chamber of the pharaoh Khufu at Giza.

The construction of what we call Monks Mound was a monumental task and certainly involved the work of a large and highly coordinated labor force directed by overseers with a deep and practical knowledge of engineering and soils, laboring diligently for an extended period of time, likely over several decades. Workers didn't simply pile up random

FIGURE 13.2, COLOR PLATE 4. The truly monumental Monks Mound, the primary earthwork at Cahokia, technically is a truncated pyramid. The house of a ruler stood at the apex of the mound, about 30 meters (100 feet) above the city. Kenneth L. Feder

basket loads of dirt. Coring of the mound shows the differential use of separate kinds of earth depending on where in the body of the mound the soil was being positioned, with denser clay being used along the sloped surfaces for greater stability and longevity. Monks Mound was the most elevated of the mounds of Cahokia and its apex was home to the most elevated of Cahokia's citizenry, its version of a pharaoh, emperor, or king.

In our time-travel visit, we hear the chatter of artisans as they create works of remarkable skill and beauty in clay, wood, and stone. Merchants have just arrived bearing raw copper, a material brought downstream from a far-flung outpost likely directly tied to Cahokia, located more than 625 kilometers (almost 400 miles) away in what is today Wisconsin.[2] There, a site now called Aztalan looks like a miniature version of Cahokia. It was perhaps a colony located to exploit the precious raw material available only in its environs. That copper was destined for the workshops of artists who would pound the metal into thin sheets and then cut out beautiful forms of birds and geometric shapes with which they would then adorn the houses and burials of Cahokia's elites.

In the distance we hear the labored breathing and pounding footsteps of young men vigorously engaged in a sporting event, each holding the equivalent of a hockey stick. Their attention is focused on a small stone shaped like a puck in the middle of a large open playing field in a game that appears to be a version of ice hockey but played on grass. The "puck" was called a "chunkey" stone by Native People who were seen playing the game by European explorers in the sixteenth century.

We wander to the west of Monks Mound and enter into a fascinating structure consisting of a series of large timbers. Depending on the year we visit, as it was rebuilt and enlarged a few times, there are between twenty-four and sixty tall wooden posts evenly positioned in a circular formation of between 75 and 145 meters (240 and 476 feet) in diameter. A single large post is positioned within the circle of posts, located just off center. If we are visiting on the twenty-first of March, June, September, or December, we might see Cahokia's astronomers carefully noting the location on the horizon of the rising sun from the central timber. Cahokia's astronomers are assessing the sun's location relative to the posts along the circle in order to determine the day of the vernal equinox (the first day of spring, when the sun rises due east), the summer solstice (when the sun rises the farthest north and the day with the most hours of sun), the autumnal equinox (when the sun rises due east again), and the winter solstice (when the sun rises farthest south and the day with the fewest hours of sun). In other words, the wood circle at Cahokia represents a calendar based on the apparent movement of the sun during the year as it shifts across the horizon at sunrise. This is very similar to the way ancient people of England used the well-known monument Stonehenge, which explains why Cahokia's researchers call the circle of wooden posts Woodhenge.

Everywhere around the city, especially in the outskirts, we see a vast expanse of richly productive agricultural fields providing an enormous harvest of the domesticated crops of maize (corn), beans, and squash, the food that fuels the engine of this society.

In our visit to the Cahokia of eight hundred years ago, we have entered into the equivalent of New York City—or maybe it makes more sense to say that when we enter New York City we are visiting modern America's version of Cahokia—a place at the core of an aboriginal Native American empire. It is a place you can today visit as part of Cahokia Mounds State Park in Collinsville, Illinois. As noted elsewhere in this book, Cahokia is one of only six current Native American sites included on the World Heritage List of the United Nations.

A King and Queen of Cahokia

One of the hallmarks of civilizations, both ancient and modern, is the existence of stratification, inequality in terms of wealth, political power, and social standing. Put bluntly, in most civilizations, both ancient and modern, there are rich and powerful people. In modern parlance, these were and are the so-called 1 percenters, the folks in that top 1 percent in terms of their accumulation of wealth and power. Most of the rest of the people in civilizations, again both ancient and modern, are the poor and mostly powerless folks, and then a bunch of folks who fit in the middle.

At the top of the economic, political, and social heap is the great ruler. They may be called pharaoh, or king or queen, or emperor or empress, or a host of other names, but they are essentially the "dear leader," the person who, often by divine fiat, is in charge of everything, at least here on Earth. At the same time, one of the material hallmarks of the existence of great rulers from the perspective of an archaeologist is their graves, as well as their near monopoly on wealth reflected in the stuff with which they are buried. As in the burials of King Tut in Egypt, the rulers of the Shang dynasty in China, and Queen Pu Abi in Mesopotamia, the grave goods enclosed in the burial of Cahokia's rulers serve as a symbol, a signifier of the wealth accumulated while they were alive and the power they maintain even in death.

Let's go back to King Tut. Sure, he's really just an avatar for the power of the ruler and was actually not an important pharaoh. He really didn't accomplish much in his very short life other than to be buried with a lot of "wonderful things," as his excavator Howard Carter famously phrased it when he first gazed into the Boy King's unplundered tomb. The concentration of wealth in the form of finely made objects of gold, ebony, lapis lazuli, ivory, and on and on in his tomb reflects the concentration of wealth and power he commanded in life.

Not surprisingly, there is just such a burial at Cahokia, the final resting place of likely a king and queen or emperor and empress of the great city in the Mississippi River valley.[3] Called Mound 72, the burial is inauspiciously marked by little more than a raised ridge of earth, but the contents are astonishing. Two primary burials, one male and one female, appear to be the heart of the grave with additions made over the course of about one hundred years between 1050 and 1150 CE. The male and female were young, between just twenty-five and thirty years old when they died. The "king," interred very close to the female, had been laid out on a remarkable platform of twenty thousand marine shells. Cahokia is located almost 1,000 kilometers (more than 600 miles) from the coast (and that's as the bird flies; it's substantially more than that if you just follow the course of the Mississippi River), so marine shells would have been a commodity that was obtainable, but at great expense and effort. Nearby these two burials are concentrations of wealth in the form of a profusion of artfully produced objects that either took a long time to make or were crafted from material that would have been difficult to obtain: 750 stone spearpoints, sheets of mica, copper tubes, and thousands more shells, many of them perforated and likely strung together.

Perhaps even more impressive than these artifacts was the inclusion in the overall tomb of individuals who appear to have been human sacrifices, people perhaps intended to be retainers, servants to fulfill the needs of the primary inhabitants of the burials in their afterlives. Among those placed in the tomb was a cluster of burials including the bones of fifty-three young women; their skeletons indicate that they were between the ages of thirteen and thirty when they died. Evidence of fracturing of the cervical vertebrae (neck bones) of many of these young women indicates that they were killed by strangulation. The "isotope signature" seen in the bones of the young women suggests that they were "foreigners," at least people not born or raised in Cahokia itself.

This chemical isotope signature of a person's bones can often be used to trace the person to the region where they were born and grew up. The isotopes in the foods they ate were derived from the soils in which those foods grew and become imprinted in the person's growing bones, allowing archaeologists to trace their geographic origin. Near the fifty-three female sacrifice victims were the remains of thirty-nine young men. Their remains also reflect the violence of their deaths. Some had their heads smashed in and many had been decapitated, likely as part of a ritual ushering those men into their eternal life of servitude to the great rulers.

Mound 72 is a complex feature, the result of about one hundred years of use, containing the graves of multiple high-status individuals and lots of sacrifice victims. However we interpret the burial's details, it does seem clear that in it we have the social stratification, inequality, and concentration of power and perceived importance of certain individuals that characterized life in Cahokia, made manifest and concrete.

Cahokia, indeed, was a busy hub of activity in a Native American civilization, a place characterized by a noble class, engineers and architects, merchants and soldiers, artists and craftspeople, workers and farmers, sacrifice victims and people for whom others were sacrificed. Cahokia was a place with an expansive reach, perhaps best interpreted as the capital of a loosely organized empire that dominated the Mississippi Valley during its tenure between 1050 and 1250 CE and maybe beyond. Raw materials flowed into the city and finished goods made by Cahokia's artisans were concentrated in the homes and burials of an elite class. Some of those high-status objects flowed back out to local, secondary elites beholden to the preeminent ruling class at Cahokia. Everyone throughout the Midwest likely knew of Cahokia at its peak, everyone recognized it as the dominant force in the region, and everyone participated in the social, economic, and political entity that was Cahokia.

Though Cahokia was unique in North America in terms of its size and geographical reach, it certainly wasn't the only large and densely occupied community in the American Midwest and Southeast at the time of its ascendance (see Map 12.1). For example, Moundville, on the

Black Warrior River in Alabama, though an order of magnitude smaller than Cahokia, nevertheless was an impressive community characterized by an open plaza of flat ground measuring 81,000 square meters (20 acres) surrounded by twenty-six sizable, truncated pyramids of earth. The main platform pyramid, though smaller than Monks Mound, stands nearly 18 meters (60 feet) in height and, as was the case for Monks Mound, provided the elevated location for the house of a ruler of the community.

Etowah, in Georgia, is another example of a site characterized by impressive pyramids of earth, remarkable art, and subsistence based on agriculture. Etowah's Mound A is an impressive platform mound about 18 meters (60 feet) high with two smaller but equally impressive platform mounds in its shadow. Perhaps these were the residences of secondary rulers, the equivalent of the U.S. vice president's house at Number One Observatory Circle, in comparison to Mound A, the equivalent of the White House.

As we saw at Cahokia, the primary mounds at Etowah, though small in number, are surrounded by a fortified palisade and, to add protection for the rulers of Etowah, residents excavated a ditch surrounding the center of the community that served, effectively, as a moat.

Artifacts recovered in excavations at Etowah are extraordinarily impressive in their artistry and sophistication. Those objects include painted marble sculptures of kneeling and seated individuals and absolutely stunning works in seashell, including two disclike objects called gorgets (Figure 13.3).

In both cases, the shell was cut and inscribed in the image of a warrior carrying weapons and wearing the costume of a bird of prey replete with a beak, talons, a cape in the form of wings, and a birdlike headdress. Fine artistry in the form of works likely produced by specialists is a common element of complex state societies that exhibit a social and political hierarchy where some people can spend much of their time perfecting their art while others labor in the fields and supply the food needed to support those people not producing food on farms. The art found at sites like Cahokia, Moundville, and Etowah appears to reflect this element of the complexity of their societies.

FIGURE 13.3. This stunning pendant cut from a shell and depicting what appears to be a soldier resplendent with a feathered cape, a bird mask, and a serrated weapon in his right hand was recovered from the mound site called Etowah, located in Georgia. Kenneth L. Feder

Many other sites that show a similar pattern of the building of platform mounds; the construction of protective palisades; the sumptuous burial of a social, political, and economic elite; and the presence of a class of artists or specialists, all underpinned by a large population of farmers whose food surplus supports the elites, is seen throughout the American Midwest and Southeast at places like Angel Mounds in Indiana, Kolomoki and Ocmulgee Mounds in Georgia, Crystal River Mounds in Florida, Grand Village of the Natchez and Emerald Mound in Mississippi,

Town Creek Mound in North Carolina, Toltec Mounds in Arkansas, and Spiro Mounds in Oklahoma (see Map 12.1). Not all of these communities were at their peak at the same time, but they certainly indicate that the general pattern seen at Cahokia on a grand scale was replicated across a broad expanse of territory and a wide span of time. All of the sites just listed are open to the public and have on-site museums that display some of the remarkable works produced by the talented and skilled artists of those places. If you want to know more about visiting these places, I have a book for that.[4]

Sadly, having peaked before 1250 CE, largely as a result of internal forces, Cahokia was a shell of its former greatness by the time eyewitnesses from other cultures, explorers sent by the Spanish or the French, arrived in the Mississippi River Valley in the mid-1700s. But those same invaders were eyewitness to some of the smaller population centers that had continued to flourish into the seventeenth and eighteenth centuries. Because they traveled with chroniclers whose job it was to record everything they encountered for their benefactors back in Europe, we can read of vast cornfields that stretched for miles around these communities. These writers also recorded what certainly sounds like a hierarchical, stratified society with a class of nobles and a powerful leader at its head and with farmers, merchants, artists, traders, soldiers, workers, and priests making up the bulk of the population. In a work first published in 1557, the Spanish explorer Hernando de Soto's chronicler, the so-called Gentleman of Elvas, described encountering palisaded communities and estimated their individual populations in the thousands.[5] In the mid-sixteenth century, another Spanish explorer, Garcilaso de La Vega, actually provided an eyewitness account of the process of mound building, indicating that the Native People in Florida built them to a height of about "two or three pikes high" with three steep sides and one not as steep with steps for access. A "pike" is about 5 meters, so the mounds he saw were between 10 meters (33 feet) and a little more than 15 meters (50 feet) high. La Vega went on to add that there were sometimes multiple houses built on their apexes, all intended for their "cacique," the term he used to refer to the king or prince, and his family.[6]

Later, in the eighteenth century, French missionaries and explorers wrote in some detail about daily life in a still-thriving mound-building society in Mississippi. For example, traveling down the Mississippi River in 1718–28, Antoine-Simon Le Page du Pratz reached the location of what is today called the Grand Village of the Natchez, where he encountered and described a clearly socially stratified society with a ruling class supported by farmers and workers.[7] Having taken the time to learn the local Native language, he could speak to the local people and could write with some authority (though one must get past his bias). For example, he recorded that the people called their ruler the Great Sun and that, indeed, his house was located on a tall, artificially raised earth eminence, the same kind of truncated pyramid as that seen at the older sites already mentioned. The Great Sun's mound can still be seen today at the Mississippi state park that memorializes the eighteenth-century village. Other eyewitnesses recorded the practice of human sacrifice upon the death of the Great Sun in 1728, matching what we've already seen at Cahokia.

However, in most of the American Midwest and Southeast, the period of interaction between the intruders and the complex Native American societies was brief. As a result, there wasn't a lengthy period during which the invaders could provide detailed descriptions of the Native People. The Spanish and French travelers unknowingly brought with them infectious diseases that the Native People had not previously been exposed to and to which they therefore did not have the opportunity to develop immunity. These diseases quickly became epidemics resulting in death on an unimaginably vast scale. For example, the American Southeast had first been explored by the Spaniard Pánfilo de Narváez in 1536. A scant four years later, explorer Hernando de Soto landed on the Gulf Coast of Florida and entered into the interior of the American Southeast, exploring the states of Mississippi, Georgia, Kentucky, Tennessee, and Arkansas. De Soto's chronicler, mentioned previously, described an abandoned community encountered in 1540 in this way: "Within a league and half a league about this town were great towns dispeopled, and overgrown with grass; which showed that they had been long without inhabitants. The Indians said that two years before there was a plague in that country, and that they removed to other towns."[8] Vibrant, thriving communities inhabited just a few centuries after the decline of Cahokia and encountered by Narváez in 1536 lay abandoned and in ruin just four years later. Disease had rapidly decimated the Native population, leaving only history and archaeology to tell us their stories.

14

Great Houses and Cliff Castles

> In beauty I walk
> With beauty before me I walk
> With beauty behind me I walk
> With beauty above me I walk
> With beauty around me I walk
> It has become beauty again.

You may have heard that or a similar version of the very well-known Navajo prayer called "The Beauty Way." I am not Native and I am not Navajo, but I always think of that prayer when I have traveled to the American Southwest. To me, it is the ineffable beauty of sky and earth, of mountain and canyon, of history and people and culture that makes me want to return again and again. The Southwest possesses a beauty that is, indeed, before me and behind me, above me, and around me. I think that beauty in part explains why the sites I will discuss in this chapter are among the most highly visited of our national parks and monuments, and why they draw in visitors from all over the world for whom the Native Southwest simply embodies American history and the American experience on so many levels. So put on your hiking books, slather yourself with sunscreen, bring lots of water, and don't mind the scorpions. Let's take a little journey and visit the landscape and the First People of the American Southwest.

First Encounters

The Spaniard Francisco Vázquez de Coronado was the governor of a province in New Spain (Mexico) in the mid-sixteenth century. Coronado had heard rumors of the existence of enormous quantities of gold in seven cities to the north. His expedition in search of the so-called Seven Cities of Gold in 1540 resulted in the first encounter by the Spanish with the Native People of what would become the four states of the American Southwest: Arizona, New Mexico, Utah, and Colorado. His are the first written descriptions we have of large and impressive pueblos holding multiple families and configured like modern apartment houses, surrounded by well-tended agricultural fields burgeoning with maize, beans, and squash. This cultural pattern that included the construction of large, multifamily, stone and adobe pueblos and an economic system reliant on agriculture already had very deep roots in the Southwest when Coronado reported on it.

Discovering the Southwest

Following Coronado and other Spanish conquistadores, Catholic missionaries arrived in the American Southwest in the sixteenth century in great numbers, saw and wrote about Native People living in the region, and reported the presence of apparently ancient "ruins." Unlike in the American Midwest and Southeast, the Spanish visitors to the American Southwest for the most part recognized that the living people they encountered were the descendants of those who had constructed those buildings that now lay in ruins.

When, following the Spanish, Anglos arrived in the Southwest, this same pattern of first encounters was replicated. Some of those encounters between, first, the explorers, and then the colonists and archaeological sites were accidental and incidental. For example, an agency of the federal government, the Army Corps of Topographical Engineers (which still exists as the Army Corps of Engineers), had as one of its major functions the collection of information about the Southwest, explicitly looking for places where the government might build roads and establish railway routes. Included in those expeditions were naturalists who could record the plant and animal resources in the region. There also were geologists whose purpose was to investigate the area for minerals and other natural resources. Among the things those scientists encountered and recorded were archaeological sites that included freestanding pueblos, structures built into cliffs, and lots of rock art. Photography was in its infancy and required quite a bit of heavy, finicky, and specialized equipment, often making it impractical to photograph these places. So the corps actually embedded artists in their expeditions who, in the manner of court reporters, produced initial drawings of the places they encountered. Those same artists then went on to produce painted images based on their drawings.

As did many European travelers beginning in the late 1500s, a leader of one of those army expeditions, Lieutenant James H. Simpson, and his embedded artist, the very talented Richard H. Kern, left their signatures at the base of a large stone promontory in New Mexico in 1849. The Zuni call the place A'ts'ina, the Place of Writing on the Rock. A'ts'ina is today known by its Spanish name, El Morro, and it is a national monument open to the public. And sure enough, the marks left by Simpson and Kern in their "I was here" moment 175 years ago are still there for all to see. It's all kind of meta, with the pair mentioning in *their* inscription that while they were there, they "visited and copied" all of the other inscriptions.

> Lt. J.H. Simpson & R.H. Kern Artist,
> visited and copied these inscriptions,
> September 17–18, 1849

Following these explorations by representatives of federal agencies in the mid-1800s, and inspired by their reports of seemingly ancient remains, experienced and trained archaeologists, often at the behest of the Smithsonian Institution in Washington, D.C., and the American Museum of Natural History in New York City, sought out the places where the ancestors of the Native People living in the Southwest had left behind sometimes enormous, freestanding pueblos, amazingly impressive cliff dwellings, and lyrical and engaging rock art, etched or painted onto expansive sandstone or volcanic rock faces (see chapter 16). I'll be highlighting a lot of the most impressive and informative of those places in this chapter.

A Note About "Discovery"

Much in the manner that Columbus is credited with discovering America (chapter 4), unfortunately, you will also read that European explorers and colonists "discovered" the archaeological sites I will discuss here. But that's simply not true. There is no great break in Native history. Native People have lived in the Southwest for more than twenty thousand years (see my discussion of the White Sands footprints in chapter 5). Of course the Native People already living in the region when Europeans arrived were well aware of these places and features and considered some of them sacred as places inhabited by the spirits of their ancestors. In multiple instances, it was those Native People who expressly alerted white visitors to the existence of these sites, sometimes even personally taking them there.

Perhaps the most egregious example, if only for its banality, is this. In the late nineteenth and early twentieth centuries, Byron Cummings was the head of the archaeology program at the University of Arizona and John Wetherill was a member of an archaeologically active family whose name is intimately associated with the fabulous cliff dwellings of Mesa Verde in Colorado (discussed later in this chapter). Cummings and Wetherill combined forces in the summer of 1909 to explore Tsegi Canyon in northeastern Arizona in their search for archaeological sites.

Cummings and Wetherill were spectacularly successful and one of the sites they "discovered," Betatakin (Navajo for "Hillside House"), is so impressive it is now showcased as part of Navajo National Monument. The place is truly amazing, featuring a spectacular, multistoried, nine-hundred-year-old pueblo nestled in a soaring alcove in the red rock cliff (Figure 14.1). It really is a breathtaking site, a testament to the Native American architects responsible for its design.

You can still read in multiple places about how Cummings and Wetherill "discovered" Betatakin; the National Park Service included that assertion in the pamphlet about the park that it published in 1947. Even

FIGURE 14.1. Close shot of the breathtaking Betatakin cliff dwelling, located in what is now Navajo National Monument in Arizona. This site was not discovered by John Wetherill or Byron Cummings, though they are sometimes so credited. Kenneth L. Feder

today, lots of websites repeat this claim (for example, the *Encyclopedia Britannica*).[1] But that is a comical mischaracterization of what happened.

Here's the real deal as the National Park Service now clarifies it. Cummings, who had brought along his wife and kid, and Wetherill, who had brought along his kids, were exploring Tsegi Canyon, expressly looking for an impressive, natural stone arch they had been told about, a great "rock rainbow" in fact today called Rainbow Bridge. Along the way, they stopped at the homestead of a Navajo man whose name was Nedi Cloey. When Cloey's wife (whose name we do not know) heard that the white men were looking for ruins, she approached Cummings's wife, Louisa, and told her of an impressive dwelling at the base of a cliff located up a side canyon about two miles away. Cloey's wife made it very clear to Louisa that the place had actually been brought to her attention years ago by her two little kids, who came across it while they were wandering the canyon tending sheep. Cummings was intrigued and excited, going so far as to pay the Cloeys' son-in-law, Clatsozen Benully, five dollars to take them to the site that today generates so much interest; I've been there and it is absolutely stunning.

So it certainly wasn't discovered by Cummings and Wetherill. It was "discovered" years before their expedition by two Navajo kids (and almost certainly they weren't the first to encounter it, so "discovered" isn't the correct word here anyway), and Cummings and Wetherill paid the husband of one of those then grown-up kids five bucks to take them to it. By the way, another impressive site in Navajo National Monument, Inscription House, was also encountered by Cummings and Wetherill. Did they discover that one? Nope. They weren't even the first Europeans to see it; their kids found the following inscription on one of the walls of the dwelling: "1661 *Anno Domini*," memorializing the date that an anonymous Spanish explorer encountered the place.

My point? I will avoid crediting people other than Native Americans for the discovery of the sites I discuss in this book for this simple reason: Euro-Americans didn't discover the sites.

Dendrochronology: I Talk to the Trees

A number of the dates I cite in this chapter were obtained from the technique called dendrochronology, commonly referred to as tree ring dating. Now, you're likely familiar with the fact that many tree species add one tree ring each year they are alive. So if you cut down a tree and count the number of rings, you can tell with some degree of certainty how old the tree was when it was cut down. Just count the rings.

Okay, that's interesting if you're an arborist, but another characteristic of tree rings, at least in some areas of the world, including the American Southwest, is that the width of each ring a tree lays down varies by the amount of rain that falls in each year. If there's a lot of rain, the ring is wide. If there's very little rain, the ring is thin. Nearly all the trees in a region will show the same proportional ring widths each year. Further, the overall sequence of rings over a long period of time is unique; the exact number and sequence of thick, medium, and thin rings doesn't ever repeat itself. If there's a ten-year-long drought in a region, the ten very thin rings laid down by all of the trees there likely never appear again. That's a key feature.

The way in which dendrochronology becomes very useful in archaeological dating begins with a living tree whose rings are collected by boring through it from its bark toward its center all the way to the ring laid down in its first year of life, extracting a sample, and then counting and examining the pattern of ring widths through time. Next the same process is applied to trees that are no longer alive—for example, a log in an old cabin. The derived sequences for the living and the dead trees are then compared for any sign of an overlap showing the same patterned sequence of thin and thick rings. If there's overlap, that means the trees were both alive during at least a part of the other's existence. This allows us to determine the actual year in which the tree in the cabin was cut down. For example, if the final sequence of thick and thin rings from the cabin log matches closely with the pattern of thick and thin rings in the first ten years of the living tree's life, we have a firm anchor, the living tree, to use in dating the year the dead tree was cut down. Counting from the current ring in the living tree to the period of ring sequence overlap allows us to determine a year for the cabin log's final ring.

In that way, we can at least determine the year each of the logs in the cabin was cut down, which tells us the age of the cabin itself. Now we can continue the process of looking at the rings in dead trees, looking for overlap in the sequence of ring widths and continuing to count backward. This process of searching for overlap in unique thick and thin sequences proceeds further back in time and then further still. In this way, in the American Southwest, a sequence of about thirteen thousand rings has been determined; this is called the master sequence. With that sequence in hand, any dead tree from the region can be matched to the master sequence and, in at least most cases, the precise year (over the course of about 13,000 years) that the tree was cut down can be calculated.

Where Native People used logs and where those logs have been preserved—both of these apply in the American Southwest—we can core the logs used in, for example, the construction of great houses and cliff dwellings and compare those tree ring width sequences with the master sequence. Assuming the logs were used in construction soon after they were harvested, we can reasonably apply that date to the pueblos themselves.

Sure, there are complications, including possible stockpiling of logs for later use, the reuse of old timbers in construction, and the use of new logs in a renovation project. This is why dates for the construction of a dwelling are based on tree ring sequences from multiple construction timbers. But there is no more accurate and no more precise a method for dating a structure and, by implication, the site itself.

Diversity and Commonalities

The Native People of the Southwest about one thousand years ago were generally divided into four similar yet distinctive archaeological cultures whose core territories are more or less geographically distinguishable: Ancestral Puebloan (formerly called Anasazi), Hohokam, Mogollon, and Sinagua (Map 14.1).

As noted, the lifeways of these groups, though far from indistinguishable, were nevertheless very similar, and they all trace to the Desert Archaic culture briefly discussed in chapter 8. They relied on a similar agricultural base of maize, beans, and squash and their architecture exhibits some fundamental commonalities. Nevertheless, they differ sufficiently in their details—in what is admittedly a sort of "inside archaeology" way—that, while anyone other than a specialist might not immediately recognize those differences or think that they amount to much of anything, it is at least plausible that were we to go back in time, the people themselves would generally agree with these distinctions. In a "Yeah, those are relatives, but they're not us" sort of way.

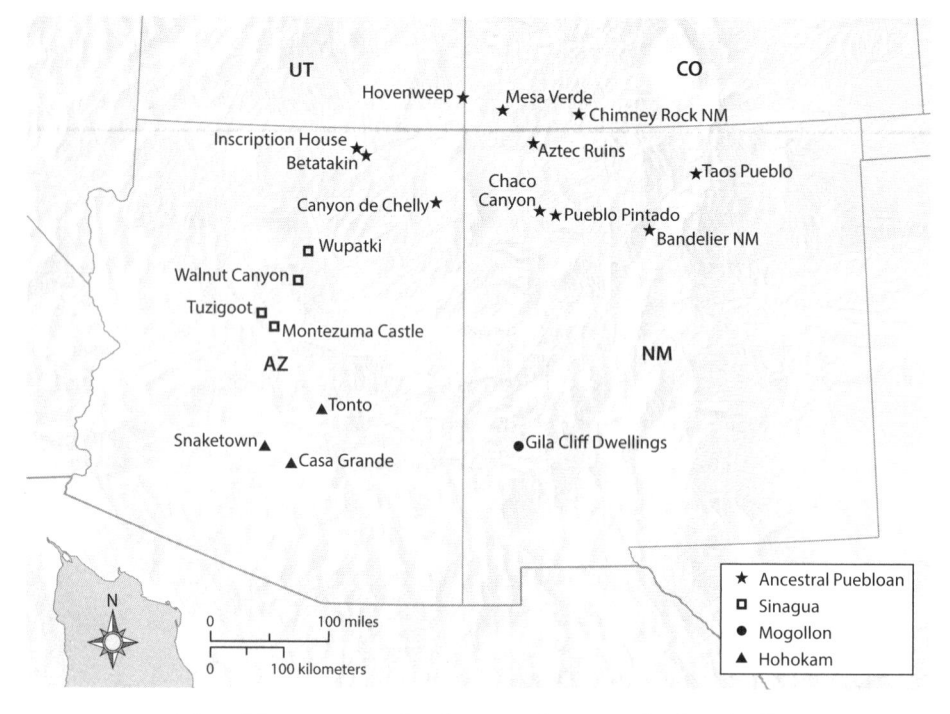

MAP 14.1. Map of the American Southwest with sites and cultural affiliation indicated. Kenneth L. Feder

Ancestral Puebloans: 100–1600 CE

Let's start with the Ancestral Puebloans. As noted, they used to be called Anasazi, but there was always a problem with that name. To begin, Anasazi is not a word in the language of the descendant people, the Pueblo Indians and their various subgroups, including the Hopi and the Zuni. Here's the key issue: Anasazi is a Navajo word. The Navajo and Hopi especially have a contentious history. Perhaps predictably, when the Navajo pointed out the abandoned great houses and cliff dwellings in or near their homeland in northeast Arizona to Europeans, they described the people who had made those buildings as Anasazi, which can be translated as "enemy ancestors." Now, some modern Navajo object to that translation, asserting that it just means "ancient ones." A Navajo man I spoke to, in fact, took umbrage at the "enemy ancestors" translation, substituting it with "ancient people who have turned to dust." I'm not sure who is right, and I certainly am not a Navajo speaker. But it doesn't matter. To be fair to the modern Pueblo people, the label used to name their ancestors should not be given by a different people, even if ultimately the term is judged to be relatively innocuous. This is why most, though not all, archaeologists use the term Ancestral Puebloan for these Native People.

Draw a flattened oval with the Four Corners region of the United States at its center and you've inscribed the home territory of the Ancestral Puebloans (see Map 14.1). Four Corners is the only place in the U.S. where four states meet at right angles, those four states being Arizona, New Mexico, Utah, and Colorado. It's located on the Navajo reservation and, the last time I checked, costs eight bucks to visit. Each year, about 250,000 people avail themselves of the opportunity to see a plaque on the ground denoting what really is an arbitrary location. Anyway, folks line up for the opportunity to have a photo taken with them sitting on the plaque so they can tell their friends and relatives that their butt is in four states at the same time. I don't want to get all judgy or anything, but in an area with piercingly beautiful blue skies, breathtaking geology, and fascinating archaeology, if you want to take the time and pay eight bucks to sit your butt in four states (eight bucks, four states, two butt cheeks; you do the math) AT THE SAME TIME, well, you do you. But really? Oh, and by the way, while the marker is now the legally accepted location where those four states meet, the surveyor who established the location for that marker in 1868 actually messed up and put it eighteen hundred feet away from where he was supposed to.

There are lots of very specific details used to define the people who live in that oval area around Four Corners, the Ancestral Puebloans, but the most important features that define the culture are the construction of large, multistory, stone and adobe buildings called great houses as well as cliff dwellings; a heavy reliance on the cultivation of maize, beans, and squash; long-distance trading networks; and the production of a distinctive kind of pottery with black, geometric designs painted on a white clay body. The modern descendants of the Ancestral Puebloans include nineteen sovereign communities living in pueblos in northern New Mexico, the Hopi people who live on their own reservation in Arizona, and the Zuni people who live at Zuni Pueblo (also called Halona) in New Mexico. Showing the level of continuity exhibited by Native history, the large structure called Taos Pueblo in northern New Mexico was built about six hundred years ago, is considered an Ancestral Puebloan great house, and is still occupied by the Puebloan people. Taos is open to the public and is a wonderful place to visit and commiserate with living Hopi (Red Willow) people who are proud of their history and heritage, and many of them enjoy sharing that history and heritage with visitors. Taos Pueblo is a place where the beauty of a preserved, maintained, and occupied great house can be seen up close. It is listed on the United Nations World Heritage List.[2]

Mogollon: 200–1450 CE

The Mogollon division of Native American culture in the Southwest is geographically centered south of the Ancestral Puebloans, especially the mountainous canyon region of western New Mexico, eastern Arizona, and northwestern Texas and extending into northern Mexico (see Map 14.1). Some Mogollon houses are pit houses, semi-subterranean structures. Also, because the Mogollon lived in a rugged territory, like the Ancestral Puebloans they built many of their later homes in niches in cliffs. The largest and most architecturally impressive of the Mogollon cliff houses are Gila Cliff Dwellings in southwestern New Mexico (Figure 14.2).

Perhaps one of the clearest differences, from an archaeological perspective, between Mogollon and the other named Southwestern groups is in their ceramics, particularly the style called Mimbres. Like the Ancestral Puebloan pottery, Mimbres is mostly black paint on white, and while the Mogollon painted often intricate geometric designs on their pottery, in their distinctive Mimbres style they also painted whimsical animal forms on their dishes, cups, and bowls, including images of insects, snakes, rabbits, bighorns, lizards, fish, and birds (Figure 14.3). It's really quite beautiful.

FIGURE 14.2. One of the Gila Cliff dwellings, located in a national monument in New Mexico. The people who lived in the Gila Cliff dwellings are, based on their artifact styles and architecture, considered to represent the Mogollon culture. Kenneth L. Feder

A subgroup of the Mogollon culture is the Jornada Mogollon. They produced the distinctive rock art that festoons the volcanic boulders in what is now called the Three Rivers Petroglyph Site in southern New Mexico. Today the site is administered by the Bureau of Land Management (a federal agency), and the twenty thousand or so individual petroglyph images are open to the public. I've been there four times and always

FIGURE 14.3. A stunning example of Mimbres ceramics. The combination of black designs on white clay, the sometimes intensely detailed geometric designs, and the often whimsical animals make Mimbres uniquely identifiable and truly beautiful. Andreas Praefcke. Wikimedia Commons.

find images I've never seen before. Among those images are lots of insects, snakes, rabbits, bighorns, lizards, fish, and birds. The subjects in many of the Jornada Mogollon petroglyphs at Three Rivers are similar both in their identity and in their style to the designs on Mimbres ceramics. See chapter 16 for a more detailed look at Three Rivers rock art.

Hohokam: 300–1500 CE

The Hohokam division of culture in the Southwest is located in southern Arizona and nestled immediately to the west of the border generally used to demarcate the Ancestral Puebloans to the north and the Mogollon to the south (see Map 14.1).

As seen at the Hohokam communities at Snaketown and Casa Grande, both located near the modern city of Phoenix, the two most distinguishing features of their culture are their reliance on and perfection of the art of irrigation and their trading connections to Mesoamerican societies to the south.

To a far greater degree than any of the other manifestations of culture in the American Southwest more than a thousand years ago, the Hohokam were expert engineers of water management. In a region far too dry for an agricultural system reliant on rain falling directly onto their fields, the Hohokam designed, built, and maintained sometimes enormous networks of canals. They derived much of the water for their agricultural fields from the Salt and Gila Rivers, and Hohokam habitation sites are concentrated in those river valleys. To give you an example of the extent of some of those irrigation networks, in the geological basin in which the city of Phoenix is located, the primary channel of the canal—dug entirely by the Hohokam people beginning in 600 CE—was 5 meters (15 feet) deep and 14 meters (45 feet) across. Secondary and tertiary channels brought water even farther from the Salt and Gila Rivers. The combined length of all of the irrigation channels in the Phoenix basin is estimated to be about 800 kilometers (500 miles). It is further estimated that the resulting network of water channels could have irrigated, at its peak in about 1300 CE, more than 400 square kilometers (100,000 acres). It is fair to say that the Hohokam made the desert bloom through the application of their sophisticated irrigation technology. It is estimated that the previously dry desert land could, at the network's peak, produce enough food to feed as many as eighty thousand people.[3]

Another feature of Hohokam village sites are oval masonry enclosures, generally about 30 meters (100 feet) long and 15 meters (50 feet) wide, surrounded by low walls about a meter high and with openings at either end of the long axis through which a person can enter and exit. There are a couple hundred of these enclosed spaces at Hohokam village sites, and they are hypothesized to have been used in the playing of a ball game, likely inspired by the ball courts seen at sites south of the border. It is believed that the idea for a ritualized ball game—a sort of cross between soccer (you couldn't use your hands) and basketball where the goal was to shoot a rubber ball through a vertically oriented stone hoop—originated in Mesoamerica. The Mesoamerican version of the game has some brutal aspects, including the sacrifice of at least some members of the losing team.

Sinagua: 500–1425 CE

If you place a point at the very impressive volcanic cone today called Sunset Crater, now the centerpiece of Sunset Crater Volcano National Monument, located about 24 kilometers (15 miles) north-northeast of the city of Flagstaff, Arizona, you have pinpointed the geographic center of the Sinagua people. You've also identified the site of a catastrophic but crucial event in defining and distinguishing the Sinagua as a distinct and vibrant element of cultural developments in the Southwest, the explosive eruption of the volcano that resulted in the creation of Sunset Crater.

Positioned at the margins of the territories of both Ancestral Puebloan culture and the Hohokam, the Sinagua began their moment in history as a group of Archaic Period (chapter 8) hunters and gatherers who slowly added elements of agriculture to their subsistence quest, lived in pit houses in small villages, and made black-and-white ceramics in a style they likely borrowed from the Ancestral Puebloans. In an area so dry it was named by Spanish interlopers *sin agua*, meaning "without water," bestowing on the Native People a name that continues to be used to identify and define them, the people built irrigation works to supplement the meager amount of rain that watered their crops. Here again, this practice likely was inspired by contact with another set of neighbors, the Hohokam.

There might be little else to say about the Sinagua but for the fact that between 1064 and 1067 CE, the Sunset Crater volcano erupted and—while, yes, it had some immediately catastrophic consequences, especially to anyone in the immediate path of its devastation—once the volcano became quiescent, people recognized that the soil in the region had become dramatically better for agriculture as a result of the ashfall. Coincidentally, rainfall increased in the region and agriculture became far more productive.

FIGURE 14.4, COLOR PLATE 5. The multiroomed, multistory great house called Wupatki. Considered to have been built by the Sinagua people. Kenneth L. Feder

At this point, the Sinagua produced a cultural amalgam, further combining elements of Ancestral Puebloan and Hohokam patterns. For example, 24 kilometers (15 miles) north of the crater they built the Wupatki Great House, an impressive, three-story pueblo with more than one hundred rooms (Figure 14.4, Color Plate 5).

The builders used a red sandstone, available as flat slabs in the immediate vicinity of its construction. Beyond the clearly different color of the raw material, Wupatki's architectural style certainly is reminiscent of the general appearance of at least some of the enormous great houses clustered in Chaco Canyon in northern New Mexico; I'll talk more about Chaco later in this chapter. A number of smaller pueblos, all within walking distance of Wupatki, dot the landscape. By counting up these sites and all of their rooms, it has been estimated that by fifty or sixty years after the eruption, the population of the general area around the Wupatki pueblo exceeded two thousand people.

A significant feature at Wupatki is an elongated oval enclosure demarcated by a low-lying masonry wall. Yup, it's a ball court. But ball courts

FIGURE 14.5, COLOR PLATE 6. Montezuma Castle in Arizona. It may not be the largest cliff dwelling, but it certainly is one of the most impressive and accessible. This is another Sinagua site. Kenneth L. Feder

aren't part of the Ancestral Puebloan tradition. This element of Sinaguan tradition likely was borrowed from or inspired by the Hohokam.

Some of the Sinagua appear to have migrated southward, searching for literally greener pastures, which they found 113 kilometers (70 miles) to the south-southwest in the Verde Valley, literally the "Green Valley." There they built the 110-room pueblo called Tuzigoot (a national monument) on the top of a hill overlooking the Verde River. From a distance Tuzigoot resembles a medieval castle.

They also built readily defendable cliff dwellings, including the absolutely stunning Montezuma Castle, a twenty-room, three-story pueblo built into a natural alcove about 27 meters (90 feet) up from the base of a cliff and adjacent to a permanent water source, Beaver Creek (Figure 14.5, Color Plate 6). It really is a stunning bit of architecture, and its location is breathtaking.

Montezuma Castle was one of our country's first national monuments, granted that honor by President Teddy Roosevelt in 1906, the same year the American Antiquities Act was approved by Congress. That law enables the president of the United States to designate places as "national monuments," providing those places with protection and preservation. Most presidents since the act's passage have availed themselves of that power and named national monuments.

The Sinagua built a very different set of cliff dwellings in Walnut Canyon (another national monument) in Arizona. There, a series of niches were eroded into the softer layers in what is now a narrow and deep canyon (about 120 meters, or 400 feet, from top to bottom). Where the niches were tall and deep enough, the Sinagua builders used the tops as ceilings and the backs as the rears of their structures. The Sinaguans then built a masonry wall to serve as the front of each house, then added masonry walls perpendicular to the front walls and backs of the niches, creating a series of about three hundred rooms making up eighty separate apartments of three or four rooms each.

It would have been a real challenge to live in Walnut Canyon. Just commuting to agricultural fields on the top of the canyon would have been time consuming and even a little treacherous. Bringing in water and firewood would have been tedious. Let's not even talk about the chore of keeping kids from falling over the narrow edges of the pathways adjacent to their homes. But their residences would have been pretty difficult for invaders to attack. Having been there, I can also attest that the interiors of the unique structures are significantly cooler than outside them.

A "Lost World" Called Chaco

Sir Arthur Conan Doyle, who is best known for his fifty-six short stories and four novels sharing the exploits of the great "consulting detective" Sherlock Holmes, was a prolific writer. One of his non-Holmes works is a 1912 novel about an imaginary mesa deep in the heart of Brazil where remnant populations of dinosaurs still roamed. He titled the book *The Lost World*. In the end, it wasn't really "lost" at all. A hardy group of explorers led by the rather eccentric Professor Challenger found and explored that world in the novel.

I have used the phrase "lost world" in this section's heading because it seems like a poetically melancholic way to phrase it. However, in truth I am using the adjective "lost" ironically, thus the scare quotes. The Chaco world was never lost, at least not to Native People living in the region. They knew of its presence as a vortex of sacred power, a center where the ancestors continued to communicate with their descendants. While not lost, it initially was unknown to non-Native Spanish and later Anglo explorers, missionaries, and settlers. So it was not a lost world but a new one to these invaders. Let's explore this new world now.

A Not Lost World Called Chaco

It was and continues to be quite a haul getting to Chaco Culture National Historical Park. Today, it takes patience, commitment, and a casual attitude about your rental car's shock absorbers. The road we most recently took leading to the park originates in Grants, New Mexico. From Grants it's a 134-kilometer (83 mile) slog to the visitors' center that takes just about two hours. While, under ordinary (dry) conditions, you don't really need a four-wheel- or all-wheel-drive vehicle to get there, much of the route is a pretty crappy, distressingly unmaintained dirt road with lots of pot holes, exposed bedrock, and washboard surfaces that rattle your teeth and vibrate the hell out of your insides. It gets even worse if it rains. The resulting clayey muck that constitutes the road surface can make the road impassable. While noises have been made about paving the route, the inherent challenge in accessing Chaco actually has its positive points. Sure it's hard to get to, but as a result the site is not inundated by crowds and, especially if you take one of the longer hikes available in the park, you may have parts of the place all to yourself. Before COVID-19, yearly attendance at Chaco peaked in 2018 at fifty-seven thousand, which, broken down, means that, on a weekly basis, only a little more than a thousand people a week visited Chaco, really a very small number for the 138 square kilometers (53 square miles) that constitute the park. Compare that with Mesa Verde (which is 1.5 times larger in area), where the attendance in 2018 was ten times that. I highlight Mesa Verde later in this chapter.[4]

GREAT HOUSES AND CLIFF CASTLES   243

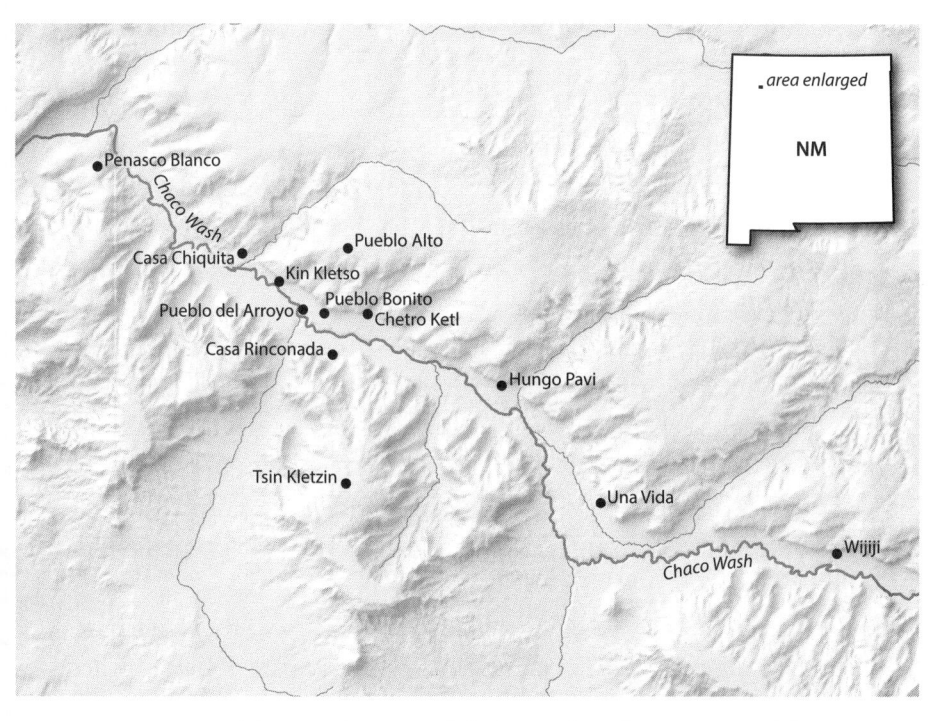

MAP 14.2. Map of the great houses and the largest kiva (Casa Rinconada) in Chaco Canyon. Kenneth L. Feder.

Once you finally arrive at the entrance to Chaco Canyon, there is a paved park road that loops by and provides easy and direct access to some of the most impressive examples of the Chacoan great houses. These are impressively large, freestanding, multistory pueblos built primarily of sandstone bricks collected from the nearby canyon walls between about 850 and 1250 CE. Altogether there are about 12 great houses scattered across the relatively small area of Chaco Canyon itself and 150 additional great houses within the greater Chaco influence region (Map 14.2). The Chaco world was a very big deal.

As you walk around and even into these enormous structures, most built in the footprint of a giant *D*, there is an uncanny feeling that you have entered into another world and another time, a distinct moment and place where a unique culture of Native People lived, worked, and worshiped. The place, as the National Park Service describes it, was the "ceremonial, administrative, and economic center" of the region and its people.[5]

Chaco is indescribably beautiful and awe-inspiring, impressive and melancholy, both vibrant and haunted. As a modern person and perhaps especially as a non-Native person, I feel vaguely out of place there. Oh, it definitely draws me in, but I feel that I am at best a guest and at worst an intruder. It is somewhere else and "somewhen" else. It definitely produces an uncanny feeling in the mind of the visitor.

Its name, Chaco, likely derives from a map drawn in 1776 by the Spanish cartographer Bernardo de Pacheco where he labeled the place Chaca, which at the time meant "a large expanse of unexplored land, desert, plain or prairie."[6] The modern Hopi who descend from the people who built the great houses there call the place Yupkoyvi, "the place beyond the horizon," and I think that name applies both literally and figuratively.

Perhaps the earliest Anglo encounter with the world of Chaco occurred on August 26, 1849 (just 175 years ago), as part of the so-called Washington Expedition led by Lieutenant James H. Simpson. This is the same Simpson who, along with his embedded artist Richard Kern, left his signature at the place now called El Morro National Monument in western New Mexico during the same trip. Simpson's record of the expedition, which included some of Kern's work, was published in book form in 1852 as *Journal of a Military Reconnaissance from Santa Fé, New Mexico, to the Navaho Country*.[7] The book contains some wonderful examples of Kern's work, including his images of Chaco, Canyon de Chelly, El Morro, Taos Pueblo, and more. Kern's depictions of Chaco Canyon are splendid works of art representing moments frozen in time when the artist and the rest of the military contingent with which he was associated first encountered them. You can view many of them online.[8] There's also a wonderful book focusing on his life and art.[9] His original works can be seen at a number of museums, especially the Amon Carter Museum of American Art in Fort Worth, Texas.

Simpson and his troops were led by local guides, among whom were Carvajal, a Native Mexican man who lived in San Ysidro, New Mexico. He may have been a descendant of a Spanish soldier usually called Juan

FIGURE 14.6. The artist Richard Kern's drawing of Pueblo Pintado, the first Chaco outlier Lieutenant Simpson's expedition encountered on their way into Chaco Canyon itself.

de Victoria Carvajal, who arrived in Mexico in the late sixteenth century. Simpson mentions another of his guides, a Diné man named Sandoval, along with a handful of unnamed Pueblo people. After leaving Santa Fe, the guides brought Simpson and his crew to the site Carvajal called Pueblo Pintado. Called Kin Teel by the Navajo, Pueblo Pintado is a 135-room, three-story great house located about 26 kilometers (16 miles) east of the main cluster of great houses in Chaco Canyon. So for Simpson and his troops, Pueblo Pintado was an opening act for the amazing show that would begin when they entered the main canyon.

Simpson was amply impressed by the masonry produced by the builders of Pueblo Pintado, describing it as "a combination of science and art which can only be referred to a higher stage of civilization and refinement than is discoverable in the works of Mexicans and Pueblos of the present day."[10] Simpson's embedded artist Richard Kern produced a drawing of the building that was included in the published version of Simpson's journal (Figure 14.6).

Dendrochronology has been applied to some of the wooden logs that served as beams in the building. Those tree rings indicate that the pueblo was built in about 1060 CE. Today Pueblo Pintado is administered by the National Park Service as a detached, separate unit of Chaco Culture National Historical Park. It is accessible to the public from the modern, small Navajo community that bears the same name as the great house (Pueblo Pintado).

After he completed his detailed examination of Pueblo Pintado and thoroughly recorded what he observed, Simpson's expedition continued westward and entered into the main part of Chaco Canyon on August 27. Simpson mentions their initial encounter with the great house he called Weje-ge, now spelled Wijiji, which today is the farthest east of the great houses in the main unit of the park. On the next day, the crew continued west into the canyon, encountering and naming individual great houses including Una Vida, Hungo Pavie, Pueblo del Arroyo, Chetro Kettle, Pueblo Bonito, and Pueblo Peñasca Blanca (I have used the names and spellings supplied by Simpson in his journal).

Pueblo Bonito is by far the largest of the great houses anywhere in the Southwest and certainly earns that descriptor; it is a multitiered, freestanding structure five stories at its highest along the curved wall of this D-shaped structure (Figure 14.7, Color Plate 7). Archaeologists count more than eight hundred rooms in Pueblo Bonito, whose vast footprint covers 12,000 square meters (3 acres).

In his journal, Simpson notes the fact that the vast majority of the rooms in the great houses are rectangular. However, he also noted that each Chaco great house also had a number of circular rooms. Pueblo Bonito has the greatest concentration of these round spaces with about thirty-five of them. Most are built into the flat plaza provided by the roof of one of the lower tiers of the pueblo. As in the rest of the structure, the construction material consisted of stone gathered from the surrounding sandstone walls of the canyon that then was shaped into flat bricks.

Most of these round rooms are between 3 and 4.5 meters (10 and 15 feet) in diameter. Evidence shows that most had timber-framed, thatched roofs. The roofs were supported by either large wooden logs or masonry posts. The beams and posts were placed into sockets on the floor of the buildings, sometimes with large limestone discs set at the bottom, ostensibly to better distribute their weight. Most of these round structures also

FIGURE 14.7, COLOR PLATE 7. Largest of all the great houses in the American Southwest, Pueblo Bonito consisted of more than eight hundred rooms divided into apartments spread out across as many as five stories. This view is from the ridge overlooking the canyon. Kenneth L. Feder

had niches built into their curved walls. Large square and circular features are found on the floors of most of these round rooms, perhaps for storage, along with a hearth on their floors with a flat, upright stone acting as a heat deflector, what appears to be a ceremonial hole in the floor (the modern Hopi call it a *sipapu*, representing a hole to the underworld), and a bench in the form of a ring along the interior. Some of the largest of these circular structures are freestanding, not integrated into a great house structure, and semi-subterranean. Many of the largest of these rooms had additional rooms connected to them, also perhaps for storage. The largest of these independent structures in all of the Southwest is close to Pueblo Bonito. Called Casa Rinconada, it also contains an underground passageway leading from below the floor and outside the building into the interior, providing access up onto the floor (Figure 14.8).

There's no archaeological evidence that these circular rooms were inhabited; there's no debris of the kind we all accumulate just by living

FIGURE 14.8. Casa Rinconada is the largest kiva in Chaco Canyon and, for that matter, the largest of all kivas. You can see in the center back the subterranean entrance from which people, dressed as spirit beings, would enter the sacred space of the kiva during ceremonies. Kenneth L. Feder

in a place. There's no evidence of storage of much of anything either. If these round structures weren't bedrooms, living rooms, kitchens, or storage rooms, then what were they? Well, we know exactly what these structures were, their function, and even what the Native People called them because they were seen in use and Native People told Simpson, who reported, "At different points about the premises were three circular apartments sunk in the ground, the walls being masonry. These apartments the Pueblo Indians call *estuffas*, or places where the people held their political and religious meetings."[11]

Today, these round rooms are called kivas (kiva, singular) by the modern Pueblo people who still incorporate them into their religion. The smaller ones were gathering places for families, and the large ones served as community centers, potent combinations of houses of worship and houses of congress where ceremonies were conducted and political discussions were held.

Kivas have been called theaters where sacred ceremonies weren't just carried out, they were performed. Casa Rinconada in Chaco and a handful of huge kivas including the kiva at Aztec Ruins National Monument in northwest New Mexico are called great kivas. Casa Rinconada is the largest at about 24 meters (80 feet) in diameter. The misnamed Aztec Ruins site (it has nothing whatsoever to do with the Aztecs in Mexico in the fifteenth century) is considered to be a Chaco Outlier, a site similar in so many ways to the great houses at Chaco that it is deduced to have been part of the same polity or society as the Chaco great houses. Today you can experience the beautifully restored great kiva at Aztec. It engenders the same kind of feeling most get walking into any house of worship and really is quite impressive.

There are underground passageways up and into the great kivas that connect the mundane, outside world to the sacred world of spirits and ancestors residing within the kiva. They were both actual and symbolic pathways from the outside underworld to the interior and were used as entrances during ceremonies by costumed people representing spirit beings. Just imagine the dramatic scene in a night-darkened kiva, its interior illuminated only by a hearth fire and smoke filling the circular room, as, perhaps with drums beating, a human-sized spirit being rises up into the sacred realm of the kiva to perform a ceremony. It is a riveting scene and one likely repeated hundreds of times at Casa Rinconada.

And there's this: years ago I took a tour of Acoma—"Sky City"—a truly beautiful little Pueblo community in central New Mexico. One of Acoma's claims to fame is that it may be the oldest continuously occupied community in North America, having been occupied since about 700 CE (take that, St. Augustine, Plimouth, and Jamestown). Our guide was a very informative resident of the community. At one point during the tour, we walked by a structure she identified as one of the village kivas, which perplexed me a little. I wasn't perplexed that the people at Acoma have maintained their traditional use of kivas in their ceremonies, but there was something unexpected about this one. There was an old-school television satellite dish on the roof. I inquired, very politely I promise, about the use of the dish on the roof of a sacred space. Our guide smiled and responded bemusedly, "Oh, that's because this kiva is used by our men in their new religion. Football." And sure, that's funny, but it's also meaningful. In a sense, this kiva is being used as kivas always have been, as a place for people to meet, talk, commiserate, and get away from the vexing issues of everyday life.

Chaco was a central place, a capital of Ancestral Puebloan life. Surrounding this central place were "outliers," sites that match the architecture and material culture of the great houses in Chaco Canyon but are located outside that geographical core. Outliers include the aforementioned Pueblo Pintado in Arizona, Aztec Ruins in New Mexico, Hovenweep in Utah and Colorado, and the great houses and cliff dwellings of Canyon de Chelly in Arizona (that canyon is now inhabited by Navajo families).

Trade

All over the world, sometimes even thousands of years ago, people traveled great distances for valued raw materials or traded, sometimes across a long geographic string of intermediaries, to access useful stuff they wanted but that wasn't available locally. I have mentioned that the source for steatite bowls found on Long Island, New York may have been Connecticut (chapters 8 and 10) and that the copper found in Hopewell sites in Ohio (chapter 12) and Cahokia in Illinois (chapter 13) can be traced to Michigan and Wisconsin. Many past people were accomplished traders.

For example, people at Chaco and other sites in the Southwest used the iridescent, brightly colored feathers of macaws in their art and clothing. Macaws are tropical birds, native to rainforests, woodlands, and savannas in a swath from southern Mexico to northern Argentina. They are absolutely not native to the desert and semidesert conditions of the Southwest. Yet we find not only their teal, blue, yellow, and red feathers at places like Chaco Canyon but actually the bones of macaws there. It appears that, once the Chacoans became aware of the existence of their colorful feathers, likely through exploration to the south but also through traders who brought feathers or maybe even captive birds north, they managed to obtain living birds and created a breeding colony of closely related birds, based on DNA obtained from their bones.[12]

Another resource Chacoans obtained from a great distance and likely at great expense was a material near and dear to my heart: chocolate. A residue was noticed in a number of the 111 cylindrical jars found in a cluster of high-status burials in a crypt in Room 28 at Chaco, strikingly beautiful white vessels with painted black designs in geometric patterns. That residue was collected from the cups and subjected to a chemical analysis. The results indicated the material contained theobromine, a chemical found in cacao, the source of chocolate. Now, the "black drink" imbibed by people in Central America and the American Southwest wasn't the sweet chocolate beverage most of us are used to. No sugar was added, so it must have been bitter, and I wonder if people drank it at least in part for the caffeine buzz you get from it. Whatever the case, it reflects the existence of an active trading network in the American Southwest beginning more than a thousand years ago.

This raises an interesting question. What did the Chacoans have that traders from the south might want and could, using a modern term, monetize in their trading business? The most obvious answer to that question is the quite beautiful, richly blue and green and black stone that can be found across much of the Southwest but was largely unavailable in Mexico. I refer here to the semiprecious stone called by the Navajo, who use it to great effect in their jewelry, *Doo tl' izh ii*. Non-Native people like me call it turquoise. During my recent visit to Zuni Pueblo in New Mexico, the little shop and restaurant where we got breakfast and supplies had a sales display, intended for local Zuni jewelers, with a bunch of containers filled with varieties of green and blue stones with names like New Enchantment, Cerrillos, Castle, and Hachita. Here is just another example of the cultural continuity we see among Native Americans, perhaps especially in the Southwest.

Archaeologists have long known of the appreciation of the Native People of Mexico for turquoise. It is found in archaeological sites there in many different artworks, as beads, as tiles in mosaic masks, and as sculptures. However, sources for turquoise in Mexico are very few in number. So where did they obtain their turquoise?

When I was an undergraduate, I worked as an intern for my professor Phil Weigand, a specialist in the archaeology of western Mexico. Phil was interested in answering questions about turquoise sources and spent at least some of his summers scrambling through caves in the Southwest that were known to have turquoise. He brought some of that raw material back to his campus lab at the State University of New York at Stony Brook, now Stony Brook University.

Part of my job was to drill holes in that turquoise to create dust that was then sealed in ampules and placed in a research-focused nuclear reactor for irradiation at Brookhaven National Laboratory on Long Island. That process was carried out by the brilliant physicist Garman Harbottle, Weigand's coleader of the research team. When retrieved from the reactor, the turquoise could be "read" for all of the elements that made up the rock. That allowed the team to identify what amounts to a distinctive or even a unique chemical signature for each turquoise source. The process was similar to how two geographically distinct obsidian sources were identified at the Lindenmeier site in Colorado (chapter 6). The trace element recovery technique used by Weigand and Harbottle is called neutron activation analysis and has been used by other researchers to obtain the chemical signatures of other raw materials.

With those unique and diagnostic signatures in hand, Weigand obtained access to actual artifacts found in West Mexico to apply the same analytical technique. This provided signatures for the turquoise artifacts. Those chemical signatures were then compared with their possible sources in the American Southwest. The result was exactly what was expected: most of the turquoise artifacts found in the West Mexico sample Weigand had obtained had been made from turquoise derived from Arizona and New Mexico.[13] Turquoise, therefore, had been at least one of the locally available and highly sought-after raw materials Chacoans used in trade for materials they wanted but had no direct access to. Trading was mutually beneficial and a reflection of an economic system that got people on both sides of the modern border between Mexico and the U.S. stuff that they wanted to obtain.

On the Road Again

Central places, places of pilgrimage, political capitals of nations; these locations all need a transportation system that allows merchants, traders, workers, and pilgrims to travel to and from them. Think of Grand Central Station in New York City, which I mentioned in chapter 13. It is no surprise, then, that the Chacoans built a series of roads, the combined extent of which exceeds 290 kilometers (180 miles), that facilitated travel and the movement of resources to the canyon and finished goods to the outside. Remember, Chaco Canyon was a social, economic, and political hub, and roads radiated out from it like the spokes of a wheel, both physically and ceremonially connecting people who were a part of the society. Think of the hub-and-spoke routing system of Southwest Airlines as an analogy. For Southwest, all routes lead to Denver. In ancient Italy, "all roads led to Rome." And in northwestern New Mexico beginning about twelve hundred years ago, "all roads led to Chaco Canyon."

The Chaco roads were more than simply a way to make travel easier. Among the features that define the roads are the following:

- At 9 meters (30 feet) in width for much of their extent, they are far wider than they needed to be to simply provide people with an avenue by which they could travel to the canyon. The roads were a huge project and an enormous amount of work was invested in their construction. But the Chacoans didn't attempt to minimize the amount of work they did on the roads; they didn't try to make them useful but with the least work necessary. That implies that something more was going on than simply creating a route of transportation or travel.
- When animals create pathways as part of their migratory patterns or simply as they move within their territory, they tend to take the path of least resistance—for example, circumventing areas

with steep slopes, either upward or down. When they encounter a steep hill or a steep drop, they tend to walk around it if they can—and if they're not mountain goats. Human beings often exploit those paths or trails when they make their own pathways. Even in many modern scenarios—and even with modern equipment when building highways—designers will avoid having their roads climb steep slopes or descend into deep canyons, preferring to circumvent them. It's simply easier to walk a little farther if, in so doing, you avoid a steep route. The Chacoans did not follow this simple rule or pattern. For them, it is clear, roads needed to be built in the straightest lines possible, and when that meant climbing straight up mountains or descending into washes or canyons, so be it. Rather than simply going around, they cut stairs directly into the rock or, when that wasn't possible, they constructed masonry steps. Some of these stone stairways can still be seen in Chaco as they descend from the mesa top into the canyon (Figure 14.9, Color Plate 8).

The fact that the Chacoan roads weren't constructed in such a way as to minimize the labor involved in making an otherwise quite useful system of serviceable roads, routes of travel that would have admirably suited practical purposes, suggests to some archaeologists that, at least, their function was not only utilitarian. One hypothesis proposes that the roadways leading to and from Chaco were at least in part, maybe even largely, symbols of the centrality of the canyon to the people who were a part of its polity. In other words, sure, the roads were useful—they certainly facilitated the transportation, for example, of the more than the estimated two hundred thousand (!) logs used in building the great houses and great kivas. Many of these logs were imported from the Zuni Mountains, 80 kilometers (50 miles) to the south of the canyon, and the Chuska Mountains, 80 kilometers to the west. But the roads were also symbolically meaningful, a physical manifestation of the spiritual connection of the people in the region to their ceremonial center, their central place where their political and religious leaders resided.

FIGURE 14.9, COLOR PLATE 8. Pictured here is one set of steps, carved into the bedrock, leading travelers into and then back out of Chaco Canyon. Kenneth L. Feder

Moving Stories

Of course, even with the existence of a route along which the enormous number of logs used in construction at Chaco may have been moved, we are still left with the question of how people, with no beasts of burden and no wheeled carts, could have accomplished the feat. The logs were quite heavy, and the estimated two hundred thousand used in construction of the Chacoan great houses is a lot of logs.

One possibility for accomplishing this feat has recently been tested. In what amounts to a preliminary feasibility study, a team of two people, physiologist Rodger Gram and undergraduate student James Wilson, paired up to attempt to jointly carry a 60-kilogram (130-pound) timber by suspending it from their foreheads with what's called a tumpline. The log actually was supported crossways on their backs, perpendicular to their direction of travel.[14] People all over the world have used tumplines to carry heavy burdens—for example, by resting the woven handle of a basket on their foreheads with the full basket resting on their backs. It took Gram and Wilson ten hours to carry the 2.5-meter (8-foot) timber along 24 kilometers (15 miles) of a dirt path serving as a model for a Chacoan road.

Now, that would have been a pretty small timber by Chaco standards, and the overall trip a thousand years ago would have been four or five times longer, but the task didn't kill the researchers (and, as far as I know, they didn't end up crushing any of their vertebrae). With a coordinated, trained, and experienced team the method might have worked for the Chacoans, though, it must be admitted, there is no direct evidence for the use of tumplines there. At least as a feasibility study, it was a successful application of experimental archaeology, in which modern researchers attempt to replicate an ancient technology. But my back hurts just thinking about it.

The most important takeaway, beyond how the logs may have been transported along the roads, is that, whatever their precise meaning and purpose to the Chacoans of nearly a thousand years ago, the roads are yet another example of their accomplishments, which also include their widespread trading networks and the construction of their monumentally scaled great houses. These accomplishments reflect their ability to organize the labor of hundreds and probably thousands of people. They also reflect their genius at designing and engineering enormously challenging work projects. The Chacoans were an impressive people indeed.

Curious, Not Baffled

Archaeologists hate it when, in relation to some new and perhaps unexpected discovery about Stonehenge or the pyramids, a clueless and hyperventilating headline writer claims that "archaeologists are baffled!" No, we are not stinking baffled about a fascinating new data point that probably adds incrementally to what we already know and have known for a long time about Stonehenge, the pyramids, or whatever.

Got it? But here's my admission: there is something about Chaco that I am willing to say that I do find at least somewhat, if not baffling, then at least intriguing. When archaeologists began working at Chaco in the twentieth century they speculated, as archaeologists do, about the population in the canyon. Their estimates were usually in the thousands. It makes sense when you consider that there are twelve great houses there, the largest of which consists of eight hundred rooms. The structures have multiple stories, each including an extraordinary number of often carefully shaped stone bricks, and some of the enormous number of very heavy wooden logs obtained for roof and ceiling beams had to be transported for tens of miles to the canyon. So it was assumed that only a settlement intended for lots and lots of people, probably numbering in the thousands, would have had the need and the human-power for so many structures with so many rooms. That seemed to make a lot of sense.

But there were always unanswered questions and skepticism about the size of Chaco's resident population. Most important, in a very dry region without a lot of arable land and no evidence of the use of irrigation to expand the agricultural productivity of the surrounding territory that is seen in other regions of the Native Southwest, there always were questions concerning the ability of the residents of Chaco to feed the inferred large, dense population in the canyon.

Then there is the pesky archaeological fact about trash. When large numbers of people live in proximity to one another, they produce enormous amounts of trash that they often accumulate in middens, which is just archaeology-speak for trash dumps. But here's the deal. There simply isn't anywhere near the amount of trash outside Pueblo Bonito or Hungo Pavi, or Chetro Ketl and the rest of the great houses, that you would see if the place had been densely occupied. Using this standard metric of archaeology, Chaco Canyon simply could not have had the human population size that was initially deduced from the combined number of living spaces available in the great houses.

And there it stands. Was Chaco purely an administrative and religious center where only a relatively few important leaders lived, died, and were buried, a place of pilgrimage for a large and dispersed population who congregated in large numbers there seasonally to build enormous and impressive structures that few would actually live in and that were used primarily for the purpose of communal worship? Maybe. Were the great houses of Chaco used mainly for storage, with participants in Chacoan society contributing food surpluses to feed the elite members of society and to redistribute during years of low agricultural yields as a consequence of, for example, drought? Did Chaco actually have a large population but archaeologists simply don't have a clue about whatever became of the mass of trash that its large population must have produced? So, yeah. Not baffled, but curious.

Chaco's Elites

Make no mistake: though the evidence simply doesn't support the presence of a large resident population at Chaco of the size that past archaeologists expected and that common sense (of non-Native People) might suggest, Chaco certainly wasn't a ghost town a thousand years ago. We know some people lived there and that some of those people appear to have been members of an elite class, based on burials excavated under the flooring of Pueblo Bonito.

I will discuss this evidence only briefly. There is some controversy about whether descendant people in the region were consulted sufficiently concerning the disinterment of their ancestors. That's never a good look in archaeology. I don't know the archaeologists involved and I am not privy to the details of the story. But I feel comfortable sharing this.

Between about 800 and 1130 CE, fourteen individuals were buried in a mortuary crypt located in what is designated Room 33 at Pueblo Bonito.[15] One of the excavated burials was of a male, and his remains were richly ornamented with a staggering trove of more than eleven thousand turquoise beads, thirty-three hundred shell beads, and bracelets and anklets.[16] That's a lot of very impressive stuff. In another of the Room 33 burials, the deceased was interred with fifty-eight hundred turquoise beads. In this same group burial, archaeologists recovered conch shells likely used as trumpets. Remember Chaco is nowhere near the coast—it is more than 720 kilometers (450 miles) from the nearest possible source for these shells, the Gulf of California—so clearly those had to be obtained through long-distance trade.

Along with recovering artifacts, the researchers also were able to extract genetic material in the form of mitochondrial DNA from fourteen of the people buried there. As noted previously (chapter 11), mitochondrial DNA (mtDNA) is housed in the mitochondria of our cells and passed down exclusively from mother to offspring. Of those fourteen individuals from whom mtDNA was recovered, nine could be shown to be very close relatives all in the female line. Nuclear DNA (that's the stuff you learned about in high school biology; it represents the genetic instructions found in the nucleus of each of your cells, and you inherit it from both of your parents) was recovered from six of the people buried there. The relationships of two pairs of those six could be identified precisely. One of those pairs was a mother and her daughter and the other pair was a grandmother and her grandson.

Finally, an analysis of the chemical components of the bones of the people buried in Room 33, particularly the strontium signature in those bones, which varies according to diet and region, indicates that among these fourteen folks and also among an additional forty-seven people whose remains were excavated in another group burial in Pueblo Bonito—so sixty-one people altogether—fifty-eight of them exhibited a signature that shows that they were local folks, likely born, raised, and dying either in the canyon or nearby.[17]

I began an earlier section by calling Chaco Canyon a "lost world" but have shown throughout my discussion here, I hope, that we are able to call Chaco not a lost world but one that has always been there as a part of history told by descendants and by the application of archaeological methods.

Castles in the Air

I've been to Mesa Verde National Park in Colorado a few times. It is a truly stunning and unique place. It's not surprising that Mesa Verde, along with being a national park, as mentioned a number of times in this book, is also one of the six Native American sites in the U.S. included on the World Heritage List of the United Nations.

I promise this is the last time I'll harp on this issue: Mesa Verde is another example in which settlers have been credited for discovering the place but didn't. Here, the tale is often told of Richard Wetherill, one of the sons of a wealthy rancher in southwestern Colorado, and his brother-in-law, Charlie Mason, who were out on horseback on a cold and snowy December day in 1888 looking for some of their wayward cattle. As the story is told, they approached the edge of the mesa, looked down into a canyon they had not seen or explored before, and marveled at the remarkable remains of what looked like a castle hidden in a niche at the bottom. It was a stunning sight in the newly fallen snow. All thoughts of finding errant cows were abandoned, and the two scrambled down the cliff to investigate. And yeah, I've been there and I'm sure they were stunned by what they saw.

It's a romantic story of rugged cowboys getting first distracted and then excited by archaeology, but not much of it is true. A professional photographer, William Henry Jackson, had already photographed some of the cliff dwellings there more than ten years earlier, in 1874. Beyond this, the Wetherills were grazing their cattle in that location with the permission of local Native People, a group called the Utes. It was their territory at the time and they knew it well. It is even recorded that one of those Utes, a man called Acowitz, had very explicitly told the Wetherill clan that there were large, abandoned houses perched in the cliffs that demarcated the canyons cutting through the mesa and that the Ute people didn't like visiting them because they were haunted: "Deep in that canyon and near its head are many houses of the old people—the Ancient Ones. One of those houses, high, high in the rocks, is bigger than all the others. Utes never go there, it is a sacred place."[18]

So yes, the Wetherills were responsible for announcing the presence of the cliff dwellings in Mesa Verde and for "excavating" or "looting" (both of those terms apply to what they did) artifacts from some sites there, and they then became tour guides to the sites. But they didn't really discover them. They just advertised and monetized them.

By the way, once word got out about the remarkable cliff dwellings at Mesa Verde and a host of curious visitors arrived to see them for themselves and maybe pick up an artifact or two as souvenirs, the

Wetherills attempted unsuccessfully to convince the federal government to help protect and preserve the cliff dwellings. The patriarch of the family, B. K. Wetherill, wrote a letter to the Smithsonian Institution in 1890 exhorting them to use the power of the federal government to protect the site: "We are particular to preserve the buildings, but fear, unless the Govt. sees proper to make a national park of the Canyons, including Mesa Verde, the tourists will destroy them."[19] His letter went unanswered. It actually took the lobbying of a consortium of women's organizations in Colorado that were organized by two women, the writer Virginia McClurg and Colorado activist Lucy Peabody, to get it done. McClurg and Peabody had an eventual falling-out over whether Mesa Verde should be designated a state or a federal park (McClurg thought it would be better administered by the state). Peabody's perspective won out and President Teddy Roosevelt designated Mesa Verde a national park in 1906. As a result of the roles of McClurg, Peabody, and the women's groups they conscripted for help, Mesa Verde has been called "the women's park."

Today, a lot of Mesa Verde is very visitor friendly. There is a paved loop road around the mesa with pullouts where folks who don't want to do a lot of hiking can park, walk short, well-maintained trails, and obtain spectacular views of the iconic palaces secreted in the cliffs demarcating one of the canyons that cut through the mesa.

Life in the Cliffs

The National Park Service highlights some of the most striking of the cliff dwellings at Mesa Verde, including Cliff Palace, Balcony House, Square Tower House, Step House, and Long House, but these represent only a tiny sample of the "castles in the air" (Figure 14.10, Color Plate 9).

There are some six hundred individual cliff dwellings scattered across two mesas: Chapin Mesa, named for F. H. Chapin, one of the first to publish about the cliff dwellings there; and Wetherill Mesa, named for the guy who didn't discover it but who certainly brought it to the world's attention. You will note that neither canyon is named for Acowitz, the Ute who first mentioned its existence to the Wetherills, nor for Virginia

FIGURE 14.10, COLOR PLATE 9. Square Tower House in Mesa Verde. It really does look like a castle tucked into a natural niche in the vertical wall of the mesa. The view from the top of the mesa (shown here) is spectacular. The National Park Service also conducts guided tours down into Square Tower House. Kenneth L. Feder

McClurg or Lucy Peabody, whose tireless efforts led to the protection and preservation of the cliff dwellings of Mesa Verde. Oh well.

Cliff Palace, the first of the cliff dwellings encountered by Wetherill and Mason, is located at the base of a canyon that runs through Chapin Mesa (Figure 14.11, Color Plate 10). It is enormous, stretching about 90 meters (300 feet—the length of an American football field) across a natural rock alcove located just below the top of the mesa.

My thesaurus simply isn't big enough to help me come up with all of the right superlatives to describe the place—beautiful, impressive, amazing, gorgeous, brilliant, spectacular, remarkable, effing incredible (okay, that wasn't in my thesaurus). Those all apply but somehow don't sufficiently convey the incredible beauty of Cliff Palace. There are about 150 rooms, 21 of which are kivas, perhaps each serving as the ceremonial space for an extended family. There are six or seven square towers (depending on how you actually identify a tower) and one delicate round

FIGURE 14.11, COLOR PLATE 10. Cliff Palace is the largest and perhaps the most beautiful of the six hundred or so cliff dwellings in Mesa Verde. It was the first of the cliff dwellings encountered by Richard Wetherill and Charlie Mason, having been told about them by local Native People. Kenneth L. Feder

tower in the structure. An Ancestral Puebloan artist decorated the interior near the top of the tallest of the square towers with a mural all in red paint of what appears to be the distant horizon as seen from the location of Mesa Verde. It is estimated that at its peak, the population of Cliff Palace exceeded six hundred people.

Also on Chapin Mesa is another large dwelling, Balcony House, perched in a shallow cave, getting its name from a very well-preserved wooden balcony that would have been accessible from the second story of the dwelling. The view down the canyon from that balcony must have been spectacular. Another cliff dwelling, Spruce Tree House, is a particularly photogenic and readily accessible dwelling (though it has been closed down for a few years as a result of rock falls).

From the loop road on Chapin Mesa you can see several impressive cliff dwellings located across the canyon, including House of Many

Windows, Hemenway House, Oak Tree House, Fire Temple, and New Fire House. The point of this litany of Mesa Verde sites—I was a college professor for more than forty years but I promise there won't be a test—is only to show how incredible the place is in terms of its great number and dense concentration of cliff dwellings. It seems that homes have been built in virtually every available niche and hollow in the cliffs that demarcate the canyons that cut through the green mesa.

Wetherill Mesa has several large cliff dwellings, including Step House and Long House. These can all be visited with a ranger guide. A hike across Wetherill provides views of yet more impressive cliff castles, including Kodak House and Nordenskiold.

Imagine the Native People who built the cliff dwellings of Mesa Verde and the other places I mention in this chapter, such as Montezuma Castle, Gila Cliff Dwellings, and Canyon de Chelly, not as archaeological data points but as living, breathing people. Imagine the designers investigating the alcoves in which they decided to build their homes; measuring their height, their depth, and the configuration of their floors; and addressing the metrical attributes that constrained the size and shape of the structures they would build in them. Now imagine the mathematically astute architects determining the sizes and shapes of elements of the building necessary to satisfy the practical needs of the people who would live there. How large could each apartment be, and how many of them could be accommodated under the existing alcove? How many kivas were needed, and how many could be incorporated into the building? How many storage rooms could be included? How tall could the towers be? And how could the entire thing be situated seamlessly within the alcove, looking not like it was jammed into place but appearing to be almost an inherent, organic, and natural part of the alcove? Now consider the engineers, experts in the strengths, weaknesses, and capabilities of the raw materials used in construction. How thick must the lower parts of walls be to be strong enough to support the upper part of the structure, including second and third floors? How tall can a freestanding tower get and still be stable? Should we shift the towers to the back where they can lean against the rock face? How many logs would be needed to create floors and ceilings? Where could those raw materials be obtained? Finally, consider the construction workers, the people who took the plans of designers, architects, and engineers and who, in practical and real-world terms, were tasked with translating those plans into a viable structure, a home to people living in Mesa Verde. It was a remarkable task and, eight hundred years after they were built, continue to amaze and delight visitors.

Which brings us to this: there's one more thing that needs to be pointed out. Cliff Palace, Balcony House, Step House, and the rest clearly were not built only to fulfill specific and practical requirements. The designers, architects, engineers, and builders (they weren't necessarily different people) made something—however we measure aesthetics cross-culturally—beautiful, impressive, amazing, gorgeous, and all of the other synonyms for "beautiful" I gleaned from the thesaurus and listed earlier.

Why Cliffs?

This all leads us to the obvious question: Why build houses in cliffs? We can't know for sure, but there are a few reasonable answers to that question:

- Defense: Certainly, if access to your home is challenging, requiring the use of hands to climb up or down a steep rock slope or on ladders, invaders are at a distinct disadvantage. They can't very well aim a bow and arrow at you when their hands are otherwise engaged. If lowered down by rope, invaders will find themselves in the midst of a shooting gallery where they are the targets. So perhaps the folks who built cliff dwellings had nasty neighbors they didn't want to arrive unannounced. The extra work involved in building structures in niches in cliffs and the inconvenience of having to climb to access your own house may have been deemed worthwhile costs to enhance safety.
- Land: The American Southwest possesses a hot, dry environment. Arable land is at a premium. Perhaps houses were situated in cliffs as part of an effort at land conservation. Sure, access to your home can be a challenge, with resources available mostly on top of the mesa, so climbing up and back down nearly every day becomes a part of your routine. But perhaps it's worth it if you produce lots of

food on land where otherwise a large structure would have been built.
- Temperature: It gets hot in the summers in the American Southwest, with temperatures reaching the mid-eighties, even at the elevation of Mesa Verde, which varies between 1,828 and 2,590 meters (6,000 and 8,500 feet). A large adobe or stone structure subject to the sun all day is simply going to bake, and interior rooms, with no direct access to air, are pretty quickly going to become the equivalent of ovens and unlivable. But a fairly shallow building positioned in a natural stone alcove, shielded from the sun on top and in the back, and in shadows for at least part of the day as a result of its location, is going to be a lot more comfortable at midday. I can tell you this: on the hottest summer days, when you walk into a building constructed in a shaded location with thick, adobe walls, it is considerably cooler than it is out in the sun. It's not air conditioning, but it's a lot more pleasant than baking in the sun. Further, in winter the temperatures in Mesa Verde descend into the mid teens at night. And it snows. The raw material used to build the cliff dwellings possesses what is called a high thermal mass. It warms up when sun hits it during the day and radiates that heat back into the exterior rooms, warming them up at night.

We don't definitively know which of those three hypothesized explanations is the most accurate. Maybe a combination of all of them explains it. Ultimately, we have to simply marvel at their beauty, even if we can't entirely explain the cliff dwellings.

Diné: The People

Oh, the wind blows cold
On the trail of the buffalo,
Oh, the wind blows cold
In the land of the Navajo
In the land of the Navajo

—PETER ROWAN, "LAND OF THE NAVAJO"

Most people call the folks who today live on an enormous reservation mainly located in northeast Arizona the Navajo. However, that name is not their word for themselves. The Navajo name comes from the Tewa Pueblo word for "place of large planted fields." The Navajo—it's so commonly used as their name that it's hard to avoid it, and even they will use it, so I will do so here—actually call themselves and prefer Diné (pronounced "di-neh"), which simply means "the People."

In Diné oral history, the People have always lived in the Four Corners of the American Southwest, having been placed there by the Creator, specifically in the place called Dinétah (the Place of the People). Dinétah's exact location is a point of contention, but maybe it is more or less the entirety of their reservation as bounded by the Sacred Mountains: Blanca Peak (Colorado), Mount Taylor (New Mexico), the San Francisco Peaks (Arizona), and the La Plata Mountains (Colorado).

So everything bounded by the Sacred Mountains is generally Dinétah, but one of the places expressly called that by the Navajo for special consideration is located in what Anglos today call Crow Canyon in northwest New Mexico near the town of Farmington. For archaeology aficionados who thought that Crow Canyon was located in Colorado and the location of a major archaeological project and institute, it is, but that's a different Crow Canyon. And the Dinétah in New Mexico's Crow Canyon has direct evidence of a Navajo presence in the form of stone masonry towers called pueblitos, along with a wealth of astonishing Navajo rock art. The subjects depicted in the art include recognizable Diné deities seen in other forms of Navajo art, including paintings and weavings: corn plants, assorted recognizable deities, and people riding horses (Figure 14.12).

The style of the imagery and, especially, the presence of horses in the art prove that it was produced after the Spanish *entrada*. As noted in the prologue, there were no horses in the New World before the Spanish brought them here in the sixteenth century.

The archaeological record often is like a palimpsest, a fancy word for a communication that involves a series of messages recorded sequentially, each message superimposed one upon another, and often separated by a substantial amount of time. It is the job of the archaeologist to peel away and identify those individual and discrete messages from their separate layers to make sense of each of the stories they tell.

FIGURE 14.12. One of the very impressive Navajo petroglyph panels in Crow Canyon, New Mexico, the place the Diné call Dinétah. Note the portrayal of people riding horses, a corn plant, and Navajo deities. Kenneth L. Feder

In the archaeological palimpsest of the American Southwest, the first people, like those at White Sands, reside at the base (chapter 5), the Clovis and Folsom people appear above them. Superimposed over Clovis and Folsom are the sites left by the people of the Desert Archaic. Above them we find the Pueblo people and their likely ancestors. The initial appearance of the Diné is above that and, therefore, later. Above them are the Spanish, and above the Spanish are the Anglos.

Archaeologists have determined that the Diné are late in the sequence from two streams of data: linguistic and archaeological. Genetic data might provide an additional stream, but the Navajo, concerned that the data might be used to harm or exploit them, imposed a moratorium on human genetic research in 2002.[20] Genetic research was conducted in the past, most of it pre-2018, but none of that showed any significant genetic markers that can be used to distinguish Navajo from Hopi.[21]

The Navajo Language

The language of the Diné people is entirely distinct from the Native languages spoken by the Pueblo people, including Hopi, Keres, Tewa, Tiwa, Towa, and Zuni. The first five on that list are closely related, technically in the Uto-Aztecan language family. Zuni is an isolate and very different. The Diné speak an entirely different language placed in the Athabaskan linguistic family, which is common not in the American Southwest but in southwest Canada. Interestingly, the only other Native People in the Southwest whose language is in the Athabaskan family are the Apache. Navajo and Apache are, to an extent, mutually intelligible. It is inferred from this that the Navajo and Apache, though through time diverging substantially in terms of their cultures, descend from the same relatively recent migrants from the north.

Think of it this way. If you are even marginally fluent in Spanish, you likely can pick up some words in Italian without too much trouble, but you'd be clueless trying to understand someone speaking in Japanese. That latter scenario is a pretty good analogy for a Hopi speaker listening to someone speaking Navajo. There's nothing in common. Therefore, Navajo is considered to be intrusive to the region compared with the languages spoken by the Pueblo people.

As a result of their being distinctive and unknown to the German and Japanese militaries, several Native American languages, including Choctaw, Cherokee, and Comanche, made a major contribution to the Allied war effort during World War II. In particular, the language spoken by the Navajo people is extraordinarily difficult for non-Native people to pick up and, in many ways, is unique. Twenty-nine Navajo Marines, the so-called code talkers, devised a code that substituted words in their language for specific military actions. The Japanese military was never able to break that code. U.S. military records indicate that during the key battle for the Pacific island of Iwo Jima in 1945, the code talkers transmitted more than eight hundred vital messages, helping the U.S. Navy and Marines secure the island and its two significant airfields.[22] Major Howard Connor gave credit where credit was due when he said, "Were it not for the Navajos, the Marines would never have taken Iwo Jima."[23]

The Battle of Iwo Jima ended with the raising of the American flag on the tip of Mount Suribachi, signifying victory. By the way, one of the heroes of that battle, memorialized by a now-iconic photograph and then a statue of an exhausted group of six men raising that flag, was Private First Class Ira Hayes, a twenty-two-year-old warrior and member of the Akimel O'odham (Pima) people of Arizona. Ultimately, he was one of only five of his platoon of forty-five men who survived the battle. In hindsight, it is clear he suffered from post-traumatic stress disorder and felt enormous guilt that so many in his "band of brothers" died while he lived. His disorder contributed to alcoholism, which led to his death in 1955. He was only thirty-two. His death moved songwriter Peter LaFarge to memorialize his life in song in "The Ballad of Ira Hayes," which gained national attention when it was recorded by Johnny Cash:

> And when the fight was over,
> And Old Glory raised,
> Among the men who held it high,
> Was the Indian, Ira Hayes.
>
> —PETER LAFARGE, "THE BALLAD OF IRA HAYES"

I Want This to Be a True Story

On the topic of the Navajo language and on a lighter note, the wonderful science fiction author Arthur C. Clarke—the iconic 1968 movie *2001: A Space Odyssey* was based on a Clarke novel—was recorded telling the following tale. It's apocryphal, meaning that, well, it's interesting, instructive, and maybe even funny, and while it may be true, it just as likely may not be.

When the National Aeronautics and Space Administration (NASA) was training the astronaut corps for their planned moon landing, they used various locations on Earth as stand-ins for the lunar landscape in a test of their mettle. One of those places was located on the dry and rugged Navajo reservation in Arizona. When Navajo people saw these strangers walking around their homeland in spacesuits, they of course asked what they were doing. When the astronauts told them they were training for their mission to the moon, the Navajo responded by telling them that their ancestors lived there and asking if NASA might bring them a message recorded in their language. The NASA administrators thought that would be a nice public relations move for them, using modern technology to help the Native folks, with their ancient culture, talk to their ancestors. So they brought out a tape recorder and a representative of the tribe, speaking in the Navajo language, intoned a brief message intended for the ancient ones.

Initially nobody at NASA understood the recorded Navajo-language message, and when they tracked down Navajo speakers to translate it to English, most just laughed and said it was a secret and they couldn't reveal its meaning. Eventually NASA did find a fluent Navajo speaker who was willing to tell them what the message to Navajo ancestors actually meant. His translation was, "Don't let these bastards steal your land." All right, I don't know if it's a true story, but it ought to be.

Early Navajo Archaeology

Adding to the linguistic argument for the relatively late appearance of the Navajo in the American Southwest, archaeology shows the same thing and provides us with a time frame for the Diné. The earliest archaeological evidence for the remains of identifiable, typical Navajo houses, their "hogans," has been dated to not much before 1500 CE. Many believe that this may be a little late as a date for the Navajo's first entry into the Southwest and estimate a date of about one hundred years before this, about 1400 CE. Whatever the actual date, it's still a relatively recent migration.

Hogans are round or octagonal structures, and they are still built and used by modern Diné both as dwellings and as ceremonial structures. In association with those dwellings, archaeologists find an arrow point style with side notches and a basal notch. Three notches allow for a very secure and tight fit of an arrow to its shaft, and the style is found at Navajo sites but not Pueblo sites. Also, new ceramic types show up in this period of around 1500 that don't look like any of the older pottery seen at Pueblo sites. The appearance of new styles of artifacts in a region with no developmental sequences for those new styles from existing styles is a hallmark in archaeological interpretation of the appearance of a new group in a region.

Another new kind of architecture that is seen in the Southwest around and maybe a bit before 1500 CE are the pueblitos I mentioned in relation to Crow Canyon, New Mexico. These are usually small masonry towers placed on mesa tops in inaccessible locations, likely for protection and storage. Again, the pueblitos are a new form and appear quickly in the region. The Navajo are credited with their construction.

When the Navajo arrived in the Southwest, they largely were hunter-gatherers. They appear to have learned the agriculture of corn, beans, and squash from the Pueblo people already there, rug weaving from those same people, and then silverwork later on, perhaps from Europeans. I remember once talking to a couple of young Hopi guys and making the mistake of asking them about "Navajo culture." "Nope," one of them said. "The Navajo don't have culture of their own. They just stole everything from us." Yikes. While my Hopi informants chided the Navajo for stealing everything about their culture from the Hopi people, that isn't entirely true since they borrowed the most important part of their economy, raising and tending sheep, from the Spanish.

None of this reflects negatively on the Navajo. Just the opposite. They entered into a new territory more than five hundred years ago, wisely adopted some of the successful adaptations of the locals, thrived, and are now, by most measures, the most populous of the Native American tribes. Theirs is a success story embodied in resilience and the ability to adapt as circumstances change.

Archaeology, History, and Spirituality: An A:shiwi Perspective

The A:shiwi or Zuni origin story explains how the people got to what they call the Middle Place, the location of their village called Halona in central New Mexico.

The first Zuni ancestors left the underworld beneath the Grand Canyon at a location today called Ribbon Falls and, led by their gods, they migrated some 320 kilometers (200 miles) to the east to the Zuni River, where they built the village in which they continue to live today. As my colleague Zuni archaeologist Kenny Bowekaty told me, the Zuni were never removed to a reservation by the federal government; they have always lived at Halona, a place chosen for them not by Uncle Sam but by their gods (see Figure 1.2 and Color Plate 2).

Ribbon Falls is a lovely, diaphanous cascade of water. For the Zuni, it is the Place of Emergence, the precise location where their ancestors climbed up the great trees placed there by the Ahayu'da, the gods, from the fourth underworld, leading all the way up and into the World of Light that is the modern surface of the Earth. As the place where their world began, Ribbon Falls is sacred to the Zuni. It is, in a sense, their Garden of Eden.

As a result of the great spiritual connection they feel to Ribbon Falls, it has long been their tradition for Zuni elders and leaders to make annual pilgrimages there; to leave offerings of salt, corn, and minerals for their ancestors; and to visit those places along the route taken by their ancestors where they encamped and left descendants messages about their emergence from the underworld and migration to the Middle Place in the form of petroglyphs (chapter 16). In so doing, the pilgrims retrace the steps of their ancestors from the Grand Canyon to Zuni, but in the opposite direction, and yes, now they take part of that trip by car and part of it by pontoon boat. By the way, once the Grand Canyon was named a national park in 1919, these pilgrimages largely were forbidden by the National Park Service. While individual A:shiwi made the journey anyway, it wasn't until the 1970s that the tribe and the park service worked out an agreement to allow the pilgrimages to legally resume.

From the perspective of both non-Native archaeologists and Native People, the Zuni pilgrims encounter evidence along their ancient migration route that shows that the Zuni story of their migration is rooted in truth. It is history. For example, typical Zuni ceramics are found along the route far from the Middle Place, as well as rock art that reflects a distinctly Zuni style.

As an archaeologist, I call these places where the Zuni stop along the way to commune with their ancestors archaeological sites. They are, after all, the remains of structures built by ancient people along with the rock art they made. The Zuni certainly recognize and understand that interpretation, but these remains are so much more to them than static ruins and fading petroglyphs. These places and features emanate a living connection to their ancestors expressed in spirit, blood, and stone. These sacred places, these "sites," are not dead or abandoned. As the A:shiwi say, "Our ancestors are still here. They never really abandoned the houses they lived in. There will always be a spiritual presence in them."

Here is my point in telling you about the Zuni pilgrimages. The things I call "archaeological sites" here are, as my good friend and colleague, archaeologist Warren Perry, phrases it, "multivalent"; they are many things with many different meanings, all of which are true at the same time. No single one of those multiple perspectives about their meaning is the right one. The interpretations are not mutually exclusive. They simply mean different things to different people and they reflect different ways of looking at the same things. Folks like Kenny Bowekaty can inhabit both worlds and embrace both interpretations simultaneously, which is sort of wonderful.[24]

15

Northwest Coast

OCEAN FARMERS AND TOTEM POLES

ALMOST CERTAINLY, you have heard of totem poles. They are an iconic image of Native America in general and the northwest coast of North America in particular. Totem poles were usually carved out of the soft wood of cedar trees, resplendent with colorful, three-dimensional depictions of various animals and other beings—those are the "totems," emblems of ancestors and spirits—one on top of another from the bottom of the pole to the top. That progression reflects history, family, social status, and ancestry. The art style is unmistakable and unique, unlike that of any other group of people in the world.

Totem poles are not simply beautiful. They are dense with stories of family and ancestry. Different family groups called clans are represented by particular types of animals. A family's totem pole will often include images of animals like the grizzly bear, eagle, thunderbird, frog, killer whale, or salmon much in the manner of a medieval family crest in Europe.[1]

Totem poles were brightly painted and range in height from just a few meters to more than 18 meters (60 feet) in height. Some poles are structural, providing support as a primary beam of a house. Others are freestanding features whose purpose wasn't architectural but informational, alerting people to the family identity of those who lived in the house and to which clan they belonged. The purpose of some poles was to commemorate a deceased individual, serving as a memorial to an individual of great importance. Modern totem pole construction has deep

FIGURE 15.1, COLOR PLATE 11. Iconic of the Native art of the American northwest coast, these modern totem poles can be found in Stanley Park in Vancouver, Canada. Kenneth L. Feder

roots in time, but the practice reached its peak only about a hundred years ago. I have seen a selection of totem poles in a park as well as in a museum in Vancouver, Canada, and they are remarkable and beautiful works of art filled with bright colors, whimsical carved figures, and sacred meanings that reflect enormous skill and creativity (Figure 15.1, Color Plate 11).

The incredible beauty of the art and the enormous skill and dedication necessary for their production raise two questions: Why did this iconic form of art develop, and who were the people who produced it? To answer these questions, we need to examine the archaeological and historical record of the Native People of the northwest coast of North America.

Roots

It is commonly believed that hunter-gatherers, folks who rely on nature's idiosyncratic and not necessarily consistent or reliable bounty for their subsistence, ordinarily live a hand-to-mouth existence. The stereotypical view is that, forever on the verge of starvation, hunter-gatherers live—in the modern cliché—from paycheck to paycheck, but in their case from meal to meal. They are obliged to focus all of their attention, all of their energy, on simply putting food on the table, a roof over their heads, and clothes on their backs. In this perspective, hunters and gatherers have little time for the niceties of life. It's just wake up, hunt, gather, eat, sleep, repeat. They certainly wouldn't have the time or energy, or even the inclination, to develop the skills needed and the enormous amounts of time required for the carving of enormous totem poles. However, like all stereotypes, that view is simplistic and often flat-out wrong. It certainly doesn't apply to the Native People of the northwest coast of North America.

The people who are the focus of this chapter were not agricultural beyond the likelihood that they grew tobacco. In terms of the necessities of life, unlike many Indigenous People to their south, they didn't grow maize, beans, or squash. Beyond this, they weren't herders of domesticated animals. So they were, from their deep time up until contact with European colonists, technically hunters and gathers. However, leaving it at that is extremely misleading. Yes, they did rely on wild foods for their subsistence, but they were reliant on the very rich and productive wild resources of the northwest coast of North America, focusing on marine resources, especially fish and shellfish.

Plenty of people in the twenty-first century in modern societies eat a lot of seafood as well, but we wouldn't call modern Americans who frequent seafood restaurants like Red Lobster hunter-gatherers. Just as modern seafood eating is facilitated by a highly sophisticated, industrial level of fishing and collecting wild species with enormous fleets of ships bearing sophisticated technologies, the Native People of the coasts of Oregon, Washington, British Columbia, and Vancouver Island developed a highly sophisticated, industrial level of fishing and collecting that relied on a very detailed understanding of fish behavior, particularly as it related to seasonal schedules. They efficiently processed and preserved fish through drying, enabling the production of enormous food surpluses with a distant "sell-by date" that could be safely stockpiled and, in turn, provide food for a large human population. As a result, many of the cultural characteristics of complex agricultural societies or advanced "civilizations" (chapters 12, 13, and 14) are seen among the Native People of the northwest coast despite the fact that their subsistence was based on wild "crops."

This is an important point. The people of the northwest coast did not just cross their fingers and passively hope for a fortuitous gift of food from nature. They took a proactive and protective role in ensuring that available wild foods would be more productive by both managing habitats and creating features that massaged their local environment and made the act of collection far more efficient. In a sense, they treated the wild foods they collected from the sea and from rivers much in the way farmers treat their crops and animals. The Native People didn't just collect those vital resources. They managed, tended, and cared for them and in so doing increased their productivity.

Here's an analogy. Have you ever planted a butterfly garden—you know, where people plant the kinds of flowers that are particularly attractive to butterflies? Plant them and they will come. In so doing, you are, in a sense, gently managing nature based on your knowledge of butterflies in order to increase their local population, because they are active pollinators or maybe just because you think they're pretty and nice to have around. You're not domesticating the butterflies. You don't own them. You are not practicing artificial selection, at least not intentionally. You're just playing an active role in encouraging their presence.

Apiculture, beekeeping, is an even better example of human beings managing a wild species, this time for food and economic benefit. Beekeepers make hives that bees find appealing. The bees inhabit the artificial homes beekeepers provide, visit flowers in the area, return to the hive with nectar, and produce honey, which is then harvested by the beekeepers. In apiculture, the bees are still wild. There are no genetic changes, no artificial selection by the keepers. The bees therefore aren't domesticated; they are simply managed and their activities encouraged by people who, historically, have observed bees, examined their behavior, created a built environment that attracts them, and then taken advantage of the bees' hard work by collecting the delicious confection that they produce. Even though the bees are wild, this still qualifies as "food production," and the people of the American northwest coast used similar strategies in the management of the wild resources on which they depended for their subsistence.

Farming the Ocean

In the area including southeast Alaska, Prince Rupert Harbor (British Columbia, Canada), the central coast of British Columbia, the west coast of Vancouver Island (Canada), the Gulf of Georgia (Canada), Puget Sound (northwest Washington State), the Olympic Peninsula (northwest Washington State), and the Oregon Coast, beginning just as the Pleistocene was coming to an end, as much as eleven thousand years ago, Native People had already developed subsistence strategies focused on the extremely rich resources of the northwest American coast with a heavy emphasis on fish, both oceanic and anadromous fish (species that live in the ocean and migrate upstream into freshwater streams to spawn), especially salmon. Along with salmon, other fish species whose bones are pretty consistently found at archaeological sites in the region and spanning a time beginning thousands of years ago and continuing right up through the modern period include cod, rockfish, ling cod, herring, surf perch, and flat fish, along with multiple species of shellfish. If you lived on the northwest coast and didn't care for seafood, you would have gone hungry.[2]

One of the strategies on which the Native People of the northwest coast relied for collecting fish along the coast was their construction of sometimes massive intertidal fish weirs, which took an extraordinary amount of cooperative work and upkeep. Weirs are structures consisting of walls of wooden posts set closely together—but not so closely that they would impound water—positioned along coastal flats that were dry during low tide. When the tide rose and these structures became inundated, fish could swim over and around them but many couldn't get out when the tide went back out. Those fish would get trapped on the "wrong," beach side of the weir. When the tide got low enough, people could simply walk onto the now-exposed flats to the weirs where fish were now flopping around on the damp sand and collect them in the hundreds and even thousands when the timing was right.

Fish weirs are found in lots of coastal regions throughout the world. They are clever facilities that require considerable labor to build and, once built, require regular maintenance. However, the Native People of the northwest coast raised these structures to a level of significance, efficiency, and productivity seen in few other places. One such weir encountered by archaeologists in southeastern Alaska consisted of no fewer than one hundred thousand (!) wooden stakes. Researchers have estimated that thousands of fish could be harvested in this one weir on a yearly basis.

That's a lot of fish. Which raises the question, How can a society use all of that abundance of fish before it goes bad? For wild foods to form the basis of a complex, sedentary society, not only do those wild foods have to be available in abundance, that society needs to develop ways of preserving those foods for extended periods of time. As mentioned, the people of the northwest coast were able to solve this problem by developing effective and efficient methods of preservation through a process of sun drying and smoking. In what amounted to an industrially scaled process, the fish were collected in numbers far greater than what their local group needed for current meals, with the excess being gutted, hung out to dry, and then stored, producing an enormous surplus that supplied food over the course of the year. In other words, the Native People weren't living hand to mouth, meal to meal, forever on the brink of hunger, only able to eat what they were able to collect that day and who knows what would happen the next day. Instead, they created a productive food system, based entirely on wild foods, that provided subsistence, sustainability, and stability similar to that offered by an agricultural food base.

Beyond employing extremely productive seafood collection strategies like fish weirs, they also practiced what has been called deliberate stewardship, through "wetland cultivation" of economically valuable plants. They cleared coastal fields of rocks, divided those fields into family plots using the stones they collected while clearing, and then weeded and oversaw those fields in an effort to encourage and protect the growth of particular species of wild plants that they incorporated into their diets. Of special importance as food were silverweed and springbank clover, both edible plant species. Again, these crops weren't domesticated; there's no evidence of the practice of artificial selection. Instead, species that were entirely wild were managed and, in fact, their growth was encouraged by Native People in order to make them far more productive and easier to collect than they would have been if people merely harvested wild stands whose growth and location were entirely fortuitous without human assistance. Those same fields provided a bonus by attracting waterfowl, which people would then hunt for a part of their diets.

A similar example of a strategy of intensive management and encouragement of a wild food resource in order to vastly improve its productivity involves another seafood, in this case clams. The Native People of the region produced "clam gardens" or "clam terraces." Like good scientists and naturalists always do, they observed the habitats in which the entirely wild shellfish species they preferred for dinner—like littleneck and butter clams—thrived, and then they determined the ways in which they could expand those habitats in an effort to increase the food base. They recognized that sand flats in the intertidal zone were naturally preferred by those clams, so they cleared off areas of rocks and other debris and then built up stone walls with those rocks and gravel to keep the gardens intact in the face of waves and the tides. Then, when the tide went out, especially during spring tides, which occurred intermittently for periods of a couple of hours, diggers would walk out onto these artificially enhanced terraces and dig up the clams. In other words, they created a built environment that was conducive to the growth and expansion of wild plant and animal species on which they relied. Yes, they benefited from the fact that they lived in a region where this was possible and productive. But they also accomplished it in ways that were efficient and remarkably successful.

Peoples of the Northwest Coast

Numbering in the tens of thousands, the aboriginal peoples living on the northwest coast upon the arrival of Europeans include several well-known, named, and distinctive but closely related groups including the Tlingit, Haida, Kwakwaka'wakw (formerly known as the Kwakiutl and alone estimated to have had a population of five thousand upon non-Native contact), Makah, Chinook, Coastal Salish, Nuxalk (also known as the Bella Coola), and Nuu-chah-nulth (also known as the Nootkah), among others. Though they are recognizably distinctive cultures, if you Google any of those names you will see photographs of their well-known and remarkably beautiful woodwork, especially their plank houses, their seaworthy boats, and, most of all, their totem poles. Those traditions have continued into the present.

Moments Frozen in Fire, Moments Frozen in Mud

The vast majority of archaeological sites, including the places highlighted in this book, consist of fortuitously preserved material remains at places where people once lived, worked, made art, extracted resources, fought wars, or died. When these living places that are now sites were left behind by the residents, the heavy hand of nature inflicted its inevitable engines of decay on their houses, tools, weapons, and works of art. Without people to provide upkeep on their dwellings or maintain their facilities, cemeteries, and roads, they slowly disintegrated. Only the most durable of materials survived. This filtering out by natural processes that has led to the utter dissolution of entire categories of material culture surely is one of the saddest realities and greatest challenges of archaeology.

I think it's disconcerting to consider the fact that all of our societies, all of our cultures, ultimately are archaeological entities in the making. Nothing is forever (well, as noted in chapter 3, except for stone tools), and people need to be in a permanent and constant mode of maintaining their creations. There is the apocryphal story, for example, that the Golden Gate Bridge is in a perpetual state of being repainted. They start on one side of the bridge and by the time they have finished the entire span, it's time to start painting all over again.

On this topic, there was a terrific television series called *Life After People* that, using computer animation, imagined what the world might look like if all people suddenly disappeared. Have you ever seen the results of software that takes a current image of a person and then digitally ages them? Over the course of a twenty- or thirty-second animation, you can watch a pretty good representation of what the next twenty, thirty, forty, or more years of aging will do to that person. In *Life After People* you can watch a similar process applied, for example, to a modern highway or high-rise building in order to depict what they would look like were people to disappear and nature take the reins. It was an amazing project with utterly terrifying images of the inevitable decay, deterioration, and ultimate destruction of some of our most beloved and iconic buildings, bridges, and landmarks—the Empire State Building in New York City, Tower Bridge in London, the Eiffel Tower in Paris—without humans to repair or maintain them. Nature is ever busy wearing things down and wearing them out. Without human beings to fix, repair, maintain, and reconstruct, the laws of entropy apply and everything—well, most everything—will descend back into its constituent elements. It would take a clever extraterrestrial archaeologist to, upon encountering the remains of these iconic structures, even recognize that a once-great civilization had existed on the third planet orbiting a rather ordinary star in this corner of the galaxy.

Deterioration is the rule, and this provides a fundamental challenge to archaeologists. On occasion, however, there is a stroke of luck and communities are, in a sense, flash frozen at a single moment in time. Admittedly, it's not so lucky for the inhabitants of these communities, but it's extraordinarily lucky for the archaeologists who find the remnants of those communities. Instead of undergoing a lengthy process of abandonment and progressive deterioration, in a few known cases settlements were destroyed virtually instantaneously, but not in their entirety, because whatever caused the destruction was selective. Certainly all living things, including the people and their animals, died, but many physical elements of the village or city survived as a result of the deposition of material that enveloped the settlement, similar to what happens when insects fall into the sticky goo of tree sap, which kills them but exquisitely preserves their bodies in material that becomes amber.

I am sure you are at least aware of the bare bones of the famous story of the destruction of Pompeii. You might also know that a sister city, Herculaneum, was destroyed at the same time. You likely also know that the agent of the destruction of these two Roman cities was the volcano known as Vesuvius.

At the better-known Pompeii, a thriving city of at least ten thousand and as many as twenty thousand people, in 79 CE the city experienced a cataclysmic destruction by the paroxysmal eruption of the nearby volcano, Vesuvius. That eruption was no great surprise and most residents had already abandoned their homes following a series of earthquakes and small eruptions in the days and weeks before the fateful day. Many more escaped during a terrifying eighteen-hour period when it literally rained hot, volcanic pumice on the city, setting fire to buildings, and ash accumulated on rooftops and on the streets like a hot, swiftly falling snow.

After the ash fell, all hell—almost literally—broke loose when the volcano erupted cataclysmically, and a pyroclastic flow, an incandescently hot avalanche of rock and lava, likely more than 700° Celsius (1,300° Fahrenheit), moved down the flanks of the volcano at about 80 kilometers (50 miles) an hour. When the more than eleven hundred diehard residents—diehard is a sadly ironic term to use here—who remained looked over at the spectacle of the erupting volcano, some of them perhaps realized that they were, as the old phrase goes, "dead men walking." They had only two choices: to just sit and wait for the burning flow to inevitably catch up to and then incinerate them, or to head into the waters of the nearby bay, where, instead of burning, they would be boiled to death when the lava hit the water.

So yes, Pompeii is an understandably and deservedly famous place, and now a major tourist attraction, where people can engage with the incredibly tragic story that played out there. But have you ever heard of Ozette, a Native American whaling community located on the Olympic Peninsula in the state of Washington? The area in which the Ozette village was located had been occupied for two thousand years when a devastating natural disaster, albeit on a smaller scale than Pompeii and Herculaneum, befell the village. It wasn't a volcanic eruption, but the ultimate cause may also have been seismic. An earthquake may have been the cause of an avalanche of mud that utterly destroyed Ozette and encapsulated the community.[3]

The timing of this disaster may have been precisely determined. Radiocarbon dating of charcoal in a couple of the hearths located in the remains of houses at the site suggests that those fires were burning, warming the residents and cooking food, sometime before about 1640 CE. That doesn't mark the beginning or end of the occupation but tells us that the village was occupied at least at that time. Dendrochronology applied to one of the planks used in house siding in the village indicates that the tree from which it was derived was growing as recently as 1613 CE. That dates to the construction of the building. Finally, Japanese seismologists have identified a major earthquake that hit the northern Pacific Ocean, originating in the vicinity of the North American northwest coast. That earthquake caused a devastating tsunami that pummeled the eastern coast of Japan. Those seismologists know precisely when this earthquake hit because villagers in Japan noted its occurrence in their village records. The day was January 27 or 28, 1700 CE.[4] Though it cannot be proved definitively, it is plausible that this earthquake was the trigger for the avalanche that destroyed Ozette, thereby dating that destruction to the year, month, and even day.

One reason I opened up this discussion by citing Pompeii is this: ironically, the agent of the destruction of the living communities of Pompeii and Herculaneum in Italy and Ozette in Washington State also served as the agent of their preservation. Because both were metaphorically "frozen" (I am aware that "frozen" is an ironic term to use for a city enveloped in volcanic ash) at a moment in time, they became preserved like the aforementioned insect in amber. It was a terrible fate for the residents of those communities but a boon to scientists able to study those places in all their archaeological glory.

Unlike the people of Pompeii, the people of Ozette probably had no warning of the impending destruction of their village. In all likelihood, the residents were engaged in their usual activities at the time of the catastrophe, drying fish, preparing food, making tools like bows and arrows, eating, and sleeping while kids were playing games and telling stories. And then, in a moment of horror, an avalanche of mud inundated and utterly destroyed their community. The mud enclosed several houses in a thick slurry, destroying the structures themselves but enfolding their wooden walls and their contents, essentially removing them from the ordinary and normal processes of deterioration and decay.

Though it happened likely 325 years ago, just as Japanese villagers recorded the tsunami, the local Makah people passed down stories of this terrible moment of destruction. It wasn't until 270 years after the event that a coastal storm in February 1970 exposed parts of the preserved village, providing physical evidence of the people's stories.

In a process led by archaeologist Richard Daugherty and a team of researchers working in tandem with Makah descendants in the region, the encasing mud was removed from six longhouses using high-pressure water sprayers, resulting in the recovery of more than fifty-five thousand artifacts, of which more than thirty thousand were made of wood, a material that, when left in the open air in the environment of the Olympic Peninsula, ordinarily decays into a powder.[5]

The six excavated structures had been made with horizontal wooden planks, in a manner similar to that used in the construction of standard wood-framed clapboard houses by European settlers in New England. Archaeology also showed a rich assortment of possessions of the inhabitants, such as hunting equipment including more than one hundred bows, more than fourteen hundred arrows, and more than one hundred harpoon shafts. There also were canoe paddles, bone awls, fish hooks, wooden storage bowls, and woven mats. In other words, archaeologists were able to recover an extraordinary amount of the regular stuff that Makah families used in their daily lives, lives that ended instantaneously 325 years ago.

On top of this, the archaeologists recovered more than one thousand woven baskets. Fifty were found in one house alone and their contents were carefully examined. Archaeologists were able to determine that each basket had been dedicated to items that were used together in various tasks. For example, they recovered fish hooks in one basket and bird bone awls used in sewing in another. There also were clam baskets and baskets in which dried fish had been stored. Another basket contained a weaver's toolkit, including a spindle whorl, bone awls, and a comb. In one house, the exceedingly fragile remains of a blanket were recovered. The blanket had been woven from a combination of cattail, moss, and dog hair.

Not all of the artifacts recovered at Ozette were used for practical or utilitarian purposes. Some clearly were art, and among the more remarkably evocative pieces was a wood carving of what appears to be the fin of a whale. The carved wooden fin had been painted black and was bedazzled with seven hundred sea otter teeth, their molars arranged in the shape of a raptor, perhaps a thunderbird. Sea otter canine teeth had also been used to produce a sawtooth edge. Along one house wall, an artist had carved the image of a whale that extended for more than 5 meters (more than 15 feet).

An obvious question to ask concerns the possible loss of life at the time of the avalanche. About two thousand people are estimated to have died at Pompeii in the course of about fifteen minutes. What about the much smaller community of Ozette?

It's really impossible to come up with any kind of definitive number. Only a fraction of the site has been excavated, and it's really impossible to extrapolate from that fraction to the community as a whole. In two houses, the remains of nine individuals were recovered. Of these, only seven could be identified as to their age: two adults, one teenager, and four younger children. It is terrifying to consider their tragic fate. Were they sleeping and unaware of what was to befall them? Were they just preparing to leave following the earthquake when they were overrun by a thick and inescapable slurry of mud and debris? Were the adults hard at work, diligently making or maintaining their tools, while kids played at their feet when, in an instant, their lives were snuffed out by the avalanche of mud? We'll never know, but the recovery and reburial of their remains make concrete the fact that Ozette is not simply an archaeological site where archaeologists were able to recover thousands of artifacts. It was the scene of a human tragedy.

The Humanity in Archaeology

Look around your room, your apartment, your house, and note the things that, while useful, are artfully made. Look around your room, your apartment, your house, and note the things that serve no particular useful purpose beyond the beauty they bring into your life. The people of Ozette were exactly like this. The weapons they used in hunting, the knives they used in preparing their food, the paddles they made and used to propel their canoes, the tools they used in weaving baskets, and the baskets they used in storing their many useful things were made far more artfully than they needed to be to accomplish their intended tasks. These things reverberate with the humanity of the inhabitants of Ozette and provide a direct connection between them and us. Further, like us, they decorated their living spaces with paintings and sculptures that served no obvious purpose other than to delight the eye. We are all humans and we enjoy surrounding ourselves with beauty. The relentless irony of the reason these objects that afford us a uniquely detailed picture of life in this three-century-old Makah village were preserved should not be lost on you.

What strikes me as so tragically human about Ozette is my familiarity with at least the context of the things preserved. In a fundamental sense, Ozette doesn't seem like an archaeological site and the objects contained therein don't seem like artifacts. Each of the structures excavated was someone's home, and truly, though clearly obvious in this instance, this applies to all archaeological sites. I think of my childhood home. I see a table with my dad's stuff, his pens and extra glasses near the couch for doing the *New York Times* Sunday crossword puzzle (yes, in ink). I see my mother's stuff in the kitchen with her cluster of tools for making her magical concoctions for the family to eat. The baskets and bowls of the stuff used by mothers and fathers, grandparents, and brothers and sisters at Ozette speak so poignantly of the love and care underlying the ordinary, day-to-day work needed to keep a family fed, dressed, warm, and safe. All of that was snuffed out in the same instant that it was preserved for archaeologists, both descendants and strangers, to pore over and consider in their attempt to measure the inhabitants' lives.

Sure, from the self-centered perspective of an archaeologist I can appreciate how the story of Ozette was preserved. But I have to admit that the human story behind the site, the human story behind the artifacts, these are very tough things to accept.

If You Got It, Flaunt It: The Potlatch

The historically known ceremony practiced by the First Nations people of Canada and the Native People of the northwest coast of the United States called the potlatch was a sort of economic leveling ceremony. Because the people of the northwest coast developed an extraordinarily effective economic and food-producing system, they were capable of producing large food surpluses at a level that was far greater than what was needed for the practical purpose of feeding everybody. They also practiced a complex political system, with individuals who were leaders shouldering great responsibilities and also wielding a degree of power in overseeing the behavior and decisions of families and even individuals within those leaders' territories. In many societies where a surplus of wealth is possible, great wealth accrues to the leaders, and in many past cultures, we see the evolution of great and nearly all-powerful rulers like pharaohs, emperors and empresses, and kings and queens whose power and wealth were concentrated in their families and then passed down from generation to generation. In some instances, this concentration of wealth in the hands of a few leads to revolt on the part of the vast majority of people who are barely scraping by.

This could have but did not happen in the northwest coast. Instead, the people of the northwest coast created a sort of pressure valve by which economic inequality was zeroed out through a process called the potlatch. The potlatch, in its original configuration, was a blowout party to end all blowout parties where a leader would exercise their great wealth and power by giving it all away to the people in a huge party.

You have to admit, that strategy for showing one's power and wealth is very different from owning a hundred cars, living in a mansion with twenty bathrooms with gold-plated fixtures, or having a monumental pyramid built as your grave. I imagine, however, that it's far more sensible to try to ensure the loyalty of your subjects by giving them a bunch of desirable stuff than by hoarding it for yourself. I'll leave it to you to decide if this has any relevance in the modern world. After European contact, the potlatch got progressively more intense, in some cases including even the ceremonial destruction of all that excess wealth.

16

Art

HISTORY, HUNTING, SACRED IMAGERY, AND THE SKY

AS A WORLD WAR II baby boom baby who was born and grew up in and near New York City, I was a nerdy kid born in the right place and the right time to take full advantage of the New York World's Fair of 1964 and 1965. A world's fair is the equivalent of a temporary Epcot (at Disney World). Celebrating the theme of "Peace Through Understanding," corporate powerhouses including General Motors, Ford, and IBM sponsored sophisticated and entertaining pavilions (Ford's ride, in fact, was designed by the folks at Disney and there were MOVING DINOSAURS!). Many countries also had pavilions honoring their histories and, at the same time, dedicated to drumming up tourism. The Vatican actually sponsored its own pavilion and became one of the most popular and highly visited buildings at the fair for one simple reason: *La Pietà*, Michelangelo's truly stunning 1498/9 sculpture of the Virgin Mary cradling the body of the dead Jesus Christ, was on display there.

My parents, my sister, and I stepped onto one of the three moving sidewalks in the Vatican's fair building and slowly moved past the remarkable and moving sculpture. Now, we were not Catholics or even Christians. Mary and Jesus may have been historical characters to my parents, my twelve-year-old self was barely aware of them, and my sister, not quite nine, likely was clueless. Yet we made the effort to see this piece of religious art and we were overwhelmed by its beauty and its poetic expression of the grief of a mother for her dead son. My parents certainly—and even, on a rudimentary level, my twelve-year-old self—recognized the beauty, the sorrow, the reverence, and even the sacredness manifested in this piece of sculpted marble.

Imagine the power of the artist to create a work that, even 465 years (in 1964) after he created it, could move to tears people from all across the world, many of whom bore no particular religious reverence for the mother and son depicted in the sculpture. Though many, my family included, were not followers of a religion that viewed the scene as depicting something technically "sacred," the beauty and power of the art transcended for us any particular religious message and were, in other ways, moving and, yes, sacred.

Art can do that. It can move us, inspire awe, confuse us, confound us, make us happy or angry; it can make us laugh as easily as it can make us cry; it can convey history, inspire pride or shame. Perhaps most of all, it can make us think. Art is amazing, and America's First Peoples are a part of the human tradition of making art, and yes, even old white dudes like me can be moved—to tears, to laughter—when we encounter it. Just as we recognized in Michelangelo's sculpture, the myriad pieces of rock art I have seen in North America similarly manifest history, worship, sacredness, reverence, love, beauty, whimsy, anger, humor, and all of the other human emotions manifested in images etched or painted onto rock.

I bring this up for one reason. I have read the argument that the term "rock art" somehow disparages or diminishes the petroglyphs and pictographs I describe in this book, that somehow "art" is a limiting term that doesn't really convey the magnitude of the significance of the material I'm talking about here.

I have to say, I absolutely don't get, nor do I agree with, that argument. There is no assumed "only" or "merely" adjective in front of the term "art." In fact, "only" is a non sequitur when applied to the word "art." We can call *La Pietà* a work of art without in any way diminishing its meaning, significance, or importance. The term "art" covers a vast and vital component of human creativity. The rock art of Native America is art. Each panel, each image has many meanings conveying many messages. Denial of this is based on a misapprehension of what art is and has always been, and it ignores the capacity of Native Americans to, like people everywhere in the world, make their ideas, feelings, thoughts, and expressions concrete in the form of petroglyphs and pictographs—in other words, art.

The Context of Rock Art

Although I have used a piece of Renaissance art here as an example to put rock art in context and to support my labeling it as "art," there are fundamental and important differences between well-known traditions of European art and the rock art of North America. One important difference concerns accessibility.

By its very nature, rock art in North America was public art. Located on the soaring walls of canyons, the curved surfaces of stony alcoves, and the flat surfaces of large volcanic boulders, the art was visible and generally accessible to anyone who walked by it. While some art in the European Renaissance was placed in the public setting of a church—funded by wealthy people hoping to score points with the Church or even God—and those works were open to churchgoers, a lot of art in the Renaissance was not. It was private, funded by wealthy patrons in the nobility and intended for display in their private residences.

Another difference concerns the underpinning of how the art was produced. Publicly accessible or not, historically, in the European tradition art was largely the result of an economic transaction on the part of members of the upper class and the artist. In other words, a rich guy who wants to flaunt his wealth supports an artist, who produces classy paintings for the rich guy's house or the local church where the wealthy benefactor is then credited for supporting the art. It's an oversimplification but not untrue.

Another significant difference between Renaissance art and Native American rock art is this. Renaissance paintings usually combine a number of elements into a coherent story or setting. For example, Jesus Christ and his disciples are shown sitting at a table, having a "last supper" together before the crucifixion. Or the lady of the house is depicted

FIGURE 16.1. Here is the most famous of the so-called newspaper rocks in the American Southwest (there are several with that name). This is not a single work of art but many, with images made at different times by different artists. There are animals, human footprints, wheels, and what appear to be assorted spirit beings. Kenneth L. Feder

dressed up in her finery, sitting in an overstuffed chair in the ornately appointed living room of her house, her baby on her lap and a cat at her feet. Both of those depict a discrete, individual event or setting, as does much of Renaissance art.

North American rock art is, for the most part (though there are exceptions), not static, not intended to depict single moments frozen in time. At a place like Newspaper Rock in Utah, for example, there is a profusion of unrelated and unconnected clusters of images of deer, bison, bighorn sheep, human footprints, wheels, and people on horseback hunting a deer or an elk (Figure 16.1).

In other words, this remarkable petroglyph panel isn't intended to tell a single story or depict one scene or one moment in time. There are many moments, many scenes at Newspaper Rock, made at different times. There are also examples of elaborate petroglyph panels where all of the individual elements appear to be part of a whole, with the artist intending to convey a single elaborate story—the so-called Great Hunt Panel in Nine Mile Canyon in Utah is an example that I will highlight later in the chapter. Nevertheless, it may well be that the finished appearance of a rock art panel in aboriginal North America simply wasn't as important as the process of creating the multiple stories told over an extended period of time.

How Is Rock Art Made?

Petroglyphs are works of art produced by scratching, incising, carving, or pecking images onto a stone surface, usually with a stone tool. The artists often took advantage of those surfaces where the elements, especially wind-blown sand, darkened the surface with a patina. When that dark patina was removed by scratching, carving, or pecking, the artist exposed the lighter-colored material below. The contrast between the surrounding darker surface and the lighter rock beneath the art makes the image "pop," causing it to really stand out.

Pictographs employ the approach likely more familiar to you, in which images are painted not on a canvas but on a rock face. Native artists produced paints by combining minerals or organic material to make variously colored pigments. Dark and deep red pigments, along with shades of yellow, orange, and black, were created with the mineral ocher ground into a powder. Other minerals rich in iron oxides, especially hematite, were also used to produce a red powder that served as a coloring agent for paint. Black could also be produced by grinding manganese or even charcoal. Those powdered pigments were combined with a binder to hold them all together in a liquid or paste. Plant oil, fish oil, egg whites, and animal fat were often used as binding agents. Brushes were made from animal fur or the stringy ends of branches, and paint could even be applied directly by hand or blown through a hollow reed.

There also are some really striking examples of art that combined the techniques employed in petroglyphs and pictographs. The artist would first etch out the image on the rock face and then apply paint as a way of enhancing the carved-out image.

North American Native Art Traditions

If you took an art history course in college, you've heard about and likely seen an endless array of photographs in PowerPoints reflecting the different styles and "schools" of Western art. If you glance at an "introduction to art" textbook or just Google "artistic traditions," you will commonly find a list that looks like this: medieval, Renaissance, baroque, rococo, neoclassical, Romantic, impressionist, postimpressionist, expressionist, cubist, futurist, art deco, abstract impressionist, and contemporary. I have no idea where paintings of sad, crying clowns or of Elvis rendered on velvet fit into this sequence. As for Bob Ross and his "happy little trees," well, I'm clueless.

One of my favorite painting styles was produced by what is called the Hudson River school, a group of nineteenth-century painters who created beautiful, dreamy landscapes of the natural world around the Hudson River valley in New York State. They're simply gorgeous images, subtly glowing with a diffuse, misty light. The point is, the artists in the Hudson River school produced a series of paintings with similar themes, similar elements, and essentially a similar vibe. As with most styles of schools, once you've seen one Hudson River school landscape, it's pretty easy to identify others.

I'm sure actual experts in Euro-American art traditions would quibble with the list just given, but it does reflect, however oversimplified it may be, the nature of change in the dominant styles of art through time in Europe.

Rock art is no different. It is effectively ubiquitous, both worldwide and also within the confines of North America. Though clearly most abundant in the American Southwest, it certainly isn't present only in that region. As a result of research for my archaeological travel guides, I have personally visited Native American rock art in the following states regionally: Arizona, California, Colorado, New Mexico, Nevada, Texas, and Utah; Florida, Georgia, and North Carolina; Massachusetts and

Vermont; Ohio; Montana, Wyoming, Washington, and Oregon. That extensive list is in no way intended to impress you. Just the opposite—I need to travel more to see art in all of the other states! But it is a good indication of the widespread nature of the tradition of leaving messages in the form of etched or painted images that tell a story, record history, memorialize a place, or honor the spirits (Map 16.1).

Just as in the art traditions seen on other continents and at other times, there are many different styles or "schools" of Native American rock art that tend to be differentially distributed in both space and time. In other words, different regions tend to have had different predominant styles, and those predominant styles tended to change through time. Even just in the American Southwest, there are several named styles, including Fremont, Barrier Canyon, Archaic, Anasazi, Hohokam, Rio Grande, Puebloan, Jornada Mogollon, and many more. Of course, we have no idea what name the practitioners applied to their style or even if they called it anything in particular. We can assume that artists in the various traditions would have recognized the essential differences in style: a practitioner in the Fremont tradition looking at Barrier Canyon art would most likely have been able to say, "Yeah, that's not my work." We'll encounter a sample of the named styles in this chapter. If you are interested in a very in-depth analysis of the rock art of the American Southwest, you need to consult the work of Polly Schaafsma. Her book *Indian Rock Art of the Southwest* is the classic work on the subject.[1]

Rock Art as a Record of Hunting: The Great Hunt, Nine Mile Canyon

The rock art style called Fremont is found throughout the Four Corners region where Arizona, New Mexico, Utah, and Colorado meet at right angles. Fremont tradition art consists mainly of petroglyphs. Many individual images are of bighorn sheep, an impressive, wild species that was a mainstay in the diet of Native People in the region. Also diagnostic of Fremont are anthropomorphs. The "anthro" in the word refers to something that looks like a human being, and the "morph" here means

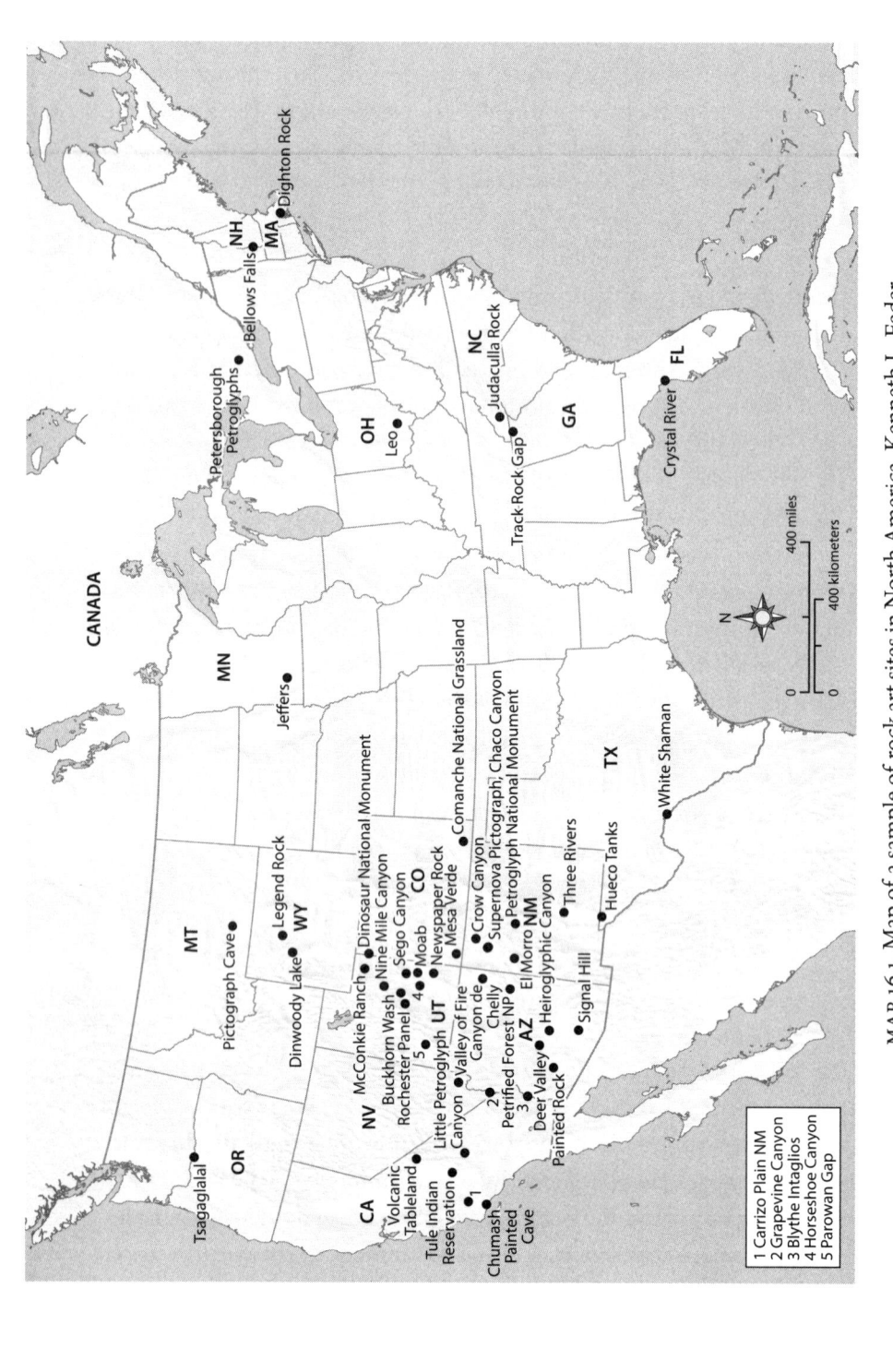

MAP 16.1. Map of a sample of rock art sites in North America. Kenneth L. Feder

FIGURE 16.2, COLOR PLATE 12. This absolutely stunning and well-preserved petroglyph was made in the Fremont style, depicting an anthropomorph with broad shoulders and a narrow waist, holding what looks like a shield. It's located at McKee Springs in Dinosaur National Monument in Utah. Kenneth L. Feder

"form." Fremont anthropomorphs consist of humanlike entities with triangular bodies, widest at the shoulders and tapering down to a very narrow waist, with either short spindly legs or no legs at all. Fremont anthropomorphs also tend to wear what appear to be elaborate headdresses, necklaces or pectoral jewelry, belts, and earrings. Many Fremont anthropomorphs appear to be holding items, perhaps shields, in their hands (Figure 16.2, Color Plate 12).

Rock art can be notoriously difficult to date. Most of the standard dating techniques simply don't apply to petroglyphs. Attempts have been made to gauge the rate of patina formation and use that as a measure. In other words, when the art was produced, the stained surface, or "patina," was removed to reveal the internal, often lighter color of the rock, so the "patina clock" was set to zero on that newly exposed rock. Once the underlying rock is exposed, the patina begins to be reestablished, and if you know the rate of patina formation, you might be able to date the art. Unfortunately, this depends on there being a constant rate of patina formation, and that can't be assumed. It also absolutely relies on artists or their descendants never returning to the art to refresh their images by removing the darkening that has occurred since it was originally produced. At a given site, you might be able to determine the relative ages of the petroglyphs, which ones are older and which are younger, based on the degree of repatination, but it isn't ordinarily possible to determine an absolute "years ago date" in that way.

In a stroke of luck, we do have another, indirect and stylistic way of dating Fremont rock art. Eleven clay figurines were found in 1950 in a canyon in Range Creek, Utah. Called the Pilling Figurines, for Clarence Pilling, the rancher who discovered them, they are anthropomorphs made of clay, each between 10 and 15 centimeters (4 and 6 inches) from bottom to top. The figurines were painted and there are remnants of red, black, and buff paint. The overall shape of the Pilling Figurines is quite reminiscent of Fremont anthropomorph petroglyphs.[2] They wear elaborate headdresses, they have wide shoulders, their bodies taper down to a narrow waist, and, as in a lot of Fremont anthropomorphs, they have no arms or legs. I have seen them—they're on display at the Utah State University Eastern Prehistoric Museum in Price, Utah—and they are stunning. Indeed, they look for all the world like three-dimensional Fremont tradition petroglyphs of humanlike entities, both male and female.

Now, the figurines were not recovered in a controlled archaeological excavation, which is problematic. However, the rock shelter where the figurines were found has been investigated by trained archaeologists who date the site to about one thousand years ago. This conforms to dates obtained from other sites in the region that are ascribed to the Fremont culture. So if a site where figurines made in an unmistakable Fremont style were crafted dates to about one thousand years ago, it makes sense to conclude that the Fremont-style petroglyphs date to about that same time.

Many Fremont rock art images depict animals that we know from the archaeological record were major food sources dating to the period when the art was produced. Even more interesting is the existence of

FIGURE 16.3, COLOR PLATE 13. One of the most photographed petroglyph panels, and unlike many other large panels (such as Newspaper Rock in Figure 16.1), the Great Hunt Panel tells a single, coherent story with hunters bearing bows and arrows hunting a herd of bighorn sheep. Kenneth L. Feder

scenes that appear to depict images of the hunts themselves, often including the presence of human hunters throwing spears or shooting arrows at the animal or animals. This is similar to animal depictions in rock art all over the world and across time. For example, more than fifteen thousand years ago, artists in the Upper Paleolithic painted an image of a severely wounded wild bull, with its viscera hanging out of its belly, on a wall in Lascaux Cave in France. Hunters all over the world painted or scratched or carved or molded representations of the animals they hunted as well as depictions of their actual hunts. The Native People of North America are a part of that tradition.

Perhaps the best-known hunting image rendered in the Fremont style is descriptively called the Great Hunt Panel. It is located in Nine Mile Canyon in east central Utah, which is described as the "longest art gallery in the world." Among the incredible wealth of art in Nine Mile, the Great Hunt Panel may be the most impressive (Figure 16.3, Color Plate 13).

Here, four hunters have their bows drawn, arrows aimed, and appear ready to fire. Their target group consists of more than thirty bighorn sheep organized loosely into three and a half or four rows, with one sheep below the rows and off by itself. The herd includes adults, some of whom, based on the configuration of the horns, are apparently female and a few of whom are pretty clearly male. Of the more than thirty sheep, based on their small size, ten are young and the smallest of these most likely are babies. The herd depicted here is out of the ordinary. In nature bighorn males and females congregate in groups segregated by sex. Some herds consist almost exclusively of males, and some consist exclusively of adult females and their offspring. The same-sex groups ordinarily combine only during mating season. The Great Hunt Panel could be depicting that, but the presence of babies suggests it's far removed from mating season.

Adult male bighorns are large animals averaging more than 135 kilograms (300 pounds). Males (rams) and females (ewes) both have horns, but the female horns are relatively short and straight, while the male horns are much larger and exhibit a big curve. If you're a truck person, think of the mascot used in Dodge Ram pickups. The rams use their gigantic horns—a set of bighorn ram horns alone can weigh 13.5 kilograms (30 pounds)—in battles with one another, literally butting heads when competing for females during mating season. They are impressive animals, they provide a lot of meat, their horns were used as pressure flakers in stone tool production (chapter 3), and they must have presented a substantial challenge to those who hunted them.

As mentioned, four hunters are aiming their arrows at the sheep in the Great Hunt Panel. Three of the hunters are proportionally small but one is much larger. Their size differences may just be a result of perspective, with the large one being closer, but it may be something else entirely. In this otherwise straightforward panel showing what obviously appears to be a hunt, there are a couple of strange geometric forms, one looking for all the world like an old-style, dome-lidded barbecue grill. There's also an apparent chimera, a beast with the lower body of a human being but a horned head looking not so much like a sheep but like a bison. Strangest of all, many of the sheep appear to be tethered to the animal in front of them, shown by an incised line carved from the tip of each sheep's nose to the butt (in one case) or the back (in most other cases) of the bighorn in front of it. One sheep exhibits this connection to the shoulder of the half-human, half-bison critter in the middle of the top row. I will not even hazard a guess regarding what any of that means. Again, the art is riveting, and it clearly reflects the practice of hunting the animal species whose bones are found by archaeologists in the living sites of the people who produced the art, but in some ways it remains intriguingly mysterious. By the way, there's a quite stunning book devoted to the rock art in Nine Mile Canyon by Jerry D. Spangler. The title is, logically enough, *Nine Mile Canyon: The Archaeological History of an American Treasure*.[3] I highly recommend it. If you are ever out that way and decide to do a drive through the canyon, which is a lot easier now that most of the road has been paved, there is a very thorough guidebook, *Horned Snakes and Axle Grease: A Roadside Guide to the Archaeology, History, and Rock Art of Nine Mile Canyon*, which examines the rock art panel by panel.[4] Using this book with your car's odometer takes you to just about all the major pieces of art along the roadway. It was coauthored by that same Jerry D. Spangler and Donna K. Spangler.

Rock Art as a Record of Hunting: Three Rivers

Among my favorite petroglyphs is that of a wonderfully rendered bighorn sheep on a basalt boulder in the Three Rivers Petroglyph Site in southern New Mexico. The animal on this boulder has enormous, curved horns and clearly is a male—that is, a ram. There are an estimated twenty thousand (not a typo or an exaggeration) images all rendered in the aforementioned Jornada Mogollon tradition, spread out across more than a mile along a ridge made up of volcanic boulders that must number in the hundreds of thousands. Remember my reference to the striking Mimbres art style seen on Mogollon ceramics in chapter 14 (see Figure 14.3)? The rock art at Three Rivers is very reminiscent of that style with images of birds, mountain lions, fish, snakes, bighorn sheep, and lots more. It is no coincidence that there is a Jornada

Mogollon site at one end of the train of boulders on which the petroglyphs are located.

The boulder with the bighorn in question is about 61 centimeters (two feet) across, its image surface inclined at an angle of about forty-five degrees, and its color is a very dark gray or even black. The artist rendered the image of the bighorn largely by pecking the black surface of the boulder with a stone pick, perhaps one hafted onto a wooden handle. The head of the animal is positioned on the narrowest part of the rock and its body is filled with intricate geometric designs.

This sheep depiction is actually just one of many along the ridge, each one unique and each one an impressive piece of art. What stands out in the image discussed here is that this sheep is clearly shown in the act of being hunted. Though there are no hunters throwing spears or shooting bows and arrows on this or an adjacent boulder, the hunt here is even more explicit; the bighorn is shown with not one, not two, but three arrows embedded in its body (Figure 16.4, Color Plate 14).

Now, I can't tell you that the image was intended to depict an actual hunt conducted eight hundred years ago, serving as an artistic celebration of the incredible skill of one or more hunters, much to the misfortune of the wounded bighorn. Imagine what it must have been like to be confronted by the fury of an angry bighorn running at you, head down, and all you have is a bow and arrow to stop it in its tracks. Instead of an actual hunt being recorded, perhaps the depiction represents an example of sympathetic magic, a kind of wishful thinking based on the belief or hope that what we render in art will happen in the real world. What we can be certain of is the great artistic skill and care with which the scene was rendered.

Rock Art as History: Canyon de Chelly

I last visited Canyon de Chelly (pronounced "shay") in Arizona in 2015. Located on the lands of the Navajo Nation, the canyon is a national monument jointly administered by the Navajo Nation and the federal government of the United States. Canyon de Chelly is a living place, and Navajo families reside in the canyon as they have for centuries.

FIGURE 16.4, COLOR PLATE 14. Three Rivers in New Mexico is located adjacent to a Mogollon village site. Among the more than twenty thousand individual pieces of rock art, this depiction of a bighorn sheep, its body pierced by three arrows, may be one of my personal favorites. Kenneth L. Feder

If you have ever visited a national park or monument, you'll know that many charge a fee to visitors or require a park pass to enter. Not Canyon de Chelly. The Navajo made a conscious decision to allow free access to their park to encourage people, including non-Natives (including *bilagáanaa*, "white people" in the Navajo language), to engage with the long history of Native People in the canyon. You can access their visitor center and drive along the north and south rims of the canyon, along which there are a bunch of pull-offs with overlooks from which you can see many of the impressive cliff and surface dwellings of past people, the Ancestral Puebloans (see chapter 14), who lived in the canyon. You can also take a public trail down into the canyon to see up close one of those buildings, a place called the White House.

To experience the canyon more fully and personally, however, you need to hire a Navajo guide. Remember, though it's a national monument, much of the land is privately owned by Navajo people. The bottom of the canyon is not a public park; it's a Diné community. This place is their home. In fact, today about forty Navajo families live in the canyon during at least part of the year. When we visited in 2015, we hired Harris Hardy as our guide, and the experience was amazing. Harris is Diné and has lived in the canyon his entire life, fulfilling the wish of his grandmother, who encouraged him to be an ambassador for their people. He is knowledgeable and passionate about the canyon's history and an absolutely wonderful guide.

Among the many remarkable places he brought us to, places imbued with the history of the Navajo as well as the Native People who preceded them in the canyon, was the site of a pictograph panel that conveys a tragic chapter in the story of the Navajo's interactions with the Spanish invaders of their homeland beginning in the sixteenth century. That relationship understandably was fraught with tension, as one goal of the Spanish was to expunge the Native presence in the area and open it up to settlement by the Spanish. Intermittent battles were fought for more than 150 years as the Navajo raided Spanish settlements encroaching on their homeland and the Spanish staged repeated raids of reprisal. In an 1805 raid, Lieutenant Antonio Narbona led a contingent of Spanish soldiers into the canyon. According to the story today told by the Navajo, a group of approximately twenty-five women, old men, and children were attempting to hide from the Spanish soldiers in a rocky alcove just below the rim of the face of a side canyon, Canyon del Muerto (Canyon of Death), that originates in the north face of the main canyon. Later accounts by the Spanish claim that ninety warriors were hiding in the same cave, but the Navajo have long disputed this, maintaining that warriors were nowhere near the shallow cave but were instead engaged in battles with the Spanish elsewhere in the canyon.

As Harris told my wife and me the story, at one point a Spanish forward scout found the Diné hiding place in the shallow cave. Had the Spaniard withdrawn to report their location, it would have spelled doom for them. A Navajo woman saw the soldier and, knowing that he would give up the location of her people, engaged him in battle, making the ultimate sacrifice by grabbing him from behind, holding on tight, and throwing them both over the edge. Both died in the fall to the bottom. This brave woman who sacrificed her life to save her people is understandably a hero to the Navajo. The spot where this happened is memorialized in Navajo history and signposted on the canyon rim, as it deserves to be. The Navajo call the place Adah Aho'doo'nili (Two Fell Off).

Sadly, despite the efforts of this woman, the Spanish eventually found the Navajo hiding place and began shooting at the cluster of them hiding in the cave, ultimately killing them all, with one exception. A young boy in the cave was shielded by his mother and grandmothers, who literally buried him under their bodies in an attempt to hide and shield him from the bullets of the Spanish soldiers. As Harris told it, they instructed the boy that just as they must die, he must live to tell the story of the massacre of his people and never let it be forgotten. The Navajo boy's name is given in English as Little Lamb or Little Sheep. The cave where the atrocity occurred has long been called by the Navajo Massacre Cave.

Miraculously, Little Lamb survived the massacre, extricating himself from the horrific scene and running far and fast, finding family living outside Canyon de Chelly and sharing with them the tragic series of events he had experienced. Fulfilling the pleas of his mother, his grandmothers, and all the other Navajo who died that day, he didn't let the story of their slaughter die and told the story again and again to Navajo living outside the canyon.

When he returned as an adult to Canyon de Chelly in about 1830, he made sure the story would outlive him and never be forgotten by creating a remarkable and permanent piece of art, a pictograph depicting the scene of men on horseback brandishing guns and wearing typical helmets worn by Spanish soldiers (Figure 16.5).

The central figure in the tableau painted by Little Lamb is a man on horseback who is dressed in a cape. On the cape is the very distinct image of a cross. Navajo history tells that the massacre of the men, women, and children cornered in Massacre Cave was blessed by a Catholic priest. The pictograph painted on the flat face of rock preserves and eternally memorializes the story of the massacre and shows the power inherent in art when it is used to commemorate a horrific

FIGURE 16.5. History is written in the art. The Diné man Little Lamb painted this image in the early 1800s, showing the Spanish invaders, led by a priest, who killed his friends and family in Massacre Cave in Canyon de Chelly in Arizona. Kenneth L. Feder

incident in the history of a people. It is an example of art preserving and conveying history. Indeed, the story of Massacre Cave will never be forgotten.

Rock Art as History: She Who Watches

There is, on a flat rock face in southern Washington State, on a bluff overlooking what is now an impounded lake that used to be the Columbia River, a truly beautiful piece of rock art, a stunning combination of petroglyph and pictograph. The image is of an ethereal face with wide-open eyes and erect ears. The art style of the image is very reminiscent of the style that typifies the art of the Native Peoples of the northwest coast of North America as traditionally seen in totem poles, wooden panels, and weavings (chapter 15). The people of the region explain its origins in the following way.

Long ago, their ancestors built a village at this spot along the great river and there arose a very wise leader. This leader was respected, trusted, and beloved. In her wisdom she recognized, of course, that she was mortal. She ruled over the people for many years but ruefully acknowledged that the time was coming, sooner rather than later, when she would no longer be able to help them as their living leader. She understood that she would die.

Because she was wracked with worry about the future, sleep eluded her, and every night she rose from her bed and walked the bluffs overlooking her village, contemplating the future and trying to devise a way that her wisdom could continue to help her people after she was gone. As she walked the bluffs, she realized she was not alone. Someone, a being who could not be trusted, had seen her and wondered how he might turn her angst to his advantage. That being was Coyote. We met him before in two entirely different contexts and in entirely different places—contending with Grizzly Bear on whether people should walk on four legs or two in the origin story of the Tule River People of Southern California and interfering with First Man and First Woman when they designed the night sky in a Navajo creation story (chapter 2).

One night, as the great leader was walking the bluff and at her lowest, Coyote revealed himself, asking, "What troubles you, my friend?" though she knew that Coyote was no real friend at all. She explained the source of her worry to Coyote, who listened attentively. He responded, telling her, "I have a solution for you. If you just trust me, I can make it possible for you to watch over your people for eternity. I would be happy to do so."

"Coyote!" she responded. "Being able to watch over my people forever would be wonderful, an answer to my fondest dreams and hopes." With a hint of sarcasm, she continued, "How do you propose to accomplish this marvelous feat?" She said this fully aware that Coyote was not one to be trusted and great care was needed to discuss her worries in the first place.

Predictably, Coyote was short on particulars, simply assuring the great leader that she only needed to trust him and he would take care of everything. She understood fully that trusting Coyote was never a particularly good idea, but when he asked her to stretch out her arm toward his outstretched front paws, she recognized his strategy. And she embraced it.

"Promise it, Coyote, for all spirits to hear and judge you. You will make it so I can watch over my people forever. Promise that, Coyote."

And he did. Standing upright before Coyote, she closed her eyes, held out her arms for him to grab onto, and took a final breath as Coyote took away her life just as she knew he would. To fulfill his promise, Coyote gathered up her spirit and then merged it with the flat-faced boulder looming over her village.

On the next morning, the sun rose brightly over the waking village, and try as they might, the people could not find their leader to answer questions, solve problems, or plan the day. As their worry grew, a child looked up to the rocks on the bluff above the village and pointed, saying, "I see her. There she is!"

The people raced up the rocky path to look at the image pointed to by the child. When they arrived, they saw her, no longer a mortal being of flesh and blood, but an eternal being of stone and pigment (Figure 16.6, Color Plate 15).

Though she no longer looked like a human being, the face they saw, with its luminous and kind eyes, was unmistakably that of their leader, her spirit now merged with stone. They realized at that moment that her great and agonizing challenge to help her people even after her death had been solved. As a sacred image etched and painted onto the rock as a combination of petroglyph and pictograph, she had become immortal and would, indeed, forever be able to watch over her people. And the people bestowed on her a new name. In their language, it was Tsagaglalal. In English it means, entirely and perfectly appropriately, "She Who Watches." I imagine this angered Coyote, who, in attempting to play an evil trick, had accomplished exactly what his "victim" had hoped he would.

Tsagaglalal still watches over the place where the village was located, though the waters of Horsethief Lake have inundated the spot. Tsagaglalal's eternal home is now a state park where visitors can sign up for a guided tour and see her great and eternal beauty. It is an example of art preserving and conveying history and magic. And it is stunning.

FIGURE 16.6, COLOR PLATE 15. The quite moving image of the great leader who traded her life for the ability to watch over her people for eternity. She is now called Tsagaglalal, "She Who Watches." Located near Horsethief Lake in Washington State. Kenneth L. Feder

Rock Art as an Expression of the Sacred: Horseshoe Canyon

The Barrier Canyon tradition concentrated in southern Utah consists of pictographs, usually rendered in shades of red, of the elongated bodies of anthropomorphs. Barrier Canyon–style anthropomorphs are large images, sometimes 1.8 to 2.1 meters (6 to 7 feet) tall, that look vaguely human, though most often they lack arms or legs. One of their most iconic features is large, wide-open eyes. This tradition is concentrated in southern Utah. Dating Barrier Canyon art has been a challenge, with estimates ranging from as little as one thousand years old to six or even seven thousand years. The most striking example I have seen is the Barrier Canyon panel at the Great Gallery in Horseshoe Canyon.

The hike to the Great Gallery in Horseshoe Canyon can be pretty intense. It's a drop of about 244 meters (800 feet) down into the bottom of the canyon and then a 5.6-kilometer (3.5-mile) slog in sand and, seasonally, through flowing streams to get there. Along the way, you encounter four sets of pictographs, mostly in deep brick-red pigments, all representing the style labeled Barrier Canyon (the art in this canyon gives the style its name, which is confusing until you learn that Horseshoe Canyon used to be called Barrier Canyon). The first, High Gallery, is seen at a distance, high up on the cliff face across the canyon, and consists mostly of elongated anthropomorphs. It certainly leaves you wondering how the artists got up there and, perhaps even more important, why.

During our visit, farther along on the trail we saw the Horseshoe Alcove, where we encountered many more anthropomorphs, some looking like chimeras, mythical combinations of human beings and animals. These pictographs are beautiful, impressive, and remarkably well preserved, and you can see them up close.

After that, we passed by Horseshoe Cave, which contains more anthropomorphs, though, unfortunately, preservation is poor and vandalism high. But we soldiered on, and at about the 3.5-mile mark, we reached our ultimate goal, the long, curved rock face protected by a bit of an overhang. The place is called the Great Gallery, and we were able to see some of the most remarkable rock art I have ever encountered in my many sojourns. It is truly mind-blowing, an accumulation of more than two dozen anthropomorphs, each one unique yet all of them sharing the fact that they are elongated, they lack arms or legs, and where eyes can be seen, they are large and hollow in appearance. Some of them are literally larger than life, more than six feet from their bottoms to the tops of their heads (Figure 16.7, Color Plate 16).

ART 313

FIGURE 16.7, COLOR PLATE 16. Seven anthropomorphic pictographs among a couple dozen, many life-size, located in a natural rock alcove in Horseshoe Canyon in Utah. Part of the Great Gallery, these armless and legless images, often with eyes wide open, are in the Barrier Canyon style. It doesn't matter what religion, if any, you subscribe to—this place is sacred. Kenneth L. Feder

Now, I freely admit to not knowing what the specific significance of the amazing art in the Great Gallery was to the people who produced it at least a thousand and perhaps as much as a few thousand years ago. Wiser minds than mine have considered the meaning of the images, only to admit that we don't really know much. I think it's abundantly clear, however, that the Great Gallery anthropomorphs are not simply people but spirit beings in the general form of human beings. The images appear to hover in space as they gaze at you with their hollow eyes from the flat face of the rock. I am not the first person to characterize them as—and with absolutely no disrespect intended—positively spooky. That ambience is amplified by the complete silence that pervades the place. Each individual image is unique. One of the anthropomorphs appears to have small beings nestled on each shoulder, perhaps speaking into its ears. Another has the image of two animals facing each other on its chest. Another, with a white face and the requisite hollow eyes, has images of two other, smaller beings rendered on its abdomen. The bodies of some of the large figures are densely filled in with bands and lines of red and white. Others are solid red.

Despite the difficulty posed in trying to figure out the intent of the artists, here's the thing. Obviously, modern visitors to the Great Gallery are removed by millennia from the artists who created the images and who understood and recognized their power and importance. Further, as a non-Native person, I am separated by a cultural barrier from those responsible for the art. However, I can tell you this. Regardless of the separation between me and the artists and worshippers, when I entered into the stunningly silent space demarcated by the gently curving rock that encompasses the alcove, I was stunned into silence myself. I could barely speak. Only whispers seemed appropriate. Though not a spiritual person, I felt I was in the presence of something special and, well, spiritual. To say I was overwhelmed by the incredible and, let's admit it, alien (to me) beauty of the art would be a gross understatement. It looked wholly different from any art I had been exposed to in that undergraduate art history course I took. To be honest, I didn't want to leave, and as I walked away and began the 3.5-mile journey back to where I parked our car, I imagined the gaze from those hollow eyes following me as I left.

Rock Art as an Expression of the Sacred: Blythe Spirits

Ordinarily, when we think of sculpture, we imagine a passionate artist laboriously carving an image in stone or wood. And that makes sense. However, sculptors are not confined to those media, and some have used the landscape itself to create what I am here calling permanent sculptures in the earth itself.

The more than two-thousand-year-old Uffington Horse in the south of England is a marvelous example. By removing the grassy turf and exposing the snow-white, chalky subsoil, ancient people created a monumentally scaled representation of a running horse; it's more than 160 meters (350 feet) across from head to tail. Using the same artistic approach, about a thousand years ago and also in England, people created the Cerne Abbas Giant, a naked guy measuring 82 meters (180 feet) tall and holding a raised club. He's infamous for having a rather obvious erection; a very late member of the species *Homo erectus*. That's a terrible joke that only anthropology students will get and groan about. Please ignore it.

You're probably aware of the Nazca Lines or Geoglyphs in the highlands of western South America. More than a thousand years ago, the Native residents of Peru exposed a hard, light ground surface by sweeping away darker stones, creating lines that stretch for miles. As monumental as the lines are, even more impressive are the geoglyphs, enormously scaled images on the ground created in the same way, of animal and insect effigies including monkeys, fish, birds, and even a gigantic spider. I can't resist pointing out that the Nazca earth art has been made famous, in part, by some very unserious (my polite way of saying "silly") people who claim they were made by ancient aliens who landed on Earth. Because, of course, the first thing a visiting alien race that has mastered interstellar space travel will do upon their arrival on another planet is make artistic images of a giant spider and a monkey. That makes perfect sense.

Remember in chapter 12 my discussion of how the Native People of North America, particularly in the Midwest, raised the creation of earth art to an astonishing level. By raising up mounds of soil and forming it into various shapes, they perfected the art of effigy mounds, often in monumentally scaled images of animals, including the iconic Serpent Mound.

Other examples of monumentally scaled works of art are the Blythe Intaglios. Created by Native People living in southeastern California and southwestern Colorado, the intaglios were created more than one hundred years ago by moving stones into what are, more or less, stick-figure images on the surface of the desert. Some are anthropomorphs, images of what appear to be, maybe, giant humans or more likely giant, humanlike spirits. Local Native People, the Mohave, have shared their insights and report that the humanlike figures are depictions of Mastamho, the creator of the universe and all life on Earth. The biggest is about 33 meters (100 feet) from its feet to its head, and its outstretched

FIGURE 16.8. One of the giant ground drawings among the one-thousand-year-old Blythe Intaglios in southeastern California. This one is about 30 meters (100 feet) from head to toe. The local Native People, the Mohave, are the likely authors of the intaglios, which represent spirit beings including their creator Mastamho. Courtesy of Desiree Ekstein

arms are 25 meters (about 80 feet) across (Figure 16.8). Outside of Blythe, I've also seen a giant snake intaglio and a character who seems to be depicted spearing a fish.

The intaglios are difficult to discern in all their beauty from the ground. I was extraordinarily fortunate on my visit to Blythe when, by sheer coincidence, I ran into a woman who was there to photograph the intaglios with her drone. Desi Ekstein calls herself "the drone diva" and has been so very generous in sharing her images with me for a number of publications, including this one (Figure 16.8). Thanks, Desi!

As we've seen in this chapter, art can be a form of worship, and in the Blythe Intaglios, we have a North American Native example of that on a monumental scale.

Rock Art as Science: Archaeoastronomy at Chaco Canyon

I don't know how many of you have ever been in a place far away from the lights of a city, way out in the middle of the proverbial nowhere, where light pollution doesn't wash out the sky with the glow of street lights. It is truly an amazing experience to look up at the sky and see the flickering glow of an uncountable number of twinkling stars that almost seem to throb against the indescribable darkness of the universe. Chaco Canyon (chapter 14) is just such a place and has earned the official designation of a Dark Sky Park, where, as the National Park Service maintains, you can see the same pristine sky that the inhabitants of Chaco experienced more than eight hundred years ago.[5]

With that level of night-sky clarity, it is no wonder that Chacoans looked up and observed patterns, sequences, and even unexpected events. One of those unexpected events would have been the explosion of a star in 1054 CE in what we today identify as the Taurus—the Bull—constellation. On the other side of the world, according to written records in China, on July 5, 1054, observers were greatly surprised to see what they explicitly labeled a "guest star" that was four times the brightness of Venus and so bright it could be seen during the day for about a month, which is astonishing considering that that stellar explosion occurred 6,500 light-years away from Earth. That's 6.15×10^{16} kilometers!

Such explosions are called supernovae and actually represent a star in the last stages of its life, when it experiences a paroxysmal release of energy visible from many light-years away. It would be surprising, even shocking, had the residents of Chaco not noticed this new, blazingly bright object in the pristine skies over the canyon, and it is at least plausible that, not only did they notice it, they depicted it in the form of a pictograph. Along what is today the trail from the main grouping of great houses to Peñasco Blanco at the western terminus of Chaco Canyon is a pictograph depicting what appears to be a star painted on the horizontal ceiling at a natural break in the cliff (Figure 16.9).

FIGURE 16.9. If you lived in Chaco Canyon in 1054 CE and looked up into the gloriously star-strewn night sky, you would have seen, on one night when the moon was a crescent, an exceedingly bright splotch of light to the right of the moon suddenly appear, as if by magic. That light was the result of a stellar explosion, a supernova. This pictograph in Chaco seems to depict that very event. Kenneth L. Feder

The star is presented in juxtaposition with a painted shape that is very reminiscent of a crescent moon, and beneath them both is a handprint. All of the images are in red. It may be a speculation that the imagery represents an eyewitness depiction of the supernova, but it's not a wild speculation when you add to the consideration the following. On July 5, 1054, the moon was in a crescent phase, and the appearance of the crescent in the pictograph, with the "horns" pointed up and the asterisk to the right, is a pretty good representation of what a resident of Chaco would have seen with their back against the cliff wall and looking out into the northeast sky on that same night. It is impossible to be certain, but it would not be at all surprising if that's exactly what we are seeing today.

There is another piece of astronomical art at Chaco. Fajada Butte is located in the eastern part of Chaco Canyon. It is an isolated eminence of hard sandstone surrounded by a flat lowland, a remnant of rock

135 meters (440 feet) high that is harder and has eroded more slowly than its surroundings. As you approach the entrance to Chaco Culture National Historical Park, you can't miss Fajada Butte. Certainly, Native People were aware of its singular presence, and Lieutenant James Simpson (chapter 14) mentions it in his diary of 1849.

The people who lived at Chaco realized that near the top of the butte two straight-edged slabs of rock, resting side by side and separated by only a few inches, allowed a shaft of sunlight to illuminate the main surface of the butte behind them in a narrow stream of light during certain times of the day. At some point, people carved a spiral petroglyph behind and between those slabs. When sunlight streams in between those slabs, it creates what looks like a dagger of light, giving it its modern name, the Sun Dagger. Remarkably, the pecked spiral is nearly perfectly bisected by the Sun Dagger, but only on certain days of the year, most significantly on the summer solstice, the first day of summer (Figure 16.10).

On that day, the rock begins in darkness but then, in the late morning, as the sun rises in the sky and sneaks through the narrow opening between the slabs of rock, a small splash of sunlight first appears immediately above the spiral. As the minutes pass, the splash of light lengthens to become the elongated dagger that lends its name to the phenomenon. The dagger grows in length and the tip appears to cut right through the center of the spiral petroglyph. As the minutes pass and the brand-new summer sun rises higher in the sky, the shadows push the shaft of light across the rock face and down the spiral, giving the impression that the entire dagger is slipping down and past the rock until it disappears completely as it is overtaken by shadows.

Though I have never experienced the Sun Dagger's dance personally, I have seen videos and it is very impressive, an extraordinarily clever, sophisticated (how many observations must it have taken for Chacoan astronomers to get a handle on the phenomenon?), and artistically evocative application of art and science as a way of memorializing and recording a significant day of the Chacoan year.[6]

By the way, as part of our tour of Zuni Pueblo, archaeologist Kenny Bowekaty brought us to the location of the Village of the Great Kivas.

FIGURE 16.10. The "sun dagger" of light that bisects a spiral petroglyph on the summer solstice (June 22). This solar calendar was created on Fajada Butte by Native People living in Chaco Canyon. Paul Charbonneau, © High Altitude Observatory, National Center for Atmospheric Research

From there we hiked to the top of the ridge to see petroglyphs created by his ancestors. Among the evocative art Kenny showed us was, in fact, the image of what appears to be a star and, immediately adjacent to it, the image of what certainly appears to be a crescent moon. Kenny called it the Supernova Panel, and I suspect that is quite accurate.

The Meaning of Art

The Native People of North America employed art to depict their exterior, natural world along with their interior, spiritual world. Animals and plants; birds and clouds; people and spirits; women giving birth; animals with babies in their bellies; weapons; mythical beasts that were half animal, half human; hunters; the sun, the moon, and the stars; insects, lizards, and snakes; pawprints, footprints, and handprints; the humpbacked flute player called Kokopelli; assorted geometric forms; and more and more. Native artists took what they saw, what they thought, what they wondered about, all things they considered important enough to record and remember, and they translated those thoughts into concrete and permanent images in paint and through etching, pecking, carving, and scratching them into rock in a way that immortalizes those ideas. But what did the art mean? It meant that the Native People of North America were creative and ingenious in producing representations of their thoughts, beliefs, and interpretations of the world around them, of life and spirit. They made art, and it is spectacular.

17

War

War, huh, yeah.
What is it good for?
Absolutely nothing.

At least those are the lyrics of singer Edwin Starr's hit song released in 1970, at the height of the Vietnam era. It was written by Norman Whitfield and Barrett Strong for Motown Records and originally was recorded by the Temptations, appearing on their album *Psychedelic Shack*. Starr's version, released as a single, sold a ton of copies. If you have heard this iconic antiwar song, his version likely is the one you've heard.

Human beings are a weird species, and along with amazing accomplishments like language, math, science, music, theater, painting, pizza, and ice cream on the good side of the ledger, there's some pretty awful stuff on the other side, and among those bad things, war may be the worst.

There is an argument that humans are not the only species to engage in the wholesale killing of members of social groups other than our own. Chimpanzees, for example, who live in discrete social groups with other chimps, have been seen patrolling the edges of their territories. When they encounter a chimp they don't know, one who isn't a member of their group, they savagely attack it, literally tearing it limb from limb. Charming. But human beings, among all the species who kill their own, have raised war to a science.

The Archaeology of War

Back to the issue at hand. I'd love to be able to tell you about the excavation of archaeological sites that reflect places where goodwill and cooperation between the Native People of the New World and European colonists have been studied, but it's difficult to find any such sites. However, and sadly, archaeological sites that represent places where Native People fought pitched and deadly battles in wars that threatened the extinction of one group or the other are depressingly common.

And yes, battlefields become archaeological sites. After all, following the definition of archaeology I provided in chapter 1, as the study of the material remains of human behavior, it must be admitted that bullets, arrows, and the bodies of dead horses and dead fighters are the material remains of the human behavior called war. There is, in fact, an entire subdiscipline of archaeology called battlefield archaeology. It uses most of the common techniques employed by archaeologists to tell stories like the ones I have presented in this book, and battlefield archaeologists have also developed some approaches unique to their work.

So the question posed in the lyrics of the song "War"—what is it good for?—has another answer. War is good for creating archaeological sites where we can study the existential clash between two cultures. In this chapter I will discuss four of those existential clashes: the battle of Pequot Fort during the Pequot War in Connecticut, the Pueblo Revolt, the Battle of the Little Bighorn in Montana, and Wounded Knee in South Dakota. In these cases, battlefield archaeologists, working in the manner of forensic scientists hoping to illuminate and investigate the scene of a crime, have revealed the sequence, course, and nature of those battles.

A Massacre in Mistick

I have long been struck by the inherent irony underlying the fact that there are international laws that govern the legal conduct of war. War! Indeed, what is it good for? In the joke definition, war is about breaking things and killing people. The International Court of Justice in The Hague actually adjudicates the conduct of how nations can legally break things and kill people. Among its rules are protections against targeting civilians and admonitions about the proportionality of one side's military reactions to attacks by the other side. The court's principle of proportionality prohibits attacks against military objectives that are "expected to cause incidental loss of civilian life, injury to civilians, damage to civilian objects, or a combination thereof, which would be excessive in relation to the concrete and direct military advantage anticipated."[1]

These laws of war were developed and applied long after the Pequot War, long after the immolation of about 150 Pequot warriors and 300 older men, women, and children in their village in a place called Mistick that is now within the borders of the modern town of Groton, Connecticut (not the modern town of Mystic as you might think). The events leading up to this massacre—there is no other word that better describes what happened on May 26, 1637, in the Pequot's palisaded village called Mistick Fort—can be best described as a slow but accelerating boil, reflecting the increasingly adversarial nature of the relationship among multiple Native and European groups including the Pequot themselves, their Mohegan and Narragansett neighbors, and the English and Dutch colonists.

Much of the hostile nature of the relationships among the Native People of southern New England was related to their complex nexus of trading interactions, with competition bubbling up into eye-for-an-eye, tooth-for-a-tooth incidents of violence. Make no mistake, the Native People in the Northeast were not a bunch of "paleo-hippies" or tree huggers, as the Thanksgiving stereotype presents them. The Pequot, Mohegan, and Narragansett were populous and powerful nations both economically and militarily. The Pequot were the most powerful of the groups in southern New England and their policy was to forge alliances with other Native groups, but these were not alliances among equals. The Pequot were in charge and everyone knew that. They sometimes were allies and other times adversaries with other groups long before the arrival of Europeans. Animal pelts were the valuable commodity everyone sought, and wampum, beads made from mollusk shells, was the currency that fueled that trade. Competition for access to fur-bearing animals and wampum-producing shell lay at the heart of the economic system, and that competition often led to violence and military action among the various Native groups in southern New England and New York State. Things got progressively more complex when the Dutch arrived in 1611 and then the English in 1630, as they became new customers and new competitors for animal pelts. The law of supply and demand certainly applied. Supply was diminishing as a result of overhunting, and demand was rising with the arrival of new customers with new stuff to trade. Of particular interest to the Natives were goods they had not previously had access to: duffle cloth, glass bottles, metal pots (which they often cleverly cut up to make metal arrow points), scissors, glass beads, and mattocks and axes.

The combinations and permutations of alliances and antagonisms among these groups became increasingly complex, but those details are beyond archaeology and beyond the focus of this chapter. Suffice it to say, no group was exclusively to blame for the increasing levels of violence that ensued and none were blameless. Each group, Native and non-Native, did some pretty bad things to maintain their position in the trading business.

For example, in 1634 the Pequot killed the English trader John Stone in what they believed was a just retribution for the callous murder of Tatobem, one of their "sachems," or leaders. Unfortunately, not only was Stone almost certainly innocent of Tatobem's murder, he wasn't even the right nationality. The Dutch, not the English, had killed Tatobem.

And then, in 1636, the body of an English trader, John Oldham, was found in his boat in Long Island Sound, near Block Island. It isn't clear which group had killed him. Nevertheless, in retaliation, in August of that year, the English sent a contingent of ninety armed men led by John Endecott, who served a few separate terms as the governor of Massachusetts, to attack Native People on Block Island. The Indians basically hid in the wetlands and had little contact with the invading forces, who were content to burn a few wigwams and cornfields and then go home declaring victory.

From Block Island, Endecott returned to the mainland and moved up the Pequot River (now called the Thames, with the "th" pronounced as it is in "the"), in southeastern Connecticut. His contingent of soldiers landed at the site of a Pequot village and insisted that the Indians give up the murderers of John Stone, the trader who had been killed two years previously. Generally unhappy with the English, the Pequot may or may not have known who was responsible but refused to share whatever they did know. The English, who had no interest in a proportionate response, then burned the Pequot village to the ground simply as retribution for the Indians ostensibly covering up the crime.

In response, in an escalating tit-for-tat, and as part of an increasing body count, the Pequot attacked and laid siege to the English settlement at Old Saybrook in Connecticut. That siege lasted for six months and any English person attempting to leave or enter the fortified village was considered fair game. Later, the Pequot attacked the English settlement of Wethersfield, Connecticut, killing nine men and women and abducting two little girls.

This ongoing series of attacks between the English and the Pequot led, on May 1, 1637, to the leaders of the British colony of Connecticut officially declaring war on the Pequot. That war resulted in a fateful battle on May 26, 1637, when a group of seventy-seven English soldiers led by Captain John Mason and a combined force of Native People including one hundred Mohegan, Wangunk, Podunk, Sucking, and Eastern Niantic warriors, along with another two hundred Narragansett, launched an attack on the Pequot. The Pequot had attempted to form an alliance with the Narragansett, but it failed due to feuds between the two peoples that had been simmering for years. The combined force attacked a major stronghold, the aforementioned palisaded Pequot village in Mistick. Ultimately, by the end of the battle, the invaders had burned the village to the ground, killing hundreds and effectively ending Pequot dominance, at least for more than three centuries. Remarkably, the Pequot persevered as a people and were finally granted official recognition as an Indian tribe by the federal agency the Bureau of Indian Affairs nearly 350 years later, in 1983.

The actual sequence of events before, during, and after the burning of the Pequot village is difficult to reconstruct, and the history of the Pequot War was written largely by one side, the victors, rendering the veracity and objectivity of those accounts suspect. In fact, one of the most important historical accounts of the war was written twenty years after the war ended by John Mason himself, the leader of the battle at Mistick Fort, who was viewed as a hero by most colonists and a monster by the Pequot. You can imagine that, at least from the Pequot perspective, and from the perspective of modern historians, the objectivity of *Major Mason's Brief History of the Pequot War*, written in 1660, cannot be assumed.[2]

However, especially when it relates to simple facts about the sequence of the battle, most historians take Mason at his word—for example, when he notes that the attack commenced at four o'clock on the morning of May 26, 1637. By five o'clock his men had breached the fort and were engaged in hand-to-hand combat with a large number of warriors who were vigorously and, at least initially, successfully defending their homes and their families. In fact, as Mason admits, the Indians were winning the battle on their home turf, so Mason, rather than focus on a losing strategy, changed his approach and set fire to the wooden structures in the village. Having accomplished this, he retreated from the fire, moving his men outside the log wall that encompassed the village, where his men proceeded to kill every Pequot who attempted to flee the blaze. In other words, the hundreds of people in the village had a choice of burning to death or being shot while fleeing that fire.

Archaeology of the Pequot War

Archaeology has been applied in an attempt to supplement the admittedly one-sided historical record and to provide an objective database on which historians and archaeologists can construct a veritable history of the war. The person most responsible for that fascinating work is the estimable Kevin McBride, a longtime colleague and friend—we were in grad school together—and a brilliant archaeologist who has directed the Battlefields of the Pequot War Project, as part of the federally funded American Battlefield Protection Program (administered by the National Park Service), for more than sixteen years. Their discoveries have been game changing. For an extremely informative discussion about how archaeology is revealing the true history of the Pequot War, see the fantastic recording of a lecture on the subject by McBride on YouTube.[3]

McBride freely admits that when he initiated the project, he wasn't particularly confident that they would find all that much in terms of archaeological remains of the war. After all, the area where the battle took place and where the combatants' encampments were located is today characterized by both residential and commercial development. Nevertheless, the project has been astonishingly successful in discovering artifacts and other material elements of the war, recovering them, and then using that material to help flesh out the story of the battle. That battle left its imprint on the landscape, and archaeology is revealing the story it tells.

Using Mason's book as a guide, McBride's team relied for the most part on metal detectors since most of the material used in battle and that likely preserved were metal objects. Though Mason likely was biased, his factual account of the timing and movement of the forces he led appears to be pretty accurate. The archaeology of the fort recovered musket balls, pieces of the armor the English were wearing, clothing buttons lost during hand-to-hand combat, gun flints, and metal arrow points belonging to the Pequot, who were vastly "outgunned" in the literal sense that they had very few firearms and relied on their bows and arrows. As noted, having little need for metal pots and pans, they had cleverly crafted arrow points from those obtained through trade.

Okay, that's interesting and a valuable complement to Mason's description of the battle. But archaeology of the war has also provided information that was previously unknown. You see, while the English and their Native allies had scored a major military victory, killing a large number of Pequot warriors, they still needed to get back to their ship in Pequot Harbor, and that was a 10-kilometer (6-mile) trek right through the middle of Pequot territory. Word had spread quickly among the Pequot of the attack on Mistick Fort and the slaughter of not only warriors there but women and children, many having been horribly burned to death. Those warriors became dedicated to exacting vengeance on their English and Native enemies.

Mentioned only briefly in histories written soon after the fight, what is now called the Battle of the English Withdrawal—a ten-hour fight from nine o'clock in the morning to seven o'clock in the evening, as the English and their allies fled from the smoldering remains of the village to the harbor—is now being illuminated by the work of archaeology. Though it is not recorded in any history, McBride found that there were six Pequot domestic sites, villages and encampments, located along that escape route, and the people in those locations were intent on attacking and killing as many Englishmen and Native enemies as they could. At that they were successful, but at a terrible cost.

McBride's crews have recovered more than twenty-five hundred artifacts associated with the fight along the route, including one thousand musket balls shot at the Pequot, broken gun barrels, assorted parts of matchlock and flintlock rifles and pistols, ramrods, and frizzens (parts of the fire mechanisms of flintlock firearms). They also recovered many of the brass and copper arrow points that the Pequot had shot at the invaders as they withdrew from the scene. As McBride describes it, the density of the remains of weapons of war clearly shows, especially across about 6.5 kilometers (4 miles) of their escape route, that the Battle of the English Withdrawal was furious and deadly.

There were times during the battle when troops rested and caught their collective breath, and McBride's team has identified the locations at which they did so by the presence of non-battle-related artifacts, things like jaw harps, buttons, and pipes. A wealth of artifacts has also been found at places where the Pequot warriors rested and reassessed the battle. Among the objects recovered were amulets, metal Jesuit finger rings, and smoking pipes. Another fascinating artifact type was pieces of brass and copper of no particular shape. We know that the Native People of Connecticut, while using these metals for utilitarian purposes, also viewed the raw metal itself as sacred, connected to a spirit creature called the Underwater Panther, a half-lynx, half-serpent animal whose tail was made of copper. One can imagine mortally wounded warriors, briefly stopped in the midst of the battle, dying as their compatriots carried them away, their metal charms falling to the ground.

Mason estimated that half of his men who survived the battle at the fort were either dead or incapacitated by the time they arrived at the harbor. It was even worse for the Pequot. As McBride points out, in every skirmish, in every battle leading up to Mistick, the Pequot had bested the English. The Pequot fought hard and they fought smart, recognizing the limitations of their weapons but taking advantage of the fact that they knew the territory better than the English. Their battle tactics can best be described as those of a guerrilla army. They didn't attempt to overwhelm their enemy in a single attack. Instead, they attacked quickly, then disappeared into the surrounding woodlands, content to kill only a small number of their enemy in each skirmish and to terrorize the larger number of survivors.

It was a brilliant approach in a war against the English. I also think it reflects a philosophy of war that conceives of it primarily as a psychological weapon to be wielded carefully, judiciously, and in small doses. Pequot tactics reflect the fact that because the English had guns, from a purely pragmatic perspective, the Pequot likely would not be successful in staging full-on, frontal assaults against them. They didn't have the ability to kill the English all at once, and maybe they didn't want to. Instead, their goal was to make the lives of the English colonists so miserable and insecure, they might just leave the Pequot alone.

Everything changed following Mistick. Perhaps as a result of the strategy I have just described, the Pequot were adherents to the philosophy of war predicated on the notion that proportionality was key. If we kill a handful of your traders who we think deserve it because they're screwing us over, we expect that you'll kill a handful of us. But you don't come into our territory and destroy an entire village filled with hundreds of people, including noncombatants. That's bad form and in fact unforgivable, a serious breach of the rule of proportionality and, in a modern sense, a war crime.

As a result, upon learning of the massacre at Mistick Fort, the surviving Pequot were so filled with rage and so despondent, they abandoned their slow and steady and previously successful approach to battle and started attacking their English and Native enemies with abandon, throwing themselves into battle without any thought of self-preservation or any interest in a long-term strategy. Unfortunately, that tactic only resulted in the deaths of many, many Pequot warriors; the Pequot assert that they lost more people, perhaps as many as five hundred, in the Battle of the English Withdrawal than they had at Mistick Fort. With that, and with the execution of their great sachem or ruler Sausacus by the Mohawk, the Pequot were, at least for a time, a finished, shattered people. You can understand, then, how the modern descendants of those shattered people feel perhaps a little bit of retribution as they see white people losing fortunes at the craps and poker tables at their very successful Foxwoods casino on their reservation in Connecticut.

The Pueblo Revolt

I started chapter 14 with a discussion of the Spanish explorer Francisco Vázquez de Coronado. He and his men traipsed around in the American Southwest between 1540 and 1542, inspired by the even then tired trope of hidden cities of gold—seven of them, to be precise. Not content to just invade the territory of the Native People living there, Coronado also initiated the so-called Tiguex War against the Pueblo people as part of a strategy to essentially annex their homeland, called Nuevo (New) México by the Spanish, to Spanish holdings in the New World, which, at this point, amounted to New Spain (Mexico). The Tiguex War has the distinction of being the first "named" war between European invaders and Native Americans, which is not exactly something Coronado should be lauded for. That war initiated more than a century of a fraught relationship between the Spanish colonists and the Native People of the Southwest, with episodes of violence, periods of relative calm, and lots of exploitation of the labor of the Pueblo people.

Though there were explicit policies articulated back in Spain about how the country's representatives in New Spain should be fair and magnanimous to the Native People, let's say they didn't quite live up to those goals. For example, when the Spanish were attempting to colonize an area near the Rio Grande, the local Acoma Pueblo people objected and rebelled against the invaders. In putting down the rebellion, the first governor of New Mexico, Juan de Oñate, ordering the killing of hundreds of Native People and the enslavement of many others, and in a policy that ranks him among the great monsters of history (there should be trading cards), he took all of the men of Acoma Pueblo over the age of twenty-five and ordered the amputation of each man's right foot purely as an act of terror.

On April 16, 1605, Oñate was the first European to inscribe his name on the rock face at El Morro, the national monument mentioned in chapter 14. I can't imagine what the other visitors to El Morro in April 2023 thought when they saw this short, white-haired weirdo (that would be me) flipping the bird to the place on the rock where Oñate had left his inscription. It's been more than four hundred years, but I don't think there should be a statute of limitations or an expiration date on that level of depravity.

The Archaeology of Conversion

One of the things that motivated the Spanish was religious conversion of the Pueblo people. The Spanish took literally and very seriously Pope Paul III's claim in 1537 that the Indians "desire exceedingly" to become Catholics (see chapter 4). With that in mind, the Spanish developed a clever strategy to facilitate conversion of the Native People by building churches adjacent to existing pueblos or even incorporating Catholic churches into those Native buildings. So the Native People didn't need to come to the church. The church came to them.

You can see the results of that strategy at archaeological sites in a couple of national monuments in New Mexico. Pecos National Monument includes the nine-hundred-year-old village called Cicuye, which had an Indigenous population of about two thousand people in the seventeenth century. The Spanish built a church at Cicuye, a gigantic structure consisting of three hundred thousand adobe bricks, and consecrated it in 1625. There is also Salinas National Monument, which includes three pueblos, Abo, Gran Quivira, and Quarai, along with their associated Catholic churches. It was a brilliant, if nefarious, strategy that allowed for easy and direct access to large concentrations of Native People who, apparently, needed their souls saved, and it also provided direct access to a labor pool that could be exploited by the Church.

The strategy worked, sort of, in that the missionaries were able to convert a lot of people, but it is apparent that the conversions weren't really all that life changing for the Pueblo people. Especially during the early years, you couldn't exactly call the Native folks deeply committed or enthusiastic Catholics. Sure they went through the motions, going to church on Sundays and wearing crosses, but they largely continued to practice their Native religion at home. They were, in a sense, casual Catholics or Sunday Catholics. Going to church on Sunday bought them access to cool European "stuff," but, if anything, they adhered to a kind of syncretism in their religious practices and beliefs where they reinterpreted and reimagined Catholic theology within the context of their traditional beliefs. Catholicism didn't replace their traditional religion; it complemented it.

I am reminded of the really quite amazing murals, measuring 15.2 meters (50 feet) long, painted by the Zuni artist Alex Seowtewa in the 1970s in the church at Zuni Pueblo in New Mexico, which was built in 1629. The images in the murals are not of Jesus, Mary, Joseph, or the saints as you might expect. They are depictions of the various Pueblo spirits! It is wonderful on so many levels—remember my discussion of Michelangelo's *Pietá* in chapter 16—that in a 1991 article the *Albuquerque Tribune* called Seowtewa the "Michelangelo of the Southwest."[4]

I think things might have been much better between the Church and the Pueblo people had the former accepted that the Native People embraced some elements of Catholicism but wanted to maintain many of their religious traditions. Instead, the Church came to view the Native traditions and practices as sorcery and devil worship and attempted to repress those beliefs and practices and oppress believers and practitioners, going so far as to execute them. That level of oppression was one of the most significant factors in inspiring the otherwise peaceful and unflappable Pueblo people to engage in a violent and bloody uprising in which they killed a lot of Spaniards.

The policy imposed by Fray Alonso de Posada in 1656–65 of confiscating and then destroying Pueblo religious paraphernalia, including effigies, masks, and prayer sticks, was initiated as part of his scheme to eliminate any vestiges of traditional worship and ceremonies. It didn't work and only succeeded in convincing the Native People that any hope of accommodating the quaint beliefs of the invaders, with their obsessive and intrusive desire to control the local people, was doomed to failure.

Next, in an attempt to exert even further control over the people, in 1675 Governor Juan Francisco Treviño had forty-seven Pueblo priests arrested and then had three of them executed. Among those released was a man named Po'pay, who turned out to be a brilliant military strategist who spent the next five years coordinating with other Pueblo leaders in planning a rebellion to expunge the Spanish from their homeland. In August 1680 in a well-planned and coordinated military action, the united Pueblo army rose up and handily defeated the Spanish invaders, killing more than four hundred of them, including nearly every Catholic priest in the territory, and effectively pushing about two thousand Spanish colonists out of New Mexico. It was payback for years of religious persecution and murder, and maybe—just spitballing here—for having rounded up young men and amputating their feet. In the revolt, the Pueblo people destroyed all of the Catholic churches—every one of them—and burned down every Spanish settlement. As impressive as their victory was, it was short lived, lasting for a little more than a decade. The Spanish returned in 1692 with an overwhelming military force.

Along with engaging in military action, the people at the aforementioned Cicuye village appear to have left a symbolic message representing their rejection of Catholicism and of all things Spanish. Incorporated into the *convento* of the burned-out church—the part of the building complex where the priest, Fray Andrés, had lived—there was a kiva, built at the same time as the priest's quarters, around 1620. As you might remember from chapter 14, a kiva is generally a round structure largely dedicated to traditional religious and social ceremonies. It has long been assumed that the friar in charge of building the church at Pecos disingenuously used the kiva as a tool in conversion, making the Indigenous People more comfortable being exposed to Catholicism in

FIGURE 17.1. The so-called Resistance Kiva at Pecos Pueblo, used in a revival of Native religion following the Pueblo Revolt of 1680 CE. Kenneth L. Feder

a building form with which they were already familiar and comfortable. If you visit Pecos National Monument, you'll see this structure, which, following the Pueblo Revolt, was no longer an agent of their conversion and erasure but was, instead, reconsecrated and used as a "real" kiva, a symbol of resistance against the Spanish imposing their beliefs and practices on the Pueblos and of revival and rejuvenation of their own culture (Figure 17.1).

Battle of the Greasy Grass: The Little Bighorn Battlefield

History isn't inclusive—it doesn't cover everything—and it isn't necessarily objective. In a very cynical view provided by the acerbically funny author Ambrose Bierce in his *Devil's Dictionary*, "History is an account, mostly false, of events, mostly unimportant, which are brought about by rulers, mostly knaves, and soldiers, mostly fools."[5]

Okay, maybe that's an extreme opinion, but especially in the case of a fierce battle, the so-called fog of war renders history derived from eyewitness testimony highly suspect. It's also the case that in the self-aware recording of events of a battle, one can imagine that those doing the reporting might, at the least, have a tendency to massage the facts in order to make them look better in retrospect and, at the worst, flat-out lie about events. As twentieth-century British prime minister Winston Churchill phrased it, "History will be kind to me, for I intend to write it," and I imagine that might apply to soldiers on all sides in their reporting of a battle.

Another aphorism that is often also attributed to Churchill, though there are versions of it that long precede him: "History is written by the victors [or winners]." Applying this, it is important to note that the winners and, even more potently, the survivors will have their voices amplified over those of people who lost the battle, have been imprisoned or enslaved, and, rather obviously in the most extreme case, were killed before sharing their perspectives about what happened. In the case of the Battle of the Little Bighorn, the only survivors of the battle were Lakota, Cheyenne, and Arapaho warriors; all of the combatants in the Seventh Cavalry, more than two hundred of them, were killed in the battle. So we don't have any testimony reflecting their recollections or perspectives. Despite these challenges, and especially as a result of the U.S. Army inquest, we have a pretty good idea about some elements of the battle. Here's what we know.

The Sioux and Northern Cheyenne Indian tribes were a potent military force well into the second half of the nineteenth century. In 1866, they had gone to war to prevent white encroachment into their territory in the northern plains. Look, it was their homeland, and they recognized that they were in the midst of an existential confrontation with white settlers. As succinctly phrased by Ta Sunke Witco (Crazy Horse), "We did not ask you white men to come here. The Great Spirit gave us this country as a home. You had yours. We did not interfere with yours. We do not want your civilization" (as recorded on the Native American memorial at the Little Bighorn National Monument).

The hostilities that resulted were called the Red Cloud War, which ended in 1868 with the signing of the Fort Laramie Treaty. In essence, the Native People had persevered and all of South Dakota west of the Missouri River was ceded to the Sioux. The federal government now had a treaty obligation to keep white settlers out of this hard-won territory. In return, the Native People promised to live on reservations staked out in this domain. While many Natives agreed, others refused, not wanting to settle for the land provided in the treaty or agree to the terms of the agreement, preferring to live their traditional, nomadic way of life, unrestricted by reservation boundaries or state borders. The federal government defined all of these non-reservation-living Indians as "hostiles."

In the same year the Fort Laramie Treaty ostensibly ended hostilities and confirmed Native ownership of part of South Dakota, rumors of gold in the heart of this territory—the Black Hills—began to filter east. With these rumors came a swarm of white prospectors who were willing to defy the treaty. This put the federal government in an awkward position. Given a choice, they would have locked down the territory of the Sioux from encroachment, but politically the government could not let the white people flooding into the territory be harmed, even though they were in violation of the treaty. Those white folks could vote and, at this time in history, Indians could not. So politicians felt the need to accommodate the people breaking the law and ignore the folks whose land was being encroached upon. In an attempt to control the Indians and in order to protect the white intruders, the "hostiles" were all ordered to the reservation. The consequence of disobedience in the face of this order was made explicit: war.

It is clear in hindsight that the nonreservation Natives who seemed the largest threat to the safety of the illegal prospectors had not the necessary time, the requisite weather conditions, or the inclination to respond positively to the order to retreat to the reservation. So the U.S. government decided in 1876 to initiate a war against these "intransigents." I'm not convinced that their heart was in it and that an all-out shooting war was what the government was hoping for. Instead, they hoped that an overwhelming show of force would be enough to convince the Native People living off reservation to retreat to the reservation, at which point the government could attempt to reconfigure the treaty in a way that isolated the Native People, insulated the white miners from them, and would allow them to look for gold.

So in 1876, not even 150 years ago as I write this, Lieutenant General Philip Sheridan ordered his commanders George Crook and Alfred Terry to prepare for what amounted to a search-and-destroy mission against the estimated eight hundred warriors who had refused to come to the reservation. Under Terry's command was the Seventh Cavalry, commanded by a politically ambitious, thirty-six-year-old Lieutenant Colonel George Armstrong Custer. The decision to hunt down what was presumed to be a manageably small and poorly armed group of hostiles was to set in motion a series of events that would lead to what historian Robert Utley reasonably characterizes as "the most spectacular triumph of the American Indian in his four-century struggle against the relentlessly advancing European civilization."[6]

About the battle that was to become known as Custer's Last Stand, much remains unknown. We do know that Major Marcus Reno, on a scouting mission with elements of the Seventh Cavalry, had located a sizable trail that, it was presumed, led to an encampment of Natives who had failed to comply with the government's order to remove to the reservation. On June 22, 1876, Custer set out with a contingent of not quite six hundred enlisted men (including his younger brother Thomas, who served as Custer's aid), forty Indian scouts, and twenty civilians—including three farriers (people who take care of horse hooves); another one of Custer's brothers, Boston (a civilian in charge of providing forage for the horses); and an embedded reporter—toward the presumed location of that hostile Indian camp in what is now Montana, far outside the reservation lands of South Dakota.[7] The plan was for Custer, commanding a swiftly moving cavalry, to arrive at the Native village before the other men under Terry and set in place. At this point the orders for the Seventh Cavalry were to collect intelligence and not initiate the battle. Custer's primary concern was that the Indians would become aware of his presence and slip away into the hills, where they would be difficult to track down.

So concerned was Custer over the possibility that the Sioux would escape the trap being laid for them, he decided to move more quickly than he had been ordered. He did not bypass the Native encampment and wait until June 26 to launch a coordinated attack with the other, more slowly moving regiments as originally planned. Instead, he became convinced that his presence had been detected by the Indians. So instead of being patient and prudently waiting for reinforcements, he decided to attack immediately on the twenty-fifth. He hoped and believed that the men of the Seventh Cavalry could by themselves deliver a mortal blow to a larger but poorly trained and poorly armed force of Native People.

Did anything else motivate Custer to attack before reinforcements arrived? It's not clear. However, one possibility concerns his political aspirations. He had already written a book trumpeting his exploits as a soldier with the requisite ability and experience to "pacify" the Indians, preferably by confining them to reservations but by killing them if necessary.[8] As he approached the encampment of Sioux, Cheyenne, and Arapaho, did a combination of overconfidence and ambition get the better of him? Did he think, "Oh boy. If I can score this public relations coup, the newspapers back east will print headlines trumpeting my brilliance and bravery. I will be celebrated for subduing the hostile Indians, making the northern plains safe for white American resource exploitation and settlement while the slower and timid Crook and Terry held back"? It might have occurred to him that this sort of public relations success as an "Indian killer" might become a valuable talking point in a presidential campaign.

Whatever the case, in preparation for battle, Custer had divided the men under his command into three battalions: Reno was placed in control of 140 men, Captain Frederick Benteen was given 125 men, and Custer took about 210. Following Custer's orders, these 475 men began a series of movements intended to surround, attack, and defeat an Indian force believed to be not much more than twice their number. Unfortunately for them, there had been a serious miscalculation. Instead of a maximum of 1,000, there were at least 2,000 and as many as 4,000 Native soldiers in an encampment of more than 10,000 Sioux, Cheyenne, and Arapaho. Even the Native People were surprised by the foolhardiness of Custer's attack. The Lakota warrior Low Dog is recorded as saying, "They came on us like a thunderbolt. I did not think it possible that any white men would attack us, so strong as we were" (as recorded on the Indian memorial at the Little Bighorn National Monument).

At about two fifteen on the afternoon of June 25, Reno, moving into position before the battle, encountered a small party of Native soldiers. Reno and his men gave chase only to realize too late that they had been drawn into combat with an enormous force. Hopelessly outnumbered, Reno's battalion retreated. They had been decimated, losing, in a very short time, about one-third of their men. About fifty-two soldiers were killed in this initial engagement.

Following Custer's initial orders, Benteen's battalion had marched to the southeast to prevent any escape of the Natives in that direction. As Benteen found no such escape in progress, he turned back along the trail. In the process he was met by Custer's trumpeter John Martin, who was carrying a message from Custer's Adjutant Lieutenant William Cooke. The scrawled note read, "Benteen, Come on. Big Village, be quick, bring packs. P.S. bring pacs [sic]" (the packs would have contained additional ammunition). That must have resulted in a serious "uh-oh" moment. Things were going drastically wrong in a hurry. The soldiers were about to find out that "drastically wrong" was too mild a characterization.

Benteen and his men responded but were only able to get to the scene of Reno's besiegement and join his battalion. The men under Reno and Benteen became surrounded and cut off from the rest of the Seventh Cavalry. Custer and his men were alone in the battle. Enforcements would arrive only after they were all dead.

We know about Reno and Benteen's predicament and actions because, though their battalions had been mauled, there were survivors, Reno and Benteen among them. When reinforcements arrived, the enormous Native encampment scattered and Reno, Benteen, and their men were spared. As Utley points out, however, in the case of Custer and the 210 men under his command, "no man can know with certainty how Custer's battalion met its fate for no member survived.... The details of the action, together with Custer's intentions and the factors which shaped them, must ever remain a mystery."[9]

Utley's pessimistic view is a bit of an overstatement since there are other sources of information concerning the battle. While it is true that there were no survivors among Custer's men, it is estimated that the Natives lost proportionally far fewer, only about 30 to 150 men in the entire battle. Historians have constructed elements of the battle on the basis of interviews with Native warriors who participated.[10]

Beyond the historical documentation based on eyewitness reports of the Native People who experienced the battle, there also is the physical evidence of the battle itself. The battlefield became, as a matter of course, an archaeological site. And the material remains of the battle were confronted as soon as the day following the battle.

On June 28, 1876, Reno's battalion arrived at the battlefield to find a scene of absolute horror. The Native warriors and their families were gone. But the bodies of the Seventh Cavalry soldiers, in some cases mutilated, were found where the soldiers fell. It was hot and the bodies were decaying. The sight and smells must have been both physically and psychologically devastating. Reno's men quickly buried the dead, often in extremely shallow graves, not in a formal cemetery but, as they later reported, precisely where they had fallen in battle. In a sense, then, in their disposal of the bodies of their comrades, they were preserving the geography of the last moments of the battle.

The battlefield was almost immediately viewed by many people as what amounts to a sacred site. In 1877 and 1879, the soldiers killed in the battle were disinterred and then reburied in deeper, more secure graves, but again in the locations where they had died—in other words, where each man had made his "last stand." Each burial location was then marked with a wooden cross, with the names recorded of the soldiers who were recognizable when found immediately after the battle. The bodies of the officers and civilians were exhumed and returned to their families for reburial. Custer's remains were removed to West Point, his alma mater in New York State. Finally, in 1881, all of Custer's soldiers—at least, all that could be found on the battlefield—were disinterred and

FIGURE 17.2. When the bodies of the members of the Seventh Cavalry were found by the U.S. Army the day after their defeat, they were buried where they lay and markers were placed at each soldier's "last stand." Those makeshift markers were later replaced with permanent marble ones. In this image, you'll see Custer's with its inscription on a black background. Kenneth L. Feder

reburied in a mass grave at the location of a granite battlefield memorial, but the crosses that formerly marked their burial sites were left in place.

That joint monument is located at the top of a high point on the battlefield adjacent to the final position of Custer and a cluster of about thirty of his troops, the infamous location of the "last stand," where they all were killed in battle (Figure 17.2).

That monument bears the names of all of the soldiers and the members of their entourage who died that day. I realize this comment will seem mysterious to many readers, but no, three additional names did not suddenly appear on that monument in the early 1960s. That was the paranormal payoff at the climax of a particularly creepy and very well-done episode of the original *Twilight Zone* series ("The 7th Is Made Up of Phantoms," 1963).

In 1890, the original wooden crosses were replaced with permanent marble markers, again with the soldiers' names inscribed where

FIGURE 17.3. More recently placed, these markers memorialize two of the Native Americans who died during the Battle of the Little Bighorn: A'Kavehe'Onahe (Limber Bones) and Hahpehe'Onahe (Closed Hand). Kenneth L. Feder

known. Far more recently, a few stone markers were placed to memorialize the lives of three Native warriors who died in the battle: A'Kavehe'Onahe (Limber Bones; Cheyenne), Hahpehe'Onahe (Closed Hand; Cheyenne), and Wasicu Sapa (Black White Man; Lakota) (Figure 17.3). Another marker was placed in recognition of the horses killed on that day.

The positioning of the markers, apparently reflecting the final locations of Custer's men at the climax of the battle, has long been used to reconstruct the final moments of the struggle. Several writers have suggested that the markers' positions, often grouped in pairs, reflect the final strategy of the Seventh Cavalry soldiers. Surrounded and outnumbered, the soldiers clustered in groups of two, it has been suggested, to better defend themselves. In an official report of the Custer National Monument prepared in 1890, O. J. Sweet proposed that forty-three pairs of markers represented the locations of "bunkmates" who bravely fought and died together.[11]

Though approximately 210 men died with Custer on June 25, the number of markers has fluctuated through the years: today there are 252, and there have been as many as 262. How can the discrepancy between the number of soldiers who died with Custer and the number of markers be explained? This is a crucial consideration if the location of the markers is used to reconstruct the last moments of the Battle of the Little Bighorn. The mystery has been approached through archaeology.

As archaeologist Douglas Scott points out, there was an immediate and morbid interest in the battlefield.[12] Indeed, soon after the battle, people arrived hunting for grisly souvenirs. One in particular was a human neck vertebra of one of the soldiers that had an iron arrow point still nestled in the bone (found in 1878 or 1879).

Initial, formal archaeological excavations at the battlefield site were conducted in 1984 and 1985.[13] Following a prairie fire in 1991, a surface survey was conducted that entailed a careful walkover and recovery of battlefield artifacts revealed on the surface, including bullets and stone arrow points. Also, excavations were conducted in the vicinity of 37 of the 252 extant markers. Though the remains of most of the soldiers had been exhumed by 1881, the archaeologists felt certain that the army's reburial detail could not have recovered 100 percent of the skeletal and archaeological material. What remained, the archaeologists hoped, would provide important information concerning the final moments of the Battle of the Little Bighorn.

The hope and expectation were well founded. The excavators indeed discovered human and artifactual remains surrounding most of the thirty-seven marble markers investigated. Interestingly, none of the paired markers, however, produced the bones of more than a single soldier. For example, in the excavation around Markers 67 and 68, fragments of human ribs, vertebrae, and skull were found, but they were all from the same person. Also found in this unit, however, were the osteological remains of a horse. Perhaps the 1881 reburial detail had not the expertise to distinguish fragmentary horse bones from human and assumed that two soldiers had fallen in this spot.[14]

Another scenario explains some of the paired markers. After the battle, each of Custer's soldiers was indeed buried where he fell. The soil was dry and hard, and shovels were in short supply. While some effort was made to bury the officers deeply enough so that animals, wind, or rain would not disturb their remains, most enlisted men were covered only with a thin layer of earth taken from either side of their bodies. Later details may have interpreted the dual depressions left from this process as two shallow graves and marked them as such.

Thus, the position of the markers does not support an interpretation of pairs of soldiers fighting in tandem against insurmountable odds. More often than not, the markers were placed where individual men of the Seventh Cavalry fell on the battlefield.

The archaeology of the battlefield therefore has helped dispel one battle scenario at the same time it has, in a general sense, validated the significance of the location of the markers. As a result, we can today obtain a better understanding of the final moments of the battle; archaeology has provided tangible evidence where the testimony of the participants does not exist.

When the Native warriors testified about the battle, they made sure to praise the courage of their adversaries: "It was a terrible battle . . . a hard battle because both sides were brave warriors" (from the testimony of Red Feather, included as part of a National Park Service memorial at the site for the Indians who fought on that day).

It is no surprise that the Little Bighorn Battlefield has been designated a national monument, representing as it does a definitional moment in the relationship between Plains Indians, including the Lakota Sioux, the Northern Cheyenne, and the Arapaho, on one side and the federal government of the United States, represented by the Seventh Cavalry, on the other. It is a melancholy place where brave men, on both sides, died for what they thought was a noble cause, a place that haunts the history of America.

Wounded Knee

One gruesome though common element of war is the defiling of the corpses of enemies and the appropriation of their stuff. The drive to violate the body of an enemy on the battlefield may result from a combination of, on the one hand, anger and terror and, on the other, an attendant adrenaline rush experienced by the victors.

The appropriation of their stuff may occur for purely practical reasons. Maybe it's winter, maybe it's snowing, and maybe your feet are cold and you don't have a good pair of shoes. Those boots on the feet of your slain enemy look really good and really warm and, hell, he's not going to need them where he's going anyway, so why not take them? And the coat, socks, hat, and muffler? Again, useful for you, not so useful for the dead soldier or warrior. That rifle won't be of use to him, but it certainly may be to you.

The appropriation of their stuff also might be yet another show of force on your part, a way of dominating yet again an enemy who has entered into your territory, has killed your friends, and would have killed you if given a chance. It may seem gross, and we might think we'd never do such a thing. But it has happened and likely is continuing to happen wherever people engage in combat. I raise this issue because there's an example of this in the case of the Battle of Wounded Knee, another massacre of Native Americans by the U.S. Army.

The Wounded Knee massacre occurred just fifteen years after the Lakota Sioux and their Native allies had defeated the Seventh Cavalry. Much had changed in those years and the details are beyond the scope of this book. For those details, the best-selling book *Bury My Heart at Wounded Knee*, by Dee Brown, is a great place to start an investigation of this heartbreaking story. Suffice it to say, the federal government had decided that the best strategy for protecting white settlers from Native Americans on the Great Plains—most of whom, ironically, wanted nothing to do with white people—was to congregate and concentrate them in what amounted to internment camps. One goal was to enculturate Native People (see chapter 18) in the ways of Euro-American culture, make them farmers living in nuclear families, and convert them to Christianity.

Many Lakota, especially older people, were resigned to their fate, recognizing that their defeat of Custer, as important a victory as that had been, had been a one-off, one that would not be repeated, and that the U.S. Army was now far too powerful to resist in terms of numbers and weaponry. Many younger people, especially young warriors, however, vowed to never bow to subjugation of their way of life by the U.S. government.

Many of the resisters became adherents to a new belief system called the Ghost Dance movement. The belief was that, as bad as the situation seemed, white people were doomed and would soon all die and a heaven on Earth for Native People was about to be established. All that needed to happen was for Indians to dance a new dance introduced by a Paiute prophet named Wovoka. As part of that belief system, warriors would don a sacred shirt to wear into battle that would make them impervious to attack.

When the army showed up to try to round up Native People, many Lakota escaped into the Black Hills of South Dakota and prepared to wait it out until the whites had all died. Followers of the Ghost Dance religion believed that Jesus Christ (who was deemed to be a Native American) would raise all the living Natives up into the sky and cause a massive, Noah-like flood to drown all non-Natives. Following this he would replenish the bison herds, then resurrect all dead Native People and gently set them back on the ground for a life in a paradise on Earth.

However, as the old saw goes, you can run, but you cannot hide, and the army, determined to carry out the orders they had received from Washington, D.C., caught up with a large contingent of these "hostiles" at the place called Wounded Knee, in South Dakota. Negotiations ensued for a hoped-for peaceful resolution to the situation and many Lakota, seeing how badly they were outgunned and outnumbered, gave up their weapons and were therefore unarmed. At that point, with the Natives essentially helpless, there was a series of miscommunications, mistakes, and accidents. Tension was very high, soldiers had their fingers on the triggers of their guns, and then, sadly, a gun went off—no one knows whose—and the army, convinced that a battle of biblical proportions had just started, began shooting their automatic weapons called Hotchkiss guns, a nineteenth-century version of machine guns. Using those guns, the soldiers mowed down more than two hundred men, women, and children, even chasing down people running away from the battle and no longer a threat to the soldiers. It was, by any objective measure, a massacre. In many ways, Wounded Knee was a knockout punch to the Ghost Dance movement and to the desires of the Lakota to simply be left alone on their land.

To the best of my knowledge, there has been no archaeological study of the Wounded Knee killing field. I use that term rather than "battlefield" since most of the Sioux had just had their weapons confiscated. While there is no archaeology in the strict sense of the word, the discipline is, after all and as defined in this book, "the study of the material remains of human behavior," and there were things stolen from those slain at Wounded Knee. These objects, these artifacts, help tell the story of the people who made and used them. Some of these things were collected at the massacre site as soldiers and perhaps other onlookers approached the dead bodies and removed items in their desire for souvenirs. Morbid, I know.

It's hard to know where a lot of those items ended up. Many of them likely were passed down in families without any documentation. However, in a few cases there is pretty good evidence of a chain of custody of the material, some of which ended up in museums in places as far away from Montana as Massachusetts and even Scotland.

For example, just a few years ago the Founders Museum in Barre, Massachusetts, about 113 kilometers (70 miles) west of Boston, still housed objects ostensibly stripped from Lakota people killed at Wounded Knee. They have, among other things, pipes, moccasins, necklaces, and assorted articles of clothing. At one time the museum also had what was purported to be a lock of hair taken from the scalp of a Lakota warrior, Spotted Elk. The museum returned that to the descendants in 1999.

All of the items from Wounded Knee were donated to the museum by a peripatetic showman from Barre who claimed to have purchased the artifacts from men who had been tasked with burying some of those killed. The Sioux, who have been trying to get the objects returned since 1990, believe the museum has a couple hundred items plundered from the Wounded Knee dead. The museum maintains that it's probably no more than a dozen and they aren't really certain that any of the material actually was from Wounded Knee.[15] The tribes and the museum continue to negotiate about the repatriation of tribal material.

There's a similar story at the Kelvingrove Art Gallery and Museum in Glasgow, Scotland, where they have possessed moccasins, a necklace, and a child's bonnet since 1891. Another item, a blood-stained Ghost Shirt in the museum's inventory, was repatriated in 1999. According to the museum, the items were obtained from George Crager, an ex-soldier and performer with Buffalo Bill's Wild West Show, when they were performing in Scotland. Concerning these items, Charles New Holy, a Lakota member of the Wounded Knee Survivors Association, has eloquently and passionately stated, "Those items belong to our grandfathers and grandmothers—their spirit is still connected to them—but people see prestige and money in them. These are spiritual items that should not be displayed anywhere."[16] When confronted with the child's bonnet, New Holy stated it even more passionately: "Why would you strip children of clothing after you murder them? We have every right to our ancestors' belongings." Indeed.

When Contact Led to Cooperation

This chapter has been pretty grim. And I don't want to leave you with the impression that contact between the Indigenous People of North America inevitably led to death and destruction. There are examples of cooperation informed by the historical and archaeological records.

It isn't too often that an archaeologist can point to a Native American archaeological village site and identify it as the historical home of a person whose name is recognized by most people, Native and non-Native alike, American and non-American as well. That, however, certainly applies to what is called the Knife River Indian Villages National Historic Site located in North Dakota, which was designated as such in 1974.

The five villages that constitute the historical site were home to the Hidatsa and Mandan people, closely related Native folks living in the northern plains. While their ancestors likely arrived in the area more than eleven thousand years ago, the Knife River villages were occupied, variously, from the early 1500s through the middle of the 1800s, leaving an archaeological footprint in the form of large, circular depressions, each one demarcating the home of a Hidatsa or Mandan family group. The architectural form of each structure was that of an earth lodge, a dome-shaped structure with a wooden framework covered with earth and sod. These earth lodges were not small, with a footprint of about 112 square meters (1,200 square feet). That's the size of the average single-family home in America in 1960. Each of the five villages had at least a few dozen such houses and, with an extended family in each (mom, dad, kids, grandparents), this would mean that each village had a population in the hundreds. The largest of the five villages, called Hidatsa Village, had more than one hundred earth lodges and a population estimated in excess of one thousand. The houses in each village were very closely packed together, likely for reasons of protection, which makes sense considering that the houses in one of the villages were burned to the ground during hostilities with another Native group, the Sioux, in the mid-1800s.

Further, we know what their homes looked like because they were still living in them when Europeans first entered into their territory. Those Europeans wrote about the earth lodges, and the well-known artist of the West George Catlin, whose primary artwork consists of paintings of Indigenous People and their possessions, quarries, and villages, produced a painting of one of the Knife River villages (Hidatsa Village) based on his visit in 1832 (Figure 17.4).

Catlin is a sort of ambiguous character in terms of his relationship to Native People, but one can't help but be struck by the obvious vitality of village life reflected in his painting.

Archaeology shows that the Hidatsa and Mandan used the area surrounding the Knife River as their home base, where they relied on agriculture for part of their subsistence. The "three sisters"—maize, beans, and squash—provided the bulk of the plant food in their diet. Hunting was a major component of their diet as well, primarily bison, white-tailed deer, mule deer, elk, pronghorn antelope, and bighorn sheep. They are sometimes labeled semisedentary, meaning that members of their families did move around in the food quest, especially during the winter.

Remember I teased the presence of an important historical figure who lived in one of the Knife River villages? Here's a hint: Meriwether

FIGURE 17.4. This painting by the artist George Catlin shows the vibrancy of life he witnessed at Hidatsa Village along the Knife River in North Dakota in 1832.

Lewis and William Clark, of the Lewis and Clark Corps of Discovery Expedition (1804–6), visited the villages on the Knife River in 1804. One of the ultimate goals of the expedition was to reach the Pacific coast, but that entailed traveling through Native territory, where they would need a translator to smooth the way, certainly someone who could speak both English and the Shoshone language of the region they were about to enter. They found that person in a young woman living in the Knife River village called by its people Awatixa. You have almost certainly heard her name: Sacagawea (sometimes written and pronounced Sakakwea).

Hers is a remarkable story of perseverance. Born Shoshone, she was kidnapped at the age of twelve and then sold to a white trapper to be his second wife. No, his first wife didn't leave him or die. He just wanted two wives. I do wonder if Sacagawea saw her opportunity to help Lewis and Clark also as an opportunity to get away from her husband. To make things even more interesting for her, when the expedition arrived at the Knife River settlement, she had recently given birth. Yes, Sacagawea led Lewis and Clark and their men from North Dakota to the Pacific, across mountains and rivers, all while carrying a baby on her back.

The Corps of Discovery kept a detailed account of their travels and of the Native People with whom they came into contact. Archaeology has been able to confirm at least part of their story. The Oregon Archaeological Society has done an admirable job of tracking down and identifying both the Native settlements listed by Lewis and Clark and the large encampments of the corps along the Columbia River from its confluence with the Snake River in eastern Washington and Oregon west to the Pacific Ocean.[17] The ability of the archaeological record to both complement and supplement the real-time account kept by Lewis and Clark is very impressive.

18

Archaeology and Ethnic Cleansing

"ETHNIC CLEANSING." It's an ugly term and an even uglier practice. It means to target an entire ethnic group for elimination, perhaps by merely erasing their culture and replacing it with the dominant one, maybe even through actual genocide. I use the term "ethnic cleansing" here not to be provocative or particularly political but because I can't come up with a better or more accurate term to describe the official policy of the federal governments of the United States and Canada toward the populations of Native People living within the borders of those countries in the nineteenth century. Let's look at a few examples.

The Tunxis People of the Farmington Valley

The Tunxis people of Farmington, Connecticut, were not forcibly removed from their home territory or escorted away by an armed guard, but they lost their homeland nevertheless and were given little choice but to remove themselves from the Farmington Valley. I include their story under the category "ethnic cleansing" at least in a geographic if not an existential sense. No, no act of genocide was visited upon the Tunxis, but they saw their homeland taken away from them, and in order to survive as a people, they had to remove themselves from that homeland.

During my forty-plus years as an archaeologist, I have conducted much of my research in the Farmington (Tunxis) River valley in northwest Connecticut. During that time, working with my colleague Marc Banks, we have located and identified close to two hundred archaeological sites and excavated twenty of them, some over multiple field seasons. Recently, researchers from the University of Connecticut discovered and excavated the Brian Jones site in the valley. Radiocarbon dating of charcoal recovered at the site provides dates of more than eleven thousand years ago.[1]

My point here is that people who are most likely, directly or indirectly, the ancestors of the Tunxis people encountered by European settlers in 1640 or 1650 have lived more or less continuously in the valley for more than eleven thousand years. So it seems perfectly reasonable that the Tunxis living in what is today the town of Farmington wondered in 1650 who in the hell these Europeans were who were moving into their homeland and how in the world they thought they now "owned" the land on which the Tunxis traditionally lived. A series of treaties, agreements, statements, and letters convey the tragic events that led the Tunxis people of Connecticut to move to, of all places, Wisconsin, where they relocated in the mid-eighteenth century and where they continue to live in the twenty-first. How did this bit of ethnic cleansing occur?

The Tunxis Have the Receipts

We do know that the English settlers of the Connecticut River valley, who were already living in Hartford in the 1630s, had explored to the west by 1640, crossing over the ancient volcanic ridge today called Talcott and Avon Mountains, which was a source for basalt and hornfels for the people at Alsop Meadow, as discussed in chapter 8. These colonists saw the beautiful and fertile river valley that local Native People called Tunxis, which was also the name of their group. Clearly the English coveted the rich farmland the area offered but recognized that there were people already living there. However, instead of approaching local people to attempt to negotiate a sale of some of their land, they negotiated the purchase of the entire valley of 775 square kilometers (300 square miles) with someone else entirely, not a resident of the valley and not a Tunxis but the sachem (chief) Sequassen, a self-described leader of Native residents of the Connecticut valley. Makes sense? Well, not really. To be sure, it very well may be that Sequassen was spoofing the English, knowing full well he had no ownership rights to the Tunxis valley and no legal power to sell it but, hell, if the English were willing to pay him for it, why not take the money?

Needless to say, but I'll say it anyway, the Tunxis were extremely confused and massively irritated when, beginning soon after 1640, English people began arriving in Tunxis territory, cutting down trees, putting up fences, plowing, planting on the land, and effectively sealing off the property to the Native residents of the valley. In response, the Tunxis filed a formal complaint with the institution called the General Court in Hartford of the colony of Connecticut. As a result of that complaint, the General Court generally acknowledged the Tunxis concerns in a 1650 document, part of which reads (I have kept the original spelling in the documents associated with this case; I examined the original, handwritten documents, where they are curated in the Connecticut Archives housed in the Connecticut State Library in Hartford):

> A Discovery in writing of such agreements as made by ye magistrates with ye Indians of Tunckses Sepus concerning the lands and such things in reference to thereunto as tend to settle peace in a way of truth and righteousness betwixt ye English and them. . . .
> "Therefore, ye Indians have reason to live loveingly among ye English by whom theyer lives ever are blessed and theyer estates and comforts advantaged."[2]

In their investigation, the General Court acknowledged the fact that the Tunxis were upset about losing their lands. The court then expressed the desire to come to an agreement that avoided violence and would lead to the Indians living "loveingly among ye English." And, oh boy, the Indians' lives would be so much better for the mere presence of those colonists.

It was a nice sentiment but, as we will see, it wasn't realized, and in 1672 the Tunxis, almost certainly with the assistance of English-speaking allies, filed another complaint with the General Court, making it clear that they were still upset. Obviously, the Tunxis wanted to go through the legal channels established by the English because they understood that going to war wouldn't work. The Tunxis knew full well the lesson of the Pequot War. Remember, that war had occurred just thirty-six years before, in 1636, and resulted in the utter defeat of that much more powerful group (chapter 17). The 1672 complaint letter reads, in part, "Wee, being now of small power and not willing to otherwayes contend, do hereby desire the honored court to take our said aggreivance into thayer serious consideration."[3] Again, by implication, the only "otherwayes" they might have contended was through a war they were not willing to initiate since they were "of small power."

The General Court responded to the 1672 grievance in 1673, acknowledging, "In process of time, some dissatisfaction growing amongst ye Indians in respect to ye premises upon which account ye town of Farmington gives them a meeting."[4] Here's where a bit of archaeology enters into the picture. When the English first entered into the Tunxis valley, there was an established Tunxis Indian village located north of a sizable bend in the Farmington River. The location of the village is apparent from English commentaries, and when we did a surface walkover of the plowed field where the English situated it, in fact we recovered flint flakes, a flint arrow point, and seventeenth- and eighteenth-century British-made ceramics. So archaeology confirms the presence of a Tunxis village in the same spot where historical documents placed it. The place was called Indian Neck, in reference to the location of that village. In 1673, the English acknowledged that the location of the Tunxis village still belonged to the Natives: "It is understood that ye land in ye Indian Neck which ye Indians stand possessed of doth yet remain firm and good to ye Indians, theyer heirs as firmly as ever tho not mentioned in ye above deed of sale they have given to the town of Farmington being bounded as on page 2 of this book we hereby declare that the town of Farmington hath neither right, title, claim or interest in aforesaid land by the above deed."[5]

That sounds pretty definitive. The location of Indian Neck village in the seventeenth century belongs to the Tunxis and their heirs. But only thirty-five years later, in 1738, the Tunxis formally complained again, this time about the fact that even the small amount of land on Indian Neck left to them was being taken over by Englishmen. Seeking to redress their grievances, the Tunxis requested that "the encroachments of the Englishmen may be removed and ye right and property of ye poor Memorialist [Tunxis] Indians may not be sacrificed to satisfy the avaricious humour of designing Englishmen." You have to love that phrasing: "the avaricious humour of designing Englishman."[6]

The Tunxis certainly had their supporters in the form of Englishmen who recognized that what was happening to them was not only illegal, it was unconscionable. One of those supporters was a very well-known resident of eighteenth-century Hartford, the lawyer and all-around righteous guy John Hooker, who, along with lending support to the Tunxis cause, was an abolitionist and supporter of women's suffrage. He wrote a letter of support for the Indians in 1738 that admirably summarized the Tunxis predicament:

> This may certify all whom it doth or may concern that there is in Farmington a certain tract of land within ye common field in a place going by the name Indian Neck containing by estimation about ninety acres, which hath always been esteemed land belonging to ye Indians belonging to Farmington, and when the Town of Farmington purchased the land in theyer township of the Indians there is mention made that ye tract of land was not intended to be sold but still remains firm and fast unto the tribe of Indians where they improved, plowed, and planted & raised corn for theyer subsistence.[7]

So there were English settlers who knew that the valley had been illegally snatched from the Tunxis in the first place, and now what little was left to them according to every duly signed legal document that followed the original and illegal land sale, the ninety or one hundred acres on Indian Neck where their village was located, was being encroached on by English settlers.

Sounds like a slam-dunk case. Everyone seemed to understand that the Tunxis, at the very least, deserved restitution and a return of at least the one hundred or so acres where their village was located.

Nevertheless, the fact that the case seemed so clear made little difference. The General Court essentially told the Tunxis that the best they could do was offer to pay them a pittance for the land on Indian Neck if they would only just go away. Fortuitously, I guess, at the same time, the Mohegan Christian Indian Samson Occom became the linchpin behind a movement to take the beleaguered Natives of southern New England who had converted to Christianity and relocate them to a joint reservation among the Oneida Native People of New York State.[8] Elijah Wimpey, a Tunxis man living in Farmington, became an active supporter of what became Occom's Brothertown movement, named for the community he established for landless, displaced, and basically disenfranchised Native People who had been treated poorly by the English authorities. The Tunxis, seeing few options and little chance of the restitution of their lands in Farmington, packed their bags and dispersed, most of them leaving Connecticut behind. Some joined the Stockbridge Native People in Massachusetts. Many followed the Reverend Occom to the Oneida reservation in New York. Unfortunately, that didn't last for long as there too, white encroachment on reservation lands became problematic. The Tunxis ended up removing yet again, this time to Wisconsin, where they joined with other displaced eastern Native People. It's ironic that the Tunxis had little choice but to leave Connecticut because they lost their land base there and ended up in Wisconsin, where they—wait for it—still don't have a land base. There is no Tunxis reservation in Wisconsin. All they have is a community center, which they use jointly with other folks from the Northeast including the Mohegan, Montaukett, Narragansett, and Niantic people.[9]

I fully recognize that some of you will dispute my inclusion of the tale of the Tunxis in a chapter about ethnic cleansing. The Trail of Tears for the Cherokee and the Long Walk of the Navajo discussed later in this chapter resulted in the deaths of hundreds and even thousands of people. While the Tunxis lost their land, none of them directly lost their lives as a result. So the Tunxis situation was different, I agree. They were not forcibly removed from the Farmington Valley. However, the application of English law was insidious, effectively making it impossible for the Tunxis to maintain their traditional way of life there. It may have been conducted with a soft glove, but I see it as a kind of ethnic cleansing done with *some* empathy on the part of *some* Englishmen.

The Trail of Tears

I began this chapter trying to explain my use of the admittedly loaded term "ethnic cleansing." Maybe you thought I was being a little much with that. However, when you title the most relevant federal legislation concerning the government's policy on Native People east of the Mississippi in 1830 the Indian Removal Act, you're saying the quiet part out loud and showing your true self.

The act was the brainchild of President Andrew Jackson, a noted protector and defender of Indigenous Americans and African Americans. I'm kidding—he owned hundreds of Black slaves on his Tennessee plantation, the Hermitage, and he was a noted killer of Native People in his role as a general in the U.S. Army during the Creek War in 1813–14 in what is now Alabama and in the First Seminole War in 1817 in what is now Florida. This all happened before he was elected president in 1829.

Please don't respond by telling me he was just a product of his time. Plenty of Americans were products of that same time and never owned slaves or killed Native People. In fact many of Jackson's countrymen actively opposed those things. Famous frontiersman Davy Crockett, who had served in the army as a scout under Jackson, vociferously opposed the Indian Removal Act when he was serving as a congressperson representing Tennessee. When confronted by the likelihood of his being politically attacked for supporting the fair treatment of Native Americans, Crockett responded, "I would sooner be honestly and politically damned than hypocritically immortalized." And, sure enough, Crockett lost his bid for reelection.[10]

Let's allow Jackson to speak to us directly. The following is taken from his remarks to Congress concerning the Indian Removal Act:

> The tribes which occupied the countries now constituting the Eastern States were annihilated or have melted away to make room for the whites. The waves of population and civilization are rolling to the

westward, and we now propose to acquire the countries occupied by the red men of the South and West by a fair exchange, and, at the expense of the United States, to send them to land where their existence may be prolonged and perhaps made perpetual. Doubtless it will be painful to leave the graves of their fathers; but what do they more than our ancestors did or than our children are now doing? To better their condition in an unknown land our forefathers left all that was dear in earthly objects.[11]

If you take Jackson at his word, he was divesting the Native People of the East and Southeast of their traditional lands, marching them to land to which they felt no connection and about which they had no knowledge, and despite the fact that the people most affected by this, the actual Native People, were never consulted about any of this, it was all for their own good. Right.

Enforcement of Jackson's plan resulted in the forced relocation of upward of sixty thousand people living in the southeastern United States between 1830 and 1850 to what maps designated as the Indian Territory in what is now Oklahoma. Most were members of the so-called Five Civilized Tribes—Cherokee, Creek, Choctaw, Chickasaw, and Seminole—and those relocated included people, young and old, able bodied and not so able bodied, who were unified in their fervent wish not to be removed from their ancestral homelands.

It is estimated that about one thousand Cherokee escaped the military roundup in North Carolina and Tennessee. Their descendants, along with folks who escaped the trail while they were en route, represent the nucleus of what later became the Cherokee population on a reservation in North Carolina. Their resistance to the ethnic cleansing embodied by the Indian Removal Act is an enormous point of pride for modern Cherokee. We will see this same pattern of resistance, renewal, and defeat of the government plan for the removal of Native People from their ancestral homelands by the Navajo people in their Long Walk of 1864.

The Native People of the Southeast traveled on foot, some up to a distance of 1,600 kilometers (1,000 miles), along the Trail of Tears.

Many died. Estimates vary but doubtless it was thousands, due to exposure, starvation, disease, and, surely, heartbreak. Among just the Cherokee, sixteen thousand people were rounded up and "escorted" by soldiers in a forced march to Oklahoma from North Carolina, Tennessee, Alabama, and Georgia. As noted, it is estimated that at least one thousand of those people died en route, and it is believed that two or three thousand more died as a result of the move after they arrived in Oklahoma. Calling it by its formal, legal name, "Indian removal," sanitizes what it actually was. It is far better to call it by the name given by the Native People who endured it: the Trail of Tears. The route of the Trail of Tears is today commemorated by the National Park Service as a national historic trail.

Some call the forced removal of the Native People of the Southeast and the egregious death toll an act of genocide. Others argue that it shouldn't be called genocide because the deaths were unintentional and accidental. I suppose it's like the difference between first-degree murder and involuntary manslaughter. In the end, dead is dead and all else is semantics.

The Long Walk of the Navajo

As I mentioned in chapter 14, the Navajo Nation today is, depending on who you include in the enumeration, the largest or second-largest Native American group in the U.S. The Cherokee are the other but have a different way of defining who is a member of their tribe. The Navajo have about four hundred thousand enrolled members (about half of whom speak the Navajo language) and an enormous reservation of 65,000 square kilometers (16 million acres), including a huge swath of northeastern Arizona, a slice of southeastern Utah, and a sliver of northwest New Mexico. They are a strong and powerful people living in a starkly glorious part of the country.

All of this is true, but what also is true is that the Navajo have not always been on the best of terms with their non-Navajo Native neighbors, including the Hopi, the Apache, and the Utes. The Navajo were relative latecomers to the region (chapter 14), migrating from the north no earlier than about the fourteenth century CE. As such, upon their arrival in the Southwest, the Navajo displaced the Hopi from some of their home territory and the Hopi have really never forgiven them for that. Also remember that the Navajo word once used to define the cliff-dwelling ancestors of the Hopi, Anasazi, means "enemy ancestors" in the Navajo language (although the precise meaning is disputed). The Hopi, Apache, and Utes have long-standing issues with the Navajo and the Navajo have issues with everybody else, though things have improved in recent times with all of these groups formally working together in their support for the establishment of Bears Ears National Monument in southeastern Utah in 2016.[12]

By the way, well aware of the antagonism between the Hopi and the Navajo, the federal government, in its infinite wisdom, located the Hopi reservation, consisting of twelve villages, on three mesas, smack-dab in the middle of the Navajo reservation in Arizona. In other words, the Hopi homeland concocted through the reservation system is located on an island in the vast ocean of Navajo territory. Oh, and there's a chunk of Navajo land located within the Hopi reservation. When the Hopi need to leave their reservation—for example, for a medical appointment in Flagstaff—they have to drive across the vast expanse of the Navajo reservation.

In the past and certainly in the nineteenth century, some of those animosities erupted into hostilities among the Native groups that resulted in raids where people were killed, villages were burned, and horses were stolen. When first the Spanish and then English-speaking Americans entered into the region, things got even worse, adding yet more nationalities to the complex web of often hostile relationships.

By the mid-1800s, the Americans decided that they had experienced enough of the instability, chaos, and violence that wracked the area, especially when they often were the target of the Navajo's wrath. I'm certainly not going to chime in on who was right and who was wrong in all of the violence that characterized the region. In all likelihood, every group shares a portion of the responsibility. But as the Navajo were the largest and most powerful group in the Southwest, the federal government recognized that if they wanted to stabilize the region, they were going to have to pacify the Navajo, something the Navajo, as you might well understand, were not about to accept.

As populous and as powerful as the Navajo were, the Americans had the guns, if not the numbers, and moved to diminish Navajo power with those guns. Colonel Edward Canby, the commander of Fort Defiance in New Mexico, carried out a plan to cut the Navajo down to size, saying, "There is now no choice between their absolute extermination or their removal and colonization at points so remote . . . as to isolate them entirely from the inhabitants of the Territory."[13] Here we confront the same rationalization we saw in the Indian Removal Act. Indians would be removed from their homelands for their own good, and in a choice between death and removal, removal was viewed as preferable by the U.S. government. So take away their homes in order to save them.

When I was a kid, Kit Carson was presented on various television shows as a brave and noble frontiersman. Like Daniel Boone. Like Davy Crockett. It turns out that, well, not so much. In order to soften up the Navajo and make them more amenable to their eviction from their homes mostly in northeastern Arizona, Carson launched a savage and relentless assault on Navajo communities in early 1864, burning many of their hogans (Navajo houses) to the ground, destroying their crops, killing their livestock, and destroying their irrigation channels. Nice guy.

Carson's goal was pretty clear. He wanted to destroy the Navajo way of life, to end their independence, take away their ability to take care of themselves, and to put them at the mercy of the American government. At this he was, at least for a time, horribly successful. As a result, the government told the Navajo in the spring of 1864, Pack your belongings, grab your children, and say goodbye to your homes, your homeland, and the graves of your ancestors because we're moving you, and a lot of other Native folks, to a place called Bosque Redondo (the Navajo name for their new home was Hwéeldi) in New Mexico. For most Navajo, the distance from their homes to their internment camp was more than 480 kilometers (300 miles); for some, it was 630 kilometers (400 miles). All of them—elderly men and women, young women far along in pregnancy, little kids, disabled people, sick people—had to travel the entire distance on foot. It should come as no surprise that during the eighteen-day Long Walk (the name the Navajo gave to their eviction), of the eight thousand or nine thousand who made the trip, at least two hundred Navajo died.

Bosque Redondo wasn't nearly large enough to accommodate the population the government had concentrated there. There was little way the Natives living there could produce enough food to feed themselves, and it's not paranoid to suggest that the government's plan was to inculcate dependency in the Native mindset and gratitude for the government's largesse in feeding them. Even with that, there never was enough food, and what foods were available often were rotten and infested with insects. Beyond this, in its usual cluelessness about Native culture, the government clustered Navajo side by side with Apache and Comanche, which only led to more violence.

The Long Walk and their imprisonment at Bosque Redondo was a horrible fate to impose on a group of people. Remarkably, the government soon came to recognize that Bosque Redondo simply wasn't working and it was a failed attempt to control and manage Native People. This led to a new treaty being drawn up, the Treaty of Bosque Redondo signed on June 1, 1868. Another Long Walk ensued, this one in the opposite direction, back to the ancestral homes of the Navajo in Arizona, with the government promising to provide for their needs until such time that the Navajo regained the self-sufficiency that same government took from them as part of the original Long Walk. I suppose the good news here is, although the Long Walk disrupted Navajo culture and history; resulted in the deaths, albeit unintended, of hundreds of people; and forged a deep resentment between them and the American government, this attempt at ethnic cleansing was unsuccessful, abandoned by the cleansers, who either recognized the immorality of their actions or recognized its great economic and psychological cost. The Navajo, like the Cherokee, Choctaw, Creek, Chickasaw, and Seminole, are proud, powerful, and resilient people, survivors burning with a desire to live that the federal government of the United States could not extinguish.

Residential Schools

Imagine the following dystopian scenario. It's the distant future. A wealthy and powerful nation of immigrants has, living among them, an Indigenous population, a minority group living ways of life very different from the immigrant population's. Unemployment is high among them and they tend to be quite poor. The government of this mythical nation decides to initiate a program intended to "help" this minority, a plan to assimilate them into the larger society as citizens. The government determines that this minority is being held back by their culture, which the government views as primitive and not congruous with modern thoughts and values.

So what to do? The government concludes that adults in this minority group are too invested in their inferior way of life to ever change, to ever fully embrace modern society. So the adults are largely written off. They are a lost cause. But the kids, oh yes, the kids. They can be saved, their lives can be salvaged, but we need to disassociate them from the backward ways of their parents. Though it will be difficult and while it sounds cruel, the only way to effectively save them is to take them, forcibly if need be, away from their parents, away from their families, away from their friends and homes, away from the places in which they're growing up, the places they love. They must be taken—"kidnapped" is such an ugly word but seems to fit here—and moved hundreds and in some cases even thousands of miles away from their homes and families and placed in boarding or residential schools with others of their kind and taught to be valuable and productive members of society until even the memory of their ethnicity and their identity will be gone and they will be just like "regular" people.

You don't need to imagine too wildly here concerning this fantasy. I have just described not some wild fiction but the actual policy of the federal governments of the United States and Canada in the period from 1801 to 1969 (yes, 1969!) concerning Native American, Native Alaskan, and Native Hawaiian children. In the U.S., legislation was passed and funded in March 1819 as the Indian Civilization Fund Act. The explicit goal was to eradicate traditional Native cultures among children, including their languages, religions, dietary practices, dress, and more, in order to assimilate them into mainstream American society. So yes, forced assimilation. When they reached adulthood, the plan was for them to merge into the greater population, live in apartment buildings in cities or live in houses in nonurban areas, go to church, and so on. The phrase coined by Lt. Richard Henry Pratt (who played a major role in administering the program) succinctly summarized the purpose in a speech he gave to the National Conference of Charities and Correction in 1892: "All the Indian there that is in the race should be dead. Kill the Indian in him and save the man."[14] I am not making that up.

The federal government of the United States established new schools or took over existing residential schools run by church groups where they could indoctrinate—oops, I mean teach, yeah, teach—Native kids a better way to live. Altogether, there were more than five hundred residential schools located in thirty-nine states and virtually every Canadian province.[15] These schools were concentrated in the West, Southwest, and northern plains of the U.S., but they stretched as far east as Pennsylvania and across much of Canada. Native kids at these schools were punished for speaking their Native language, boys had their hair cut short, amulets and talismans were confiscated, any hint that they were worshiping in their traditional ways was punished, and even their names were taken from them, replaced with Anglo names. Oh, and by the way, their growing up to live within the larger culture would eliminate the need for reservations at all and, in a final act of divesting Indians of a homeland, the plan was to dissolve reservations and sell the land, water, lumber, and mineral rights to the highest bidder. So the tribes would cease to exist as nations and the individual members of those tribes would fade into the general population as "Americans" whose skin was just a little bit browner than that of Euro-Americans.

Please understand, in the nearly 170 years the boarding schools were used, they didn't house hundreds or even thousands of students. In 1925 alone there were about sixty thousand Native kids in the schools, some as young as four years old. Babies. As I write this we've just celebrated my Ellie's fifth birthday, and even thinking about government thugs arriving at my house to steal my baby away "for her own good" absolutely enrages me. By the 1930s, more than 80 percent of all Native kids in the United States had spent at least some time in the boarding schools. More than 150,000 were sent to residential schools in Canada.

Records are pretty bad and even the government doesn't have a complete enumeration, but it's believed that hundreds of thousands of kids were caught in the boarding school net.[16]

Now, lest you think that the boarding schools were voluntary or that the majority of Native parents welcomed having their children taken off reservation for an education or vocational training, read this chilling account of the removal of children from the Mescalero Apache reservation in Arizona provided directly by the very federal agent in charge of the tribe:

> Everything in the way of persuasion and argument having failed, it became necessary to visit the camps unexpectedly with a detachment of police, and seize such children as were proper and take them away to school, willing or unwilling. Some hurried their children off to the mountains or hid them away in camp, and the police had to chase and capture them like so many wild rabbits. The unusual proceeding created quite an outcry. The men were sullen and muttering, the women loud in their lamentations, and the children almost out of their wits with fright.[17]

Imagine your children being hunted like "wild rabbits" by an armed police force whose plan it was to take them away for the elimination of their culture with little expectation that you would ever see them again. "Kidnapping" is too mild a word.

Call it kidnapping, ethnic cleansing, erasure, or cultural genocide—in 2022, the Parliament in Canada voted unanimously to label their historical residential school policy flat-out genocide—but whatever you call it, it involved the conscious attempt by the U.S. and Canadian governments to destroy Indigenous ways of life by stealing children from their families. There's simply no way around it. Sorry; I summarily reject any response that relies on the tired cliché of "Well, things were different back then." Nonsense, and by that I actually mean "bullshit." It should never have been and never was an acceptable practice to kidnap children. Ever. The people who implemented the Indian boarding school policies knew they were splitting up loving families. They knew they were breaking hearts and breaking spirits. It was wrong and it was evil. Period.

As despicable as the practice sounds, it actually was even worse. It became common to take Native boarding school kids and put them up for adoption by white families even if they had families back on the reservation who were perfectly capable of taking care of them and desperately wanted them returned. That was criminal, as was the entire operation.

And at the risk of repeating myself, as bad as that sounds, the truth is actually worse than the "worse" I just described. Conditions at many of the boarding schools were beyond terrible. So terrible that just plain old terrible would have been an improvement. Food was crappy and certainly not what the kids were used to back home. Many of the boarding schools were cold in the winter, likely a lot colder than a cozy Navajo hogan or Hopi apartment. Remember, these kids had had their world turned upside down. They were isolated from the people who loved them and the people they loved, they were punished for speaking their own language or practicing their religion, and despair and depression must have been rampant. As a result of these inhumane conditions, many children died. Diseases like smallpox, tuberculosis, influenza, measles, and whooping cough readily spread through the crowded schools and killed thousands and maybe tens of thousands. Recordkeeping was sketchy and numbers are hard to come by. I'm not sure if I'm being paranoid, but maybe the poor recordkeeping was intentional, a convenient way to keep quiet about the enormity of the situation.

That's not just me blowing smoke or handwaving. That's based on government records that do exist. According to the current, incomplete count, in the U.S. one thousand guileless, innocent kids guilty only of the fact that they were Native Americans died in the schools where records exist and have been examined as I write in December 2024. The Canadian National Centre for Truth and Reconciliation has records of more than four thousand kids who died in those schools.[18]

There were more than 500 schools in the U.S. and Canada. The enumeration has really just begun for this tragic and forgotten part of American history, and estimates for the entire number of student deaths vary. A recent year-long investigation by researchers from the *Washington Post* newspaper documented the deaths of more than 3,100 Native children in residential schools in the U.S. between 1828 and 1970.[19] Most died of tuberculosis, exacerbated by the crowded conditions at the schools. Meningitis, typhoid, pneumonia, and the flu also took terrible tolls on the children. Ninety-nine of the documented deaths were due to accidents or suicide.

The *Post* investigation likely has just scratched the surface. Some estimates suggest as many as forty thousand Native children died at the schools. The "lucky" ones were given gravestones to mark their graves, though in the photos I've seen, there are no names recorded on the markers. Many Native children were buried in unmarked graves on the grounds of the schools and are only now being discovered through the discipline of archaeology, as discussed in the next section of this chapter.

In case you think the story of boarding schools is sad, sure, but it's ancient history, consider the following. Deb Haaland was (2021–2025) the director of the Department of the Interior of the United States, the government agency responsible for administering and caring for America's national parks and national monuments, many of which have within their borders Native American archaeological sites that I have described in this book and that are also highlighted in my guide.[20] Haaland is a Native American, a member of the Laguna Pueblo tribe. Two of her grandparents were eight years old when they were taken to Indian boarding schools. Her grandparents! As she has eloquently stated concerning her grandparents, "Many children like them never made it back to their homes. Each of those children is a missing family member, a person who was not able to live out their purpose on this Earth because they lost their lives as part of this terrible system."[21]

In chapter 14, I mentioned the American Antiquities Act of 1909, which gave U.S. presidents the power to designate a place, whether it's an archaeological site, a building, a battlefield, and more, as a national monument deserving of protection and preservation. Many of the places listed in this book, especially in chapters 12, 13, and 14, have been so designated. In one of his final acts in office, President Joe Biden named another national monument, the buildings and grounds of the Carlisle Indian Industrial School, founded in 1879 in Pennsylvania. This national monument, like Manzanar National Monument in California (a World War II Japanese internment camp), memorializes a tragic and awful episode in American history, one that is crucial to remember and acknowledge.

The Archaeology of Boarding Schools

The story of the boarding schools tends to be given short shrift in telling the story of America. How many of you knew about their existence and policies of cultural erasure before reading this discussion? Not many, I imagine. One reason I know about them is that I follow my brilliant colleague archaeologist Kisha Supernant on X. As she reports, the skill set of archaeologists is now being applied especially to those areas where the schools buried the bodies of deceased Native kids in unmarked graves. The goal of what she characterizes as "heart centered archaeology" is pretty straightforward: an accounting of those deaths.[22] Supernant is the director of the University of Alberta's Institute of Prairie and Indigenous Archaeology in Canada and chair of the Unmarked Graves Working Group of the Canadian Archaeological Association.[23] She is Métis, a descendant of Papaschase people and the British settlers of Canada. She has spoken about the potential of ground-penetrating radar to identify those unmarked graves. Using this technology, for example, the Tk'emlúps te Secwépemc Nation of British Columbia has enumerated 215 soil anomalies that might potentially be graves at a school in British Columbia. This entire process is very recent and Native People are still trying to reach a consensus about what's next. Some people want the possible human remains disinterred and returned to reservations for culturally appropriate reconsecration. Other Native People are opposed to recovery, as this would result in disturbance of the graves. Of course, it is for Native People to decide what the most appropriate course of action should be in order to obtain some degree of closure.

Remember my discussion in chapter 1 of archaeology's "new purpose" of serving the needs of Native People? In an example of that, archaeology is playing a role in the recovery and repatriation of the remains of some of the children who died at the schools. In the abovementioned *Washington Post* article, the authors tell the story of Almeda Heavy Hair, a member of the Gros Ventre tribe in Montana and held at the aforementioned Carlisle School between 1890 and 1894. She died when she was barely sixteen years old and buried on school grounds, one of the more than 230 children whose deaths at Carlisle were documented by the *Washington Post*. Following her family's wishes, archaeologists employing their skill set have exhumed Almeda's bones, which were returned to her family. Though she was never able to see her home again in life, she has now returned in death. Almeda Heavy Hair. Say her name.

I am not a Native person but am tremendously ambivalent about the whole concept of "closure" for the families of the children who became enmeshed in the boarding school system. It sounds so, "Okay, let's just move on now." I can't imagine people ever embracing complete closure when it concerns the deaths of their children. We can only hope that, at this late date and on some level, recognition and memorialization of these kids can supply some degree of, if not true closure, at least a measure of acknowledgment of what happened and a bit of comfort to their families and their people.

Epilogue

A STORY STILL BEING WRITTEN

I GET IT. Having had two kids pass through a high school in a very highly rated public school system in Connecticut, I am well aware that Native American history gets short shrift in the standard social studies curriculum. My impression that this is generally true throughout the U.S. was upheld during forty years of teaching at a public university. I would regularly ask my students how much of Native American culture and history was covered in their high school social studies or American history courses. The results were invariably discouraging. With a few notable and laudable exceptions, American history begins in those courses with the exploration and then colonization of North America by Spanish, English, Dutch, and French explorers and settlers. Sure, students are informed that there were people already living in the New World when Europeans arrived, and they are taught the whole "Indians helped the Pilgrims" bit around Thanksgiving, but the coverage of Native America, even in AP history courses, is generally brief and perfunctory, resulting in a focus on only five hundred years of an American history that, as I have shown in this book, actually stretches back at least twenty thousand years. That's only at most 2.5 percent of the time human beings have lived in North America. Obviously, that ignores most of the story.

Ask the average American kid about the other 97.5 percent of American history, the story before the arrival of Europeans. They certainly have heard about corn (chapter 9) and maybe cliff dwellings (chapter 14), but they likely have never been taught about the Late Pleistocene settlement of, expansion into, and adaptation to the New World (chapters 5 and 6); the Native American agricultural revolution (chapter 9); the time depth of the earliest settlers of the Arctic North (chapter 11); the mound builders (at least outside of the region where the mounds discussed in chapters 12 and 13 are located); or the Native People of the northwest coast (chapter 15). The history ordinarily taught in most social studies courses in most high schools in the U.S. isn't inclusive, and it's far from covering the entire story. In other words, it's incomplete and, as such, is inherently misleading. When students of mine have gone out into the world to teach in high schools where they have suggested incorporating more of the Native American story in their history or social studies classes, they have run into roadblocks, not because their principals or other school administrators are bad people or ignorant, but because the curriculum is set and often inflexible. There's little room or time for adding anything outside of the established curriculum. Also, especially in AP courses, teachers need to "teach to the test," which doesn't usually leave a lot of time for telling the story of America's original inhabitants because that's not on the test. I am afraid that in some cases this leads people to accept or even embrace stereotypes of Native People as ignorant, backward, and primitive. They don't know better because they haven't been taught better.

The story of Native America told through oral histories, archaeology, and written histories, and as I have tried to present it here, is one of the perseverance and survival of a people who explored and expanded across two entire continents beginning more than twenty thousand years ago. It is a story of ingenious adaptation to hundreds of widely varying habitats while, simultaneously, those habitats were being disrupted by climate change, including species extinctions, at the end of the Pleistocene Epoch, or Ice Age. It is a story of crafting novel and creative ways of surviving in new territories, including the invention of new ways of feeding people through Indigenous modes of agriculture. It is a story of the development of architectural practices that exploited local raw materials, provided local environmental necessities, and developed and conformed to the people's own standards of beauty that even thousands of years later we can continue to appreciate. And yes, that included tipis and wigwams. It is a story of the creation of vast trading networks with neighbors both close by and distant to obtain raw materials that made life easier and better. It is a story of architects and engineers, hunters and gatherers, travelers and traders, farmers and scientists, artists and explorers. It is a story of the evolution of complex social and political practices that resulted in societies we may rightly label "civilizations" as we apply that no longer fashionable term to cultures like those of ancient Egypt and Mesopotamia, as well as the Maya and Aztecs. It is a story of people who, like people everywhere, possess and reflect the genius of the human mind and the enormous capabilities of human beings who, when they work together with a common goal, can accomplish truly remarkable things and provide a safe and comfortable environment in which people can be born, grow, learn, contribute, be productive, maybe have kids of their own, age, and then die in peace and comfort, having lived useful and satisfying lives. It is a story worthy of telling. And a story you can personally encounter at the many places where the ancestors of the Native People of North America still speak to us, Native and non-Native alike.[1]

It is, ultimately, a story of people who are still here and who, as Angie Mitchell phrased it so wonderfully in her diary in 1880 and as I quoted it in chapter 1, may have been "unlike us in appearance but who had known joy and grief, pleasure and pain same as our race of today knows them, and who had laughed, cried, sung, danced, married & died, mourned or rejoiced their lives away."[2]

NOTES

A Practical Preface

1. Stephen Jay Gould has a nice discussion about this in his 1999 book, *Questioning the Millennium*.

Prologue

1. Coffeekid99 2007.
2. Dunaway 2017.
3. Taylor et al. 2023 discusses the evidence.
4. Smithsonian Institution, n.d.
5. Institute for American Indian Studies, n.d.

Chapter 1. Archaeology

1. Moss 2011.
2. Angie Mitchell's remarkable diary has been published in an edited form with commentary as *A Frontier Teacher in Tonto Basin* (Mitchell 2014).
3. Mitchell 2014, 28.
4. National Park Service, n.d.-d.
5. Mitchell 2014, 114.
6. Questions Worth Asking Symposium 2023.
7. Zuni Pueblo Department of Tourism, n.d.
8. Beaulne-Stuebing 2023.

Chapter 2. In Their Beginning

1. Shameless plugs: Feder 2017, 2023c.
2. The book I am citing here is Johnstone 2008.
3. I gleaned this Inuit origin story from Qitsualik-Tinsley and Qitsualik-Tinsley 2015 (quote on p. 13). Rachel Qitsualik-Tinsley is Inuit Cree and Sean Qitsualik-Tinsley is Scottish Mohawk. The book is lavishly illustrated by Emily Fiegenschuh and Patricia Ann Lewis-MacDougall. Their artwork is stunning.

4. For a uniquely beautiful illustrated treatment of the story of Coyote and the stars, see Oughton and Desimini 1992.

Chapter 3. Are You Ready to Rock?

1. Ritchie 1971.

Chapter 4. European Encounter with a "New World"

1. National Archives 2017.
2. Feder 2023a.
3. Feder 1992.
4. Tremlett 2006.
5. Vespucci's statements and letters were published in English in 1894 under the title *The Letters of Amerigo Vespucci and Other Documents Illustrative of His Career*, translated by Clements R. Markham. The quote is from p. 42.
6. Ray 1743 (this is the eleventh edition of the book originally published in 1691). I find Ray to be an amazing combination of theologian, philosopher, and scientist.
7. Paul III 1537.
8. Lepper and Gill 2000.
9. The published diary of Lucas Barger (2013; titled *Life on a Rocky Farm*), who lived in the Hudson Valley in the late 1800s and early 1900s, contains his very informative eyewitness account of seeing the construction of a stone chamber by a farmer in that period.
10. Chartier 2007.
11. Godfrey 1951.
12. You can read English translations of *The Saga of the Greenlanders* in Clark and Friðriksdóttir, n.d., and of *The Saga of Erik the Red* in Icelandic Saga Database, n.d.
13. The Ingstads summarized their archaeological excavation of L'Anse aux Meadows in their book (Ingstad and Ingstad 2000).
14. Parks Canada, n.d.
15. Kuitems et al. 2022.
16. Guðmundsdóttir 2023.
17. Ruiz-Puerta et al. 2024.
18. Magnusson and Pálsson 1966, 100.

Chapter 5. First Peoples: Origins

1. Archaeologist David Hurst Thomas's 2001 book *Skull Wars* is a terrific source for information on this less than exemplary element of American history.
2. Native American Graves Protection and Repatriation Act, H.R. 5237, 101st Cong. (1989–90), https://www.congress.gov/bill/101st-congress/house-bill/5237.
3. This saying can be traced to political adviser James Schlesinger.
4. From research reported in Hublin et al. 2017.

5. Dates taken from Becerra-Valdivia and Higham 2020.
6. Institute of Arctic and Alpine Research, n.d.
7. The research at On Your Knees Cave was reported in Dixon 1999.
8. The Cooper's Ferry site was described in Davis et al. 2019.
9. Reported in Bennett et al. 2021.
10. Bennett et al. 2021.
11. C. G. Oviatt and colleagues presented their skeptical view of the White Sands footprints dating in Oviatt et al. 2023.
12. Pigati et al. 2023.
13. Jennifer Raff's 2022 book *Origin: A Genetic History of the Americas* is the definitive work on the topic. Raff is simply a wonderful writer.
14. The genetic investigation of the Anzick child was conducted by M. Rasmussen and colleagues and published in Rasmussen et al. 2014.
15. The genetic investigation of the Upward Sun River babies was conducted by J. Moreno-Mayar and colleagues and published in Moreno-Mayar et al. 2018.
16. Lippert used this phrasing in Lippert 1996, p. 126.

Chapter 6. First Peoples: Clovis and Folsom

1. There is a biography of McJunkin: Folsom 1973.
2. Nash 2017.
3. Buchanan et al. 2022.
4. The Casper site's excavator, George Frison, wrote a book about it (Frison 1974).
5. Wheat 1972.
6. Archaeologist Joe Ben Wheat compiled a number of historical descriptions of mass bison kill sites in Wheat 1972.
7. Martin et al. 2009; archaeologist Edwin Wilmsen focuses on the site in Wilmsen 1974.
8. Waters, Stafford, and Carlson 2020.
9. You can read about Lehner in Haury, Sayles, and Wasley 1959.
10. For the publication aimed at archaeologists that describes the site, see Surovell et al. 2021.
11. There's a very nice summary of work at the La Prele site in Stirn 2023.
12. Pelton et al. 2024.
13. Faith and Surovell 2009.

Chapter 7. First Peoples: Older Still?

1. Paulette Steeves presents her case for a much older occupation of America in her 2021 book *The Indigenous Paleolithic of the Western Hemisphere*.
2. Calico Early Man Site, n.d.
3. The very well-known paleoanthropologist Mary Leakey expressed this in her 1984 autobiography, *Disclosing the Past*, 143.

4. Leakey 1984, 142.
5. Calico Early Man Site, n.d.
6. Holen et al. 2017.

Chapter 8. Learning to Live in a New World

1. Feder 2016.
2. Bourque 2012.

Chapter 9. More Than Maize

1. Champlain's description of sunflower farming in the Great Lakes region is reported in Wales et al. 2019.
2. A determination of the ultimate source of domesticated sunflowers was made by B. Blackman and colleagues and reported in Blackman et al. 2011.
3. These dates were provided in B.D. Smith 2014.
4. Wales et al. 2019.
5. Museum of Classic Chicago Television 2019.
6. NY Retro Vault 2017.
7. Matsuoka et al. 2002.
8. From the iconic Piperno and Flannery 2001.
9. Reported in Coelho et al. 2021.
10. A summary of the evidence for the origin of domestic dogs in Native America is in Leathlobhair et al. 2018.
11. Simon 2016 provides an analysis of the earliest dates for maize at the Holding site.
12. Hart 2022 provides a breakdown for the dating of maize domestication in the American Northeast.
13. Hart and Lovis 2013 provides a summary of the dating of maize agriculture in northeastern North America.
14. Abel 2016.

Chapter 10. Into the Woods

1. New York State Museum, n.d.
2. Oneida Indian Nation, n.d.
3. Shannon, n.d.
4. Albany Congress Committee 1754.
5. Research Laboratories of Archaeology 2022.
6. Reynolds 2009.
7. Hart 2011 is the best source for this.
8. Hart et al. 2011.
9. Hansen 2018.
10. Hansen 2018; V. Thompson et al. 2022.

Chapter 11. Into the Cold

1. Raff 2022.
2. Though published more than twenty years ago, Robert McGhee's *Ancient People of the Arctic* (2001) is still a terrific source of information on the topic of this chapter. The quoted phrase appears in that book on page 73.
3. Raff 2022.
4. D. F. Pelly's book *Ukkusiksalik: The People's Story* (2016) is a wonderful ethnography of the people of the Canadian Arctic.
5. Science 2.0 2015.
6. McGhee 2001, 73.
7. American Museum of Natural History, n.d.
8. E. Thompson 2020.
9. Peary-MacMillan Arctic Museum, n.d.

Chapter 12. Monument Builders of the Midwest

1. J. D. Baldwin, *Ancient America* (1872), as cited in C. Thomas 1894, 615.
2. Silverberg 1989, 48.
3. Colavito 2020.
4. Feder 2023b.
5. The Watson Brake site was reported in Saunders et al. 1997.
6. UNESCO World Heritage Centre, n.d.-b.
7. Lepper 2005.
8. Lepper 1995 provides a detailed discussion of this.
9. Lepper 2018, 2024.
10. Lepper 2020 presents a detailed discussion of the meaning of Serpent Mound.
11. Lepper et al. 2018.

Chapter 13. City Dwellers

1. See Iseminger 2010 for a wonderful presentation about the place. Iseminger worked for years as the assistant director there and knows the site as well as anyone.
2. Robert Birmingham and Lynne Goldstein wrote the definitive book about the site: *Aztalan: Mysteries of an Ancient Indian Town* (2006).
3. Emerson et al. 2016 provides a detailed analysis of the Mound 72 burials at Cahokia.
4. Feder 2017.
5. The Gutenberg Project is a very helpful online source for digital scans of historically significant publications that might otherwise be difficult to track down. You can read the report of de Soto's Gentleman of Elvas (1557) there.
6. La Vega 1881 contains his eyewitness description of mound building.
7. Le Page du Pratz 1774 contains a description of the Grand Village of the Natchez base on Le Page du Pratz's visit in the early eighteenth century.
8. Gentleman of Elvas 1557.

Chapter 14. Great Houses and Cliff Castles

1. Encyclopedia Britannica 2023.
2. UNESCO World Heritage Centre, n.d.-a.
3. Rose 2014.
4. National Park Service, n.d.-b.
5. National Park Service, n.d.-c
6. National Park Service, n.d.-a.
7. Simpson 1852.
8. Amon Carter Museum of American Art, n.d.
9. Weber 1985.
10. Simpson 1852, 34.
11. Simpson 1852, 35.
12. George et al. 2018.
13. I was so pleased, many years after graduating from what was then called the State University of New York at Stony Brook, to read Eric Powell's 2005 article in *Archaeology* magazine highlighting my old mentor's work tracing turquoise from the American Southwest.
14. Ouellette 2023.
15. Plog and Heitman 2010.
16. Kennett et al. 2017 reports on the analysis of the human remains from Pueblo Bonito.
17. Price 2016 reports on the isotopic analysis of human remains recovered at Chaco Canyon.
18. As quoted in McNitt 1966, 22.
19. Wetherill's letter to the Smithsonian can be found in Harrell 1987.
20. R.L. Begay, who is Diné, and colleagues present the Navajo perspective about genetic research in Begay et al. 2019.
21. R. Williams et al. 1981 reports on genetic comparisons between the Navajo and Hopi.
22. Office of the Director of National Intelligence, n.d.
23. National WWII Museum, n.d.
24. To see an informative and moving Zuni perspective about their pilgrimage to the Place of Emergence, check out the video "Zuni in the Grand Canyon" (Byers 2020) and join a group of elders and leaders making their annual pilgrimage.

Chapter 15. Northwest Coast

1. Huang, n.d.
2. Madonna Moss's 2011 publication, *Northwest Coast: Archaeology as Deep History*, is my primary source for the archaeology of the northwest coast. And yes, I used her subtitle in chapter 1 as a way of describing my approach in this entire book.
3. Ruth Kirk's lavishly illustrated book *Ozette: Excavating a Makah Whaling Village* (2015) is my primary source and a great read if you'd like to know more about this remarkable site. It's a gorgeous book.
4. As noted in Kirk 2015, 79.
5. Many of the details of the Ozette excavations were provided in the National Register nomination to the federal government.

Chapter 16. Art

1. Schaafsma 1990.
2. Pitblado et al. 2013.
3. Spangler 2013.
4. Spangler and Spangler 2003.
5. DarkSky, n.d.
6. Cactus Atlas 2022.

Chapter 17. War

1. Maroonian 2022.
2. Mason (1897) 1736.
3. SEC-TV 2023.
4. Gallegos 1991.
5. Bierce, n.d.
6. Robert Marshall Utley is the author of a long-standing excellent source on the Battle of the Little Bighorn, the guidebook titled *Custer Battlefield National Monument, Montana* (Utley 1969), written for the National Park Service. The quote is from page 10.
7. Utley 1969.
8. Custer discusses his attitude about Native Americans in his autobiography titled *My Life on the Plains: Personal Experiences with Indians* (Custer 2015).
9. Utley 1969, 31.
10. See Utley (1969, 50–55) and Graham (1953) for transcripts of some of the testimony.
11. Mentioned in the book written by archaeologist Douglas Scott and colleagues, *Archaeological Perspectives on the Battle of the Little Bighorn* (Scott et al. 1989).
12. Scott's 2013 book, *Uncovering History: Archaeological Investigations at the Little Bighorn*, is a great source of information, written by the most active archaeologist who has worked at the battlefield.
13. Scott and Fox 1984; Scott et al. 1989.
14. This was suggested in Scott et al. 1989.
15. Marcelo 2022.
16. Kindy 2022.
17. Oregon Archaeological Society 2004.

Chapter 18. Archaeology and Ethnic Cleansing

1. Leslie, Sportman, and Jones 2020.
2. From a 1650 statement by the General Court in Hartford. Indexed in the Indian Series of the Connecticut Archives, Connecticut State Library.
3. From a 1672 letter written by the Tunxis People. Indexed in the Indian Series of the Connecticut Archives, Connecticut State Library.
4. From a 1673 statement by the General Court in Hartford. Indexed in the Indian Series of the Connecticut Archives, Connecticut State Library.

5. From the 1673 statement by the General Court in Hartford. Indexed in the Indian Series of the Connecticut Archives, Connecticut State Library.

6. From the 1673 statement by the General Court in Hartford. Indexed in the Indian Series of the Connecticut Archives, Connecticut State Library.

7. From a 1738 letter written by John Hooker in support of the claims of the Tunxis. Indexed in the Indian Series of the Connecticut Archives, Connecticut State Library.

8. Love 2000 is a biography of the fascinating historical figure Samson Occom.

9. Brothertown Indian Nation, n.d.

10. Nix 2024.

11. Jackson 1830.

12. Bears Ears Inter-Tribal Coalition, n.d.

13. Wikipedia 2024.

14. From the federal proclamation designating the Carlisle School as a national monument. The White House 2024.

15. National Centre for Truth and Reconciliation, "Interactive Map," https://nctr.ca/records/view-your-records/archival-map/. Accessed December 16, 2024.

16. American Indian Resource Center, n.d.

17. From the heart-wrenching 2020 book *Education for Extinction* by David Wallace Adams, p. 233.

18. Canadian Press 2023.

19. From a lengthy article published on December 22, 2024. Written by Dana Hedgpeth, Sari Horwitz, Joyce Sohyun Lee, Andrew Ba Tran, Nilo Tabrizy, and Jahi Chikwendiu.

20. Feder 2023c.

21. Brewer 2022.

22. Supernant 2024.

23. Gault 2024.

Epilogue

1. Feder 2017, 2023c.

2. Mitchell 2014, 114.

REFERENCES

Abel, T. 2016 The Iroquoian occupations of northern New York: A summary of current research. *Ontario Archaeology* 96:65–75. https://ontarioarchaeology.org/wp-content/uploads/oa096-07_Abel.pdf

Adams, D.W. 2020 *Education for Extinction: American Indians and the Boarding School Experience, 1875–1928*. University of Kansas Press, Lawrence, Kansas.

Albany Congress Committee. 1754 Short hints towards a scheme for a general union of the British colonies on the continent. June 28. Founders Online, National Archives. https://founders.archives.gov/documents/Franklin/01-05-02-0100

American Indian Resource Center. n.d. Native American boarding schools. UC Santa Cruz. https://airc.ucsc.edu/resources/boarding-schools.html

American Museum of Natural History. n.d. Ahnighito. https://www.amnh.org/exhibitions/permanent/meteorites/meteorites/ahnighito

Amon Carter Museum of American Art. n.d. Richard H. Kern. https://www.cartermuseum.org/artists/richard-h-kern

Barger, L. 2013 *Life on a Rocky Farm: Rural Life Near New York City in the Late Nineteenth Century*. State University of New York Press, Albany.

Bears Ears Inter-Tribal Coalition. n.d. Homepage. https://www.bearsearscoalition.org/

Beaulne-Stuebing, L. 2023 "We were anything but primitive": How Indigenous-led archaeology is challenging colonial preconceptions. CBC Radio, May 27. https://www.cbc.ca/radio/unreserved/indigenous-led-archaeology-1.6854258

Becerra-Valdivia, L., and T. Higham. 2020 The timing and effect of the earliest human arrivals in North America. *Nature* 584:93–97.

Begay, R.L., et al. 2019 Weaving the strands of life (liná Bitl'ool): History of genetic research involving Navajo People. *Human Biology* 91(3):189–208.

Bennett, M.R., et al. 2021 Evidence of humans in North America during the Late Glacial Maximum. *Science* 373(6562):1528–31.

Bierce, A. n.d. *The Devil's Dictionary*. https://www.gutenberg.org/files/972/972-h/972-h.htm

Birmingham, R.A., and L. Goldstein. 2006 *Aztalan: Mysteries of an Ancient Indian Town*. Wisconsin Historical Society Press, Madison.

Blackman, B., et al. 2011 Sunflower domestication alleles support single domestication event in eastern North America. *Proceedings of the National Academy of Sciences* 108(34):14360–65.

Bourque, B. 2012 *The Swordfish Hunters: The History and Ecology of an Ancient American Sea People*. Bunker Hill Publishing, Piermont, New Hampshire.

Brewer, G.L. 2022 U.S. counts Indian boarding school deaths for first time but leaves key questions unanswered. NBC News, May 11. https://www.nbcnews.com/news/us-news/indian-boarding-school-deaths-interior-department-report-rcna28284

Brothertown Indian Nation. n.d. About our heritage and culture. https://brothertownindians.org/

Buchanan, B., et al. 2022 Bayesian modeling of the Clovis and Folsom radiocarbon records indicates a 200-year multigenerational transition. *American Antiquity* 87:567–80. https://www.cambridge.org/core/journals/american-antiquity/article/abs/bayesian-modeling-of-the-clovis-and-folsom-radiocarbon-records-indicates-a-200year-multigenerational-transition/4EE32E6542352CB5C517AD471DD5D9B8

Byers, D. 2020 Zuni in the Grand Canyon. YouTube video, 27:36. August 17. https://youtu.be/wMSLgYb3M8Y

Cactus Atlas. 2022 Gallo Campground review & info | Chaco Culture National Historical Park | New Mexico. YouTube video, 23:37, August 25. https://www.youtube.com/watch?v=_4edKY62OO8

Calico Early Man Site. n.d. Homepage. http://calicoarchaeology.com/

Canadian Press. 2023 How ground-penetrating radar is used to find unmarked graves at residential schools. Saanich News, June 19. https://www.saanichnews.com/national-news/how-ground-penetrating-radar-is-used-to-find-unmarked-graves-at-residential-schools/

Chartier, C.S. 2007 *Report on the Site Examination Testing and Monitoring of the Reconstruction of the Acton Stone Chamber, Acton, Massachusetts.* Town of Acton.

Clark, S., and J.K. Friðriksdóttir. n.d. *The Saga of the Greenlanders. Víðförul: The Women Pioneers of the Vinland Sagas.* https://vidforul.wordpress.com/the-saga-of-the-greenlanders/

Coelho, F., et al. 2021 An early dog from southeast Alaska supports a coastal route for the first dog migration into the Americas. *Proceedings of the Royal Society B* 288(1945):20203103. https://royalsocietypublishing.org/doi/10.1098/rspb.2020.3103

coffeekid99. 2007 The Crying Indian—full commercial—Keep America Beautiful. YouTube video, 1:00, April 30. https://www.youtube.com/watch?v=j7OHG7tHrNM

Colavito, J. 2020 *The Mound Builder Myth: Fake History and the Hunt for a "Lost White Race."* University of Oklahoma Press, Norman, Oklahoma.

Custer, G.A. 2015 *My Life on the Plains: Personal Experiences with Indians.* Cirignani Enterprises.

DarkSky. n.d. International Dark Sky Places. https://darksky.org/what-we-do/international-dark-sky-places/

Davis, L.G., et al. 2019 Late Upper Paleolithic occupation at Cooper's Ferry, Idaho, USA, ~16,000 years ago. *Science* 365:891–97.

———. 2022 Dating of a large tool assemblage at the Cooper's Ferry site (Idaho, USA) to ~15,785 cal yr B.P. extends the age of stemmed points in the Americas. *Science Advances* 8(51).

Dixon, E.J. 1999 *Bones, Boats, and Bison: Archaeology and the First Colonization of Western America.* University of New Mexico Press, Albuquerque.

Dunaway, F. 2017 The Crying Indian ad that fooled the environmental movement. *Chicago Tribune.* https://www.chicagotribune.com/2017/11/21/the-crying-indian-ad-that-fooled-the-environmental-movement/

Emerson, T.E., et al. 2016 Paradigms lost: Reconfiguring Cahokia's Mound 72 beaded burial. *American Antiquity* 81:405–25.

Encyclopedia Britannica. 2023 Navajo National Monument. September 1. https://www.britannica.com/place/Navajo-National-Monument

Faith, J.T., and T.A. Surovell. 2009 Synchronous extinction of North America's Pleistocene mammals. *Proceedings of the National Academy of Sciences* 106(49): 20641–45. https://www.pnas.org/doi/10.1073/pnas.0908153106

Feder, K.L. 1992 Christopher Columbus wasn't a hero. *Hartford Courant*, January 13.

———. 2016 *Walter Landgraf Soapstone Quarry*. Barkhamsted Historical Society, Barkhamsted, Connecticut.

———. 2017 *Ancient America: Fifty Archaeological Sites to See for Yourself*. Rowman and Littlefield, Lanham, Maryland.

———. 2023a *The Barkhamsted Lighthouse: The Archaeology of the Lighthouse Family*. Rowman & Littlefield, Lanham, Maryland.

———. 2023b *Frauds, Myths, and Mysteries: Science and Pseudoscience in Archaeology*. Oxford University Press, New York.

———. 2023c *Native American Archaeology in the Parks: A Guide to Heritage Sites in Our National Parks and Monuments*. Rowman and Littlefield, Lanham, Maryland.

Folsom, F. 1973 *The Life and Legend of George McJunkin: Black Cowboy*. E.P. Dutton.

Frison, G. 1974 *The Casper Site: A Hell Gap Bison Kill on the High Plains*. Academic Press, New York.

Gallegos, M.J. 1991 Michelangelo of the Southwest. *Albuquerque Tribune*, May 21. https://nmdc.unm.edu/digital/api/collection/vf_zuni/id/27/download

Gault, Caroline. 2024 The Canadian Archaeological Association working group on unmarked graves receives Governor General's Innovation Award. University of Alberta, May 22. https://www.ualberta.ca/en/arts/faculty-news/2024/05-may/governor-generals-innovation-award.html

Gentleman of Elvas. 1557 *The Discovery and Conquest of Terra Florida by Don Fernando de Soto and Six Hundred Spaniards, His Followers*. Burt Franklin, New York. https://www.gutenberg.org/files/34997/34997-h/34997-h.htm

George, R.J., et al. 2018 Archaeogenomic evidence from the southwestern US points to a pre-Hispanic scarlet macaw breeding colony. *Proceedings of the National Academy of Sciences* 115(85):8740–45. https://www.pnas.org/doi/full/10.1073/pnas.1805856115

Godfrey, W. 1951 The archaeology of the Old Stone Mill in Newport, Rhode Island. *American Antiquity* 17:120–29.

Gould, S.J. 1999 *Questioning the Millennium*. Harmony Books, New York.

Graham, W.A. 1953 *The Custer Myth: A Sourcebook of Custeriana*. Bonanza Books, New York.

Guðmundsdóttir, L. 2023 Timber imports to Norse Greenland: Lifeline or luxury. *Antiquity* 97:454–71.

Hansen, T. 2018 How the Iroquois Great Law of Peace shaped U.S. democracy. PBS, December 13. https://www.pbs.org/native-america/blogs/native-voices/how-the-iroquois-great-law-of-peace-shaped-us-democracy/

Harrell, D. 1987 "We contacted Smithsonian": The Wetherills at Mesa Verde. *New Mexico Historical Review* 62(3):229–48.

Hart, J.P. 2011 The death of Owasco-Redux. In *Current Research in New York Archaeology: A.D. 700–1300*, edited by C.B. Rieth and J.P. Hart, pp. 95–107. New York State Museum, Albany.

———. 2022 Tracing maize history in Northern Iroquoia through radiocarbon date summed probability distributions. *Open Archaeology* 8:594–607.

Hart, J.P., L.M. Anderson, and R.S. Feranec. 2011 Additional evidence for cal. seventh-century maize consumption at the Kipp Island site, New York. In *Current Research in New York Archaeology: A.D. 700–1300*, edited by C.B. Rieth and J.P. Hart, pp. 27–40. New York State Museum, Albany.

Hart, J.P., and W.A. Lovis. 2013 Reevaluating what we know about the histories of maize in northeastern North America: A review of current evidence. *Journal of Archaeological Research* 21:175–216.

Haury, E.W., E.B. Sayles, and W.W. Wasley. 1959 The Lehner Mammoth site: Southeastern Arizona. *American Antiquity* 25(1):2–30.

Hedgpeth, D., et al. 2024 More than 3,100 students died at schools built to crush Native American cultures. *The Washington Post*, December 22. https://www.washingtonpost.com/investigations/interactive/2024/native-american-deaths-burial-sites-boarding-schools/

Holen, S.R., et al. 2017 A 130,000-year-old archaeological site in southern California, USA. *Nature* 544:479–83.

Huang, A. n.d. Totem poles. Indigenous Foundations, First Nations and Indigenous Studies, University of British Columbia. https://indigenousfoundations.arts.ubc.ca/totem_poles/

Hublin, J.-J., et al. 2017 New fossils from Jebel Irhoud, Morocco and the pan-African origin of Homo sapiens. *Nature* 546:289–92. http://dx.doi.org/10.1038/nature22336

Icelandic Saga Database. n.d. The saga of Erik the Red. https://sagadb.org/eiriks_saga_rauda.en

Ingstad, H., and A.S. Ingstad. 2000 *The Viking Discovery of America: The Excavation of a Norse Settlement in L'Anse aux Meadows, Newfoundland*. Breakwater Books, St. John's, Newfoundland.

Institute for American Indian Studies. n.d. Institute for American Indian Studies Museum and Research Center homepage. https://www.iaismuseum.org/

Institute of Arctic and Alpine Research. n.d. Postglacial flooding of the Bering Land Bridge: A geospatial animation. https://instaar.colorado.edu/groups/QGISL/bering_land_bridge/

Iseminger, W. 2010 *Cahokia Mounds: America's First City*. History Press, Charleston, South Carolina.

Jackson, A. 1830 Speech to Congress on Indian removal. National Park Service. https://www.nps.gov/museum/tmc/manz/handouts/andrew_jackson_annual_message.pdf

Johnstone, E.B. (editor). 2008 *Bigfoot and Other Stories*. Tulare County Board of Education, Visalia, California.

Kennett, D.J., et al. 2017 Archaeogenomic evidence reveals prehistoric matrilineal dynasty. *Nature Communications* 8:14115. http://dx.doi.org/10.1038/ncomms14115

Kindy, D. 2022 Native Americans urge Scottish museum to return artifacts from Wounded Knee massacre. *Smithsonian Magazine*, February 24. https://www.smithsonianmag.com/smart-news/native-americans-urge-scotland-museum-to-return-wounded-knee-massacre-artifacts-180979589/

Kirk, R. 2015 *Ozette: Excavating a Makah Whaling Village*. University of Washington Press, Seattle.

Kuitems, M., et al. 2022 Evidence for European presence in the Americas in AD 1021. *Nature* 601:388–91. https://www.nature.com/articles/s41586-021-03972-8

La Vega, G. de. 1881 History of the conquest of Florida. In *The History of Hernando De Soto and Florida: Or, Record of the Events of Fifty-Six Years, from 1512 to 1568*, edited by B. Sharp, pp. 221–487. Robert M. Lindsay, Philadelphia. https://louisiana-anthology.org/texts/vega/vega--florida.html

Leakey, M. 1984 *Disclosing the Past: An Autobiography*. McGraw-Hill, New York.

Leathlobhair, M.N., et al. 2018 The evolutionary history of dogs in the Americas. *Science* 361:81–85.

Le Page du Pratz, A.-S. 1774 *The History of Louisiana*. T. Becket, London. https://louisiana-anthology.org/texts/du_pratz/du_pratz--history_of_louiaiana_english.html

Lepper, B.T. 1995 Tracking Ohio's great Hopewell road. *Archaeology* 48(6):52–56.

———. 2005 *Ohio Archaeology: An Illustrated Chronicle of Ohio's Ancient American Indian Cultures*. Orange Frazer Press, Wilmington, Ohio.

———. 2018 Archaeology: Serpent Mound might depict a creation story. *Columbus Dispatch*, February 11. https://www.dispatch.com/story/news/technology/2018/02/11/archaeology-serpent-mound-might-depict/14828999007/

———. 2020 The Mississippian iconography of Serpent Mound. *Journal of Ohio Archaeology* 7:38–55.

———. 2024 The Great Hopewell Road: A biased assessment thirty years on. *Journal of Ohio Archaeology* 10:1–37. https://ohioarchaeology.org/file_download/inline/53989b92-2905-43d5-9feb-fa2de43dae6c

Lepper, B.T., et al. 2018 Arguments for the Age of Serpent Mound. *Cambridge Archaeological Journal* 28(3):433–50.

Lepper, B.T., and J. Gill. 2000 The Newark Holy Stones. *Timeline* 17(3):16–25.

Leslie, D.E., S.P. Sportman, and B.D. Jones. 2020 The Brian D. Jones site (4-10B): A multicomponent Paleoindian site in southern New England. *PaleoAmerica* 6(2):199–203. https://www.academia.edu/41790349/The_Brian_D_Jones_Site_4_10B_A_Multi_Component_Paleoindian_Site_in_Southern_New_England

Lippert, D. 1996 In front of the mirror: Native Americans and academic archaeology. In *Native Americans and Archaeologists: Stepping Stones to Common Ground*, edited by N. Swindler et al., pp. 120–27. AltaMira Press, Walnut Creek, California.

Love, W.D. 2000 *Samson Occom and the Christian Indians of New England*. Syracuse University Press, Syracuse, New York.

Magnusson, M., and H. Pálsson (translators). 1966 *The Vinland Sagas: The Norse Discovery of America*. New York University Press, New York.

Marcelo, P. 2022 Wounded Knee artifacts at Barre museum highlight slow pace of repatriations. WBUR, July 28. https://www.wbur.org/news/2022/07/28/wounded-knee-artifacts-repatriation-barre-museum

Markham, C.R. (translator). 1894 *The Letters of Amerigo Vespucci and Other Documents Illustrative of His Career*. Burt Franklin, New York.

Maroonian, A. 2022 Proportionality in international humanitarian law: A principle and a rule. Articles of War, Lieber Institute, West Point, October 24. https://lieber.westpoint.edu/proportionality-international-humanitarian-law-principle-rule/

Martin, B., et al. 2009 The Excavation of Lindenmeier: A Folsom Site Uncovered 1934–1940. Fort Collins Museum and Discovery Science Center, Fort Collins, Colorado.

Mason, J. (1897) 1736 *A Brief History of the Pequot War*. S. Kneeland and T. Green, Boston. Reprinted in *History of the Pequot War: The Contemporary Accounts of Mason, Underhill, Vincent and Gardener*, edited by C. Orr, 1–46. Helman-Taylor, Cleveland. https://archive.org/details/briefhistoryofpeoomaso

Matsuoka, Y., et al. 2002 A single domestication for maize shown in multilocus microsatellite genotyping. *Proceedings of the National Academy of Sciences* 99:6080–84.

McGhee, R. 2001 *Ancient People of the Arctic*. UBC Press, Vancouver.

McNitt, F. 1966 *Richard Wetherill Anasazi*. University of New Mexico Press, Albuquerque.

Mitchell, A. 2014 *A Frontier Teacher in Tonto Basin: The 1880 Diary of Angeline Mitchell*. Edited by S.C. Brown. Rim Country Museum Press, Prescott, Arizona.

Moreno-Mayar, J.V., et al. 2018 Terminal Pleistocene Alaskan genome reveals first founding population of Native Americans. *Nature* 553:203–7. http://dx.doi.org/10.1038/nature25173

Moss, M. 2011 *Northwest Coast: Archaeology as Deep History*. Society for American Archaeology, Washington, D.C.

Museum of Classic Chicago Television. 2019 Mazola Margarine—"we call it maize" (commercial, 1977). YouTube video, 0:30, September 16. https://www.youtube.com/watch?v=W96AVpiu7cI

Nash, S.E. 2017 Why the famous Folsom point isn't a smoking gun. SAPIENS, September 19. https://upcolorado.com/about-us/news-features/item/3312-why-the-famous-folsom-point-isn-t-a-smoking-gun

National Archives. 2017 American Indians in the federal decennial census, 1790–1930. Last reviewed June 26. https://www.archives.gov/research/census/native-americans/1790-1930.html

National Centre for Truth and Reconciliation. 2024 https://nctr.ca/records/view-your-records/archival-map/

National Park Service. n.d.-a Chaco Canyon place names. https://www.nps.gov/chcu/learn/upload/Chaco-Culture-Place-Names.pdf

———. n.d.-b Chaco Culture National Historic Park. https://www.nps.gov/chcu/index.htm

———. n.d.-c Chaco Culture National Historic Park: History and Culture. https://www.nps.gov/chcu/learn/historyculture/index.htm

———. n.d.-d Tonto National Monument. https://www.nps.gov/tont/index.htm

National WWII Museum. n.d. American Indian code talkers. https://www.nationalww2museum.org/war/articles/american-indian-code-talkers

New York State Museum. n.d. Haudenosaunee or Iroquois? Video, 3:56. https://www.nysm.nysed.gov/education/videos/haudenosaunee-or-iroquois

Nix, E. 2024 At least 3,000 Native Americans died on the Trail of Tears. History, last updated April 3. https://www.history.com/news/7-things-you-may-not-know-about-the-trail-of-tears#

NY Retro Vault. 2017 Mazola Margarine ad—1980. YouTube video, 0:30, May 25. https://www.youtube.com/watch?v=CBfLJFATjOo

Office of the Director of National Intelligence. n.d. 1942: Navajo code talkers. https://www.intelligence.gov/people/barrier-breakers-in-history/453-navajo-code-talkers

Oneida Indian Nation. n.d. There is strength in unity: American democracy and the Haudenosaunee. https://www.oneidaindiannation.com/there-is-strength-in-unity/

Oregon Archaeological Society. 2004 *Archaeological Sites of the Lewis and Clark Expedition Through Oregon and Washington 1805–1806*. Oregon Archaeological Society, Portland, Oregon.

Ouellette, J. 2023 These scientists lugged logs on their heads to resolve Chaco Canyon mystery. Ars Technica, February 24. https://arstechnica.com/science/2023/02/these-scientists-lugged-logs-on-their-heads-to-resolve-chaco-canyon-mystery/

Oughton, D., and L. Desimini. 1992 *How the Stars Fell into the Sky: A Navajo Legend*. Houghton Mifflin, Boston.

Oviatt, C.G., et al. 2023 A critical assessment of claims that human footprints in the Lake Otero basin, New Mexico date to the Last Glacial Maximum. *Quaternary Research* 111:138–47.

Parks Canada. n.d. L'Anse aux Meadows National Historic Site. Government of Canada. https://parks.canada.ca/lhn-nhs/nl/meadows

Paul III. 1537 Sublimus Dei. May 29. https://www.newadvent.org/library/docs_pa03sd.htm

Peary-MacMillan Arctic Museum. n.d. Exhibition: Caught in the middle: The tragic life of Minik Wallace. https://www.bowdoin.edu/arctic-museum/exhibits/2020/caught-in-the-middle-the-tragic-life-of-minik-wallace.html

Pelly, D.F. 2016 *Ukkusiksalik: The People's Story*. Dundurn, Toronto, Ontario.

Pelton, S.R., et al. 2024 Early Paleoindian use of canids, felids, and hares for bone needle production at the La Prele site, Wyoming, USA. *PLOS ONE* 19(11). https://journals.plos.org/plosone/article?id=10.1371/journal.pone.0313610

Pigati, J.S., et al. 2023 Independent age estimates resolve the controversy of ancient human footprints at White Sands. *Science* 382:73–75.

Piperno, D.R., and K.V. Flannery. 2001 The earliest archaeological maize (Zea maize L.) from highland Mexico: New accelerator mass spectrometry dates and their implications. *Proceedings of the National Academy of Sciences* 98(4):2101–3.

Pitblado, B.L., et al. 2013 Archaeological fingerprinting and Fremont figurines: Reuniting the iconic Pilling collection. *Advances in Archaeological Practice* 1(1):3–12. https://www.academia.edu/4279131/Archaeological_Fingerprinting_and_Fremont_Figurines

Plog, S., and C. Heitman. 2010 Hierarchy and social inequality in the American Southwest, A.D. 800–1200. *Proceedings of the National Academy of Sciences* 107(46):19619–26. https://www.pnas.org/doi/10.1073/pnas.1014985107

Powell, E. 2005 The turquoise trail. *Archaeology* 58(1):24–29.

Price, T.D. 2016 Great house origins and population stability at Pueblo Bonito, Chaco Canyon, New Mexico: The isotopic evidence. *Journal of Archaeological Science, Reports* 11:261–73.

Qitsualik-Tinsley, R., and S. Qitsualik-Tinsley. 2015 *How Things Came to Be: Inuit Stories of Creation*. Inhabit Media, Iqaluit, Nunavut.

Questions Worth Asking Symposium. 2023 Advocating for archaeology's new purpose. SAPIENS, March 15. https://www.sapiens.org/archaeology/archaeological-reclamation/

Raff, J. 2022 *Origin: A Genetic History of the Americas*. Twelve, New York.

Rasmussen, M., et al. 2014 The genome of a Late Pleistocene child from a Clovis burial site in eastern Montana. *Nature* 506:225–29.

Ray, J. 1743 *The Wisdom of God Manifested in the Works of the Creation*. W. and J. Innys, London. https://archive.org/details/wisdomofgodmanifooray/mode/2up

Research Laboratories of Archaeology. 2022 *The Jesuit Relations and Allied Documents*. Updated December 21. https://rla.unc.edu/Louisiane/jesuit.html

Reynolds, N. 2009 Early Iroquois encounters with Samuel de Champlain. *Weekly Historical Note*, July 6. https://oneida-nsn.gov/wp-content/uploads/2016/04/8-09.07.06-Champlain.pdf

Ritchie, W.A. 1971 *New York Projectile Points: A Typology and Nomenclature*. New York State Museum, University of the State of New York, State Education Department, Albany.

Rose, D. 2014 The Hohokam. ArizonaRuins.com, February. http://www.arizonaruins.com/articles/hohokam/hohokam.html

Ruiz-Puerta, E.J., et al. 2024 Greenland Norse walrus exploitation deep into the Arctic. *Science Advances* 10(9). https://www.science.org/doi/10.1126/sciadv.adq4127

Saunders, J.W., et al. 1997 A mound complex in Louisiana at 5400–5000 years before the present. *Science* 277:1796–99.

Schaafsma, P. 1990 *Indian Rock Art of the Southwest*. University of New Mexico Press, Albuquerque.

Science 2.0. 2015 Paleo-Eskimos and Neo-Eskimos migrated from Alaska's North Slope. April 29. https://www.science20.com/news_articles/paleoeskimos_and_neoeskimos_migrated_from_alaskas_north_slope-155179

Scott, D.D. 2013 *Uncovering History: Archaeological Investigations at the Little Bighorn*. University of Oklahoma Press, Norman, Oklahoma.

Scott, D.D., and R.A. Fox Jr. 1984 *Archaeological Insights into the Custer Battle*. University of Oklahoma Press, Norman, Oklahoma.

Scott, D.D., et al. 1989 *Archaeological Perspectives on the Battle of the Little Bighorn*. University of Oklahoma Press, Norman, Oklahoma.

SEC-TV. 2023 Mystic River Historical Society: Prof. Kevin McBride and the Pequot War. YouTube video, 1:17:41, March 23. https://www.youtube.com/watch?v=FA4IEvZxxHc

Shannon, T.J. n.d. Albany plan of union. Bill of Rights Institute. https://billofrightsinstitute.org/essays/albany-plan-of-union#

Silverberg, R. 1968 *Mound Builders of Ancient America: The Archaeology of a Myth*. New York Graphic Society, New York. Reprint, 1989 *The Mound Builders*. Ohio University Press, Athens, Ohio.

Simon, M. 2016 Reevaluating the evidence for Middle Woodland maize from the Holding site. *American Antiquity* 81:140–50.

Simpson, J.H. 1852 *Journal of a Military Reconnaissance from Santa Fé, New Mexico, to the Navajo Country*. Lippincott, Grambo, Philadelphia. https://archive.org/details/journalamilitar00simpgoog/page/n10/mode/2up

Smith, B.D. 2014 The domestication of Helianthus annuus L. (sunflower). *Vegetation, History, and Archaeobotany* 23(1):57–74.

Smithsonian Institution. n.d. National Museum of the American Indian homepage. https://americanindian.si.edu

Spangler, J.D. 2013 *Nine Mile Canyon: The Archaeological History of an American Treasure*. University of Utah Press, Salt Lake City.

Spangler, J.D., and D.K. Spangler. 2003 *Horned Snakes and Axle Grease: A Roadside Guide to the Archaeology, History, and Rock Art of Nine Mile Canyon*. Uinta Publishing, Salt Lake City.

Squire, E.G., and E.H. Davis. 1848 *Monuments of the Mississippi Valley*. Smithsonian. Contributions to Knowledge. Vol. 1. New York. Edward O. Jenkins.

Steeves, P.F.C. 2021 *The Indigenous Paleolithic of the Western Hemisphere*. University of Nebraska Press, Lincoln, Nebraska.

Stirn, M. 2023 High Plains mammoth hunters: A chance discovery in Wyoming leads archaeologists to a unique 13,000-year-old hunting camp. *Archaeology* January/February:40–45.

Supernant, K. 2024 An Indigenous archaeologist's journey to find the lost children. *Scientific American*, April 25. https://www.scientificamerican.com/article/an-indigenous-archaeologists-journey-to-find-the-lost-children/

Surovell, T.A., et al. 2021 The La Prele Mammoth site, Converse County, Wyoming, USA. In *Human-Elephant Interactions: From Past to Present*, edited by G.E. Konidaris et al., pp. 303–20. Tübingen University Press, Tübingen.

Taylor, W.T.T., et al. 2023 Early dispersal of domestic horses into the Great Plains and northern Rockies. *Science* 379:1316–23. https://www.science.org/doi/10.1126/science.adc9691

Thomas, C. 1894 *Report on the Mound Explorations of the Bureau of Ethnology*. Smithsonian Institution, Washington, D.C.

Thomas, D.H. 2001 *Skull Wars: Kennewick Man, Archaeology, and the Battle for Native American Identity*. Basic Books, New York.

Thompson, E.L. 2020 As we protest statues that glorify racist ideology, we also need to think about the things that ended up inside of museums because of assumptions about white superiority. X post, July 17. https://twitter.com/artcrimeprof/status/1284114081859985413?s=20

Thompson, V.D., et al. 2022 The early materialization of democratic institutions among the ancestral Muskogean of the American Southeast. *American Antiquity* 87(4):704–23. https://www.cambridge.org/core/services/aop-cambridge-core/content/view/5B00F098F5A279B3EDC97E2BB0944FC5/S0002731622000312a.pdf/early_materialization_of_democratic_institutions_among_the_ancestral_muskogean_of_the_american_southeast.pdf

Tremlett, G. 2006 Lost document reveals Columbus as tyrant of the Caribbean. *Guardian*, August 7. https://www.theguardian.com/world/2006/aug/07/books.spain

UNESCO World Heritage Centre. n.d.-a Taos Pueblo. https://whc.unesco.org/en/list/492

———. n.d.-b World Heritage List. https://whc.unesco.org/en/list

Utley, R.M. 1969 *Custer Battlefield National Monument, Montana*. National Park Service, Washington, D.C.

Wales, N., et al. 2019 Ancient DNA reveals the timing and persistence of organellar genetic bottlenecks over 3,000 years of sunflower domestication and improvement. *Evolutionary Applications* 12:38–53. https://onlinelibrary.wiley.com/doi/pdfdirect/10.1111/eva.12594

Waters, M.R., T.W. Stafford, and D.L. Carlson. 2020 The age of Clovis—13,050 to 12,750 cal yr B.P. *Science Advances* 6(43):eaaz0455. https://www.science.org/doi/abs/10.1126/sciadv.aaz0455

Weber, D.J. 1985 *Richard H. Kern: Expeditionary Artist in the Far Southwest 1848–1853*. University of New Mexico Press, Albuquerque.

Wheat, J.B. 1972 *The Olsen-Chubbuck Site: A Paleo-Indian Bison Kill. Memoirs for the Society for American Archaeology 26*. Society for American Archaeology, Washington, D.C.

The White House. 2024. *A Proclamation on the Establishment of the Carlisle Federal Indian Boarding School National Monument*. https://www.whitehouse.gov/briefing-room/presidential-actions/2024/12/09/a-proclamation-on-the-establishment-of-the-carlisle-federal-indian-boarding-school-national-monument/.

Wikipedia. 2024 Long Walk of the Navajo. Last updated October 22. https://en.wikipedia.org/wiki/Long_Walk_of_the_Navajo

Williams, R.C. 1981 The HLA loci of the Hopi and Navajo. *American Journal of Physical Anthropology* 56:291–96. https://onlinelibrary.wiley.com/doi/10.1002/ajpa.1330560309

Wilmsen, E. 1974 *Lindenmeier: A Pleistocene Hunting Society*. Harper and Row, New York.

Zuni Pueblo Department of Tourism. n.d. Experience Zuni. http://www.zunitourism.com/tours.htm

INDEX

Abel, Timothy, 154
Abo Pueblo, 332
Acoma Pueblo (Sky City), 249, 331–32
Acosta, Father José de, 55–58, 67, 73–74
Acowitz, 260–61
Acton Stone Chamber, 59
AD (meaning), xviii–xix
Adah Aho'doo'nili (Two Fell Off), 307
Adam and Eve, 53, 55
Adams, President John, 70
Adena, *192*, 201–2, 204, 208
Adovasio, James, 70, 82
Aivilingmiut, 179–80
Ak&lungiqtautitalik site, 173
A'Kavehe'Onahe (Limber Bones, Cheyenne), *343*, 343
Aleut, 7, 171
Aleutian Islands, 171
alluvial fan, 106–7, 109
Almeda Heavy Hair, 371
Alsop Meadow, 124, *126*, *127*, 127–28
amaranth, 152, 154
American Antiquities Act, 241, 369
American Association of Physical Anthropologists, 68
American Battlefield Protection Program, 327
American Graves Protection and Repatriation Act, 67
American Revolution, 158, 166
anadromous fish, 279
Ancestral Puebloan (Anasazi), 169, 231–34, *232*, 238–40, 250, 263, 297, 362
Ancient America, J. D. Baldwin, 193

Ancient People of the Arctic, Robert McGhee, 185, 379n2 (chap. 11)
Andrés, Fray, 334
Angel Mounds, Indiana, *192*, 220
Aniyunwiya (Cherokee), 3
antler, 34, 37, 71–72, 90, 132
Anzick, Susan, 89
Anzick site, 90–91, 99, 377n14
Apache, 3, 7, 269, 361–62, 364, 367
Aqsarniit (Northern Lights), 27
Arapaho, 7, 336, 339, 345
Archaeoastronomy, 317
Archaeological Perspectives on the Battle of the Little Bighorn Battlefield, Douglas Scott and colleagues, 381n11
archaeology (definition), 11–14
archaeology's new purpose, 16, 371
Archaic Period, 118–19, 134, 238
Arctic, 26, 28, 65, 74–76, 78, 78, 118–19, 169–76, 178–85, 187–90, 373
Arctic char, 180
Arctic Culture Area, *171*
Arctic Small Tool Tradition, 173
Arikara, 3, 7
Arizona Territory, 12
Army Corps of Topographical Engineers, 225
arrow point, 35, 37, 39, 121, 173, 271, 325, 328–29, 344, 356
artificial selection, 137–39, 142, 144–45, 147, 149–50, 153, 278
A:shiwi (Zuni), xxii, 7, 17–18, 226, 232, 234, 251, 272–74, 333

393

atlatl, 172
A'ts'ina (Place of Writing on the Rock), 226
Australopithecus afarensis, 112
Awatixa Village, 351
Aztalan Mounds, Wisconsin, *192*, 214, 379n2 (chap. 13)
Aztec Ruins National Monument, 232, 249–50

Baffin Island (Markland), 62
Balcony House (Mesa Verde), 261–63, 265
Ballad of Ira Hayes, The, Peter LaFarge, 270
ball court, 237, 239
Barrier Canyon (art style), 297, 311–12, *313*
Barringer Meteor Crater, 186
basalt, 36, 108, 124–26, *125*, 303, 354
Bat Creek Stone, 194
Battle of the English Withdrawal (Pequot War), 329, 331
Battle of the Greasy Grass, 335
Battle of the Little Bighorn, 323, 335–45
Battle of Wounded Knee, 346
BC (meaning), xviii–xix
BCE (meaning), xix
beans, 50, 134, 140, 144, 154–55, 164, 215, 225, 231–33, 272, 277
"Beauty Way, The," 224
Bella Coola (Nuxalk), 282
Benteen, Captain Frederick, 339–40
Benully, Clatsozen, 229
Bering, Vitus, 57
Beringia(n), 74, 78, *78*–80, 85, 90, 107, 171, 174–75
Bering Land Bridge, 74, 77, 133, 174–75
Bering Strait, 57, 88, 173
Betatakin (Hillside House; Navajo National Monument), 227, *228*, 232
bifacial tools, 127
bighorn sheep (bighorns), 134, 234, 236, 294, 297, *301*, 302–4, *305*
bilagáanaa (white people), 305
bison, 4, 76, 92–98, 100, 102, 115, 134, 294, 302, 347, 350
Bison antiquus, 92–93, *93*, 96, 102

Bison bison bison, 4, 92
Bison occidentalis, 97
black drink, the, 251
Black Hills, South Dakota, 337, 347
Block Island, 325
Blythe Intaglios, *298*, 314–15, *316*
boarding schools (residential schools), 365–67, 369
Bosque Redondo (Hwéeldi), 363–64
Bowekaty, Kenny, xxii, 17–18, 273–74, 319
BP (meaning), xix, 72
brass, 194, 329
Brian Jones site, *99*, 354
bronze, 61, 63, 194
Bureau of Indian Affairs, 326
Bureau of Land Management, 109, 235
burial mound, 191, *192*, 193, 199, *200*, 201–2, 204
Bury My Heart at Wounded Knee, Dee Brown, 346

^{14}C dating (carbon dating, radiocarbon dating). *See* radiocarbon dating (^{14}C dating, carbon dating)
Cahokia, xvii, *192*, 199, 211, *212*, 213, 214, *214*–19, 221–23, 250
calcined bone, 122, 124
Calico Early Man Site, 105–9
Canadian National Centre for Truth and Reconciliation, 368, 382n15
Canassatego, 158
Canby, Colonel Edward, 363
Canyon de Chelly, 232, 244, 250, 264, *298*, 304–5, 307, *308*; Canyon del Muerto, 306; Massacre Cave, 307, *308*; Two Fell Off, 307; White House, 305
carbon dating (^{14}C dating, radiocarbon dating). *See* radiocarbon dating (^{14}C dating, carbon dating)
caribou, 76, 102, 131, 172, 176–79, 182
Carlisle Indian Industrial School, 370–71, 382n14
Carson, Kit, 163
Cartier, Jacques, 162–63

Carvajal, Juan de Victoria, 244–45
Casa Grande, 232, 237
Casa Rinconada (Chaco Canyon), 243, 247, 248, 249
Casper site, 96–98, 99, 377n4 (chap. 6)
Catarrhini (Old World monkeys), 112
Catholic churches, 332, 334
Catlin, George, 350–51
Cayuga, 165
CE (meaning), xix
Central Connecticut State University, 10, 16, 124
Ceramics, 61, 128, 130, 157, 234, 236, 238, 273, 303, 356
Cerutti site, 109–10
Chaco burials, 258–59
Chaco Canyon, 199, 232, 239, 242–43, 243, 244–245, 245, 246–47, 248, 250–55, 255, 257, 259, 298, 317–18, 318, 320; Casa Chiquita, 243; Casa Rinconada, 243, 247, 248, 249; Chetro Ketl, 243, 246, 257; Fajada Butte, 318–20; Hungo Pavi, 243, 246, 257; Kin Kletso, 243; Peñasca Blanco, 243, 246; Pueblo Bonito, 243, 246–47, 247, 257–59; Pueblo del Arroyo, 243, 246; Pueblo Pintado, 245, 245–46, 250; Sun Dagger (petroglyph), 319, 320; supernova pictograph, 298, 318, 318; Tsin Kletsin, 243; Una Vida, 243, 246; Wijiji, 243, 246
Chaco Outlier, 250
Chaco roads, 253–54
Chaco steps, 254, 255
chalcedony, 36, 40, 106, 109
Champlain, Samuel de, 142, 162–63
Chang, K. C., 15
Chapin, F. H., 261
Chapin Mesa (Mesa Verde), 261–63
chenopodium, *141*
Cherokee (Aniyunwiya), 3, 7, 28, 269, 358, 360–61, 364
chert, 36, 101, 106, 109, 132
Chetro Ketl (Chetro Kettle; Chaco Canyon), 243, 246, 257

Cheyenne, 7, 336, 339, 343, 345
Chillicothe, Ohio, 199, 207
Chinook, 7, 282
chocolate (at Chaco Canyon), 251
Choctaw, 3, 7, 18, 269, 360, 364
Chukotka, 175
chunkey stone, 215
Chuska Mountains, 254
Cicuye Village, 332, 334
clam garden (clam terrace), 281
cliff dwellings, xvii, 12, 13, *13*, 226–27, 231–34, 235, 240–41, 250, 260–63, 263, 264–66, 272; Betatakin, 227, 228, 232; Gila, 232, 234, 235, 264; Montezuma Castle, 232, 240, *240*, 264; Tonto, 12, 13, 14, 232; Walnut Canyon, 232, 241. *See also* Mesa Verde
Cloey, Nedi, 228
Cloudsplitter Rockshelter, 141, *142*
Clovis (culture), 69–70, 80, 83, 89, 92, 94, 98–100, 102, 104, 110, 119, 268
Clovis First, 69–70, 104
Clovis Mafia, 70
Clovis points, 69, 83, *94*, 98, 100
Coastal Salish, 282
Cody (point type), 97
Colorado Museum of Natural History (Denver Museum of Science and History), 94
Columbus, Christopher, 8–9, 47, 47–51, 58–59, 61, 63, 64, 74, 186, 195, 227
Columbus Day, 46
Comanche, 7, 269, 364
conchoidal fracture, 35, 125
Conestoga, 165
Connecticut Archives, 355
Connecticut State Library, 355
Cooke, Lt. William, 340
Cooper's Ferry site, 80, *81*, 82, 99, 377n8 (chap. 5)
copper, 97, 120–21, *122*, 131, 187, 194, 202, 203, 212, 214, 217, 250, 329
coprolites (paleofeces), 134

Cordilleran ice sheet, 78–80
Coronado, Francisco Vázquez de, 225, 331
Corps of Discovery, 351–52
Corti, Espera de, 2
cottontail (rabbit), 134
council houses (Muskogee), 168
Coyote (the trickster), 24, 24–25, 28–30, 31, 309–10
Coyote Throwing the Stars (Navajo/Diné), 30, 30–31, 376n4 (chap. 2)
Crager, George, 349
Creek, 3, 7, 360, 364
Creek War, 359
Crockett, Davy, 359
Crook, Commander George, 338
Crow Canyon (New Mexico), 267, 268, 272, 298
Crying Indian ad, 1–3
Crystal River Mounds, Florida, *192*, 220
Cummings, Byron, 227–29
Cummings, Louisa, 228–29
Custer, Boston, 338
Custer, Colonel George Armstrong, 338–44, *342*, 346, 381n8
Custer, Thomas, 338
Custer Battlefield National Monument, Montana, Robert Marshall Utley, 381n6 (chap. 17)
Custer's Last Stand, 338

Dark Sky Park, 317
Darwin, Charles, 68, 136, 211
Daugherty, Richard, 286
Davenport Stones, 194
Dawn twilight child-girl (Yełkaanenh t'eede gaay), 90
dead carbon, 86–87
deer, 23, 120–21, 123, 134, 154, 176, 202, 294, 350
de La Vega, Garcilaso, 221
Denbigh Flint Complex, 173
dendrochronology (tree ring dating), 229–30, 285
Desert Archaic, 119, 133–34, 156, 231, 268

Devils Dictionary, The (Ambrose Bierce), 335
Dezhnyov, Semyon Ivanovich, 57–58
diffusion, 150–51
Dillehay, Tom, 70
Diné (Navajo), 3, 7, 9, 28–31, 169, 224, 227–29, 245, 266–68, *268*, 271–72, 306, *308*, 309, 358, 360
Dinétah, 267, *268*
Dinosaur National Monument, 298–99
dinosaurs (not archaeology!), 10
disruptive innovation, 158
DNA, 90
dog (domestication), 147, 378n10 (chap. 9)
dog (Inuit), 26, 28, 181
Dog (meteorite), 187
domestication (domesticated), 139–40, 142–44, *142–43*, 146–47, 154, 157
Donner Party, 114
Doo tł' izh ii (turquoise), 251
Dorset, 175, 179, 186, 188, 190
drive lane, 131, 177
Dunaway, Finis, 2

earth lodge, 4, 350
Eastern 8-Row maize, 153
Eastern Agricultural Complex, 140–41
eclipse (lunar), 24
ecoregion, 116
Eden's Bluff site, 143
Edwin Harness site, 151
effigy mound, *192*, *193*, 204, 207–8, *208*, 315
Effigy Mounds National Monument, *192*, 207, 209
egalitarian, 6, 203
18.6-year lunar cycle, 206
Einstein, Albert, 39
Ekstein, Desi (the Drone Diva), *316*
Ellesmere Island, 183
El Morro National Monument, 244
enclosure (mound), *192*, 200, *200*, 202, 204–7, *205*, 209, 213
Endecott, John, 325
Erikson, Leif, 61–62, 64

esker, 124
"Eskimo," 26, 169–70, 172, 182
estuffas, 248
Etowah (Georgia), *192*, 219, *220*
experimental archaeology, 37, 39, 256

Fajada Butte (Chaco Canyon), 318–19, *320*
Farmington Valley, 125, 353, 358
federal census, 43–44
Fiddler on the Roof (musical), 41, 128
Fire Temple (Mesa Verde), 264
First Seminole War, 359
fish weir, 279–80
Five Civilized Tribes, 360
flint, 36–38, 40, 153, 173, 356
fluted (channeled) points, *94*, 97–98, 100, 102–3
Folsom (culture), 69–70, 92, *93*–94, 95–98, *99*, 102, 119, 268
Folsom points, *94*, *95*, 97–98, 102
Food and Agriculture Organization, 149
footprints (human), 83–84, *85*, 87–88, 227, 294, 321
Fort Ancient, *192*, 199, 209
Fort Defiance, 363
Fort Laramie Treaty, 336–37
Founders Museum, Barre, Massachusetts, 348
Four Corners, 233, 267, 297
fox, 102
Franklin, Benjamin, 160, 166
Fraser, James Earle, 6
Frauds, Myths, and Mysteries: Science and Pseudoscience in Archaeology, Kenneth L. Feder, 196
Fremont (art style), 297, *299*, 299–301

Garden of Eden, 53, 273
Gault site, 83, *99*
General Court in Hartford, 355–56, 358, 381n2 (chap. 18), 381n4 (chap. 18), 382nn5–6
Genesis (Book of), 33, 52
genetics, 88, 380n21

genocide, 353, 361, 367
genome, 136, 139, 149
Gentleman of Elvas, 221, 379n5 (chap. 13)
Ghost Dance Movement, 347–48
Gila Cliff Dwellings, 232, 234, *235*, 264
goosefoot, 135, *141*, 141, *142*, 202
gorget, 219
Grand Banks, 151
Grand Central Terminal, New York City, 210
Grand Village of the Natchez, *192*, 220, 222
Gran Quivira Pueblo, 332
Grave Creek Mound, *192*, *201*, 201
Grave Creek Mound Tablet, 194
Great Circle Earthworks, *192*, 199, 204, 206
Great Council of Chiefs, 166
Great Gallery (Horseshoe Canyon), *298*, 312–14, *313*
Great Hopewell Road, 207
Great Hunt Panel (rock art), *295*, 297, *301*, 302
Great Law of Peace, The, 166–67
"Great Peacemaker, The" (Skennenrahawi or Deganawida), 165
Great Sun, the, 222
Greenland, 61–64, 169–71, *171*, 175, 183, 187–88
Gros Ventre, 371

Haaland, Deb, 369
Hahpehe'Onahe (Closed Hand, Cheyenne), *343*, 343
Haida, 7, 15
half-life, 72
Halona, 17, 234, 272–73
Harbottle, Garman, 252
Hardy, Harris, xxii, 16
harpoon, 131–32, 182, 286
Hart, John, 164
Harvard University, 67–68
Haudenosaunee (Iroquois), 7, 158–67, *159*
Hawass, Zahi, 14
Hayes, Private First Class Ira, 270
Hayes site, *142*, 143
Hebrew (inscription), 58, *59*, 194
Hebrew (people), 31

Hebrew Creation Story, 31–32
hematite, 295
Hemenway House (Mesa Verde), 264
Herculaneum, 284–85
Herjólfsson, Bjarni, 61–62
Hiawatha, 165
Hidatsa, 7, 349–51
Higgs site, 141
High Bank Works, 199
Hohokam, 231, 232, 236–40, 297
Holden, 218
Holyoke basalt, 121
Homo erectus, 112, 315
Homo habilis, 112
Hooker, John, 357, 382n7
Hopeton Earthworks, 199
Hopewell, 192, 199–204, 202–3, 206–7, 250
Hopewell, Mordecai, 200
Hopewell Ceremonial Earthworks (sites), 199, 200
Hopewell Mound Group, 199
Hopi, 3, 7, 9, 232, 234, 244, 247, 269, 272, 361–62, 368
Horned Snakes and Axle Grease: A Roadside Guide to the Archaeology, History, and Rock Art of Nine Mile Canyon, Jerry D. Spangler and Donna K. Spangler, 303
hornfels, 36, 38, 125, 127, 129, 354
horses, 4–5, 100, 344
Horseshoe Canyon, 298, 311–12, 313
House of Many Windows (Mesa Verde), 263
Hovenweep, 232, 250
Hrdlička, Aleš, 67–68, 89, 92
Hudson Bay, 116, 171, 173, 179
human sacrifice, 222
Hungo Pavi (Hungo Pavie; Chaco Canyon), 243, 246, 257
Huron (Wendat), 7, 161, 165

Ice Age (Pleistocene Epoch), 4, 57, 69, 76–77, 93, 95, 100, 102–3, 156
ice-free corridor, 79–80
Icehouse Bottom site, 142, 151

igloo (snow house), 4, 169, 173
Ikhine site, 75
Indian Civilization Fund Act, 365
Indian Neck (Farmington, Connecticut), 356–58
Indian Removal Act, 359–61, 363
Indian Rock Art of the Southwest, Polly Schaafsma, 297
Indigenous People, 1, 4, 9, 19, 47, 49, 54, 56, 119, 135, 195, 277, 334, 349–50
Ingstad, Anne Stine, 62, 376n13
Ingstad, Helge, 62, 376n13
Inscription House (Navajo National Monument), 229, 232
inscriptions (fake): Bat Creek Stone, 194; Davenport Stones, 194; Grave Creek Mound Tablet, 194; Los Lunas Decalogue Stone, 194, 195; Newark Holy Stones, 194
Institute for American Indian Studies, 9, 159
Institute of Prairie and Indigenous Archaeology in Canada, 370
intertidal, 279, 281
Inuit, 3, 7, 26–27, 31, 132, 170–72, 174–90
Inuit creation story, 26–28
inuk (person; plural for inuit), 170
Inuktitut (language), 132
Inupiaq, 170
Iñupiat, 170, 171, 183–84
iron (Native), 186–88, 194, 344
iron (Norse), 63–64
Iroquois (Haudenosaunee), 7, 158–67, 159
irrigation, 50, 151; Hohokam, 237–38
Iseminger, William, 212, 379n1 (chap. 13)

jack rabbit, 134
Jackson, President Andrew, 359–60
Jackson, William Henry, 260
jasper, 36
Jebel Irhoud site, 73
Jemez Cave, 142, 148
Jesuit Relations, The (*Relations des Jésuites de la Nouvelle-France*), 162–63

Jesuits, 155, 161–64
Johnson, Norma, 19
Jornada Mogollon, 235–36, 297, 303
Journal of a Military Reconnaissance from Santa Fé, New Mexico, to the Navaho Country, Lt. James H. Simpson, 244

Kalaallit, 170
Kamchatka Peninsula, 175
Karlsefni, Thorfinn, 64–65
kayak, 169, 173, 174, 181
Kelvingrove Art Gallery and Museum, Glasgow, Scotland, 349
Keres, 269
Kern, Richard H., 226, 244, 245
Kin Teel (Pueblo Pintado), 245
kiva, 17, 243, 248, 248–50, 254, 262, 264, 319, 334, 335
Knife River Indian Villages National Historic Site, 349–52
Kodak House (Mesa Verde), 264
Kolomoki Mounds, Georgia, *192*, 220
Koster site, 134–35, 141, 143
Kwakiutl (Kwakwaka'wakw), 3, 7, 282
Kwakwaka'wakw (Kwakiutl), 3, 7, 282

Labrador (Helluland), 62, 131–32
Laetoli site, 83
Laguna Pueblo, 369
Lake Forest Archaic, 119–21, 132, 156
Lakota, 7, 336, 339, 343, 343, 345–49
lamb's quarters, 152, 154
L'Anse Amour site, 132
L'Anse aux Meadows site, 62, 63, 64, 199
Laplace, Pierre Simon, 70
La Prele Mammoth site, 99, 100–102, 377n11 (chap. 6)
Late Glacial Maximum, 74, 77, 110, 175
Laurentide ice sheet, 78–79
Leakey, Louis, 105, 107–8
Leakey, Mary, 83, 107–8, 377n3 (chap. 7)
Lehner site, 99, 100, 377n10 (chap. 6)

Le Page du Pratz, Antoine-Simon, 222, 379n7 (chap. 13)
Lepper, Bradley L., xxi–xxii, 207–9, 379n10 (chap. 12)
Levy, Jay, xxi, 16, 18
Lewis and Clark, 351–52
Life on a Rocky Farm, Lucas Barger, 376n9
Lindenmeier site, 97–98, 99, 101, 252
Lippert, Dorothy, 18, 91, 377n16
Little Lamb (Little Sheep), 307, *308*
Long House (Mesa Verde), 261
longhouses, 4, 132, 163–64
Long Walk (Navajo), 358, 360–64
Los Lunas Decalogue Stone, 59
Lost Tribes of Israel, 54, 195
Low Dog (Lakota), 339
lunar cycle (18.6 years), 206

macaws, 250
Magellan, 56
Magnusson (Magnuss) and Pálsson (Hermann) (translators of sagas), 65
mahiz, 144
maize (corn), 144–55, 164, 202, 215, 225, 231, 233, 277, 350, 378nn11–14
Major Mason's Brief History of the Pequot War, John Mason, 327
Makah, 282, 286, 288
Mal'ta, 90–91
Mandan, 3, 7, 349–50
Manganese, 295
Manis site, 80, 99
Marble Bluff Shelter site, 143
Maritime Archaic, 119–20, 123, 130–33, 156
marsh elder, 135, 141, *142*
Martin, John, 340
Mason, Captain John, 326–27
Mason, Charlie, 260, 263
Massacre Cave, 307–8, *308*
Mastamho, 315, *316*
master sequence (dendrochronology), 230–31
Mast Forest Archaic, 119, 121, 123, 156
mastodon, 95, 98, 102

Mazola TV ads, 145
McBride, Kevin, 327
McClurg, Virginia, 261–62
McGhee, Robert, 175, 185, 379n2 (chap. 11)
McJunkin, George, 92, 377n1 (chap. 6)
McKee Springs (petroglyphs), *298*, *299*
Meadowcroft Rockshelter, 70, 81–82, *82*, 99
Medieval Warm Period, 184–85
Meherrin, 165
Mesa Verde, xvii, 199, 227, 232, 242, 259–62, *262–63*, *263*–66, *298*; Balcony House, 261, *263*, 265; Cliff Palace, xvii, 261–63, *263*, 265; Fire Temple, 264; Hemenway House, 264; House of Many Windows, 263; Kodak House, 264; Long House, 261; New Fire House, 264; Nordenskiold, 264; Oak Tree House, 264; Spruce Tree House, 263; Square Tower House, 261, *262*; Step House, 261, 264
Mescalero Apache, 367
metallurgy, 42, 105
meteoric iron, 187
Métis, 370
metric scale, xvii
Middle Passage, 44
Middle Place, 272–73
Milagro, *142*, 148
Mimbres (art), 234, *236*, 303
Minik, 189
missionaries (Catholic), 11, 161–62, 222, 225, 242, 333
Mississippian, *192*
Mistick, Connecticut, 323–24, 326
Mistick Fort, 324, 327, 330–31
Mitchell, Angeline, 11, 12, 74, 375n2 (chap. 2)
mitochondrial DNA (mtDNA), 183, 259
Mogollon, 231, 232, 234–36, *235*, 297, 303–4, *305*
Mohave (people), 7, 315
Mohave Desert, 105
Mohawk, 7, 165, 331
Mohegan, 3, 7, 17, 324, 326, 358
Mohs Scale, 128–29
Monks Mound (Cahokia), xvi, xvii–xviii, 213–15, *214*, 219

Montaukett, 358
Monte Verde site, 70
Montezuma Castle, 232, *240*, 264
moose, 102, 120
Mound 72 burials (Cahokia), 217–18, 379n3 (chap. 13)
Mound Builder Myth: Fake History and the Hunt for a "Lost White Race," The, Jason Colavito, 195–96
Mound Builders, The, Robert Silverberg, 195
Mound City, *192*, 199–200, 203
Moundville, Alabama, *192*, 218–19
Mount Ararat, 56
mtDNA haplogroup D2a, 183
mukluks, 174
Muskogee, 167–68

Nahuatl, 146, 172
Napoleon Hollow site, 141, *142*
Narbona, Lt. Antonio, 306
Narragansett, xxii, 7, 324, 326, 358
Narváez, Pánfilo de, 222–23
National Centre for Truth and Reconciliation, 382n15
National Conference of Charities and Correction, 366
National Museum of the American Indian, 9
Native American Graves Protection and Repatriation Act, 67, 376n2 (chap. 5)
native copper, 120
Natural and Moral History of the Indies, The, Father José de Acosta, 55
natural selection, 68, 136–37
Navajo (Diné), 3, 7, 9, 28–31, 169, 224, 227–29, 245, 266–68, *268*, 271–72, 306, *308*, 309, 358, 360
Navajo Code Talkers, 269
Navajo language, 232–33, 245–46, 250–52, 269–71, 361–62
Navajo Long Walk, 358, 360–64
Navajo National Monument, 227, *228*, 229
Navajo Reservation, 28, 233, 270, 362
Navajo rock art, *268*, *298*, 304–7, *308*

Nazca, 315
necropolis, 199, *200*
needles (sewing), 102
neutron activation analysis, 252
Newark, Ohio, 204, *205*, 207
Newark Earthworks State Memorial, *192*, 204, *205*
Newark Holy Stones, 194
New Fire House (Mesa Verde), 264
Newfoundland (Vinland), 62, *63*, 64
New Holy (Lakota), 349
Newport Tower, 60–61
New Spain, 225, 331
Newspaper Rock, *294*, *295*, *298*, 301
Newt Kash Hollow, 141, *142*, 143
Niantic, 326, 358
Nine Mile Canyon, 30, 295, 297, 298, *301*, 301, 303
Nine Mile Canyon: The Archaeological History of an American Treasure, Jerry D. Spangler, 303
Noah's Flood, 55–56
Noah's sons, 54–55
"noble savages," 5
Nootkah (Nuu-chah-nulth), 282
Nordenskiold (Mesa Verde), 264
Norse (Viking), 48, 55, 60–65, 180
Northwest Coast: Archaeology as Deep History, Madonna L. Moss, 11, 380n2 (chap. 15)
Nottoway, 165
nut foods, 71, 100, 121–22, 134, 154, 211
Nuu-chah-nulth (Nootkah), 282
Nuvugmiut, 184
Nuxalk (Bella Coola), 282

Oak Tree House (Mesa Verde), 264
obsidian, 36, 40, 98, 252
Occom, Samson (Mohegan), 358
ocher, 101
Ocmulgee Mounds, Georgia, *192*, 220
Oconee Valley, 168
Octagon Earthworks, 199, 204–6, *205*
Old Copper Culture, 121, 122, 187
Oldham, John, 325

Olsen-Chubbuck site, 96–97, *99*, 377n6 (chap 6)
Olympic Peninsula, 80, 279, 284, 286
Oñate, Juan de, 331–32
Oneida, 165, 358
Onondaga, 165
On the Origin of Species, Charles Darwin, 136
On Your Knees Cave, 79, 377n7 (chap. 5)
optically stimulated luminescence, 87
Oregon Archaeological Society, 352
Orient Fishtail (point type), 39, 128
origin stories, 20–33
Origin: A Genetic History of the Americas, Jennifer Raff, 88, 377n13 (chap. 5)
over-hunting hypothesis, 102–3
Ozette site, 284–85, 287–89
Ozette: Excavating a Makah Whaling Village, Ruth Kirk, 380n5 (chap. 15)

Paiute, 7, 90, 347
paleofeces (coprolites), 134
Paleoindian, 96, 99, 101
Paleo-Inuit, *171*, 175–88, 190
paradigm, 51, 53, 55, 66, 68–69, 73, 93, 95, 104, 109, 111
parka, 169, 173
Parker Pallan, Bertha, 16
Parks Canada, 63
patina, 295, 299–300
Peabody, Lucy, 261–62
Peace Queen of the Seneca, The (Jigonsaseh), 166
Peary, Admiral Robert, 188–89
pelagic, 131, 133
Peñasco Blanco (Chaco Canyon), 243, 317
Pequot, 324–31
Pequot War, 323–24, 326–28, 356
percussion flaking, 37, 132
Perry, Warren, 274
petroglyph, xvii, xxii, 30, 235, 268, *294*, 294–95, 298–99, 301, 303, 308, 310, 319, 320
Phoenician, 55, 194

Phoenix, Arizona, 12, 237
Phytoliths, 164
pictograph, 90, 208, *298*, 306–8, *308*, 310, *313*, 317–18, *318*
Picture Cave, 208
pigweed, 135
Pilling Figurines, 300
Pima, 7, 270
Place of Writing on the Rock (A'ts'ina), 226
Plains Archaic, 119
Platyrrhini (New World monkeys), 112
Pleiades, 29
Pleistocene Epoch (Ice Age), 4, 57, 69, 76–77, 93, 95, 100, 102–3, 156, 175, 373
pollen, 87, 153
Pompeii, 284–85, 287
Po'pay, 334
Port aux Choix site, 132
Posada, Fray Alonso de, 333
postglacial, 110, 139
post molds, 163
potlatch, 289–90
pottery, 8, 128, 157, 200, 212, 233–34, 271
Poverty Point site, *192*, 197–99, *198*, 204
Pratt, Lt. Richard Henry, 366
pre-Dorset, 175, 179, 186, 190
prehensile tail, 113
pressure flaking, 37
primates, 112
projectile point, 39, 41, 98
pronghorn antelope, 134, 350
Pueblo (people), 7, 169, 232–35, 245, 248, 268–69, 272, 331–35
pueblo (structures), 4, 225–26, 231, 234, 239, 243, 245, 332
Pueblo Bonito (Chaco Canyon), 242, *243*, 246–47, *247*, 257–59
Pueblo del Arroyo (Chaco Canyon), *243*, 246
Pueblo Pintado (Kin Teel), 232, *245*
Pueblo Revolt, 323, 331
pyramid, xvii, 191, 199, 213, 219, 256

Qablunatt, 180
Quarai Pueblo, 332
Questioning the Millennium, Stephen Jay Gould, 375n1 (A Practical Preface)
qulliq, 180

rachis, 138
radioactive, 71–72
radiocarbon dating (^{14}C dating, carbon dating), xix, 71–73, 80, 83, 86, 90, 95, 100, 123, 285, 354
Raff, Jennifer, xxii, 88, 175, 177, 183
Rainbow Bridge, 228
Ray, Reverend John, 52, 376n6
receiving vault, 60
Red Cloud War, 336
Red Feather, 345
Red Paint People, 133
Red Willow, 234
Reno, Major Marcus, 338–41
residential schools (Indian boarding schools), 365–67, 369
Resistance Kiva, 335
Ribbon Falls, 273
Rio Balsas, 146
Riverine Archaic, 119
Riverton site, 143
rock art, *18*, 22, 30, 226, 235–36, 267, 273–74, 292–305, *294*, *298*, *299*, 299–301, *301*, 303–4, *305*, *308*, 308, *311*, 311–12, *313*, 314, 317, *318*, 320
Rocky Mountains, 78
Room 28, Chaco Canyon, 251
Room 33, Chaco Canyon, 258–59, 380nn16–17
Roosevelt, President Teddy, 4, 240, 261
Ruppia cirrhosa, 84–85, 87

Sacagawea (Sakakwea), 351–52
sachem, 325, 331, 355
Sacred Mountains (Navajo), 267
Sagan, Carl, xxii, 70, 109
Saga of Erik the Red, The, 61, 376n12

Saga of the Greenlanders, The, 61, 376n12
Salinas Pueblo, 332
Salts Cave, 141, *142*
San Andres, 142
Sandoval, 245
San Pedro River, 100
Saqqaq, 184
Scott, Douglas, 344, 381nn11–12
seal, 131, 172–73, 179, 181–82
sea lion, 172
Seip Earthworks, *192*, 199
Seminole, 3, 7, 360, 364
Seneca, 16, 165–66, 207
Seowtewa, Alex, 333
Sequassen, 355
Serpent Mound, *192*, *208*, 208–9, 315, 379n10
Seven Cities of Gold, 225
Seventh Cavalry, 336, 338–41, 343, 345–46
shell midden, 123
Shell Mound Archaic, 119
Shem, Ham, and Japheth, 54–55
Sheridan, Lt. General Philip, 338
Sherlock Holmes, 83–84, 241
She Who Watches (Tsagaglalal), *298*, 308, 310, *311*
Shield Archaic, 119
Shinnecock, 3
Short Hints Towards a Scheme for a General Union of the British Colonies on the Continent, Benjamin Franklin, 161
Shoshone, 3, 7, 351
Siberia, 73–77, 88–90, 147, 170–71, *171*, 173, 183
Silva, Cecilia, 22
Simpson, Lieutenant James H., 226, 244–46, *245*, 248, 319
Simpson, Ruth DeEtte, 105
Sinagua, 231, 232, 238–39, 239–40, 240–41
Siouan origin story, 208
Sioux, 3, 7, 336–39, 345–46, 348, 350
sipapu, 247
Site 211-1-1, 151

Six Nations, the, 160, 165
SK Mammoth site, 75
Skraelings, 65
Skull Wars, David Hurst Thomas, 376n1 (chap. 5)
smartweed, 135, 154
Smithsonian Institution, 9, 18, 67, 226, 261
Smithsonian National Museum of Natural History, 68
Snaketown, 232, 237
snow house (igloo), 4, 169, 173
soapstone (steatite), 63, 128–30, *130*, 157, 180
Society for American Archaeology, 16, 18
Soto, Hernando de, 222
South America, 16, 44, 54, 68, 98, 112, 140, 315
Spanish (explorers/invaders), 5, 47, 49, 55, 73, 144, 152, 194, 221–22, 225–26, 238, 242, 244, 267–69, 272, 306–8, 331–32, 334–35, 362
Spotted Elk, 348
Spruce Tree House (Mesa Verde), 263
Square Tower House (Mesa Verde), 261, *262*
squash, 50, 140, 142, 144, 154–55, 164, 202, 215, 225, 231, 233, 272, 277, 350
steatite (soapstone), 63, 128–30, *130*, 157, 180
Steeves, Paulette, 18, 104, 377n1 (chap. 7)
Step House (Mesa Verde), 261, *264*
Stockbridge, 358
stone age, 34, 120
stone chambers, 60
Sublimis Deus, Pope Paul III, 53
Sugpiaq, 170
Sun Dagger (petroglyph; Chaco Canyon), 319, *320*
sunflower, 135, 140, *142*, 142–43, *143*, 151–52, 154, 202, 378nn1–2 (chap. 9)
Sunrise child-girl (Xach'itee'aanenh t'eede gaay), 90
Sunset Crater Volcano National Monument, 238
sunshades, 174
Supernant, Kisha, 18, 370

supernova pictograph (Chaco Canyon), 298, 317–18, *318*
Swordfish Hunters, The (Bruce Borque), 131
syncretism, 333
Synopsis Methodica Stirpium Britannicarum, Reverend John Ray, 52

Taino, 144
Talcott basalt, 108, 124, *125*, 129
Tales from Azlantis (podcast), 19
Tallbear, Kim, 18
Taos Pueblo, 199, 232, 234, 244
Tapleras, Martha (Tule), 22
Tatobem, 325
Tent (meteorite), 187–88
teosinte, 145–47, 149
Terry, Commander Alfred, 338–39
Tewa, 9, 267, 269
Three Rivers Petroglyph Site, 235–36, *298*, *303*, *305*
three sisters (maize, beans, and squash), 144, 164, 350
Thule, 170, 184
Tiguex War, 331
Tionontati, 165
tipi, 3–5, 91
Tiwa, 269
Tk'emlúps te Secwépemc Nation, 370
Tlakatekatl, Ruben Arellano, 19
Tlapoyawa, Kurly, xxii, 19
Tlingit, 7, 282
tobacco, 154–55, 277
toggle harpoon, 133, 173, 182
Tonto Basin, 12
Tonto National Monument, 13
Tonto site, *13*, *14*, 232
totem pole, 275–77, *276*, 282, 308
Towa, 269
Town Creek Mound, North Carolina, *192*, 221
trace element (analysis), 97, 252
Trail of Tears, the, 358–61
Trappist monks, 213
Treaty of Bosque Redondo, the, 364

tree ring dating, 229–30, 285
Treviño, Governor Juan Francisco, 334
truncated pyramid, 191, 213–14, 219, 222
Tsadeyohdi (Denise Waterman; Turtle Clan), 159
Tsagaglalal (She Who Watches), *298*, 308, 310, *311*
Tsegi Canyon, 227–28
Tule River People, 3, 7, 22–24, *24*, 25–26, 29, 31, *298*, 309
Tumamoc Hill, *142*, 148
tundra, 76, *116*, 118
Tuniit, 179, 182
Tunxis, 353–58
turquoise (Doo tl' izh ii), 28, 251–52, 258
Tuscarora, 7, 165

Ukkusiksalik National Park, 173, 179
Ukkusiksalik: The People's Story, David Pelly, 179, 379n4 (chap. 11)
ulu, 132, 181
umiaqs, 181
Unangax̂, 171
Una Vida (Chaco Canyon), 243, 246
Uncovering History: Archaeological Investigations at the Little Bighorn, Douglas Scott, 381n12
Underwater Panther, 329
United Nations World Heritage List, 216, 234, 259
Unmarked Graves Working Group of the Canadian Archaeological Association, 370
Upton Stone Chamber, 59
Upward Sun River site, 90, 377n15
Utah State University Eastern Prehistoric Museum, 300
Utes, 260, 361–62
Utley, Robert, 338, 340–41

Verrazzano, 56–57
Vespucci, Amerigo, 9, 48, 51, 376n5
Viking (Norse), 48, 55, 60–65, 180
Village of the Great Kivas, 17, 319

Walnut Canyon National Monument, 232, 241
walrus (ivory trade), 65, 132, 178–80
Walters, Holly, xxii
wampum, 324
Washington Expedition, 244
Washington Post (on boarding schools), 369–71, 382n19
Wasicu Supa (Black White Man, Lakota), 343
Watkins, Joe, 18
Watson Brake site, *192*, 196
Weigand, Phil, 252, 380n13
Wendat (Huron), 161, 165
Wetherill, B. K., 261, 380n19
Wetherill, John, 227–28, *228*
Wetherill, Richard, 260, 263
Wetherill Mesa, 261, 264
When the World Began (Tule), 22, 28
White, Tim, 83
White House (Canyon de Chelly), 219, 305
White Sands site, 83, *85*, 87–88, 99, 115, 227, 268
Wigwam, 4, 325, 374
Wijiji (Weje-ge; Chaco Canyon), 243, 246
Wilcox, Beatrix, 22
Wilcox, Dan, 130
wild cat, 102
Wild Horse Arroyo site, 92–94

Wimpey, Elijah, 358
Wisdom of God Manifested in the Works of the Creation, The, Reverend John Ray, 53
Woman (meteorite), 187
Woodhenge, 215
Woodland Period, 37, 129, 156–58, 161–62
woolly mammoth, 75, 80, 84, 95, 98, 100, 102, 110
World Heritage Center of the United Nations, 199
Wounded Knee, 323, 345–49
Wounded Knee Survivors Association, 349
Wovoka, 347
Wupatki, 232, 239, *239*

Yana River RHS site, 75
Yupkoyvi (The Place Beyond the Horizon), 244

Zuni (A:shiwi people), xxii, 7, 17–18, 226, 232, 234, 251, 272–74, 333
Zuni in the Grand Canyon, 380n24
Zuni language, 269
Zuni Mountains, 254
Zuni pictograph, 18, *298*
Zuni Pueblo, 17–18, 234, 251, 333

A NOTE ON THE TYPE

This book has been composed in Arno, an Old-style serif typeface in the classic Venetian tradition, designed by Robert Slimbach at Adobe.